FOXY LADY

The Authorized Biography of **Lynn Bari**

JEFF GORDON

Published in the USA by:
BearManor Media
PO Box 1129
Duncan, Oklahoma 73534-1129
www.bearmanormedia.com

ISBN 978-1-59393-523-8

Printed in the United States of America.
Book design by Brian Pearce | Red Jacket Press

TABLE OF CONTENTS

ACKNOWLEDGEMENTS 7

I KNOW WHY (AND SO DO YOU) 13

SPEED TO BURN 19

I'M MAKING BELIEVE 37

THE STOCKGIRL AND THE STUDIO 51

QUEEN OF THE 'B' HIVE .77

CITY OF CHANCE 113

MOON OVER HER SHOULDER 151

HOLLYWOOD CAVALCADE 179

THE BARI BOOM 223

SHOCK 243

SERENADE IN BLUE 263

ON THE LOOSE 285

BOSS LADY 305

ENTER: THE SHRINK 339

TRAUMA 355

THE GASLIGHT TREATMENT 375

EARTHBOUND 409

AT LAST 437

FILMOGRAPHY 463

TELEVISION APPEARANCES 481

INDEX 487

To Peggy Fisher

In loving memory

ACKNOWLEDGEMENTS

My journey with *Foxy Lady* took place over a period of two decades. During this time, many people gave of themselves most generously to this book. Their contributions proved invaluable — and, with heartfelt thanks, I'd like to recognize each of these wonderful individuals, a good number of whom are no longer with us.

I was quite fortunate to have made contact with an array of Lynn Bari's professional associates, personal friends and family members. While only some are quoted directly in this volume, the reflections of all who had known Lynn were ever so enlightening to me.

Those who'd been part of Bari's professional life to whom I'd like to express my gratitude: Robert Arthur, Tony Aylward, Dick Baldwin, Dixie Dunbar, Gene Evans, Alice Faye, Conrad Janis, June Lang, June Gale Levant, Lon McCallister, Roddy McDowall, Maeve McGuire, George Montgomery, Dick (Dickie) Moore, Terry Moore, Anthony Quinn, William Roerick, Jean Rogers, Cesar Romero, Gloria Stuart, Claire Trevor, Barbara Whiting, and Yvonne Wood.

Three of Lynn's personal friends were of great assist to me. The thoughts of Wilson Blaine gave insight to Bari's early childhood in Virginia. Eyvind Earle drew an illuminating portrait of a young Lynn, from the time she and her family settled in California through her first years on the soundstages of Hollywood. The Lynn Bari of the 1960s and 1970s was vividly brought to life by Jerry Walston, whose spirited manner and devotion to the star proved particularly inspiring to me.

The helpfulness and kindness of Lynn's family is something of which I'm deeply appreciative. Bari's beloved son, John Luft, was especially thoughtful toward me. Lynn's stepfather, the Reverend Robert H. Bitzer, came through under circumstances which I'm certain must have been difficult, given that he had been predeceased by Bari. The animated remembrances of Jay Fisher, Lynn's nephew, made clearer the shared history of Bari and her brother John. Most illuminating to me was Jay's mother, Eugenie Ediss Fisher. A charming, perceptive woman, Eugenie had come into my life in 1993. She has, over the years, provided me countless insights into Lynn and the unusual dynamics of her family. Eugenie also facilitated my interviewing others who had known Bari well. I cannot adequately express how much this book owes to Eugenie Fisher. Her friendship with me is something I truly treasure.

The research that went into this book drew upon the remarkable resources of the New-York Historical Society Library, the New York Public Library of the

Performing Arts, and Photofest, Inc. I am immeasurably indebted to all those affiliated therein; their helpfulness guided me greatly.

The undertaking of telling Lynn Bari's life story involved the able assistance of many other people who had held no personal connection to the star. The support I received from these individuals played a significant role in bringing this book to fruition. My sincere thanks to: Ed and Mary Atwood, Helen C. Barranger, Jeanine Basinger, Roger Blunck, Leonard Charney, John Cocchi, Ed Colbert, Tom Cullen, Rita Dubas, Henry Fera, Lester Glassner, Elizabeth J. Hamilton, Ron Harvey, Bryant Hoven, Amanda Jarrett, Kevin Kaufman, Bob King, Richard Lamparski, Doug Lee, Jerome Levin, Doug McClelland, Cheryl Messina, Patricia Moore, David Schaublin, Tom Toth, George Ulrich, Lou Valentino, Mark Vieira, and Doug Whitney.

Brian Pearce is this book's designer. It is with a sense of admiration that I wish to convey my appreciation to Brian for his truly artful work herein.

My gratitude also to my family: my brothers, Andy and Jimmy; and my dear late mother, Cynthia Gordon, a grammarian without equal and my biggest champion.

There are five people whom I'd especially like to single out for their contributions to this book. All are cherished friends who share my tremendous affection for vintage movies. Immensely encouraging to me, they brought to *Foxy Lady* their inherent wisdom and their knowledge in their particular areas of expertise.

My lifelong pal, Anne Katherine Markowitz, had been with me here from the very beginning. Untold were the times I called upon Anne's command for English syntax and her professional understanding of familial relationships.

Howard Mandelbaum, another longtime buddy, forever proved to be a fountain of inspiration and learning about things pertaining to Lynn Bari and the construction of movie-star biographies.

Patricia Emerson, a distinguished editor, had since 1993 devoted countless hours to my manuscript. Pat gave of herself freely, her good humor making our work together a totally pleasurable experience.

Great is my debt of gratitude to Laura Wagner, a gifted writer and editor. Laura saw this book to its completion and she facilitated its publication. Her perceptivity throughout left me in a state of wonder. A quality of goodwill complemented Laura's discerning nature, the combination thereof helping to move me forward in a most positive direction.

Tom Turton had been with me every step of the way for this book. I cannot begin to imagine how many times I had called upon Tom's insightfulness, his encyclopedic knowledge of film, and his extraordinary familiarity with Lynn Bari. Tom is, in this writer's mind, Bari's number one admirer. His affection for Lynn is absolute, yet he views her with a very realistic eye. His approach toward her had both inspired and grounded me these past twenty years. It is with sincerest thanks that I'd like to acknowledge Tom Turton.

To the subject of this book, I'd like to express my profound appreciation. There's no way for me to properly quantify Lynn Bari's contributions to her biography; they were incalculably large in dimension, going on to resonate within me in unexpectedly wondrous ways. All that was good about Lynn came to the fore during her participation in this volume; throughout, I found her to be a warm, witty and benevolent person, a woman of great intelligence, admirable bearing and high principles. I will be eternally thankful for the way in which Lynn Bari graced my life.

FOXY
LADY

A World War II snapshot: Lynn Bari for "Victory."

I KNOW WHY
(AND SO DO YOU)

Lynn Bari's star was poised to rocket in the summer of 1942. If and when it did catapult, the actress's many champions would be there to cheer her on.

She had just received a Star of Tomorrow citation from the Motion Picture Exhibitors of North America. The honor was heavily publicized by Lynn's studio, 20th Century-Fox, as something that "was to determine which names among the Hollywood younger set possess sufficient box-office draw to shoulder the responsibility that goes with top billing in expensive pictures."

The Magnificent Dope was one of those pictures. Co-starring Henry Fonda and Don Ameche, the comedy afforded Lynn her best performance to date. The film went into release in July, about the time Bari's next assignment, *Orchestra Wives*, was wrapping up production. Destined to become a blockbuster, the musical featured Glenn Miller and his orchestra. Lynn played the sultry band singer, introducing two songs, "At Last" and "Serenade in Blue," which would go on to become standards.

No stranger to the heaviest of workloads, Bari was rushed into *China Girl*, her sixth film of the year, in mid-July. Director Henry Hathaway requested that she lighten her long chestnut tresses to an ash blonde; lending a visual contrast to his other leading lady, Gene Tierney, an actress of similar frame. Lynn ended her first week of filming on a high note; the *China Girl* crew was all in agreement that their old reliable was stealing the picture out from underneath Tierney's chiseled nose.

Bari was always at her professional best when her pressure-cooker existence was escalating to the boiling point. Before the Hathaway set folded, she found herself working double-time in the Fox photo gallery: *Orchestra Wives* promotions, *China Girl* portraits, pinup shots, fan magazine layouts and four-color Sunday rotogravure covers. In concert with the endlessly clicking camera shutter, her cherubic smile kept widening. A dream was now becoming an actuality.

By Labor Day, Lynn was participating in the first full-scale Victory Tour. Her fellow travelers included Greer Garson, Irene Dunne, Hedy Lamarr and Ronald Colman. Working around the clock, she and her new peer group sold war bonds and spread morale throughout the West. Naturally, the tour was a huge success. While Bari thoroughly enjoyed contributing her time for the effort, once again the

conflicts that had motivated her advancements would build to an almost unbear-
able point of stress, turning the entire trip into a two-month personal disaster.

I was married to an agent named Walter Kane. At the time, I was on the verge
of divorcing him. During the Second World War, Walter was on The Victory
Committee. He booked me to go out with Ronald Colman, selling war bonds.

Lynn strikes a provocative pose in the Fox photo gallery.

He [Kane] knew my mother and how she was a terrible drunk. Mother had been
in love with Colman her whole life. When she heard that I was going on tour
with him, she insisted, "My daughter is not going alone, unattended, on that
trip!" So my dear ex-husband-to-be thought, I'll show dear Lynn something —
and he booked my mother to go on the trip, too.

Before we left, Ronald Colman sent his henchman, Joe Steele — a writer who handled his publicity — over to the still department at Fox. I was taking pictures on a tiger skin for some magazine. He said that Mr. and Mrs. Colman would like to have me over for tea the next day. So I said fine. The whole thing turned out to be very proper, very stiff.

Then I heard whispers that Ronnie didn't know whether he should go out

Five stars reviewing their Victory Tour itinerary. Left to right: Irene Dunne, Lynn, Ronald Colman, Hedy Lamarr and Greer Garson.

with a twenty-two-year-old divorcée. And I thought, "Holy…*this* old man?" To me, he was just an old man and a short one. I didn't care if he was a Greek god. And here he was going to Wyoming and all these places where they never heard of him.

When we boarded the train in LA, everything was lovely. I'm with Marge — she never allowed me to call her mother. She was a very beautiful woman. Butter wouldn't melt in her mouth when she was sober — then, she was a charming person. But when she took a couple of drinks, it was Jekyll and Hyde. I'm afraid I took after her in that respect. *(laughing)* Soon after the train pulled out, my mother started nudging me, "Oh, we haven't met him yet. When do you think Ronald will be by?" I said, "You call him Mr. Colman, Marge. Don't start in with that crap now."

Morning comes and there's this knock on our compartment door. In comes Colman with a bottle of Johnnie Walker Black Label held high above his head.

"Let's have a little nip before we go to breakfast," he said. I said, "Oh God, no thank you, Mr. Colman. I can't drink in the morning." My mother then said that she'd have one. Oh, brother! We were off to the races. Well, she passed out.

Eventually, the people on the tour would say, "Lynn, we're going out for supper. We'd love to have you join us, but don't bring Marge." I would have to get away from her or else I'd have gone screaming mad.

Unfortunately, the government had a per diem for everybody, and each day my mother was given an envelope with thirty bucks. So even if I hid the booze, she could get it. She'd just send a bellboy out for it. She knew all the things to do.

Then came the incident that happened when we were driving through Nevada. I was sitting in the middle of the car. My mother was on my right and Colman, on my left. He reached over and took my hand. He had never done anything like this before — made a pass or anything. My mother just happened to look down and saw what was going on. That's when it all started. From there on, it was all just horrible.

After eight weeks of touring the West in everything from jeeps to covered wagons, we were coming home on the *Super Chief*, the big new train of the year. On the last night, I was sitting in my stateroom with my mother. I had a hostess robe on. Joe Steele came by and said, "Lynn, Ronnie would like you to come by and have a farewell drink this evening." I said, "I'd love to." Then he whispered, "Don't bring Marge." A half an hour later, I told my mother I was going over to have a farewell drink and that I'd see her later. She said, "I'm going too!" I said, "You're not, Marge. I don't want you to." So I went out without telling her what compartment they were in.

We were there for about ten minutes, laughing and having a wonderful time. We let our hair down, discussing everything that had happened on tour. All of a sudden, there's a horrible noise. It's the emergency whistle. Everything stops.

We all ran out to see what it was. My mother had been *that* furious that she had pulled the cord and stopped the train! I could see the conductor trying to pry her door open, so they could turn the alarm off. She wouldn't open it. She was screaming, "Ronald Colman is raping my daughter!"

I wanted to die. I turned to everybody and said, "Oh, my God. What can I say?" Ronnie just turned his back on me and walked away. So did Joe. Joe was a pantywaist, but I was so shocked at Colman's behavior. Finally, I got back to my mother. I said, "I could kill you!" She was stinking drunk. I don't know how she had managed to get that way in ten minutes. Maybe she was already, when I left, and was hiding it.

She had ruined the whole thing. We were stuck in our compartment, and I had to listen to her ravings all night. I had to take her into the dining car in the morning. I didn't want to; but I hadn't eaten in a day-and-a-half. There they were: no recognition at all. We got off the train in LA. Mrs. Colman was there. Nothing! No words were spoken. I got my mother into the car. I was going to take her right to the sanitarium, but by the time I got home all hell had broken loose on something else and I had to stick with her and go through her sobering-up process by myself.

That SOB Colman, who had been my dear friend for all that time, never spoke to me again. I'd see him out at different places and he'd always turn his head and walk away. I wouldn't make a move. I was embarrassed to death and I didn't feel that I should be judged by what my mother did. Colman was just cruel and terrible and he told everybody in Hollywood about it. It was in the paper, alluding to the thing, but not mentioning any names.

Don't get me started on my mother. Don't ever mention her name out here; you'll be clubbed to death! *(laughing)*

People ask me, "Why didn't you do a little better in your career, Lynn?" My mother was a terrible problem. I think that I would have had an entirely different life if she had not been that way. And, of course, I'm scared to death that I'm going to wind up like her.

Roanoke, Virginia, January 1921; Marge Fisher takes delight in her one-year-old daughter, Peggy.

CHAPTER TWO

SPEED TO BURN

Lynn Bari was born Marjorie Schulyer Fisher on December 18, 1919. The
second child of Marjorie and John
Fisher, she would always be called
"Peggy." Her brother, John ("Johnny"),
was five years her senior. The first five
years of Peggy's life were spent in Roanoke, Virginia, a medium-sized city set
into the heart of a pastoral landscape.
Located at the entrance of the Shenandoah Valley, Roanoke was bordered on
the east by the Blue Ridge Mountains
and, on the west, by the Allegheny. The
Fishers lived in the center of the town
until 1922, at which point they moved
up to Mill Mountain, where they settled
into the middle-class district of Walnut
Hill. Their new neighbors on the hill
were impressed by the fact that John
Fisher had built a multiple-car garage
adjacent to his two-story stucco home.

*Peggy Fisher, age four, in Roanoke;
January 1924.*

It soon became apparent to everyone that John and Marge had money and
were the worldly type. Their sophistication, however, did not prevent them from
becoming one of the most well-liked couples in the area; they were extremely
gracious people. And when the Fisher family prepared to move to Lynchburg in
the summer of 1925, most of Walnut Hill bade them a teary goodbye.

The very young Peggy Fisher would be remembered by her Walnut Hill neighbors as a "cute lil' old thing," a sunny child who bore a striking resemblance to the
Kewpie Doll. Her face was very round, she had huge hazel eyes and her figure
was a bit on the plump side. Whenever she smiled — which was often — her
snub nose would become lost between two enormous apple cheeks. Unlike the
popular doll, though, Peggy did have a full head of hair; it was ash blonde and
cropped into a Buster Brown, complete with bangs.

Peggy appeared to be as uncomplicated as she was adorable. There was nothing about her character that distinguished her from the other children on the hill. Had she not gone on to become a movie star, she probably would have faded from memory.

Daughter or no daughter, folks would never have forgotten Marge Fisher, however. Over six decades later some would still recall her tale that she was once a George Eastman model. There was never any reason to doubt this fiction because Marge was an extraordinarily beautiful woman. Her body was willowy, perfectly proportioned and topped by a lush, curly brown mane. She had brilliant blue eyes, a finely-sculpted face and creamy pink skin which practically glowed when she lapsed into one of her endearing smiles. Her precise mode of speech and impeccable taste in clothes complemented her natural grace; it was clear she was from a cultured background. This fact stood in startling contrast to her excitable demeanor, which often took on a note of theatricality. She could play the rowdy, the coquette and Mother Courage with equal ease and somehow managed to convey a childlike charm while assuming any of these poses. She also had a wildly independent streak which manifested itself into various displays of female emancipation. If a thirty-one-year-old mother of two could be called a "flagrant flapper," Marge Fisher certainly fit the bill. She smoked, drank, bobbed her hair and drove fast cars. By 1925, the gasps had subsided into chuckles as she sped by in her roadster on one of her daily excursions up Mill Mountain; people had come to accept Marge as a loveable eccentric. They would later realize that, in certain respects, she was way ahead of her time.

Although Marge's looks and behavior were attention-getting, her conversational skills left something to be desired. She had a hard time moving beyond banal pleasantries — except when she was drinking; then her remarks bordered on the absurd. Nothing she ever said, drunk or sober, invited closeness and her friendships, though numbering many, were purely of the superficial variety. Walnut Hill's great extrovert was, in essence, insecure in the company of adults.

With children, however, Marge could really communicate. They were more on her level; they shared the same outlook: life was meant to be fun, fun, fun! Kids never judged her and, in turn, she never judged them. By all accounts, she was in heaven when she was around them.

Marge was extremely affectionate toward her own children when they were small. Both were bright, agreeable and well-mannered youngsters; they seemed to be turning out just fine. Johnny had his mother's curly brown hair, the greenest of eyes and a sturdy little frame. He was an active boy, one who also had a pensive side. When he stood beside his adoring baby sister, he always assumed an air of protectiveness. Peggy's personality was more animated than her brother's, but the two basically shared the same character traits. They were both certainly devoted to their mother, unwaveringly so.

Their affection for their father appeared to be less intense. This was understandable because he wasn't around the house much. John Fisher's energies were almost exclusively directed toward his work. He was the co-owner of the Harper Motor Company, an agency at the corner of Luck Avenue and Second Street. His

SPEED TO BURN 21

establishment sold Durants, Oaklands, Overlands, Stars and Willys-Knights. It was a prosperous concern, due in large part to the fact that Fisher put in much overtime, at night and on out-of-town business trips. Weekends found him more at liberty, and this is when he spent time with family and friends.

Fisher's consuming career drive belied his persona, which was rather low-key. At fifty, he bore a resemblance to the Arrow Collar Man, Madison Avenue's quintessential upright gentleman. His regular features were offset by penetrating brown eyes and dark hair, which was now graying at the temples. Although dignified in appearance and well-versed in social etiquette, Fisher didn't project the self-assurance associated with one who excelled professionally. He came across as the quiet type and almost faded into the woodwork when in the presence of his bubbly young wife. However, he was genuinely interested in what others had to say and this enabled him to form acquaintanceships that were of greater substance than those of Marge. People who got to know John Fisher more than casually found him to be thoughtful, intelligent and affable.

Despite their vast differences in age and temperament, Peggy's parents presented themselves as a harmonious pair. They spoke of one another in positive terms and never quarreled in public. Both came from privileged backgrounds and were strongly motivated toward external achievement. They seemed to be very concerned about their children's well-being and were intent on giving them the best life had to offer. According to Marge, her kids would have more than they'd ever need because her husband was on a path to tremendous success. Friends sensed that it was Marge herself who provided Fisher with the incentive to push forward in such a determined manner. For quite a while, she had been pressing him to relinquish his partnership in Harper Motor and go into business for himself. He did so in 1925, the year he decided to set up a car dealership in Lynchburg. Marge was elated by this move. In no time at all, she had everyone's belongings packed up and ready to be transported to the greener pastures she saw ahead.

The family exchanged farewells with the folk on Walnut Hill and headed fifty miles east. Driving blithely across the mountains in her husband's touring car, Marge pacified her already-homesick kids, promising them nothing but fun and good times in Lynchburg. Seated behind the wheel of his wife's beloved roadster, John Fisher was immersed in thought about the responsibilities that lay before him.

The Fishers settled in Lynchburg and a new automobile business took form. Within two years, the family would be shattered by an unforeseen tragedy.

Marge Fisher could always turn to her family for comfort. Not the family that had just moved Lynchburg, but the one that had raised her. The fact that she wasn't on speaking terms with many of her relatives was beside the point; it was their line of descent that mattered. Her family heritage was her anchor, a source of pride that enabled her to carry on.

Marjorie Babcock Halpen was born in 1893 in Albany, New York. Albany had also been the birthplace of Marge's older sister, Ellen (b. 1891), and her parents, William and Hannah. William Halpen's mother's family had been residents of the Hudson Valley for several generations. The Halpens had settled there as Irish immigrants in the mid-nineteenth century. They had come to America as people of means, having been prosperous tradespeople in Western Europe. By the time William was born, in 1865, the Halpens had established themselves among Albany's upper crust. At the very highest circle of this social class were the Babcocks, the family of Hannah Halpen (b. 1869). The Babcocks were part of the Schuyler dynasty, a powerful Hudson Valley clan of Dutch heritage that had figured prominently in the first two centuries of US history. The Schuylers had, indeed, boasted many an illustrious descendent. Among them: Alexander Hamilton and Philip Livingston, one of the men who had signed the Declaration of Independence.

Marge would always speak of her distinguished background with great reverence. While her familial pride was bona fide, the stories with which she gave forth about her own upbringing were severely edited for public approval. She would often describe her early life as a charmed one — and, by all appearances, this seemed to be true. Her parents sent her to the best schools, exposed her to the fine arts and catered to her material desires. At an appropriate age, she was allowed to dress to the nines and hobnob with her family's well-to-do friends, many of whose sons became bewitched by her beauty and vivacity. Could there be any doubt that Marjorie Halpen was the girl who had everything?

What Marge would constantly fail to recall, however, was her longstanding resistance to her family's self-contained way of life. Their stuffy mores made her an impatient and contrary girl, one who escaped into a world of books to alleviate her boredom. There, on the printed page, she could find people who lived exciting lives — people she wanted to emulate. The contrast between her fantasies and her actual home life only served to increase her restlessness and she finally became openly defiant to her family's conventions. After completing her formal education at seventeen, she let it be known that she had no intention of remaining in Albany, where she knew she would be expected to marry some proper young man.

Marge's mother Hannah understood her daughter's wanderlust to a certain degree; she could envision her following a more dynamic course than her own. However, she knew full well that her implacable child could not possibly fend for herself in some strange environment. Much thoughtful consideration caused Hannah to seek help from a cousin in Virginia, Tim Williams. She asked Tim if he and his wife, Grace, would be willing to have Marge come and live with them at their sprawling farmland estate, Tusculum. Tusculum was built in the eighteenth century by the Williams family (part of the Schuyler clan). It was located twenty miles east of Lynchburg in Amherst County, an area which was comprised of rural communities and small towns. Hannah had been a guest at Tusculum several times, visits which had strengthened her ties to Tim and Grace. Since her friendship with the couple was on very solid ground, it wasn't too difficult for her to make a weighty request on her daughter's behalf. The Williams responded to it positively and unconditionally. They extended a personal invitation to an elated Marge, saying she could move in with them anytime she wished. She did so almost immediately, in the summer of 1911.

Tusculum became Marge's dream world. She got along famously with the Williams, who treated her like a princess. Taking advantage of their hospitality, she saw no reason to go to work. College was another endeavor which didn't capture her interest. Instead, she chose to invest her time and energies in another pursuit: the reinvention of herself as a Southern belle. This was a task she could — and did — carry out quite well.

Life for this beguiling ex-Yankee quickly became one big party. Furthering this situation along was the fact that drinking was part and parcel of Southern entertaining; families like the Williams's always made sure their liquor cabinet was well-stocked — and Marge shared in the abundance. Right from the start, she used alcohol as a social lubricant; in unfamiliar surroundings, drinking made her feel more witty, desirable and at ease. A dependence on booze had now been established, eventually playing havoc on the lives of Marge and those closest to her.

John Fisher met Marge in 1912. From Lynchburg, he was a member of a sports club to which Tim Williams also belonged. The two men became friends, spending much time together fishing, hunting and skeet shooting. Fisher was a real gentleman, in Tim's mind's eye; a nice, steady fellow. Grace felt similarly about him and she came to believe that Marge might also enjoy his company. A dinner at Tusculum was arranged for this purpose. One glance at Marge and Fisher was cast into the spell of her beauty and charm. Marge reveled in her dinner partner's adoring attentions and thought him to be a man of distinguished bearing and innovative ideas. The two began courting.

Fisher's family had lived in the Shenandoah Valley since the late eighteenth century. They were descended from a small enclave of Pennsylvania Dutch who had settled in Strasburg, Virginia, a town where they had earned their living as master craftsmen. In 1828, Levi Fisher moved to nearby Lynchburg to open a gun shop. He turned out to be an astute businessman and his store flourished. Inspired by this success, Levi decided to enlarge his enterprise and feature a wider variety of merchandise; the United States now had its second sporting goods store. The establishment moved to much larger headquarters in 1873, on Lynchburg's Main Street. By then it had become known as the S.O. Fisher Sporting Goods Store, bearing the name of its current chief, (Levi's half-brother) Samuel Otho Fisher.

Samuel Fisher and his wife Virginia parented five children. Their second son, John Maynard, was Peggy Fisher's father. John was born in 1874, in Strasburg. He went to work at S.O. Fisher when he was a youngster, helping out in the stockroom after school. Following college, he began his swift ascent to a top managerial post at the store. The company was now in its glory days, expanding as rapidly as America itself. Sensing this parallel, young Fisher's thoughts became focused on his country's growth and the things that were propelling it forward at the dawn of the twentieth century. The burgeoning automobile industry fascinated him more than anything else.

This new industrial frontier had been gathering steam by 1910 — and John Fisher wanted to be part of the action. Leaving the family business behind, he went to work at Lynchburg's first auto dealership, where he soon became a canny master of promotion and sales. John Maynard Fisher was on his way.

Fisher was thirty-seven when he was introduced to Marge Halpen. The eighteen-year-old was the first woman to whom he ever drew close and the first person who made him feel special. Marge admired Fisher for his tenacity; despite his rather restrained character, he had broken away from his family to engage in a life pursuit that was radically different from theirs. Marge could identify with this individualism, herself having left a home steeped in tradition. In her dreamy thoughts, the two of them were renegades out to conquer the world. The truth of the matter was somewhat different: an irrepressible teenager was preparing to hitch her wagon to the star of John Fisher — a man of whom she had no real understanding.

The couple had known one another for less than a year when they married in Virginia. Their 1913 wedding had been arranged on impulse, with Hannah and William Halpen not being notified. But word soon traveled north and Marge's parents hit the roof; to say that they were furious with their daughter would be an understatement. That she had married a man nineteen years her senior was cause for much upset. More than anything else, though, the Halpens felt insulted by the fact that she had made no attempt whatsoever to introduce them to Fisher — they barely knew he existed. The results of this subterfuge would be unfortunate, driving a deep wedge into Marge's relationship with her parents.

Marge and her bridegroom moved into a small house in Lynchburg. New Year's 1914 unfolded happily for the couple. John Fisher was moving straight up the professional ladder and his wife was in a blissful state, pregnant with their first child. John Owen Fisher was born on September 8, 1914.

Johnny brought out Marge's healthier, unselfish side; without a hint of maternal anxiety, she was most attentive and loving toward her newborn. The baby's father, however, was not nearly as affectionate. A true Victorian, John Fisher, Sr. believed the handling and holding of children the domain of women and servants. Marge was disturbed by the distance he placed between himself and his son. The quality of her marriage began to disintegrate because of this — and, before long, almost everything her husband did was provoking her to annoyance. As far as she was concerned, he was unfeeling and drab beyond words. Little about him now interested her, except his professional potential.

Late in 1916, Fisher was offered a key position at the Harper Motor Company. He accepted the job, which had to be filled immediately. Because his transition was a hurried one, he relocated his family to Roanoke without first selling his Lynchburg home. So in the interim, they stayed at an enormous boardinghouse, owned and operated by Roanoke businessman George Payne and his wife, Ida. The Paynes and Fishers soon became good friends. Johnny himself would come to be pals with the Payne boys, Ralph and John. John Payne would one day go out to Hollywood and play in movies opposite Peggy Fisher.

The Fishers found new lodging several months later, setting up house in a smart two-story dwelling several blocks from Harper Motor. The company and the gentleman from Lynchburg turned out to be a good match, much to Marge's delight.

Marge was made even happier in the spring of 1919, when she once again found herself expecting. Certain her second child would be a girl, she had already chosen for her a name: Marjorie Schulyer, in honor of herself and her family. As had been anticipated, this middle name would become a conversation piece for years to come — thus giving the elder Marjorie many wonderful opportunities to boast about her lineage. Marjorie Schulyer Fisher was born at home one week before Christmas 1919.

Peggy was a hearty and even-tempered baby, one nurtured by the caresses of her doting mother. The maternal caring and concern Marge displayed

Roanoke, January 16, 1921; one-year-old Peggy sits for a portrait with her brother John, age six.

did, indeed, have its positive effects on her little girl, and Johnny as well. However, her ambivalence toward her husband precluded the possibility of the children developing a truly healthy relationship with their father. Marge was now playing upon Fisher's inherent frailties and insecurities, as she prodded him to excel in his career and turned him into a workhorse who'd devote increasingly less time to his family. The automobile business came to assume sad and ironic overtones for John Fisher. What had once been a continuing source of inspiration had evolved into a beleaguering way of life — and an escape from the demanding wife who had helped to make it so.

Fisher became a partner at Harper Motor in 1922. The same year he and his family moved to Walnut Hill, a neighborhood perfect for rearing children. Its woody and sloping terrain proved ideal for Johnny and his friends, as they spent many hours engaging in tree climbing, relay races, soapbox derbies and games of cowboys-and-Indians. Peggy herself was too young to participate in these activities but she often tagged along and sat on the sidelines, her prized pony cart in tow. There was also a lively camaraderie present among the adults in the area; they socialized with one another frequently. Marge basked in this whirl. The good front she and her husband put forth in public left their friends totally clueless to the discordant nature of their marriage. Neighbors, in fact, could witness

On April 8, 1922, two-year-old Peggy posed in front of her family's Walnut Hill home for this pair of snapshots. Brother Johnny is alongside her in the second of these photos.

a happy family scene being played out in the Fisher driveway every morning. Marge would be at the front door with Peggy in her arms, waving goodbye to her husband and son. On his way to work, Fisher would drive Johnny to The Park School, over in Highland Park. Usually invited along for the ride would be one of Johnny's car-crazy classmates, all of whom thought "Mr. Fisher" a great guy.

Johnny's impressions of his father were quite different from those of his friends. It was hard for him to like a man who was both a harsh and remote presence in his life. Fisher rarely made any effort to communicate with his son — and, when he did, it was usually to reprimand him for some childish act of mischief. Then he'd assume the role of the strict disciplinarian. Sensing no real love from his father, Johnny directed his parental affections solely toward his mother. Marge would empathize with her boy's conflict — by treating him to her ravings about his dad and the male sex in general.

Marge became a daily drinker during these Walnut Hill years. She largely confined her imbibing to the evening hours, after she had given her kids their dinner. Booze brought out her worst qualities when she was at home with her family; she tended to be hostile, directing

Albany, New York, 1923; Peggy and Johnny Fisher with their grandparents, Hannah and William Halpen.

most of her antagonism toward her husband. Fisher would usually react to her tirades in silence, retreating to the den and his ledger books. It is no small wonder why his work schedule now included frequent overnight business trips.

Returning home from one of these sojourns, Fisher found himself startled by his wife's sudden change in appearance; she had shorn her long, luxurious hair and was sporting a daring flapper bob. The bait worked this time and he threw a fit. Marge took perverse delight in this; she would do anything to get a rise out of her husband. That's one of the reasons why she had become an incessant cigarette smoker. The same could be said for her reckless driving, boisterous social demeanor and extravagant taste in clothes — behaviors which she knew full well would meet with Fisher's disapproval.

Marge's relationship with her family in New York was also marked by mounting friction. There had been a period of relative peace in this area, shortly after

Peggy's birth. Hannah Halpen had, in fact, spent several months with the Fishers in 1920, delighting in her grandchildren. Her stay, however, eventually turned into a nightmare of battles with her daughter. What had actually transpired between them is uncertain, but it had created strong feelings of enmity that still prevailed. In spite of this, Hannah and her husband William had remained in phone contact with Marge. Their calls would invariably wind up as arguments, with each party trying to put the other in their place. The Halpens had become exasperated by their daughter's willfulness and insolence. Marge, in turn, found her parents to be overly intrusive, self-righteous and stodgy. She dealt with them impatiently and tried her best to keep them at arm's length. On several occasions, though, she did vacation in Albany with her husband and children. These visits, by all accounts, were made unpleasant by her combative behavior.

Peggy and her adoring brother, Johnny, on Walnut Hill in June 1924.

In due time, Marge would be on the outs with virtually every member of her family, refusing to communicate with one or another of them for months on end. At the root of these sweeping rebuffs would be an intense jealousy of the people of whom she was also proud. Having chosen to conduct her life in a rebellious way, Marge had forfeited a world of grandeur and social distinction — and she had yet to create a lifestyle for herself that in any way approached what she had left behind.

Pride and envy would always stand in Marge Fisher's way. These emotions were the hallmark of her personality and they would continually corrupt her relationships with those whom she loved.

The Fishers' last year on Walnut Hill (1924-25) saw Marge attempting to redesign the career course of her husband, whom she felt was rotting away in a state of complacency. The fact that he was doing very well by Harper Motor didn't matter to her one bit. She told him that partnerships were all right for someone getting started in business, but he was fifty and should have long since been in a position of total authority — and headed toward something big. To achieve this end, Marge masterminded a game plan for her spouse: he should purchase his own car dealership, make a resounding success of it, and then expand his business to a national level. Relentless coercion by his wife saw Fisher taking the first step toward this lofty objective; he plunged his savings into the creation of an auto enterprise in Lynchburg, where both of their families were well-connected. The city itself might not have been Albany but, for Marge, it did hold promise.

The move from Roanoke to Lynchburg coincided with the children's summer break. Peggy and Johnny had both been attending The Park School, where they had just completed kindergarten and the fourth grade, respectively. Although they'd miss their old school, they came to like the one in Lynchburg just as much and would make many friends there. The two would also take a special liking to their new home, which was far more spacious than the house on Walnut Hill.

Marge did her best to give her kids a full life. She saw to it that they were always involved in one recreational activity or another and took them swimming, horseback riding and skating. Whenever a circus or fair came to town, she made sure they'd be on hand to enjoy it. All three shared a great fondness for motion pictures and they attended them several times a week, usually after an early supper. Peggy's favorite film, one she would see many times, would be the first screen version of *Peter Pan* (1925). Based on Sir James Barrie's play, it starred Betty Bronson in the title role. The picture held less interest for Johnny, whose taste in movies was primarily action-oriented. Marge preferred romances and historical dramas. She lost herself in these types of sagas and developed crushes on their leading men; John Barrymore, Richard Barthelmess and Ronald Colman among them. She had also come to idolize the female stars, women like Norma Talmadge, Corinne Griffith and Eleanor Boardman. Since people had often remarked that her own beauty rivaled theirs, it was easy for her to imagine herself in their roles as she gazed at their films. Marge was also very curious about the offscreen lives of her favorites and she had subscriptions to *Photoplay* and *Motion Picture*. Interestingly, Eleanor Boardman (who would later marry director King Vidor) had first come to prominence as an Eastman Kodak Girl. This was a title which Marge herself had chosen to appropriate for her own biography, subtly indicating her unspoken desire to be a movie star.

Despite the fact that she and her children were making an easy adjustment to Lynchburg, Marge had come to believe that Virginia was not a place where they should live too much longer. Fourteen years there had convinced her of this: her family would be better suited to a more cosmopolitan environment, which some other state could offer. Marge's role models had now become the movers and shakers whom she read about in magazines. She desperately wanted her family to ascend into an inner circle of these "beautiful people," and she fully expected they would — providing her husband would follow her plan for his career.

Fisher gave his all to his new venture. The car dealership opened its doors in the fall of 1925; about three months after his family had arrived in Lynchburg. The fact that it had so swiftly become a going concern had had everything to do with its owner's diligence. Experience, however, had taught Fisher that automobile businesses take time to flourish. Cars were no longer a novelty and their mass production had brought thousands more men into his field, making things very competitive. Fisher was aware of all the uncertainties with which he was dealing and was disheartened, but definitely not surprised, to see his enterprise in the red throughout the remainder of 1925. At first he dealt with this situation in a constructive way, taking a broad view and anticipating a brighter future.

In time, though, he became worn down by Marge's incessant hounding. She would berate him continually, reasoning that there was no excuse for the figures at the bottom of his balance sheets. Her means of whipping him into shape were the same as they had always been: feed his self-doubt with belittling words so that he would try even harder to prove his worth. And, once again, her ploy seemed to work; her husband's business began realizing a profit in early 1926.

Marge's tactics had another effect on Fisher, however, one she could not — or would not — see. His mind had now become numbed by her unceasing harassments. An emotionally stronger individual might have stood up to her or brushed her remarks aside. Fisher, on the other hand, usually affected a stoic silence and acceded to her demands. His children would much later come to surmise that, in all likelihood, it had been his habit from childhood to internalize his reactions to difficult situations. Adult hindsight would also find Peggy and Johnny reflecting on how Marge's aggressive manner had caused their father to retreat

Summer 1926; Peggy and Johnny Fisher, vacationing on the Virginia coast.

further and further into his shell, turning him into something of an emotional automaton. Decades after the fact, the younger Fishers would be of the opinion that their dad had suffered from what had come to be known as a "clinical depression." A probable neurological disorder notwithstanding, the John Fisher of 1926 was able to carry on with his business — an enterprise by which he was becoming increasingly less fulfilled.

The year moved on and a fledging auto company continued to gain ground. Fisher had accomplished a great deal within a brief period of time but, despite its current profits, the business was a long way from receiving a total return on its initial investment. This didn't matter much to Marge, who had become thrilled by her husband's progress, which made her certain that he had what it took to become a captain of industry. Impulsively, she had now decided that the time was ripe for him to open up a second dealership, preferably one in a metropolitan area. Fisher could not go along with this idea, explaining that he did not have the financial wherewithal to operate two businesses at once and still adequately provide for his family. Marge couldn't argue with this, nor could she bear the thought of remaining in Lynchburg for an indeterminate period of time. Consequently, in early 1927, she began to trumpet another scheme: the family would pull up stakes and relocate to a big city, to found a company that would be better poised for a more rapid expansion. Fisher's receptivity to this plan remains in question, but he did agree to pursue the matter by investigating possibilities in larger urban areas. Marge also got into the act here and, after some quick research, the couple chose Philadelphia as their target city. It was then decided that Fisher would make a trip there pronto to evaluate his options.

Fisher traveled alone to Philadelphia, where he had set up several business appointments over a three-day period. Arriving there, he called Marge. He told her he had just checked into his hotel room. All was well, he said.

The following morning, Marge received another phone call; the person on the other end was a concerned stranger. To her utter disbelief, she was told that her husband had jumped to his death from out his hotel window. Fisher's sense of inadequacy, his children would later conjecture, had apparently become overwhelming in the face of all these elaborate plans for his future. In a moment of complete despair, he had determined that taking his own life was the only way he could put an end to his torment.

Marge was stunned by Fisher's suicide. She did not voice any feelings of grief, shame or guilt about it, but instead went into a mode of extreme agitation; she became filled with anxiety about how she and her children were going to get by. She knew she wouldn't be able to think clearly in her own home, a grim reminder of the life she had carved out with her husband. Thankfully, in the wake of his death, she and the kids were invited by Tim and Grace Williams to live at Tusculum. Marge accepted their offer without hesitation, packed up her household in an instant and moved in with them. This relocation would last about four months.

Peggy and Johnny's stay at Tusculum proved to be diverting, helping to distract them from any feelings of sadness or disorientation they might have been experiencing. The two had not yet been told that their father had killed himself; it had instead been explained to them that he had died in an accidental fall from his hotel window. Both children were inherently resilient, fostering a way for them to cope with a tremendous loss and its aftereffects. At the same time, however, they were being deprived of the chance to openly talk about what had transpired because Marge refused to discuss her husband's death with them — or anyone else, for that matter. The youngsters, by their own admission as adults, consequently repressed any questions they might have had about their father and his demise.

Marge was pleased to see her kids enjoying themselves at the Williams', but she herself had come to realize that additional problems had followed her to Tusculum. Despite its ample supply of booze and the warmth of her cousins, she felt increasingly more uncomfortable there, primarily because her husband's suicide had become a hot topic of gossip with everyone in Lynchburg, Roanoke and points-in-between. This was definitely one time that Marge didn't appreciate being at the center of attention. Accordingly, she determined that she would have to hustle herself and her children out of Virginia.

Before leaving, she had to get her finances in order. She hired a lawyer to liquidate her husband's estate and discovered to her horror that it was worth far less than she had supposed. It turned out that Fisher had sold off most of his holdings to establish his Lynchburg business, and he had to take out several large bank loans to keep it going. Marge was obliged to take care of these debts — plus taxes, legal fees and various outstanding bills. When all was said and done, the sale of the dealership, her two cars, her home and its furnishings netted her comparatively little — enough to support her family for several months, at best.

Marge had originally wanted to start afresh and create a home with her children on new terrain. This plan had to be abandoned once her monetary situation became clear. If she still wanted to relocate, she was left with but one possible alternative: she would have to move in with her family up North — something she dreaded doing. She knew, though, that she had no recourse but to swallow her pride, ask for help and reconnect with people whom she felt treated her like an errant child. Marge also understood there was no guarantee that she'd be welcomed back, even if she humbled herself. Behind her doubts was the nature of Fisher's death. In that era, families of her station often treated suicide as a scandal and a disgrace, an event with which they would rather not be associated.

Marge phoned her parents, made her request and was met with a chilly reception. After this snub, she could have tried reasoning with her folks, who might very well have softened. This didn't happen because she instead chose to be spiteful — and her return to Albany was no longer an option. She then turned to her Aunt Jo, Hannah's sister. Jo was one of the few Hudson Valley relatives with whom she had been on consistently good terms. Marge spoke to her about her plight in great detail. Weighing her problems thoughtfully, her aunt suggested she seek assistance from her niece Ellen — Marge's sister — who was living in Massachusetts. Ellen was thirty-six at this point, long married to a man named Palmer. The couple had recently relocated from Albany to Melrose, a small city just north of Boston. Jo thought Ellen to be a benevolent person, one who might very well be willing to open up her home to Marge and her children. Marge told Jo she was doubtful that her sister would be so magnanimous, since their relationship had always been marked by an intense rivalry. She did, however, pursue her aunt's recommendation, realizing she was now backed into a corner.

Marge decided to approach her sister with frankness. Ellen sincerely appreciated this and was extremely sympathetic, at once welcoming Marge and her kids into her home. The three Fishers moved up to Melrose in autumn 1927. Peggy and Johnny were immediately enrolled in the local public schools. Ellen and Palmer enjoyed the children's presence; they found them to be cheerful, resourceful and cooperative. Marge, on the other hand, turned out to be an agonizingly annoying houseguest. She was full of advice about how her hosts should conduct their lives and manage their home, all the while making no effort to contribute to its upkeep by obtaining employment. The effects of her drinking were another thing that added to a situation of growing tension. One quarrel led to another and Marge was given the boot at the outset of summer.

Despite their differences, Ellen was clearly concerned about her sister. She felt even more compassion for Peggy and Johnny. Both she and her husband dearly loved the children and they were happy to have brought a sense of stability into their lives. Not wanting them to lose it, the couple thought they should live near to them. A small house across the street had just become vacant. Ellen and Palmer sang its praises to Marge, who grudgingly rented it.

Melrose, Massachusetts, 1928; Johnny extends a protective arm around eight-year-old Peggy.

Marge felt humiliated by her new home, which she thought to be dreary, confining and inadequately heated. A big freeze blew in that December and she made a resolve with herself to get out of there as soon as she could. When she would move and where she would live would be determined by her finances which, at this point, were in disastrous shape; her savings had almost completely dried up. Her impoverishment saw her resuming contact with the folks in Albany. She and the kids went to visit them over Christmas 1928 — and afterwards she began to receive monthly checks with Hannah Halpen's signature. All too soon, though, she discovered this money couldn't be stretched to support a family of three. The day finally came when Marge was forced to face the fact that she would have to go to work. Since she had already intended to break her lease and clear out, she decided to leave Melrose altogether and move to Boston, where she thought she would stand a better chance of finding an interesting job. The city would also afford her and the children the opportunity to pursue a more sophisticated way of life, something she naturally considered to be of utmost importance.

Marge made a day-trip to Boston and was able to secure a modest apartment. Then, out of the blue, she went to Ellen and Palmer with a request: she asked if Johnny could live with them for a short spell, while she tried to get on firmer footing. She explained this would also be in the best interest of her son, now fourteen. Because his life had endured so many disruptions over the past two years, she thought he should remain at his current school, which he enjoyed attending. Peggy would accompany her to Boston, she said, for she was only nine and would have an easier time adjusting to yet another new situation. Ellen was confused by her sister's logic and worried that Johnny might feel left out. Marge assured her he wouldn't, adding that it was her plan to have him visit Boston each weekend. Ellen, led to believe the arrangement very temporary, finally agreed to take in her nephew. Johnny was never consulted in the matter. He would continue to reside with Ellen and Palmer, exclusive of weekends, for more than a year — much to his great dismay. The boy, however, not once protested his mother's decision to leave him in Melrose. But years later he'd admit to his wife Eugenie that he'd experienced an intense feeling of rejection because of this displacement — one by which, according to Eugenie, he'd be emotionally scarred for the rest of his life.

Marge and Peggy relocated to Boston in early 1929. Peggy switched schools once again and adapted to it well, receiving good grades. Her scholastic record would always be above average, even though her educational history would be distinguished by a constant change of enrollment. The same would hold true for her brother. Both children felt anchored by their studies and were motivated to achieve. Their teachers' approval meant much to them, perhaps more than it did to most other youngsters.

Peggy derived much pleasure from her life in Boston. She was a popular kid, one whose friends appreciated the rather kooky sense of humor she had come to develop. She often employed it in an attempt to rally the spirits of her mother, who was having a hard time coping with her single status.

Marge's finishing school education had left her unprepared for the harsh realities of the working world. She discovered in short order that being a woman usually meant having to settle for a mundane and low-paying job. After combing the help-wanted ads, she determined that office work would be the least offensive alternative. She became a receptionist in a business firm, but was promptly let go when she got into an argument with her boss. Her second job saw her in a similar position, one to which she would manage to hold on for several months. She detested the work, though, and viewed her meager salary as a personal affront. All too soon she came to sense there existed few employment prospects that would be suitable to her, certainly none that would elevate her family to a decorous standard of living. However, she knew someone who could accomplish this advancement for her — and that person would become her second husband.

Marge hadn't known anyone in Boston when she had first moved there. Shortly after her arrival, she had joined a neighborhood church, thinking this would be a good way to meet people. She had never been a particularly religious woman; although she and Fisher had made a point of bringing Peggy and Johnny up as Episcopalians, they themselves hadn't attended services regularly. Now on her own in an unfamiliar city, Marge had become a member of the Institute of

Religious Sciences. She had quickly made friends with many of its parishioners and, to her surprise, was able to find solace in the church's teachings. She was also developing an interest in its local leader, the Reverend Robert H. Bitzer.

Soft-spoken, gentle and wise, Dr. Bitzer was thirty-three, two years younger than Marge. He was also quite attractive and definitely had a promising future ahead of him. Not long after Marge had become a part of his church, she had struck up a conversation with him and learned that he had grown up in Alexandria, Virginia. This had led to a lively dialogue about the "Old Dominion"— and the preacher became smitten with a beautiful young widow. He perceived her to be a courageous woman, one who had faced great hardship but who presented herself as a cheerful optimist and the loving mother of two fine children. Within months of their first chat, Marge and the reverend were married.

A preacher's wife and stepdaughter in 1931; Marge Bitzer and eleven-year-old Peggy Fisher are all smiles, standing on the grounds of their first home in Beverly Hills, California.

CHAPTER THREE
I'M MAKING BELIEVE

My mother married my stepfather practically the moment after we got to Boston. I don't know how she swung that one *(laughing)*, but she did.

My stepfather was a very kind man. We got along just fine. He brought us up liberally, not believing in punishing children. He had a doctorate in the ministry and was with the Institute of Religious Sciences in Boston. The Institute was run by a fellow named Ernest Holmes, who worked out of Los Angeles. Its credo was akin to that of Christian Science, Mary Baker Eddy's church. Because they were also located in Boston, and to avoid confusion, my stepfather's chapter had to be very careful about how they worded its name.

The Reverend's home was situated on Commonwealth Avenue. Peggy and her mother would live with him there for about a year. During this period, the nine-year-old became fired with the desire to act.

I wanted to be an actress ever since I can remember. There was never a thought of being anything else.

Responding to this, Dr. Bitzer helped to expose his stepdaughter to the abundance of theater in the area.

We used to see plays and tryouts for New York, like *Follow Thru*, which was my very first play. Also, E.E. Clive, the character actor, had a place where they did these horrible melodramas like *The 13th Chair* and *The Bat*. I'd always be so frightened at night, thinking about them — so I eventually stopped going there.

But I went to the movies anytime I could. Jean Arthur and Garbo I thought were the best in the world. Still do. I remember seeing Jean Arthur in a movie where she was playing a villainess. I thought that she was pretty and wondered, "How could she do those terrible things?"

Peggy's theatrical interests were also encouraged by her mother, who was finding a spotlight for herself in her husband's parish. Marge seemed to enjoy the role of preacher's wife and jumped at the chance to preside over almost every social and civic activity the church had to offer. In very little time she had managed to ingratiate herself with a congregation who had become rather wary of her, feeling that she had somehow entrapped their minister into a hasty marriage. Everyone now agreed that Dr. Bitzer had chosen a most winning partner.

Throughout his marriage to Marge, the Reverend would try in every way to be a good husband and stepfather. His relationship with his wife would be a mutually supportive one during their early years together. Peggy had warm feelings for Dr. Bitzer and would always treat him lovingly and with respect. Since her natural father had died when she was so young, she came to embrace the Reverend more as a father than a stepfather (although she would never be legally adopted by him). Her brother, however, saw him only as the stranger who had usurped his position in their family. After Fisher's suicide, Johnny had come to think of himself as his mother's protector. Now the Reverend had assumed this role and the boy felt displaced. He certainly had reason to react this way, especially since he was still living in Melrose during the school week. Even though it had been solely Marge's decision that he remain with his aunt and uncle, Johnny chose to blame his stepfather for the continued separation. Dr. Bitzer could see how much the boy was hurting and would make countless attempts to befriend him — but every time he reached out in his direction, the youngster would greet him with contempt. Johnny was, in fact, aware of his stepfather's good intentions, yet he couldn't feel it within himself to accept him. This rejection would be enduring, causing the Reverend considerable heartache.

In early 1930, Reverend Bitzer received word from Ernest Holmes that the Institute of Religious Sciences was going to dissolve its Boston chapter because of a dwindling membership. Holmes did not hold Dr. Bitzer accountable for this situation, realizing there was little way for the Institute to gain ground in the city of the mother church of Christian Science.

Holmes was greatly impressed by the Reverend's sense of spirituality and his dedication to Religious Science. Not wanting to lose Dr. Bitzer to the church of Christian Science or any other sect, he approached him with an idea he had in mind. It had long been Holmes' intention to expand his church in Los Angeles, where Religious Science was thriving. Specifically, he'd been thinking of opening a chapter in Hollywood, a community whose population had been increasing at an enormously rapid rate. It now seemed an ideal time to establish this branch, especially since Dr. Bitzer would soon be at liberty and could become its leader. Holmes asked the Reverend if he would be willing to relocate to California for this purpose. Dr. Bitzer told him he very much appreciated being offered this position but, before accepting it, he would have to consult with his wife.

Marge shouted a resounding yes to the idea of the transfer, most probably imagining a congregation filled with movie stars. She snapped into making preparations for her family — Johnny included — to head west late that spring. Somehow, she was granted permission to have her children leave their respective schools a month early. By the time the kids said good-bye to their classmates, it seemed as though their mother had told all of Boston her family was Hollywood-bound.

My mother really wanted to go there. I'm sure she had aspirations to act, but she never would admit it. However, she did have aspirations for everyone else in the family. I don't think that she ever did a damn thing in her life. Oh, she did work a couple of jobs when we first came to Boston and never let us hear the end of it — how she "slaved" so. But she'd usually just sit around and look like a beautiful "Southern Lady."

I recall telling my teacher about our plans to go to Hollywood. She said, "Oh, Marjorie, that's the city of sin! Nothing but terrible, awful people. You can't go there." Big deal.

The trek to California began in May 1930 and would include over four months of sight-seeing. Dr. Bitzer and his new family would cross the country circuitously, in a Cadillac that had been given to him by a devoted parishioner. Peggy and Johnny were assigned to the back seat, crammed together amidst luggage. The youngsters fought with one another almost the entire trip, but everyone appeared to be in one piece when they arrived in Los Angeles in September.

Naturally, we all had to go over to MGM immediately and have lunch in the drugstore next door. I remember I drank the water; it was full of sulfur, and I got just deathly ill as the extras started coming in. They were all made-up. It was such a to-do. I was so sick and excited that I couldn't eat lunch.

We then stopped and checked into this horrible hotel in Culver City. They had sent the furniture out in a van and it was already there when we got to Los Angeles, but we didn't know where to go. Then we rented a little apartment. Oh, that's another thing — we used to move every five minutes. My mother was always fighting with the managers in some way or another. We either got asked to leave or she told them that "We're goddamn leaving!" I don't know how many houses we lived in.

The family ultimately settled in Beverly Hills, south of Wilshire, which was the less affluent area of the city within LA. Peggy was enrolled at the Horace Mann Grammar School. Johnny went to Beverly High, where he would find himself a track star with a perfect scholastic record. Dr. Bitzer began what would be a nineteen-year affiliation with the Institute of Religious Sciences at their newly-established Hollywood headquarters.*

The church was first based at the Women's Club on Hollywood Boulevard. Toward the rear of the club building was a library where Marge would sell books to the congregation each Sunday. Peggy would eventually accompany her stepfather to the Institute and assist him in conducting Sunday school. She would

---

* Dr. Bitzer would leave the Institute in 1949, to found the Hollywood Church of Religious Science. The Reverend would be the spiritual director of the Hollywood Church of Religious Science — the Hallmark Church of Religious Science — until his death at age ninety-eight, in 1994.

embark on this activity in her early teens and would continue with her teaching well into her screen career (a part of her life that would never be revealed in any of her studio publicity). Dr. Bitzer was acutely aware of Peggy's intelligence and her capacity to relate to people, and he knew from the start that her association with the church would prove to be meaningful to her. There was no question that the Reverend was a strong, positive influence on his stepdaughter

Beverly Hills, 1931. Left: Dr. Robert Bitzer embraces Peggy, with sixteen-year-old Johnny Fisher to their left. Right: Peggy, Marge and Johnny.

during her formative years; he instilled within her a sense of ethics and a compassion for others.

While Marge herself would claim to be guided by the moral precepts of her husband, she would lose none of her willfulness. She would, in fact, become more controlling than ever. The reason for this was simple: she was an alcoholic.

Not long ago, I was talking to my brother and said, "Johnny, do you ever remember mother drinking when we were kids?" He said, "I don't remember her sober." He's five years older than I am, so he was more aware of what was going on and took a lot more from her than I did.

Deep down, Marge was a well-intentioned and encouraging mother. She was also a severely troubled woman, however, filled with insecurities that directed the way in which she connected with her children. Her relationship to them would grow more askew with the passage of time — and the progression of her alcoholism.

Peggy and Johnny's earliest years had seen them reared by Marge in a relatively responsible manner, with love and normal maternal concern. At that point in their lives they had been unthreatening to her; she had been at the center of their worlds and the object of their devotion. The situation in this regard changed once the children began to develop as individuals, with their own distinct personalities and interests. Their evolvement was commonplace, healthy — and intimidating to their mother. Out of her own neurotic needs, Marge would undermine their self-esteem as a means of diminishing their capacities to become independent. This subversion would be accompanied by her aggressive efforts to chart the course of their lives toward lofty achievement. She would, in effect, come to treat them in the same way as she had their father, a way in which she was now also relating to Dr. Bitzer.

Marge would constantly attempt to orchestrate Peggy and Johnny's every activity with blaring directives. Her words would be marked by distortion, cruelty and inconsistency, the levels of which would correspond to her given state of inebriation. The children would react to her harangues with feelings of inadequacy. Consequently, they would always be trying to prove to both their mother and themselves that they could do better.

Although Marge knew how to play mind games on Peggy, she couldn't manipulate her daughter's innate spirit, which would prove to be indomitable; the girl had a joie de vivre that would see her through many a trying experience. Peggy was decidedly outgoing and fun-loving and her personality easily attracted friendships. Unfortunately, though, she had a disproportionate need to be liked. The effects of this would prevent her from discussing her problems with others, for she'd be afraid people would look down upon her if she did. Accordingly, no one would ever have any cause to suspect this vivacious youngster the victim of a troubled home. Peggy had already mastered the art of putting on a happy face, a behavior that would be with her always.

Peggy's grades remained unaffected by her family turmoil. She did consistently well at Horace Mann, graduating from there in the eighth grade in June 1933. Along with many of her classmates, she planned on entering the Beverly Vista School in the fall. The high school was located on South Elm Street in Beverly Hills, about two miles from her home.

Peggy and her family were currently living on Forrester Drive. John Fisher was still part of the household. The eighteen-year-old had just completed his freshman year at UCLA, at the top of his class. His academic achievements were something of which his stepfather was very proud. Dr. Bitzer had himself been making impressive headway, his good works having contributed greatly to the rapid expansion of his congregation.

The accomplishments of the family on Forrester were varied and many, but they had no dollar translation; the four had been squeaking by financially since their move west. Like most everyone else living through the Great Depression, they had learned to make do with the little they had. John Fisher had been pulling his own weight for two years, working part-time as an instructor of both tennis and golf. His mother, on the other hand, had chosen to stay at home, twiddle her thumbs and complain about the dull life that had been inflicted upon her by her husband — with whom she was now constantly arguing. Playing the role of minister's wife had apparently been no more than a short-lived diversion for the thirty-nine-year-old coquette; she had grown impatient with everyone and everything.

Marge had been in LA almost three years and wanted more than ever to be part of the glamour and excitement of Hollywood. Peggy was thirteen at this point. Although she was looking forward to entering high school, her mind had become increasingly more focused on something other than her studies — something that was soon to intersect with her mother's longings.

From the minute I got to Los Angeles, I wanted to be in the movies. I hung around the studios and watched them film. Although it was fascinating, I felt kind of like a lost soul; I thought my family was nuts *(laughing)*, and I didn't know what was happening half the time.

Peggy had matured over the past year, flowering into a beautiful young adolescent. She was tall and slender like her mother, on her way to reaching five-foot-seven-and-one-half inches. She took pride in her appearance and knew that her meager wardrobe had to be augmented; one party outfit, a Sunday school dress and a couple of skirts would simply not do anymore. In order to acquire some new clothes, the teenager decided to find herself a job. She knew she could work for three months, her summer vacation having just begun.

The local paper seemed to be the appropriate place to look for employment. Peggy began scanning the help-wanteds and came upon a small classified ad, one that would prove to alter the course of her life.

Actually, I was looking for a babysitting job when I saw this ad: "Wanted: Tall girls for musical at MGM. Bring bathing suit." I showed it to my mother, who said, "Wonderful! We're going." She lent me a pair of high-heeled shoes for the audition. I had a very pretty red, white and blue bathing suit that some little old lady had knitted me for the Olympic Games the year before. So with the shoes and the bathing suit, we went off to MGM.

I was stunned at what I saw going on. Three thousand women showed up! It was a mob scene outside those studio gates, which weren't the grilled ones that were always photographed, but great big wooden ones in back. They herded everyone in and told us to go to this big room and change our clothes. We then went over to a tremendous, starkly-lit soundstage.

There stood this dear little man named Sammy Lee. Mr. Lee was Fox's dance director but he was working at MGM then, on a loanout. All of us were there because he was looking for showgirls. Showgirls were not the same as dancers. Chorus girls were the dancers. All you did as a showgirl was walk around in a beautiful dress and, every once in a while, you'd mouth the words to some pre-recorded music.

Groups of twenty began parading past Mr. Lee and he'd say, "You stay...you go..." I think he made a mistake and chose me.

Peggy's first movie job would be as a showgirl in *Dancing Lady* (1933), a big-budgeted backstage musical starring Joan Crawford, Clark Gable and Franchot Tone. The film would be shot throughout the summer, a perfect schedule for a vacationing schoolgirl.

There was, however, just one problem: Peggy was thirteen and labor laws required that one be at least eighteen years of age in order to gain full-time employment at a movie studio. With her mother's encouragement, the youngster told the casting department she was nineteen. The studio then handed her a form which had to be filled out and returned within several days. Once it was reviewed and approved, a thirteen-week contract would be drawn up for her and she could begin work on *Dancing Lady*. Peggy and Marge went over the document at home. In the space allotted for date of birth, Peggy wrote, "12/18/13." This fabrication would be but one of many concoctions that would go on the form.

You see, I had to falsify all the information on myself because I was underage. I was only going to work in the summer, but I was still enrolled in the Beverly Hills school system. They had all of my vital statistics. If the studio had found them out, I'd have been kicked out because you had to go to school and all that business — the truant officers were everywhere! So, I made up this long biography on myself.

On the first falsification of my age, I figured that if I said I went to private schools in New England they'd never track me down.* I gave them the name of a summer camp I went to in New Hampshire. At that point, I had begun to color my hair blonde. I had started sneaking it in at school. All the women in movies were blonde then and I thought I could get a job if I looked a little tougher. When I got the picture at MGM, I really let go with the hair because I didn't want the Board of Education to know I was working there. My mother had me so scared. I was trying to hide on a ninety-foot screen.

Marge was actually more nervous for herself than she was for her child. Once the job offer at MGM had presented itself, Peggy's future in films became the

* 1920 US Census records reflect the 1919 birth of Marjorie S. Fisher, daughter of John M. and Marjorie Fisher of Roanoke, VA. Over the years, however, film-reference sources have recorded various dates for Lynn Bari's year of birth — anywhere from 1912 to 1920. The majority of these discrepancies had been engendered by Bari's desire to gain employment while underage. To meet an age requirement, she told MGM she was born in 1913. Several months later, at Fox, she gave her birth year as 1915. In 1938, when Bari began in leading-lady roles, 1917 became the most frequently stated birth year — and it would remain such for the next decade. The situation after 1947 would find Lynn putting forth great effort to ensure that her publicity reflected her correct year of birth, 1919.

number-one priority in her own life — and the answer to many of her unrealized hopes, the ones which her husbands had been unable to fulfill. Everything now seemed to hinge on the success of her daughter, her latest vehicle for the wealth and acclaim she had so long desired.

Although Marge would eventually live out her own fantasies through Peggy, the one thing she would fail to understand from the start was the fact that her dream and her daughter's reality were not the same. This misconception would be at the heart of a lifelong resentment between the two.

Marge's tendency to live vicariously was not at all clear to Peggy in 1933, when she was trying to break into films. In fact, her mother appeared to be more of a friend to her than she had in the past. The teenager was delighted by her supportiveness and enthusiasm; Marge felt certain Peggy was going to become a movie star.

My mother and I were up the night before I was first going to report to *Dancing Lady*, figuring out what name I would use. We went over a list of twenty-five different choices. I certainly wasn't going to use the name Marjorie Fisher or the truant officer would be after me. I knew that Lynn Fontanne was a great actress and I enjoyed James Barrie's plays. So we settled on "Lynn Bari," with my mother — who was into numerology — changing the spelling of the last name.

I did get adjusted to my new name, but I was so used to being called "Peggy" that somebody would have to say it twice before I caught on. Years later, I was talking with Jed Harris, the director, who had just seen me in a picture called *Moon Over Her Shoulder* (1941). He said, "I saw your name on the credits and thought, 'Oh God, there's another one of Zanuck's new imports whose name sounds like a bad face powder.'"

Lynn Bari's first film, *Dancing Lady*, also marked the screen debuts (in features) of Fred Astaire, Nelson Eddy and The Three Stooges. The David O. Selznick production, slated for a Christmastime release, would eventually become Metro's highest-grossing film of the year. Needless to say, its success would have much to do with the star power of Joan Crawford and Clark Gable. They were listed at the top of the picture's cast sheets. Way down at the bottom one could find the names of the unbilled showgirls. A minor listing on the rolls did not, however, reflect minor participation for these young women — as Lynn was soon to discover. The costly *Dancing Lady* would make maximum use of its showgirls, enlightening Bari to how much work could be involved in strutting around and looking pretty — something she would do time and again over the next four years.

Dancing Lady was set forth in an elaborate manner by its director, Robert Z. Leonard, who was no stranger to grand-scale productions. Leonard's work here benefited greatly by the intricate and innovative choreography of Sammy Lee. Together, the two men were able to create moments of rhapsodic lushness, a rather heavenly quality that was the hallmark of many a top thirties musical. This achievement was vividly illustrated in *Dancing Lady* by an extravagant twelve-minute musical interlude. Placed near the end of the film, the sequence melded together three stylistically different songs: "Heigh-Ho," "Let's Go Bavarian" and "Rhythm of the Day."

"Heigh-Ho" begins with showgirls garbed in white satin, leaning against a circular railing. One by one, they are given both a cherished close-up and a line to talk-sing: "Heigh-ho; The gang's all here; Let's have pretzels; Let's have beer; ...Let's give; (now, Lynn's big moment:) The grand old cheer!..." The

Thirteen-year-old Lynn Bari (fourth from right) on the MGM lot in July 1933, shortly after she began work on Dancing Lady. Lynn is featured here alongside other showgirls from the musical, all waiting their turn to receive — according to Metro ballyhoo — a clean bill of health from studio physician Harry Anderson.

women finish their vocalizing and start to sashay as the railing parts in half to make way for the entrance of Fred Astaire and Joan Crawford, both dressed to the nines. The two stars assume the foreground and perform the song on a round dance platform — which is then magically lifted into space. They alight onto the Bavarian set, where evening wear has been replaced by lederhosen. "Let's Go Bavarian" bounces along, ending to thunderous applause. Franchot Tone, seated in the audience, examines his program: bold type conveys that "Rhythm of the Day" is up next. Below this notation is a listing of the "Ladies of the Ensemble" — with Lynn Barri [sic] being fourth-mentioned.

The curtain rises on a minuet in progress. Top-hatted-and-tailed Nelson Eddy bursts onto the scene chanting about rejuvenation to a historically-clad chorus. The tempo jazzes up as fair maidens and men of armor are ingeniously transformed into 1930s cuties and dapper-Dans. "Rhythm of the Day" climaxes with showgirls riding a carousel, tilting back-and-forth to a lyrical waltz melody. Beneath them are more young women, striking a swimsuit pose on a whirring circular prop. This motion and the counter-revolving carousel produce an astonishing visual effect, one which is further heightened by reflections, shadows and silhouettes created by lighting and abstract camera positioning. The kaleidoscopic number draws to a close with Joan Crawford, the dancing lady herself, sailing across the screen on a painted horse.

Lynn is featured on both the carousel and the turning wheel underneath. This dual-placement is but one of numerous indications that the number was photographed with many, many different set-ups. To carry off something so complex required a great deal of rehearsal and blocking time — and this represented only one third of a musical sequence. As Bari learned first-hand, twelve celluloid minutes could translate into months of work on a Hollywood soundstage. The film novice was in awe with all that was entailed here — and she was equally dazzled by the talent on the set.

I couldn't believe I was working with all these great stars — especially Gable, who was really a nice guy. I was surprised that he was very unsure of himself; he blew his lines a lot.

Fred Astaire had an incredible reputation from the theater and he was so lovely to work with. Such a pleasant guy to be around, so very thoughtful about whether everyone was comfortable or not. One day, when it was terribly hot, we had on these very high-heeled white satin shoes. Our feet were bleeding and swollen. Fred told everyone to take their time and cool off. He sent out for cases of Coke for all of us.

The rehearsal halls were like being at a party. Jimmy Durante would drop in and play the piano. We'd do little acts and sing. One girl would hitch up her trousers, doing an imitation of Gable, who just had his appendix out. I would do my "Garbo." It was all very gay.

Jimmy Durante was not featured in *Dancing Lady*. He had wandered over from the next stage, where he was filming another Selznick production, *Meet the Baron* (1933). As it would so happen, that picture would become Lynn Bari's second screen credit — although it would be released just prior to *Dancing Lady*. *Meet the Baron* was directed by Walter Lang (who was to achieve eminence at Fox, where he would play a pivotal role in Bari's career). The movie was a thoroughly absurd trifle about mistaken identities on a girls' campus, Cuddle College. Highlighting the whole affair was an irresistible musical number, "Clean as a

Lynn Bari, child of Hollywood.

Whistle, Fresh as a Daisy." The sequence was as lavish as it was fanciful, giving Lynn a close-up in a shower. There, underneath a spray of water, she, for a few seconds, mouthed a lyric — one that had been recorded by a singer with a preposterous Betty Boop-type voice.

That was so funny. You know, I went into *Meet the Baron* quite unexpectedly. This guy on the lot had come up to me and a couple of other showgirls and asked, "Would you like to make some extra money?" I said, "Yes. What do I have to do?" He said, "Well, after you get finished on your show, you come over to our set and we'll pay you overtime." Well, the bastards were getting away with murder! Here they were paying us three or four dollars more for working on their picture, which was shot at night, while we were working all day on the other one.

On *Dancing Lady*, we were being paid $8.33 per day for a six-day workweek. So we took home fifty bucks a week. After three months on that picture, I was rich! *(Laughing)* My God, I was living!

While working hard for the money at Metro, Bari had a most interesting encounter with another Hollywood neophyte.

I had two very beautiful friends whom I palled around with; the pictures were new for them, too. They were both tall and very lovely. The three of us were walking down from the stage to the commissary when this very handsome young man came running up to us. He said, "Could I speak with you ladies for a moment?" I turned to my friends and said, "Come on, girls, listen to this smartass." *(laughing)* I didn't know who he was and I was told not to speak to strangers at the studio. But he persisted and seemed very well-mannered and terribly good-looking. So, we did stop for a moment to listen to him:

"The reason I asked is that I'm doing a picture with Miss Garbo and they're looking for tall, lovely ladies to be maids-in-waiting in her court. Would you like to do the picture?"

"Of course," we all said — what else!

He told us to meet him at the exact same place and time the next day. Thinking that this was the most exciting thing, we couldn't sleep that night — we were going to be stars! The next day we go back and wait for him at the appointed spot. And we wait. And we wait. Finally, we realize that he wasn't going to show up. We found out later that Miss Garbo said his legs were too skinny and sent him back to England. The young man was Laurence Olivier and the picture he was talking to us about was *Queen Christina* (1933). By then, Garbo had gotten John Gilbert for the Olivier role; she had asked for her boyfriend all along.

Queen Christina went along without Olivier and his "discoveries," one of whom was a few weeks away from entering the ninth grade. Summer came to an end and this schoolgirl-turned-showgirl was back in the classroom, daydreaming about the Hollywood she had come to know.

After *Dancing Lady* and *Meet the Baron*, I wanted to go on in pictures. But I felt I had to go back to school. I thought, for the time being, this was it as far as the movies were concerned. A week after *Dancing Lady* finished, I got a call from MGM to please come back and bring a dinner dress for a party sequence they were adding. I told them, "I'm sorry, I'm working." "Really? Where?" they asked. I said, "I'm waiting for a call. I can't tell you." *(Laughing)* My God, I was such a liar then!

Peggy Fisher would be in "retirement" for about six weeks. In late October — at her mother's behest — she was able to secure day work as an extra in two movies, Fox's *I Am Suzanne* (1934) and Paramount's *Search for Beauty* (1934). The first picture had been choreographed by Sammy Lee, the man who had launched her film career — and the person who would soon be shaping her destiny.

Lynn Bari's first official studio portrait for the Fox Film Corporation, photographed in early 1934.

CHAPTER FOUR

THE STOCKGIRL
AND THE STUDIO

Peggy was at school that fateful December day when the Fox Film Corporation phoned her home. Marge answered the call and was beside herself as she took down all the information. Sammy Lee had been given the go-ahead by Fox production chief Winfield Sheehan to hire new talent. The dance director wanted to meet with Lynn Bari and other *Dancing Lady* showgirls to discuss the possibility of their signing long-term Fox contracts. Marge told the voice on the other end her daughter would contact the studio in short order.

Peggy had barely walked through her front door when she was hit off guard by the news about Fox. She dialed the studio straightway; the prospect of securing a contract at a major film company meant everything to her at the moment. An interview with Lee was arranged for the following week. Marge was in seventh heaven. Reverend Bitzer, however, met the situation with a concern about Peggy continuing her education. His doubts were pooh-poohed by his wife, for whom school was a non-issue; under no circumstances would her daughter's chance-of-a-lifetime opportunity be passed up.

The all-important day was at hand. Peggy spent the better part of the morning glued to her bedroom mirror, readjusting her hair, examining the line of her new navy suit and practicing the gestures of a seasoned actress. In a few minutes she and her mother would be on their way to Fox. Marge rushed in with the car keys and a repertoire of admonishments. Peggy was grateful that the drive would be a short one; the Fox Film Corporation was also located in Beverly Hills.

Arriving at the studio, Marge gave her daughter a prolonged embrace. Peggy melted away at this rare outward display of affection; she knew she was the object of her mother's loving pride and she treasured the moment. Genuinely encouraged, she kissed Marge, took a deep breath and walked alone through the studio gates.

More than a dozen showgirls from *Dancing Lady* were escorted into Sammy Lee's bungalow. Lee offered each a seven-year stock contract. Their salary would start at fifty dollars a week. The intensive dramatic training promised them would, hopefully, lead to stardom and the income that would go with it. One other thing — once or twice a year, Fox had the option to break the contract.

51

Peggy listened to Lee's pitch, went along with the studio's terms and signed the contract shortly before Christmas 1933. The name of Lynn Bari was on its way to becoming irrevocably enmeshed with Fox.

Lynn's contract provided her with a strong feeling of acceptance. With youthful determination, she would prove to the studio, her mother and herself that it would deserve to be renewed. This resoluteness was partnered with a sense of

Her blonde hair braided, extra Lynn Bari gazes at Charles Boyer and Annabella, as the couple is serenaded in Caravane *(1934), Fox's French-language version of their* Caravan *(in which Boyer starred opposite Loretta Young).*

enchantment; it amazed her that she, in her own small way, had become a bona fide member of the Hollywood dream factory.

Now a Fox stockgirl, Bari quickly became fascinated by every aspect of movie-making. She would cover the lot from corner to corner, immersing herself in all the excitement of the studio. Partly because she was the ubiquitous participant and spectator, she was soon known to everyone at Fox. The production personnel were amused by the starry-eyed enthusiasm of this teenage apprentice. They couldn't help but notice her buoyancy, sincerity and willingness to learn. Without affectation or calculation, she would approach them with rudimentary questions about some operation they were in the midst of executing. They responded to her thoughtfully and with kindness — and saw to it that she got work. Her considerable energies and ambitions were rapidly brought into focus.

Lynn's career drive escalated during the vulnerable time of adolescence.

A trio of Fox's Junior Stock Company players graces a garden party in Lottery Lover *(1935): left to right: Iris Shunn, Lynn and Dorothy Dearing.*

Because of this, she was denied the chance to mature normally and develop emotional independence. There were just too many goals to be met — too many welcome distractions from her very real problems. She would never properly deal with her deep sense of inadequacy, which was due in great part to an alcoholic stage mother and a father who had abandoned her by committing suicide.

The daily rewards of approval Bari would receive from members of her studio family would help to dull the wounds that had been inflicted upon her by her parents. Caught in a destructive relationship with her mother, she would continually turn to her studio for positive reinforcement and a sense of stability. Fox would be Lynn's place of work, her surrogate home and her psychological sanctuary for nearly fourteen years.

Learning to move, no less act, in front of a camera was stockgirl Lynn's first concern, and the opportunities to do so would be plentiful. From the December 21, 1933, production start of *David Harum* (a homespun Will Rogers vehicle) to the November 1937 wrap of Darryl F. Zanuck's *Love and Hisses* (a slick musical comedy), Lynn Bari would be featured in over seventy Fox films. This astonishing count would reflect the fact that she'd be sparingly utilized in almost all of these pictures. Bari was, of course, not a star moored to a lengthy shooting schedule; she was an actor-in-training who would hop around from one set to another, as an extra, bit player or showgirl. Even so, she'd do more hopping than most in her lowly position.

If it was a Fox picture produced between 1934 and 1937, chances would be better than even that Lynn would be lurking somewhere between the opening credits and the end titles. Her guises would be varied and many. The following are a small representation of those from 1934 and 1935:

Backstage extra *(Ladies Love Danger)*
Bridesmaid *(Spring Tonic, Welcome Home)*
Carnival patron *(Dante's Inferno)*
Corpse *(Charlie Chan in Paris)*
Nightclub patron *(Under Pressure)*
Party guest *(Coming Out Party, Doubting Thomas, The Gay Deception,
   Way Down East)*
Receptionist *(The Great Hotel Murder)*
Shop patron *(Orchids to You)*
Showgirl *(Bottoms Up, George White's 1935 Scandals)*
Telephone operator *(Charlie Chan in Shanghai, Thanks a Million)*
Townsperson *(David Harum)*
Waitress *(The Man Who Broke the Bank at Monte Carlo, Redheads on Parade)*

To this day, many film buffs have been kept on their toes trying to spot Lynn in her unbilled assignments (a number of which have gone unrecorded by those who compile actors' filmographies). Sometimes she came and went with the blink of an eye. On other occasions she had noticeable silent bits, some lines, or was prominently positioned in the showgirl lineup. Two men proved especially helpful to Bari in securing her this better exposure.

This December 1934 portrait of Lynn bore the following Fox caption: "Lynn Bari, who will next be seen in a tragic role with Warner Oland in Charlie Chan in Paris." *Her "role" in the 1935 mystery was that of corpse.*

Henry King was a marvelous director and so terribly nice to me. I was regularly put on his pictures as an extra or showgirl. Every time, he would give me something to do — like saying, "Happy birthday" to someone — or silent bits, where he'd focus on me; for instance, he'd open a party scene with me dancing. Allan Dwan was also one of the first directors with whom I worked who would give me bits that weren't written into the script.

Bit player Lynn was clearly on view in Henry King's Way Down East *(1935). Here, she stands alongside the stars of the drama, Henry Fonda and Rochelle Hudson.*

Lynn played a box-office cashier in the opening scene of Alice Faye's *Music Is Magic* (1935). Fifty-four years later, she ran the film on her VCR.

I still can't place that one. I don't even remember making it, or so many of my early films. So often I just opened a door or worked as an extra. Actually, I didn't even know what movie I was doing until the night before I was to report

Blonde no more — and happily so — Lynn was featured briefly as a bridesmaid in Welcome Home *(1935). She poses here with the film's leading man, James Dunn.*

for work. I'd get a call saying something like, "Be on Stage Nine at eighty-thirty a.m." Once I got to wardrobe, they'd tell me what to do. It was always like that, unless you were doing something where you had to have a costume fitting.

One early film that did jog Bari's memory was her fourth under contract to Fox, *Stand Up and Cheer* (1934). The picture was a Depression-era morale

Fourteen-year-old Lynn is pictured at the far left of this showgirl lineup from Stand Up and Cheer *(1934).*

booster headlining three of the studio's top leading men: Warner Baxter, John Boles and James Dunn. Although Lynn's footage amounted to far less than those of these stars, her presence in the movie reflected a fair amount of screen time for an uncredited player. In one scene she had a couple of lines as a receptionist. In another she was just an extra. Two big production numbers featured her as a showgirl. One of them was "Broadway's Gone Hillbilly." (**Will Rogers came in and taught us how to use the ropes on that one.**) The other, "Baby, Take a Bow," spotlighted five-year-old Shirley Temple — and made her a star. A very blonde Lynn Bari stood directly behind the tiny dynamo during this history-in-the-making moment.

Shirley was adorable — absolutely sensational. But when we were filming, I don't think anybody had any idea what would happen to her. She wound up saving the country. She really did!

Shirley Temple was responsible for keeping Lynn Bari and most everyone else at her studio employed. The once mighty Fox Film Corporation had now been on the verge of bankruptcy for four years, a grim situation brought on by the financial mismanagement of its deposed founder, William Fox. The studio's misfortunes had been exacerbated by Winfield Sheehan, its current vice president and production chief. Sheehan had launched a string of artistic and commercial triumphs at Fox during the latter half of the 1920s. Unfortunately, his golden touch had begun to rapidly wither in 1930 — a fact clearly recognized by Sidney R. Kent, the man who had assumed William Fox's presidential post in 1931. Kent had been successful in averting a total collapse of his company, but the studio was still operating at a deficit. He held Sheehan, with whom he was frequently clashing, directly accountable for the paltry revenues. The vice president's limp production schedules had served to undermine the careers of its superstars, a meager three in number; heroine Janet Gaynor, romantic lead Warner Baxter and humorist Will Rogers had been faltering at the box office since 1932. Given the weak properties Sheehan was continuing to approve, other Fox talent (e.g., Alice Faye and Spencer Tracy) found themselves with little chance to develop as stars. Only little Miss Temple emerged unscathed. The enormous profits from her vehicles were what was keeping the studio afloat during these last troubled days. Since Shirley couldn't appear in every Fox picture, Kent knew that he would have to take decisive action at once, before his company went completely under.

At this time former United Artists president Joseph M. Schenck and ex-Warner Brothers production head Darryl F. Zanuck were seeking to expand their two-year-old company, Twentieth Century Pictures. Twentieth had been releasing a limited amount of high-quality films through United Artists, from whom they also rented studio space (on the Goldwyn lot). This association had begun to go sour after Twentieth's first year in business, when Zanuck and Schenck had discovered that some manipulated accounting had allowed UA to reap the lion's share of their own company's profits. Roiled by this, the two men were now in the midst of an active search for a new base of operations — a place where they would have more financial and artistic control.

They set their sights on the Fox Film Corporation, aware that that studio was in urgent need of better product. Fox also had much to offer them: advanced film and sound technology, a well-established distribution network and ninety-six acres of property, which housed the old Western Studio in Hollywood and the recently-built (1928) Westwood Studio in Beverly Hills. Schenck approached Sidney Kent with the idea of a merger between their two companies, promising him that he and Zanuck would produce superior pictures — the kind of product that would return Fox to the Hollywood vanguard. Kent was quite receptive to Schenck's proposal. A merger took place in the spring of 1935 and Twentieth Century-Fox was born. Schenck became chairman of the board of this new enterprise, while Zanuck assumed the role of vice president in charge of production — replacing Winfield Sheehan, who was edged out with a $420,000 financial settlement.

Everything came to a grinding halt at Fox the day Darryl Zanuck arrived on the scene. With the intensity of a lightning bolt, the thirty-three-year-old production chief set out to reorganize. Heads rolled and new contracts were drawn. Shooting scripts were tossed and literary properties were purchased. In form, appearance and feeling, the new studio and its product would bear little, if any, resemblance to the Fox Film Corporation. It would instead carry the mark of Zanuck himself, the man who had propelled Twentieth Century-Fox toward greatness.

Zanuck was an uncannily perceptive person, one who involved himself in every aspect of filmmaking. He strove to challenge his audiences by utilizing contemporary fiction, controversial headlines and other topical subject matter. Each year, he undertook the role of producer on a select group of pictures, almost all of which would go on to become major box-office hits. Zanuck's creative participation was never limited to just these films, however; nearly everything that carried the Twentieth Century-Fox logo was seen through all phases of production by the studio chief. Well-versed in script writing and the art of film editing, he knew how to inject an air of freshness into even the most banal material. There was always a crystal-clear look and edge to a Twentieth Century-Fox film, yet another signature of Darryl F. Zanuck.

Darryl F. Zanuck.

Zanuck knew who was boss and let no one forget it. Daily, with a polo mallet in one hand and a cigar in the other, the sprucely-dressed young mogul would regally survey his domain. He'd sweep through the lot, rattling out demands to his minions, using his ever-present props for emphasis. He had little patience for phonies, procrastinators and no-talents. At the same time he could be very sensitive to the human condition, a quality which evidenced itself in many of his films. He also appreciated the creative contributions of others — in a selective way. Writers were held in his highest regard. Film editors were similarly valued. He generally considered directors to be of secondary importance; however, John Ford and Henry King could do no wrong and he greatly admired Walter Lang. Actors were met with varying degrees of his attention, but he did not seek their input in the creative process of filmmaking.

When it came to cultivating screen personalities, Zanuck had a very short attention span. Those who didn't capture his fancy were given no more than a year to prove their mettle. Those whom he favored generally sailed on to major stardom. He preferred touting players with a dramatic track record — actors from the stage, radio or film studios other than his own. Stock players at Fox were not nurtured to become movie stars. And, indeed, none would attain stardom — with the exception of Lynn Bari. Zanuck would only be indirectly responsible for Bari's progression, but it would be his remarkable steerage of his studio that would afford her the opportunity to succeed.

Lynn posed for this studio portrait in 1935, shortly after Twentieth Century-Fox came into being.

As a Twentieth Century-Fox stockgirl, Lynn Bari would be affiliated with all the top craftspeople under contract to her studio. Many of them, like herself, would remain at Fox for years. This group included musical director Alfred Newman and film editor Barbara McLean, both of whom worked on *Metropolitan* (1935), Twentieth Century-Fox's inaugural film.* The musical drama marked the first of Bari's thirty-seven appearances in a picture personally produced by Darryl F. Zanuck.** *Metropolitan* starred famed baritone Lawrence Tibbett and was centered on the denizens of the opera world. It went into production on July 29, 1935.

> That picture was made during such an exciting time. Zanuck came on the set every day with his little group; all of them swinging their mallets. He was very much a part of the production, watching everything and telling 'em what to do.

Lynn vividly remembered her participation in *Metropolitan's* "Toreador" number, from Bizet's *Carmen*. With this sequence, came her first publicity of note.

> That number took about a month to film. About twenty of us were in the chorus, dressed in white satin uniforms. They chose a girl named Julie Cabanne and me to pose with Tibbett for the still pictures. Those photos wound up being featured in just about every newspaper and magazine in the country. *(Laughing)* I got more publicity from that than any of the movies I did myself.

Bari was at this point a long way from being listed on film credits, but her name would soon appear in hundreds of inanely captioned "leg art" shots. She would pose for these pictures at the Fox still gallery, where she would become known as their most frequent visitor. For the next several years an endless procession of Lynn Bari cheesecake photos would march into print. The teenager would typically be attired in a bathing suit or short-shorts, skipping rope, playing ping-pong, indulging in archery or any number of other activities — all performed in high heels. Additionally, no known holiday, including April Fool's Day (hiding around a corner, holding a string tied to a wallet), would escape her pictorial salute.

When she wasn't before a camera, Lynn would be attending classes at Fox's drama school, run by Lillian Barkley (who doubled as the studio's resident schoolteacher). Bari would spend as much time as possible with Miss Barkley, finding her classes a stimulating learning experience. Drama school would also help to lessen Lynn's dismay over the fact that she hadn't pursued her formal education.

---

* Planned before the merger took effect, as Twentieth Century-Fox's first production, *Metropolitan* would actually be shot on the United Artists lot — the last Zanuck film to be lensed there.

** Lynn would also participate in the production of Zanuck's next five personal endeavors, all lensed in 1935: *Thanks a Million, The Man Who Broke the Bank at Monte Carlo, Show Them No Mercy!, King of Burlesque* and *Professional Soldier*.

The only thing I know I missed out on was an education at a college or a university. If only I had had Psych One or Two! *(laughing)* During the summer I was at MGM, I used to go over to the lending library across the street and check out a lot of books. There was a wonderful old gal there who ran it. She put me on to all the great literature; so, I became pretty well-read.

This moment from The Man Who Broke the Bank at Monte Carlo *(1935) captures Lynn's first encounter with Ronald Colman. Colman headlined the film, one in which bit player Bari donned a rather splendid waitress uniform.*

Fox would issue an untold number of Lynn Bari cheesecake photos. These two (this page, facing page) date from late 1935.

Bari would often select a favorite literary character as the subject for a dramatic reading in one of Miss Barkley's classes. The teacher would assist Lynn and her other students with their interpretations of their chosen roles, for the purpose of enacting them before a live audience. Every so often, she would showcase these young stock players in a performance comprised of these readings. Fox's producers and directors would be invited to attend, making the event an all-important one for which the students had diligently prepared.

We worked like crazy. I was nuts about Eugene O'Neill. Miss Barkley helped me with a monologue she had pasted together from *Anna Christie*. Now, could you imagine a fifteen-year-old outfitted in a tight sweater, short skirt and black stockings? *(laughing)* I came up "vis dis occent" and did it *very* seriously. Do you know; I got a big hand! Buddy DeSylva, the songwriter who'd become a producer, came up to me the next day in the commissary with all these compliments. After that, he gave me some bit parts in his pictures. But, my God, I must have been atrocious!

Back on the soundstages, Lynn appeared in *My Marriage, Poor Little Rich Girl, Girls' Dormitory* and *Sing, Baby, Sing*, all 1936 releases. The quartet represented but a small portion of the films she made for Twentieth Century-Fox during their first year. Sandwiched somewhere in between was a loanout to MGM, for *The Great Ziegfeld* (1936).

They borrowed all the tall showgirls from Fox for that because it was such an enormous picture with so many people. I remember on the "Pretty Girl Is Like a Melody" number they had us on a huge spiral prop that kept turning around. They put me at the bottom [of the top tier] and I got so dizzy.

Lynn had met with a similar situation some months earlier on her home ground, while filming *King of Burlesque*, an Alice Faye-Warner Baxter musical. In a 1942 interview she recalled the staging of the picture's "Lovely Lady" production number — and the personal agitation it had provoked:

> "A horrible experience and quite frightening. Five of us girls were swinging from single trapezes some twenty-five feet over the heads of the cast. I am scared to death of heights and for ten days straight we rehearsed and shot that sequence." *

The latter half of 1936 found Bari earthbound, doing more mundane things like answering telephones, cheering in the bleachers, taking dictation and strolling through musical numbers. *Ladies in Love, Pigskin Parade* and *Crack-Up* were among the many Fox films in which she engaged in such activities during this period.

Lynn's studio was now also utilizing her rich contralto voice for off-camera assignments. For instance, in *It Had to Happen* (1936), she could be heard over an office intercom. Her vocals would also be employed in a substitutive manner.

Publicity shot for King of Burlesque *(1936), featuring a quintet of the musical's showgirls in all their swim-suited glory. Lynn is on the far left.*

* *EveryWeek Magazine,* May 10, 1942.

Lots of times I did voice-overs for actresses when something went wrong and the studio didn't want to call them back at their salaries. I was also asked to supply a scream or two in many pictures.

The deep resonance of her voice and her cultured upbringing made Lynn seem more mature than her tender years. There was also a certain imposing quality

Eddie Fetherston, Helen Wood and Lynn in Crack-Up *(1936).*

to her character, something that would later be captured on film. Bari's overall bearing was beginning to set her apart, indicating to some that she would not be following the path of an ordinary starlet. Time, of course, would substantiate this. However, for her first four years in pictures, Lynn would usually remain silent and barely noticeable once the cameras started rolling. Bari herself felt that her many efforts in miniscule parts were on target as far as her development as

Lynn's appearance in Ladies in Love *(1936) lasted no more than seconds — but it did afford her the opportunity to share a scene with Constance Bennett.*

an actress was concerned, standing firm in her belief that her career evolved in its proper time.

Oh, I'm sure of that. At first I knew I could handle where to walk and the like. But I was nervous when I had to speak — terribly, terribly frightened. I had a real feeling of inadequacy that had been instilled in me for one reason or another. I was finally able to come on the set and say lines, but I never let my fears show with the people with whom I worked. So you see, if the larger parts had come sooner, I never would have been able to handle them.

Everybody's Old Man (1936), Bari's first relatively substantial stockgirl assignment, had served as an indicator of this. The comedy had gone into production in December 1935. It starred playwright-novelist Irvin S. Cobb, as corporate magnate William Franklin. Fox had cast Cobb in several pictures, essentially as a replacement for the recently-deceased Will Rogers. Cobb, however, possessed little of Rogers' charisma and his performance in *Everybody's Old Man* was uninspired. Lynn didn't send up any flares either, in the very small role of Franklin's secretary. Her "big scene" had her trading a few lines with her boss and reading him a letter. Nerves pitched her voice into a higher register here, and lack of experience with handling more than two lines of dialogue caused her recitation

Practically every Fox stockgirl went before the cameras of Pigskin Parade *(1936). Most also found themselves helping to publicize the movie, posing for group portraits like this one. Lynn stands tall here, sixth from right.*

to be overly precise. Although her character was given a name, Miss Burke, Bari did not receive screen credit. Billing and more self-assurance would come only eighteen months — but numerous films — later. In the meantime, Lynn would find herself content with her step-by-step progress.

> Those four years of doing bits and showgirls were perfect. I got to work with and learn from a lot of great actors and actresses — especially the character people; they were the ones who really knew how to do it, much more so than some lead who would be popular for a hot second.
>
> I just didn't want to be bad, so I spent my spare time on the sets watching anybody who was an interesting actor or actress. Loretta Young was the best picture actress I ever saw. She knew more about the camera than the cameraman. She knew exactly what to do. If I was working as an extra on her sets, I'd go someplace where I wasn't bothering anybody and just look at her and learn.

Lynn's cinematic education continued with at least twenty films in 1937, her last year as an uncredited stockgirl. She was prominent in Roy Del Ruth's *On the Avenue,* where she backed up Alice Faye in several Irving Berlin music sequences, spoke a line as a guest at a party, and had her portrait framed on Dick Powell's dressing table. She returned to the periphery of the steno pool for *Loves Is News*, sold candy in *Fair Warning*, enlivened Eddie Cantor's harem in *Ali Baba Goes to Town*, did two more musicals with Faye and worked as an extra on John Ford's *Wee Willie Winkie* set. *Café Metropole* saw her dining with Gregory Ratoff, but there she only opened her mouth to eat. Smidgens of dialogue did, though, come her way in these productions: Walter Lang's *Wife, Doctor and Nurse* (as a doctor's

Michael Whalen, George Hassell and Lynn in Woman-Wise *(1937).*

wife), Alfred Werker's *City Girl* (waitress), and Allan Dwan's *Rebecca of Sunny-brook Farm* (secretary, once more). The latter film was a Shirley Temple showcase that had started production in October. A March 1938 release, it would contain Bari's final seconds as a bit player.

Lynn delivers a sensational high kick, promoting On the Avenue *(1937).*

Tony Martin, surrounded by four lovelies, in You Can't Have Everything *(1937). Lynn is on the far right.*

Spotlight on the showgirls of You Can't Have Everything, *with Lynn positioned front-and-center.*

Lynn again assuming prominent placement (front, far left), this time in a musical number from Life Begins in College *(1937).*

Ali Baba Goes to Town *(1937) was one of the last films in which Lynn went without an onscreen credit. This publicity still from the picture finds her seated between fellow Fox stockgirl Helen Ericson and* Ali Baba *star Eddie Cantor.*

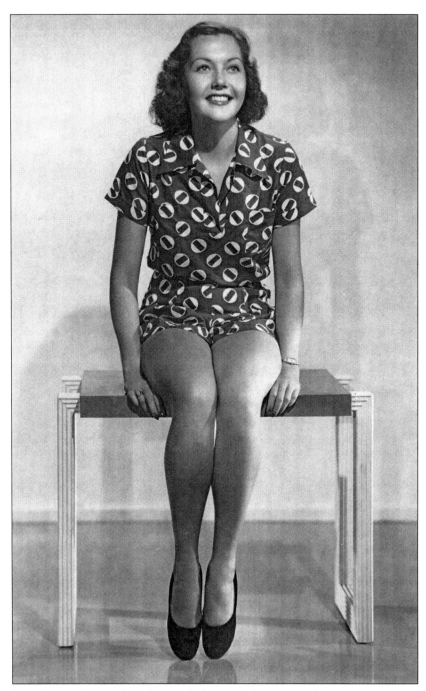

Lynn Bari, in late 1937, radiating the beauty and optimism of a movie star in the making.

Though the scope of her 1937 assignments had varied from picture to picture, Lynn remained encouraged and optimistic. Had it ever occurred to her that Fox was preparing her, albeit quite slowly, for better things?

I don't think so, honey. I was *grooming myself* to be a movie star! For instance, I learned early on that the wardrobe department got the scripts first. I was always right there reading through them. I'd look and see if there was a bit and made note of who was doing the picture. Then, I'd go over and sit myself in that producer's or director's office. When they came in, I asked them if I could do the bit. Nine out of ten times they'd say, "Yes, you can." I was insecure and shivered to death doing this, but I did it.

Lynn, as the tragic Sandra De Voe of Walking Down Broadway *(1938).*

CHAPTER FIVE

QUEEN OF THE 'B' HIVE

Four years of patience, persistence and dedication resulted in Lynn's December 1937 appointment at the Fox wardrobe department. Swathed in a muslin jacket, she experienced the strange sensation of a heavy pencil tracing the contours of her body. The seamstress drawing these lines was taking careful measurements for a dressmaker's dummy. When completed, the mannequin would bear the inscription "Lynn Bari" across its chest area. At the same time the model herself would finally see that name featured in the opening credits of a film. Bari had arrived.

A trio of movies marked her ascent from anonymity. Number one, lensed the previous summer, had given her a small role and an end credit. The second and third went before the cameras days after her mannequin was finished. Both cast her in supporting roles, her very first of this kind.

There were three pictures that were the kickoff: *Lancer Spy* (1937), *The Baroness and the Butler* (1938) and *Walking Down Broadway* (1938).

I had been working as a saloon girl in *Lancer Spy*. About two weeks later, I was dressed in street clothes going into the studio café for lunch. Gregory Ratoff, the director of the picture, stopped me.

"Vat is you name? Vere do you work?" he said in his broken English.

"I'm under contract here," I told him.

"You actress? You can act?"

"Oh, yes, I'm a very good actress." My God, the nerve I had!

"You can say lines?"

"Yes, I'm accomplished at lines."

I first thought, "This guy's on the make; something's going on." But I knew who he was. And, lo and behold, I get a call two days later. They had written in this little piece, which was set in a plane, for the beginning and the end of the picture — and I was cast.

The script afterthought, a present-day conversation between Bari's character, Miss Fenwick, and her father, Colonel Fenwick (Lionel Atwill), harked back to a tense World War I espionage story enacted by Dolores Del Rio, George Sanders and Peter Lorre. During production, Del Rio had given twentieth-billed Lynn an unexpected thrill, taking her aside and showering her with compliments. Bari had been left speechless as the glamorous actress made note of her "beautiful voice" and told her she was destined to become a star.

"Star" was certainly a word applicable to the Mexican-born Del Rio; she had been a major one on the American screen since her film debut in 1925. Her success and that of her European counterparts, Greta Garbo and Marlene Dietrich, had inspired the launching of a raft of other foreign actresses in 1930s Hollywood. With

A private exchange between two servants: Lynn and William Powell in The Baroness and the Butler *(1938).*

the notable exception of Ingrid Bergman, none of these Tinseltown newcomers would gain a firm foothold in the States. This luckless group would include Zanuck's French protégées, Simone Simon and Annabella. Lynn had worked as an extra on the sets of both. Now she was enacting a nice little part in *The Baroness and the Butler*, a comedy which starred Annabella and William Powell in the title roles.

Directed by Walter Lang, *The Baroness and the Butler* dealt with class conflict in Hungary. The costly movie had its moments of charm, but it was pulled down by the colorless performance of its miscast leading lady, one who spoke English in an almost unintelligible manner. Bari was far more comprehensible as Klari, the chambermaid with whom servant Powell carried on a mild flirtation. Her eighth-billed role, as written, had involved more scenes than those she had gone on to film.

I was so nervous. I got sick and they got another kid to come in and complete it [in an added role]. My stomach couldn't take it. I was just so excited with everything that was going on. But Walter Lang was a very good guy to work for, very nice. And, believe me; William Powell was so kind to me — God, what a good actor, what a lovely gentleman. I was shivering in my boots working with him. Plus, they were making such a fuss over Annabella. She was like a cardboard character; she didn't move — though I understand that [offscreen] she was a wild lady! *(laughing)*

Lynn saw her level of anxiety subside during the production of *Walking Down Broadway*, perhaps because the film was much smaller in scale and less intimidating than her previous effort. In terms of her career, though, *Walking Down Broadway* would hold far greater significance than *The Baroness and the Butler*; the drama was her first featured assignment in the genre of film within which she would hone her skills and make a name for herself — the 'B' picture.

'B' films had established themselves as a movie staple by 1935. These movies had originally answered a need for Depression-era audiences who had wanted the most entertainment — and escapism — possible for their nickel, dime or quarter. 'B' pictures were not to be confused with the cheapies made by minor film companies. These were films produced by the major movie studios, considerably lower in budget than their top-shelf fare but executed with the same technical resources. Also called "second features," they were made to fill out a three- to three-and-one-half-hour program that would generally be sold as a package by the studios. The 'A' film, the lure to the ticket buyers, would be handled on a percentage basis. The 'B' picture and studio short subjects would be rented out to exhibitors at a flat fixed-rate. This block-booking turned out to be quite an advantageous arrangement — particularly for the largest film companies, who owned theater chains in the big cities. An example of this type of scheduling would have *Walking Down Broadway* as the co-feature to the 'A' film, Zanuck's *Four Men and a Prayer* (1938), directed by John Ford and starring Loretta Young. The double feature in place, the bill would be completed by a rotation of shorts. Fox's one- and two-reelers included Lowell Thomas travelogues, *Movietone* newsreels, *March of Time* documentaries, *Sports Reviews* by Ed Thorgersen, and the animated *Terry-Toons*. In one sitting, audiences would view two movies, a cartoon and be brought up-to-date on world news events. This kind of programming would be reaching its height of popularity during the spring of 1938, the time *Walking Down Broadway* would go into general release.

Walking Down Broadway's executive producer was Sol M. Wurtzel, the head of the Fox 'B' unit. Wurtzel's association with the studio had gone back to its very beginnings. He had started there as a stenographer in 1914, became William Fox's private secretary in 1917 and was upped to story chief in the early '20's.* Wurtzel had developed into a shrewd producer by the time Fox's new production chief, Darryl Zanuck, had appointed him to the company's fourth highest post: Executive Producer. It was in that capacity that Wurtzel was to helm Fox's recently created 'B' unit, located at their Western Avenue studio. He worked for

---

* In the position of story chief, Wurtzel had given Darryl Zanuck his first paid job in the movies when be bought the then-aspiring writer's short story, *The Scarlet Ladder*.

Zanuck autonomously, with the implicit understanding that limited budgets and tight shooting schedules were to govern his directives. Handed a heavy production load, Wurtzel employed a talented young technical staff and efficiently churned out well-produced entertainments.

A Fox 'B' most often blended elements of comedy and intrigue into a snappy sixty-to-seventy-five-minute running time. The heroes and heroines of these photoplays were likely to be quick-witted, direct and, above all, identifiable in character. Big of heart and not particularly glamorous, they were "regular" people thrown into quasi-extraordinary situations. The minor-league players who enacted these roles sometimes attracted their own fan followings. As a box-office draw for a certain lower-case film, the popular 'B' star could save an accompanying 'A' turkey from an early demise. On rare occasions an outstanding second feature would be flipped (via advertising) into the top spot. Generally, though, 'B' pictures had no aspirations toward greatness; they were designed to support as "filler" or "programmer" material. How many filmgoers, after all, remember that *The Grapes of Wrath* had shared its 1940 play-dates with *Free, Blonde and 21*? However, those who had come to see Henry Fonda in the John Ford classic had also left with an impression of Lynn Bari, the star of the co-feature.

It's doubtful that Lynn made anything more than a momentary impression in *Walking Down Broadway*, but the backstage saga did provide her with a few flashy moments of screen time. The film was obviously meant to cash in on the success of RKO's *Stage Door* (1937). Its seventy-five minutes were crowded with melodramatic subplots that served to showcase some of Fox's more promising young actresses. Claire Trevor was assigned the linchpin role, supported by Bari, Phyllis Brooks, Dixie Dunbar, Leah Ray and Jayne Regan. All were initially seen as chorus girls in a show that had closed minutes before. It was New Year's Eve and the women had gathered together in their dressing room to toast their final performance and the coming year. Each going their separate way, the six vowed to reunite the same evening the follow year. Fifth-billed Lynn was the beautiful and tragic Sandra De Voe. Recently handed a movie contract, Sandra was run over by a truck as soon as she left the theater. Her ill-fate had been conveyed in an unsubtle bit of symbolism during the toast, when she had accidentally shattered her dressing-table mirror while raising her glass. Fan magazines would later say that Bari had gotten this "breakthrough" role after others previously considered for the part had refused to smash a mirror. Lynn denied this tale, but did admit the superstition had weighed on her mind a bit during shooting.

Walking Down Broadway was [director] Norman Foster's picture. Claire Trevor was the star, a wonderful actress and a helluva nice girl. I was a bridesmaid at her first wedding.

Claire Trevor had been Fox's premiere 'B'-picture actress for the past five years. By the time *Walking Down Broadway* was released, Trevor and the studio had parted ways. This break would prove most fortuitous for Lynn, for she'd instantaneously inherit her friend's position at the Western Avenue lot.

There were certainly many starlets in the 'B' unit with more credited roles than Bari, but she was clearly the best choice to fill Trevor's shoes. Like Trevor, she was a strong and intelligent actress with a deep commitment to her craft. These attributes had already evidenced themselves to the powers-that-be at Fox — in particular, the casting department, who had come to feel that Lynn possessed a "star quality," where her presence alone could enliven a picture — in much the

Hollywood-bound Sandra De Voe is toasted by her fellow chorus girls in Walking Down Broadway *(left to right): Claire Trevor, Lynn, Jayne Regan, Phyllis Brooks, Leah Ray and Dixie Dunbar.*

same way as Trevor's had. In light of the similarities between the two women, Trevor's career startlingly foreshadowed the course Lynn's would take.

Trevor was born in New York City and had attended both Columbia University and The American Academy of Dramatic Arts. Much experience in stock brought her to Broadway, where she was to star in two plays. During the run of the second, *The Party's Over* (1933), she was signed to a long-term contract at Fox, which commenced in 1933 with two George O'Brien westerns. Two splendid screen assignments followed later that year: *The Mad Game*, costarring Spencer Tracy, and *Jimmy and Sally*, which paired her with James Dunn. More films with Dunn followed, including Shirley Temple's *Baby Take a Bow* (1934). She had a good role as Tracy's wife in the elaborate *Dante's Inferno* (1935) and lent solid support to several other 'A's, including *To Mary – with Love* (1936) and *Second Honeymoon* (1937).

Trevor earned the "Queen of the 'B's'" title at Fox by playing the ingénue lead in an array of the studio's medium-budgeters. Among them: *My Marriage* (1936), *Star for a Night* (1936), *15 Maiden Lane* (1936), *Human Cargo* (1936), *Song And Dance Man* (1936), *Time Out for Romance* (1937), *Big Town Girl* (1937), and *Five of A Kind* (1938). The pictures themselves were moderately entertaining trifles, made more interesting by their leading lady, who could be counted on to deliver an excellent performance. Trevor's knack for elevating the quality of her films, for better or worse, secured her position on Western Avenue.

The actress herself looks back on her early years in the motion-picture business with a realistic eye:

> CLAIRE TREVOR: "Listen, I didn't know anything. I came straight from Broadway. It was the middle of the Depression, so it was a great relief for me to get out of New York; the theater there was dead. I was being offered a job at Fox. It was good money, the people were very nice, and I got promotions and bonuses. I had started out with a fairly low salary, compared to the work I did, but they kept buttering me up so I'd work.
>
> "I worked all the time. We were on eighteen-day schedules. We worked six days a week, far into the night. Even on Saturday nights you knew that you couldn't have dinner with anyone. You'd have dinner on the set and work until two or three in the morning. That was customary. It was not easy. I made so many pictures and I don't remember half the names of them. First of all, I wasn't proud of them and I wouldn't go to see them. I saw some of them, sure, but I'd squirm in my seat. *Spring Tonic* (1935) was the picture I remember Lew Ayres and ZaSu Pitts were in. After we saw it, we seriously thought of pooling our money, buying it and destroying it. That's how good it was! *(Laughing)* It was horrible! But I loved being on the set and I loved the people I worked with at Fox. I *enjoyed* it. It was a beautiful place to work."

Lynn Bari had been a bit player in almost all of Claire Trevor's Fox vehicles. While working in that minor capacity, she had come to be befriended by the star.

> CLAIRE TREVOR: "I couldn't tell you when I first noticed Lynn; it was a gradual thing. She was a darling and we became good friends. As I've said, there wasn't much time for a social life; so, there was never a chance to develop a big friendship. I liked Lynn enormously, though — well enough to have her as my bridesmaid. She wasn't a pushy, ambitious actress like a lot of them were; that's one of the things that I liked about her. I thought she had great potential. She was a serious actress and a *good* actress. I was crazy about her as a person and I thought her work was terrific."

Claire Trevor's departure from Fox was the pivotal element in Bari's sudden leap forward. Trevor sheds some light on why she came to terminate with the studio:

> CLAIRE TREVOR: "Here's what upset me: I was borrowed by Samuel Goldwyn to play *Dead End* (1937) and was nominated for an Oscar. Now, today, a young actress who would have that happen to her would immediately be put into good things. I went right back to doing 'B' pictures, obscure 'B' pictures. I was not Zanuck's type, let's face it. He didn't understand serious actresses. If I had been at Warner Brothers, I think I would have done better. I got buried under all those things at Fox. So, when my contract expired, I wouldn't sign with them again because it was the wrong place."

Free from contractual assignations, Trevor's work improved. Fine characterizations (including an Oscar-winning one, as a drunk, in 1948's *Key Largo*) were to follow over the next thirty years. Interestingly, Trevor and Bari would encounter the same casting problem as they matured. The two were certainly different in physical appearance (Trevor being a petite blonde), but they both projected a womanly assurance. This trait would loom large in the thoughts of most casting directors, who would simplemindedly stereotype them into harder-edged roles, a fact exemplified by the majority of the actresses' post-Western Avenue work.

Lynn would be put under Sol Wurtzel's guidance after assuming Claire Trevor's preeminent slot at Western Avenue. In the few short months before Trevor's spring 1938 exit, Wurtzel had come to realize that his up-and-coming star was both a quick study and a good actress, and he appreciated her unpretentiousness. He would assign Bari to the best of the 'B's, sensing she had everything it took to help place his unit on an increasingly more successful course. He grew to be quite fond of Lynn and, with his wife, came to befriend her socially. Often the Wurtzels would have her dine with them, after which she'd be invited into their private projection room for screenings. Bari, in retrospect, felt that this camaraderie had not been entirely helpful to her career. She implied that Wurtzel had liked her too much and, thereby, had kept her working at the 'B' unit longer than she would have preferred.

Over a period of four years Lynn would play the heroine in two dozen Wurtzel-supervised films, frequently finding herself cast as the wide-eyed girl reporter, the romanced ingénue or the wisecracking waitress. Simultaneously, she would be running over to the Westwood Studio for supporting roles in Fox's 'A' pictures, usually enacting the meanie. The cinematic avalanche in which Bari would long be consumed would make for an intense way of life, one that would seem to agree with her temperament. The pace of 'B' filmmaking could be especially hectic.

You better believe it, honey. You started work an hour before the 'A' pictures did. Six days a week. No laws allowing breaks for lunch, dinner or between-calls. You just worked till you dropped.

The 'B's were shot at the Western Avenue Studio, which was the first Fox studio. They had a theater set, a couple of break-away houses and office sets. They never had terribly expansive interiors or exteriors. You wouldn't find a boat sailing out in the blue Pacific over there. That would be shot at The Hills; that was where the 'A's were made. But sometimes this all switched, depending on productions schedules.

On the 'A' pictures, you took a lot of time — not that long because nothing was done slowly. These higher-budget films had more attention paid to detail. Also, they took many more shots instead of just taking a master, a two-shot and a close-up, as they did in a 'B' picture. They could photograph a cockroach going across the floor if they felt like it! *(laughing)*

The shooting schedules of my 'B's were usually about twenty-one days. They say that the ones they made with Duke Wayne were done in three-to-ten days. But the 'B's I did were of better quality. There were good stories for most of them. But I was in a few stinkers, like the one with Brian Donlevy where I was being lassoed to a camel.* Those were just terrible. They could have gotten anybody.

Sometimes the behind-the-scenes stories to Bari's 'B's were more intriguing than the plots of the films themselves. This was certainly the case with *Mr. Moto's Gamble* (1938), the picture that afforded Lynn her first lead role, as an eager young reporter. The project had initially gone before the cameras as *Charlie Chan at Ringside*, the seventeenth *Charlie Chan* whodunit featuring Warner Oland as the sage Chinese-American sleuth. *Ringside* had been at its production midpoint when Oland suddenly up and disappeared — a baffling situation that would cause the film to be completed as a *Mr. Moto* movie.

It was a prizefight mystery. We shot with Warner for a couple of days. He was having an awful lot of trouble with his lines. He always did. They used to write most of them out on something like a TelePrompTer. But, my God, he was not a young kid, and he had to do these pictures so fast. He was also given an awful lot of dialogue, intricate lines that constantly re-explained the plot. Keye Luke, who played Chan's number-one son, was very helpful to Warner. He's one of the nicest men you'll ever meet in your life.

At the end of one day, Warner said goodnight to us rather cryptically: "Goodbye, everybody, we're all continuing to go up." With that, he walked off the set and we never saw him again. He disappeared and the picture closed down. When it resumed as the "Moto" film with Peter Lorre, a postcard was delivered to us on the set. It was from Warner, now back in [his native] Sweden. He wrote, "Always going up. Warner." He died soon after we received that. I guess the poor man had gone home to die.

---

* *Sharpshooters* (1938).

They took the script and changed it into *Mr. Moto's Gamble*. J.P. Marquand, Moto's creator, got in on the act. Warner was gone, but Keye Luke had already filmed many of his scenes and was still under contract. Fox wasn't going to lose any money; so, they got their pound of flesh by keeping him in the picture [in the role of Lee Chan].

Peter Lorre smelled so funny. There was something strange he was smok-

Lynn, Dick Baldwin, Peter Lorre and Jayne Regan in Mr. Moto's Gamble *(1938).*

ing or taking — and it wasn't booze. We had been in the swamps, down in the gulch on the back lot of the studio, shooting some outdoor stuff at a prize ring. Everybody caught colds and I stayed home for a day or two, so I wouldn't get pneumonia. The morning I came back, I was lying in my make-up chair getting my face put together. I felt this tap on my shoulder and I looked at this little face standing there. It was Peter Lorre. He whispered, "Did you get rid of the baby?" Well, here I am this eighteen-year-old girl, young and impressionable, and I just thought, "You vulgar old son-of-a-bitch!"

Personally, I could have been a pushover. I believed everybody. But just by looking at people, I knew damn well what was going on with them. The naiveté had left a long time before.

In the three months following *Mr. Moto's Gamble's* March 1938 release, Lynn appeared on screen in five films which had wrapped before Claire Trevor and Fox were no longer. First up was *Battle of Broadway*, a high-quality 'B', directed by George Marshall. The peppy musical comedy saw Bari play the winsome ingé-nue role and receive fifth billing for her efforts. She was then handed a lead in the lower-budget *Speed to Burn*, a horse-drama installment in Fox's *Sports Adventure* series. *Josette* was another musical comedy, far less entertaining than *Battle of Broadway*, but produced on a large scale at The Hills. Directed by Allan Dwan, the film starred Don Ameche, Simone Simon and Robert Young. Lynn marginally supported here, as Mrs. Elaine Dupree, Young's coquettish secretary.* A somewhat better role in the first-rate *I'll Give a Million* followed. The delightful Walter Lang

comedy concerned a millionaire who assumed the guise of a tramp. Warner Baxter starred opposite Marjorie Weaver, another erstwhile Fox stockgirl. Seventh-billed Bari was featured in one scene, as Cecilia, Baxter's opportunistic ex-wife. She made the most of her brief screen time, conveying her character's shallowness subtly, while exuding an alluring quality in an equally understated manner.

Lynn figured much more prominently in the Barbara Stanwyck vehicle, *Always Goodbye*, the first 'A' film in which she would be cast as a second lead.** She would continue to appear in this light, with occasional frequency, through 1941. Being a second lead in 'A' pictures was a two-sided affair for a young actress. In a positive respect, it afforded one the opportunity to work with top-notch talent on films that would gain them greater exposure. The downside of this casting was that the roles

---

* Bari was cast as Elaine Dupree after *Josette* had completed principal photography. She replaced Jayne Regan, whose footage had been scrapped — the result of an eleventh-hour decision made by Zanuck, who felt the actress hadn't projected the sexual magnetism needed for the part. (**Jayne was a nice woman; but not the flirtatious type.**)

**Always Goodbye* was a remake of Zanuck's *Gallant Lady* (1934), a Twentieth Century production which had starred Ann Harding.

themselves were limited in nature, usually being one of three types: girlfriend to the female principal, someone's sister, or "the other woman." Bari herself would almost always portray the third kind. "The other woman" generally followed one course of action. She would descend upon a somewhat tranquil setting and stir up trouble for the leading lady. Eventually, after being exposed for the miscreant she was, she would walk off into oblivion, with nothing but a mink wrap for consolation.

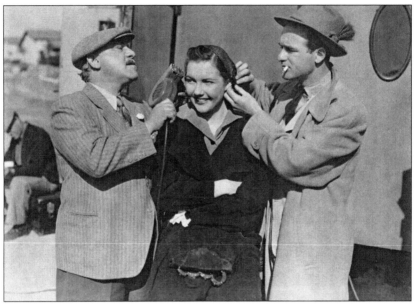

Henry Armetta (left) and Chick Chandler momentarily take over for Lynn's hairdresser on the set of Speed to Burn *(1938).*

Always Goodbye embraces "the other woman" plot formula to a tee. In this case the mischief-maker manifests herself as the cool and calculating clotheshorse, Jessica Reid (Bari). Jessica is engaged to marry Phillip Marshall (Ian Hunter), a very wealthy widower. Phillip has a young son, Roddy (Johnny Russell), whom he and his late wife had adopted at birth. Unbeknownst to Marshall, the boy's natural mother is Jessica's couturier, the unmarried Margot Weston (Stanwyck). Margot, though, had known the identities of Roddy's adoptive parents. Quite by chance, she had been in loving contact with Roddy shortly before being introduced to both Phillip and Jessica — a time in which she had come to realize that the child was her own. Her protective maternal instincts prevail when she discovers that Jessica is a gold-digger, one who has been feigning affection toward Roddy in his father's presence. Margot sets out to reclaim her son, endearing herself to Phillip — and, in a roundabout way, revealing to him Jessica's actual character. Things come to a close with Margot forsaking her true love (Herbert Marshall) for life with Roddy and his father. By this point Jessica has been edged out of the picture in disgrace.

Always Goodbye was decried by many reviewers, who thought it a pat soap opera. However, audiences, particularly female moviegoers, ate up its glamour-and-tears storyline — and the performances of those who enacted it. Fifth-billed Lynn certainly created a wave of attention for her sharp turn as Jessica. The attention she had received during filming, though, hadn't been all to the good.

Johnny Russell and Lynn in Always Goodbye *(1938).*

Except for the fact that I met wonderful people on it, *Always Goodbye* was the movie on which I had the worst experiences of my life. Here I was, eighteen years old, and I'm playing the heavy; standing up to Barbara Stanwyck, who's like a brick house! Stanwyck was marvelous, though — and she stood up for me. But the director, Sidney Lanfield, was just horrible to me. He later became a friend, but, at the time, he was a bastard; there were no two ways about it. He'd say, "Oh, they send me these goddamn stockgirls and expect me to make them act. She walks around like a duck." At one point he cleared the set, holding the cameramen outside. I was doing the best I could as we rehearsed. Finally, he got really mad at me and said some horrible things. By then I was crying. Barbara went over to him and said, "Look, Sidney, go over to the coffee stand and get yourself a cup and cool off. You're all wrong about this girl." She took me into her dressing room and consoled me by talking about all the bastards she had worked with. I had expected her to side with the director. She was so nice to me, I couldn't believe it. I had been frightened to death of her to begin with; she was such a big star. But she was very, very supportive.

Lanfield also used to carry a big riding crop and walk up in the back of unsuspecting people and goose them. Have you ever heard of anything lovelier than that? When he did it to me I turned and said, "Don't you *ever* do that to me again!" That was some picture.

Always Goodbye would represent the first of numerous instances in which Lynn's career would advance in an antipathetic climate, usually one in which her insecurities would somehow be played upon. The situation with Lanfield hit Bari

Lynn and Barbara Stanwyck, enacting a showdown between their characters in Always Goodbye.

hardest because it came with a major stepping-stone film — and the youthful hopes, fears and sense of excitement involved. The director managed to touch a most sensitive nerve with Lynn when he called her a "goddamn stockgirl." This deflating statement not only attacked her skills but, in Bari's mind, underscored the fact that she was earning next-to-nothing in salary.

Initially, Bari's paycheck raises were commensurate with those of other stock players who had started at the bottom. She had now, however, arrived at a point where her career had been ascending much more rapidly than her wages. The explanation for this was simple: she was still locked into her December 1933 contract with Fox, a seven-year agreement whose particulars had made no mention of stardom and proportional pay increases.

On *Always Goodbye*, I don't think that I was making more than a hundred dollars a week. I was so mad that one day I called the casting director, Lew Schreiber. Later he became a very good friend but, at the time, he was just the boss. I went into his office and said, "Mr. Schreiber, the extras in this picture," — girls they had *imported (laughing)* from the Copacabana nightclub — "are being paid $125 a week for just walking around as models. My God, I'm playing a lead in this thing and I'm only getting a hundred." And he said, "Don't worry, Lynn, they'll all be back on their fannies within a year."

Between May and December of 1938 Lynn made a quartet of films in the series genre. The four comprised a mixed bag of entertainment. All, however, profited by Bari's acting and her screen persona, which was quickly taking form. In a reciprocal way, the movies themselves helped to make apparent Lynn's reign over Western Avenue, which had begun upon the release of the first. Her position at the 'B' unit would be further strengthened by the publicity she received in conjunction with these pictures.

Fox favored the series film; they were, after all, the home of the successful *Charlie Chan*, *Mr. Moto*, and *Jones Family* movies. Most in this genre had followed a similar path on Sol Wurtzel's turf. A picture would click and Wurtzel would go for a sequel, in anticipation of turning out a series. This one-two formula involved the employment of familiar characters, stories and settings — all of which facilitated a speedy and economical shoot on the second film. If the public responded well to the sequel, another follow-up would be lensed and the series would probably enjoy a long run. Wurtzel's track record in this regard had been solid. However, in 1938, he began to get a few steps ahead of himself by hyping several movies as series pictures before the first entry had even been released. Bari appeared in two of these ventures, *The Big Town Girls* and *The Camera Daredevils*. Both would be scrapped after the second production. The former would come to a close because of studio ambivalence, while the latter would meet with a critical assault that would quickly seal its fate — much to Lynn's relief.

The Camera Daredevils films, *Sharpshooters* (1938) and *Chasing Danger* (1939), were preposterous tales of international intrigue, centered on two newsreel cameramen, Steve Mitchell and his comic sidekick, Waldo. Wally Vernon played

Waldo in both pictures, while Steve was portrayed by Brian Donlevy, then Preston Foster. The films cast Lynn in two different damsel-in-distress roles: the American Diane Woodward in *Sharpshooters* and the aristocratic Arabian spy, Renée Claire, in *Chasing Danger*.

Sharpshooters was not my cup of tea. The whole thing was just a mess. I towered over Brian Donlevy; he had legs like Tim Conway's "Dorf" character. *Chasing Danger* was a bit better. Preston Foster was a good actor and delightful to work with. I think Fox could have done a helluva lot more with him.

Fox, in the long run, could have done considerably more with *The Big Town Girls* because the screwball comedy series unfolded well with *Meet the Girls* (1938) and continued on a smooth course with *Pardon Our Nerve* (1939). The pictures rose above the usual 'B' fare, being smartly-scripted and polished in their presentations. Both moved along at breakneck speed, detailing the harebrained adventures of two dizzy dames. Judy was the dumb blonde, Terry (Lynn), the wisecracking brunette. In *Meet the Girls* the gals were hula dancers who accidentally wound up as stowaways on a cruse ship, where they unwittingly became embroiled in a jewel heist. *Pardon Our Nerve* featured the pair as escorts-turned-prizefight promoters. Each film saw its heroines without any sort of romantic entanglement — a story slant that was somewhat ahead of its time.

Erik Rhodes, Lynn and June Lang in Meet the Girls *(1938)*

Meet the Girls had originally been planned as a costarring assignment for Claire Trevor, in the role Bari would eventually assume. Lynn took second billing here to an actress who would not repeat the role of Judy in *Pardon Our Nerve*.

The first one I did with June Lang, the second — which was much better, much faster — co-starred June Gale. They claimed those two made a lot of money and that they were going to continue the series. But they never found another script. That's ridiculous. I would have written them one myself!

Meet the Girls would be June Lang's last picture under contract to Fox. Gentle and fair, Lang had stirred hearts in *Music in the Air* (1934), *The Road to Glory* (1936), *Nancy Steele Is Missing!* (1937) and other deluxe 'A's. In none of these films, however, had she evidenced a particularly dynamic personality and her career was on the downswing when she was cast against type as the loopy Judy. She appeared to give her all to the part, but she proved that boisterous comedy was not her strong suit — and her performance wound up being overshadowed by that of her costar.

Lynn gave every indication that she could carry a film in *Meet the Girls*. She played the crafty and kooky Terry with pluck, revealing her adeptness with humorous situations and a knack for comic timing. Her own quick wit had, no doubt, played a large part in her falling totally into sync with the fast-paced nonsense at hand. Throughout the movie her delivery was vital and assertive, something that would go on to define most of her future acting turns. The Lynn Bari screen image

Lynn was a dominant presence in Meet the Girls, *as this scene from the comedy illustrates. Here, June Lang watches the dice being thrown by Bari — whose eyes are locking with costar Wally Vernon.*

was now beginning to fall into place. Time and experience would sharpen this persona and bolster Bari's self-confidence as an actress — which had little correlation to the quality of self-assurance she had been projecting in *Meet the Girls*.

That was all painted on, believe me. I was a hot eighteen years old then. I was scared all the time and wasn't sure of myself. I also think that my part was better. June had such a silly little role. But she was a beautiful girl who photographed so well. She had had her name on the screen a long time before I did. They sent up the balloon for June when she came out of her big dressing room onto the set. I had this little canvas "chicken house." It was funny.

Billy Wilkerson, the head of *The Hollywood Reporter*, went with me and my future husband, Walter Kane, to the preview of *Meet the Girls*. We got through with the picture and he told us that he had to drop off at "the plant" for a minute. So we left him at his typewriter and stopped off at the saloon for a drink. The next day I read *The Reporter*. He wrote the review as if I were the only star in the film! The studio called me in immediately.

"Who the hell wrote this?" they asked.

"I don't know what you're talking about," I said.

"You're a good friend of Billy Wilkerson's."

"Well, he wouldn't do a thing like that."

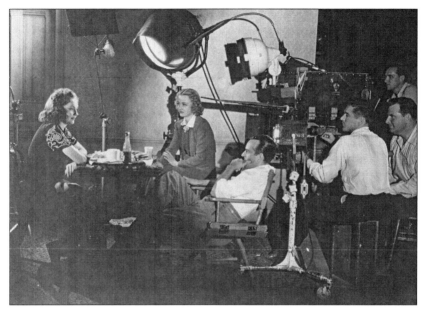

Bruce Humberstone assuming the director's chair, as Pardon Our Nerve *(1939) cinematographer Charles G. Clarke focuses on Lynn and June Gale.*

Trade papers, such as *The Hollywood Reporter*, were an important barometer for the motion-picture industry. Their terse reviews and news items often influenced the decisions of studio executives, film distributors and theater owners. In the winter of 1939, the trades' reception to *Pardon Our Nerve* was enthusiastic. *Daily Variety:* "Entertainment in any customer's language!" *Motion Picture Daily:* "65 Minutes of fast-moving laughs!" *The Reporter:* "A laugh a minute … will please all type audiences … Lynn Bari in an excellent performance … lots of charm and good looks … should go a long way!" *Box Office:* "Lynn Bari delivers a standout performance!"

Industry publications had reacted almost as approvingly to *Meet the Girls* — which, in this viewer's mind, had a stronger story than its sequel. In any event, both *Big Town Girls* movies were head and shoulders above most of the comedies being churned out by the 'B' units at the major film studios. Each benefited greatly from their directors' 'B'-picture savvy, which was marked by a talent for crisp pacing. The ever-capable Eugene Forde *(Meet the Girls)* was something of a record-holder in the world of 'B' movies, having spent his twenty years in features (1928-48) under contract to Fox where he worked exclusively at Western Avenue. H. Bruce "Lucky" Humberstone (*Pardon Our Nerve*) had also begun his affiliation with the studio as a Wurtzel standby, but his career course would be more mobile than Forde's.*

In addition to its director, *Pardon Our Nerve* profited from the casting of June Gale in the role of Judy. Gale was pretty and blonde, like June Lang — but that's where the similarities between the two Judys ended. Lang was demure, while Gale was saucy and endearingly quirky, qualities that made her better suited to the zaniness of *The Big Town Girls*. Gale also clicked with Bari in a way that Lang hadn't. Lynn's onscreen chemistry with Gale was delightful, most probably enhanced by the fact that the two shared a special personal friendship.

June Gale was a child when she began her show-business career as the youngest member of "The Gale Sisters" vaudeville act. After a few film shorts and some bit work at Paramount, Gale signed a contract at Fox. She started there in 1936, as a stockgirl who would often find herself paired with Bari; the two were side by side as showgirls (e.g., *Pigskin Parade, Wake Up and Live* [1937]), bridesmaids (*The Lady Escapes* [1937]), and Victorian "party girls" (*This Is My Affair* [1937]). Lynn broke away from the bits about nine months before her pal. Gale first received billing in Bruce Humberstone's *Time Out for Murder* (1938), one of three films she made in another Wurtzel series, *The Roving Reporters*. Having lent support in those pictures, she moved up to costarring status with *Pardon Our Nerve* — and Bari couldn't have been happier.

June Gale was a very good friend. She was one of the wittiest women I'd ever known, really fun, and made me feel good.

> JUNE GALE LEVANT: "During the late thirties Lynn and I were close friends. We worked in several movies together and double-dated off the lot. Lynn was great fun to be around and we laughed a lot and had a good time.
>
> "She was also well-liked by the members of the cast and crew, as well as the hairdresser and wardrobe woman — these last two women became her close friends.
>
> "Lynn was a talented actress and a lovely looking girl. When she married Walter Kane, I sent her a wedding present and hoped for her happiness. When I married Oscar Levant, New York became my home and our lives took different tracks.
>
> "Over the years we seldom met, yet I followed her movie career with interest — also her private life which seemed to be troublesome."

Lynn had received solo star billing for *Pardon Our Nerve*. This recognition had come little more than a year after her first onscreen credit. Now, five years

---

* Fox promoted Humberstone to their 'A' unit in 1941, at which time he began to helm a number of glossy lightweight entertainments, including two with Bari: *Sun Valley Serenade* (1941) and *Hello, Frisco, Hello* (1943).

under contract to Fox, she was being given a big push by her studio, whose publicity department praised her as a "fast-rising young actress" and one of "their brightest young players."

Bari's ascent could chart the careers of almost everyone who worked at Fox. Because she was the company's most frequently employed actress, Lynn typified the complex network of the contract system. She constantly collided with

Lynn and June Gale, October 1938.

contract talent at various stages of their development (e.g., June Gale and Bruce Humberstone) — and demise. To illustrate the downward turn, one could draw a comparison between Bari and another *Pardon Our Nerve* co-worker, actor Michael Whalen.

Michael Whalen had leapt from obscurity (model and local radio singer) to movie stardom in Zanuck's *Professional Soldier* (1935). Over the next two years, the darkly attractive Whalen went on to star in ten films at Fox, five 'A's and five 'B's. Lynn was an extra or bit player in seven of these pictures. Concurrently, she was performing similar duties in the films of two more magnetic and easygoing actors, Tyrone Power and Don Ameche. Their careers soared. In 1938, the "difficult" Whalen was demoted to working exclusively at the 'B' unit. *Walking Down Broadway* opened in March of that year. Whalen had the key male role there, while Bari was in support. The two then costarred in *Speed to Burn*, a summer release. The following February, Whalen received fourth billing in *Pardon Our Nerve* and a dismissal from the studio.

Lynn worked with a number of flash-in-the-pan actors and fading stars in the late thirties. Her progress at her studio during this period made her something of a survivor in the fickle world of movie stardom. Unlike many of her coworkers, she was on solid footing with Fox and her first big step forward there had

come about in a logical way. Bari's relationship with her studio was something she handled constructively. Her need for stability contributed to this, and she approached her career in a sound, intelligent manner. In order for Fox to remain her support base and source of advancement, she thought it important that she gain a thorough understanding of the motion-picture business. Her absorption

QUEEN OF THE 'B' HIVE

of the studio system was keen, enabling her to form a realistic perception of the stardom she sought to achieve. Her intense drive was tempered with the conviction that her career had to progress at a reasonable pace — which it would. Unwilling to compromise her ethics or abandon her sense of fellowship, she was attaining her goals with a clear conscience.

Lynn cherished the special camaraderie that existed among the young Fox stock players. Her early years at the studio had been brightened by the many friendships she had formed with other stockgirls, the majority of which would prove to be long-lasting. However, as her career was taking off, most of these women were being dropped from the studio payroll. Few lasted under contract more than several years. Some went on to act elsewhere, with lukewarm success. Others fizzled out with chorus and extra work. Nearly all would give up on their dream by the age of twenty-one, having been unable to weather the myriad frustrations and disillusionments that had so often befallen them. Many of these actresses would wind up forfeiting their careers for marriage. Bari's *Walking Down Broadway* costars, Dixie Dunbar, Leah Ray and Jayne Regan, all parted with Fox in 1938, wed shortly thereafter, and retired from films.

For Lynn, marriage might one day be there to complement her career — but it would never supplant it. She wasn't particularly motivated by thoughts of romance and had seldom dated before Western Avenue had become her domain. Her one previous involvement, six months in length, had been with actor Dick Baldwin. The handsome Baldwin had been contracted by Fox in 1937. He had made his debut there playing a second lead in *Life Begins in College*. Bari had also been in the musical comedy, as one of the many coeds who flitted in and out of the picture. While racing about the campus set, she had caught the eye of Baldwin. He approached her not too long afterwards. With sincerity, he remarked to her that she might really go somewhere with her career if she'd spend less time clowning around with the crew. Lynn's temper flared and lighthearted insults were traded, leading to a first date. The two entered into a relationship that was more a situation of loving support than a sizzling affair, with each championing the other's professional aspirations. Still, Bari and Baldwin were inseparable buddies during their off-hours and they continued to be so when they both went into *Mr. Moto's Gamble* (where the actor was cast as a prizefighter). Their special closeness had dissipated by the time the film had wrapped, but they would remain friends for years to come.*

> DICK BALDWIN: "I held Lynn in high regard. She will always
> have a dear place in my heart. She was wonderful; always encour-
> aging, helping and inspiring me. She was a beautiful person."

---

* Dick Baldwin spent one year at Fox. He would abandon acting in 1944, going on to a successful career in real estate. For over five decades, he would be married to MGM actress Cecilia Parker (Mickey Rooney's sister in the *Andy Hardy* series).

Lynn's involvement with Dick Baldwin had been responsible for some of her earliest press coverage, with several columnists reporting the couple on the verge of engagement. After becoming a known quantity, Bari was swept up into a succession of print romances. Some were with actors, others with politicians and military men. All of them were glamorous and exciting — they should have been, since they were the concoctions of Fox publicity chief Harry Brand and his staff.

My God, you would have thought I was the biggest twist in Hollywood! They had me going out every night with a different man, even the Emperor of Japan. Finally, I said to them, "What are you doing to me? I'm always home in bed, studying my lines, and you're making me sound like a two-bit hooker!"

Though irksome, these romance fabrications were a reflection of Bari's rise in the Hollywood firmament. The erstwhile stockgirl and cheesecake cutie was now a newsworthy subject — and not just in respect to her love life. For the next few years movie magazines would stress Lynn's affliction with "The Claudette Colbert Jinx," indicating that a certain resemblance to Colbert — facially, vocally, and in manner — had been inhibiting her advancement in pictures. Similar comparisons would be drawn with Barbara Stanwyck. It would further be "revealed" that Bari was sick and tired of being likened to both actresses. Lynn dismissed all of this as rubbish.

Two better people they couldn't have come up with!

In one of their wildest fictions, Brand's department issued this story of how Lynn got into films:

LYNN BARI WON FILM START BY CRASHING GATE
She Just Walked In and Went to Work — As Easy As That

Every movie-struck girl dreams of going out to Hollywood parading right past the studio gateman straight into pictures. But does it ever happen that way in real life?
No, never!
What, never?
Well ... hardly ever.
For beautiful Lynn Bari got her start in exactly that way. The actress just followed a group of actors and actresses who were returning from lunch. Once safely past the studio gateman, she strode to the stage where a picture called 'Dancing Lady' was being filmed. As she stood on the sidelines, intently watching the proceedings, a director ordered her into the scene. And the film career of Lynn Bari was launched!

That's a lie. *(Laughing)* That's beautiful. We could make a whole scenario out of that one. They must have been hard up for news.

Bari's beginnings were also charted in the following Fox publicity release:

> While most girls who have been bitten by the screen 'acting bug' just dream about it, lovely Lynn Bari did something — she upped and went straight to Hollywood.
>
> After taking part in a long succession of plays at the exclusive girls' school she attended, Lynn graduated and left for Hollywood, determined to cut a niche for herself in the movies.
>
> Once in Hollywood Lynn enrolled in dramatic school. Talented and beautiful she immediately began her screen career in chorus sequences.
>
> After a series of minor roles in pictures, Lynn was signed by 20th Century-Fox and admitted to the studio stock school where she received intensive dramatic training.

Oh, honey; you know how to become a publicist in this business — go blow your brains out, ask for a job, and then they'll hire you. Those stories are all such garbage. Never believe them.

Lynn's press coverage, fact-based or otherwise, had a reciprocal relationship with her fan mail. Her rise in popularity caused her studio to escalate their production of Lynn Bari publicity portraits, photos that would be disseminated to the print media and Bari's ticket-buying admirers.

Lynn's first big glamour buildup was initiated in 1938 and lasted well into 1939. Fox assigned their top portrait photographers, Gene Kornman and Frank Powolny, to this promotion. They treated Bari in a delicate manner, emphasizing the poised qualities she'd acquired since her anonymous "leg art" days. Lynn's pin-up sessions in the photo galleries were now dramatically reduced in number — but they were still occurring with some regularity, and would continue to be scheduled for as long as she would remain at Fox.

It was generally acknowledged that Lynn possessed a sensational figure (height: 5' 7½"; weight: 122 pounds; bust: 35"; waist: 25"; hips: 35½") — and that figure looked as well in swimsuits and short shorts as it did in the chic suits and gowns of designers Travis Banton, Herschel, Helen Rose, Gwen Wakeling and Yvonne Wood.

Bari's hours before the portrait cameras would only increase with time. The publicity department would later estimate that, between 1937 and 1941, approximately five thousand shots of Lynn had been produced for potential release to the public.

Lynn would repeatedly find herself playing opposite the major Fox stars in whose films she had once done extra or bit work. While this situation would

1938 saw Fox's portrait photographers become increasingly more careful in their treatment of Lynn. This photo, dating from October of that year, was among the first to underscore the genteel and winsome aspects of Bari's personality.

sometimes be cause for self-consciousness on her part, she eventually came to feel that most of these costars weren't even aware of her past participation in their pictures.

Among the first in this group was the aging Fox lothario, Warner Baxter. Once the mightiest of the studio's leading men, Baxter was now on his last legs at the lot. He would costar with Bari in two films. Number one was *The Return*

Another late 1938 portrait demonstrates the fact that Fox was also achieving success presenting Lynn as a glamorous screen figure.

of the Cisco Kid (1939), produced by Darryl Zanuck in the winter of 1939. The lightweight western had Baxter resurrecting the part of O. Henry's fabled gay caballero, a role which he had first played in *In Old Arizona* (1929). That turn had netted him an Academy Award, spawning a successful sequel, *The Cisco Kid* (1931), in which he had also appeared. Baxter and the Cisco Kid then parted ways for eight years, during which time the actor starred in many important films. Toward the end of this period, however, his position in the Hollywood constellation quickly descended. Baxter was not aging well; nearing fifty and paunchy, he suffered from arthritis and saw his energy level drastically decrease. *The Return of the Cisco Kid* was something of a last-ditch attempt to revive his sagging career. That didn't work, though, and the film became a sad reminder of how time had taken its toll on a screen legend, with Baxter appearing lifeless throughout. Lynn, cast as his lady-in-distress, actually fared little better. Under the limp direction of Herbert I. Leeds, she recited her birdbrained lines rather mechanically and gave an uncharacteristically weak performance. *The Return of the Cisco Kid*, needless to say, turned out to be a first-rate dud.*

Lynn is serenaded by Warner Baxter in The Return of the Cisco Kid *(1939).*

If it was a Darryl F. Zanuck production, it was an 'A' film. But they sure shot it like a 'B.' They said it was Warner's comeback, but he was very old and drinking — I think, I don't know for sure. We got along just fine, although he was furious that I had gotten married in the middle of the picture. He said to someone, "How could she do this to me?" I asked, "What did I do to him?" They said, "He considers himself a great lover, you can't do that to these guys." *(Laughing)* Can you imagine that? It was a scream!

Baxter was one of several Fox 'A' stars given to imperious behavior. The studio begrudgingly tolerated the oversized egos of these players — as long as their films continued to make money. There was no time for any sort of self-

---

* The *Cisco Kid* series would be more successfully revived the following year at Western Avenue, with the animated Cesar Romero in the star slot. Romero would play the Cisco Kid six times. He had been featured in support in *The Return of the Cisco Kid*, as Lopez, one of "The Kid's" henchmen.

indulgence, however, over at Western Avenue. To successfully adapt to the rigors of 'B'-picture shooting schedules, casts and crews were practically required to be unaffected and amiable. These qualities also worked as a performance tool for the actors, helping to create a feeling of snug interaction among the characters they were portraying. This type of harmony was no better illustrated than in Bari's next film, *News Is Made at Night* (1939).

Lynn and Russell Gleason cast their eyes on Preston Foster, as he confronts George Barbier in a scene from News Is Made at Night *(1939).*

News Is Made at Night turned out to be a superior 'B', in no small measure the result of the rapport Lynn had shared with her costar, Preston Foster, and her director, Alfred Werker. The comedy-mystery had also afforded Bari the opportunity to deliver what would be her best performance in the 1930s. The picture's story centers on two night-desk reporters. The seasoned Steve Drum (Foster) is cool, confident, and totally resistant to the idea of women entering into the newspaper business. Enter Maxine Thomas (Bari) — who is out to prove him wrong. Spunky, somewhat scatterbrained and thoroughly determined, Maxine has coaxed the son (Russell Gleason) of the paper's publisher to hire her on a probationary basis. She is put on a murder case with Steve, much to the newsman's chagrin. The two become friendly adversaries as they try to keep an innocent man from going to the gas chamber, ferreting out clues that will help to reveal to them the real killer. Their quest is one of mounting suspense, culminating in the identification and arrest of the guilty party. Maxine winds up with her very own byline — and a proposal of marriage from Steve.

Director Werker, to whom Fox assigned both 'A's and 'B's, responded well to Lynn's sensitivities and had utmost confidence in her acting abilities. His approach toward her contributed greatly to the air of abandon she projected in

Lynn delivering her best performance to date, playing Maxine Thomas, the intrepid girl reporter of News Is Made at Night.

News Is Made at Night. Bari was also ably abetted here by the tall and virile Foster. The two actors complemented one another perfectly and clicked in an informal way. Their chemistry was delightful, highlighting the good-natured aspects of their characters' battle-of-the-sexes relationship. Add to all of this a relatively exciting plotline and *News Is Made at Night* came out a winner.

> *Variety* (7/19/39): "Another somewhat fanciful newspaper yarn, but a 'B' release that ought to come in fairly handy at this time of year. Some pretty good comedy relief helps to raise 'News Is Made at Night' a bit above the run-o'-the-mill, while the story is still good enough to hold interest all the way.
>
> Both Foster and Miss Bari, latter an interesting film type, acquit themselves creditably. Their percentage as performers would rate much higher than the picture itself."

That one was fun. I would have loved to have done real comedy, the way the big kids did — but they [Fox] never wrote anything like that over there. They were so goddamned serious. The big parts were where you could weep a lot. None of those people who produced the films had any sense of humor. They were all very big on themselves. I don't think that people like that can laugh at anything but pratfalls.

An ideal pairing; Lynn and Preston Foster in News Is Made at Night.

The disastrous *Pack Up Your Troubles* (1939) was certainly no cause for laughter. Directed by Bruce Humberstone, the film defied one's imagination. It starred Fox's much-hyped comedy trio, The Ritz Brothers, and the studio's little Southern live wire, thirteen-year-old Jane Withers. The brothers Ritz played down-and-out American vaudevillians who were serving in the Army during World War I. Assigned to mule-skinning duty in France, they happened upon Withers, whose

The Ritz Brothers and Lynn in Pack Up Your Troubles *(1939), a cinematic bomb without equal.*

father (an absurdly miscast Joseph Schildkraut) had presumably perished at the front. The man turned out to be alive, however, working as a spy for France. Discovering his life threatened, his daughter enlisted the brothers' aid in bringing him back to safety. Lynn was Yvonne, a German undercover agent who posed as a dancing waitress. Espionage, the horrors of war, family crises, giddy musical numbers and slapstick antics comprised the disparate elements of *Pack Up Your Troubles*, a truly bizarre hodgepodge.

(Laughing) They tell me I made that. I don't remember that one.

Lynn's recollection of *Pack Up Your Troubles* might have been blurred by the fact that its shooting schedule coincided with that of her next film, *Charlie Chan in City in Darkness* (1939). Rushing back-and-forth between sets was something to which Lynn had become accustomed, but her situation here was no doubt made confusing by her costuming; she wore the exact same ensemble in both pictures — even though their time frames differed by twenty years!

City In Darkness was Fox's twenty-first entry in their *Charlie Chan* detective series — and the first film in which the studio utilized the actual mounting turmoil in Europe to frame a story. It found Charlie (Sidney Toler — **a really good actor**) in a blacked-out Paris, at the time of the 1938 Munich crisis. Before

Sidney Toler and Lynn, striking a dramatic publicity pose for Charlie Chan in City in Darkness *(1939)*.

long he was investigating the homicide of a munitions manufacturer (Douglass Dumbrille) who had been supplying his wares to the enemy. Second-billed Bari was Marie Dubon, a desperate young woman who was trying to smuggle her husband, Tony (Richard Clarke), out of France. It was later revealed that Tony had been framed for forgery by the murder victim. Neither he nor Marie, however, would be among the guilty parties eventually exposed by Chan.

City in Darkness ended on an uneasy note, with some cautionary words by the master sleuth himself. Commenting on the Munich Agreement and British Prime Minister Neville Chamberlain's meeting with Adolph Hitler, Charlie observed, "Wise man has said: Beware of spider who invites fly into parlor." This epigram was a perfect denouement to a most interesting screenplay that was well-enacted and set forth in a technically proficient manner. But, despite its many attributes, *City in Darkness* fell flat. The film was seriously marred by the insipid direction of Herbert I. Leeds, who stretched what could have been an exciting hour-long mystery into a seventy-five-minute exercise in tedium.

Pacing was the name of the game in 'B' pictures — and the talent for it, the mark of a good 'B' director. The majority of the directors at Western Avenue were able to keep their films galloping along on a smooth track. There were, however, the studio hacks whose deficiencies became glaringly apparent when they had to deal with either of two types of narratives. One kind was the pedestrian, where the seams tended to show. These stories required a quality of inspiration from their directors. The other sort, equally problematic, embraced the complex plotline (e.g., the *Chan* movies), which proved too difficult for some to coordinate into a neat package. In both cases, 'B' stars, such as Lynn, would have to assume the burden of pulling their pictures together themselves when those at the helm were falling short with a lackluster approach.

You don't realize what you have to do. It's so hard to be active and alive in something that's dead weight. I always tried like hell. But on some of those pictures…well, as they say, "If it ain't there, you can't paint it in."

The quality of Bari's scripts and directors had varied greatly in the ten Western Avenue movies in which she had so far played a lead; being accorded preferential treatment by Sol Wurtzel hadn't always translated into starring in film projects that panned out. Nevertheless, these pictures had been Lynn's proving ground and they had afforded her a firm step toward stardom. Time would show Fox paying closer attention to Bari with regard to her medium-budget efforts, fashioning vehicles that would be more worthy of her talents and appropriate to her personality.

While Lynn's career was moving along in a straightforward fashion, the internal path that guided her actions was anything but clear-cut. Bari's emotional development hadn't paralleled her professional maturation and she would have great difficulty confronting her personal conflicts in a healthy way. Matters would be further complicated by the rising of her stock and celebrity, accomplishments which would cause her problems at home to multiply. More than ever, Lynn would turn to her studio for reliable support and a safe harbor. An unsettling pattern of success and self-sabotage was soon to emerge.

Lynn Bari, 1940.

CHAPTER SIX

CITY OF CHANCE

He seemed like a nice man. My mother thought he was a very nice man…
He was Howard Hughes's "bushbeater" *(laughing)*.

Lynn would impulsively marry Walter Kane, a man twice her age, in an attempt to release herself from the strangulating grip of her mother. Marge's alcoholic behavior was now beginning to imperil Bari's career; and marriage to Kane seemed, for Lynn, the only way to keep her professional life from falling off track.

Bari and her mother shared an intense attachment. Although rooted in love, their relationship was warped by Marge's unbalanced nature and the chronic alcoholism that went with it. Marge had long since embraced her daughter as an alter ego, a second self who would be nurtured to live out *her* dream, one that she herself was incapable of ever achieving. In effect, a mother's frustrations had been molding a daughter's evolution. This situation had become increasingly more neurotic once the dream had turned into a reality.

Lynn was now experiencing a newfound sense of self-recognition, the result of her quick ascent at Western Avenue. For the first time in her life, she could perceive herself as being something other than an extension of her mother; at nineteen, she was finally experiencing feelings that should have arisen during mid-adolescence. Her greatest inhibitor, Marge, became threatened by this healthy mark of maturity — and, from then on, it would be obvious to Bari that her mother was both unable and unwilling to accept her personal and professional transitions with maternal grace. This matter would drive a deep wedge between the two women, causing a love/hate relationship that would last the rest of their lives.

Marge's controlling hand had a wide reach, affecting Lynn, her brother and stepfather. All had been relentlessly prodded to achieve by a woman who would resent them for their accomplishments. Because their successes could translate into personal independence, Marge resorted to manipulating the three into states of vulnerability and self-reproach. Her tactics toward attaining this end often worked, enabling the apron strings to remain unbroken.

Lynn's ferocious career drive had worked as her best defense against Marge's vicious circle of emotions. It had helped her to sustain a precarious balancing act between her movie world, which represented security, and her private world — the one of the para-alcoholic, which was centered on mother and mired in chaos. Things began to fall apart, however, when it appeared certain that Bari was on her way to becoming a star; Marge drowned herself in booze and Lynn's two worlds collided.

The situation at home had started to take a significant turn for the worse during the summer of 1938. The family had for the past two years been living on South Wetherly Drive in Beverly Hills. Lynn was then gaining a foothold at the 'B' unit, Dr. Bitzer's church was prospering and John Fisher had just been hired as insurance broker for a prominent Beverly Hills real estate firm. John had recently returned to the nest after a brief and unhappy marriage to a college sweetheart. Affecting a strong and steady demeanor, he was, like his sister, a conscientious overachiever who worked well under stress. Marge was now giving her children ample opportunity to display this latter trait, for the frequency of her liquor-induced rages had increased to almost nightly occurrences.

The scenario was becoming all too familiar. Lynn's thirteen-hour day at Fox would end at about 8 PM, at which point she'd get in her car and wave good-bye to the studio gatemen. Fatigue would never prevent her from experiencing a sense of satisfaction about her work — a feeling that would be savored fleetingly on her short drive home. Her body would already be tense by the time she'd enter her driveway. With script revisions of the next day tucked under her arm, she would open her front door and once again be swept into the insanity created by her drunken mother.

Fresh from a two-hour row with her husband and son, Marge would greet her daughter's arrival with a glazed look of contempt. Ignoring this reception as best she could, Bari would exchange hellos with John and Dr. Bitzer and head straight for the kitchen. Marge would follow her there, stopping along the way to replenish her glass. While preparing her supper, Lynn would be served a host of indigestible invectives; she'd be branded a whore, her looks would be ridiculed and her talent, savaged.

Now seated before her dinner plate, Bari was informed that the noble sacrifices of her mother were what had been keeping her from winding up on top of the trash heap — a place where she was told she belonged. Lynn would arise from her half-eaten meal and join her brother and stepfather in the living room. There, attempts at light conversation would be thwarted by a barrage of insults from Marge. Her three prey would try to suppress their hurt and exasperation, assuming an air of stoicism and becoming placaters.

Lynn, John and Dr. Bitzer's efforts of conciliation were always met with disdain by Marge; coddling led to dramatic monologues of self-pity — and apologizing, the worst tact, only incited greater fury. Bari had recently begun to employ another approach in dealing with mother, often choosing to fight back. However, every time she'd lash out, she'd either be put in her place by a crushing verbal blow or suffer some repercussion later.

It wasn't constantly an all-night fight situation. Sometimes Marge would stagger out of the house to do some serious bar drinking, only to return home in the wee hours totally out of control. Then there were the evenings when she just passed out. Those occasions gave Lynn the chance to learn her lines without having to wrap her hands around her ears.

Marge was a forty-four-year-old woman with the maturity of someone twenty-five years her junior. An irresponsible wife and mother, she was reaching for the bottle with increasing regularity. The harmful effects of her boozing were something she had long been afraid to acknowledge. She had no desire to become a sober person and her distressed family had become her unwitting enablers. As the wife of a respected clergyman, she was proving to be an embarrassment. As the mother of a rising young actress, she was being denied the attention she felt she herself deserved — and she sought to destroy.

She was impossible. She was always calling the studio, harassing them about how they should be treating me. She would phone them and scream, "When are you *bastards* going to let my daughter come home! Which one of you is trying to *do* it to her tonight?" Every time I started a picture she would be off on something or she'd do something while I was in the middle of it, and this would continue for the rest of the shooting. She'd call the newspapers, Louella Parsons, anybody whom she could think of, saying, "My daughter is sleeping with so-and-so!" These were only some of the *mild* things my mother had done.

But the studio was damned nice to me. The only thing that saved my life over there was the fact that Mr. Zanuck's mama was also a little cuckoo. But she was a nice, quiet cuckoo. When she used to come out on the lot, he'd very carefully pick her up and take her home.

Darryl Zanuck would deal with Lynn in an uncharacteristically sympathetic manner for the better part of her tenure at Fox. Perhaps their "maternal bond" helps to explain why this would be so. Of course, Zanuck was also impressed by Bari's professional dedication, her engaging personality — and her looks.

Zanuck was terribly nice to me, he really was. At first, all I did was say "hello" to him. Being just a stockgirl at the studio, he really gave me my first break. He was always very kind. I liked him and I loved being at Fox.

You hear all these wild stories about Hollywood and jumping in and out of the sack with this guy and that. They always treated me as a lady. None of that *ever, ever* happened to me at the studio. Maybe I was the most unattractive person there, but no one ever even approached me. Oh, maybe they tried to make a pass or kiss me, but nothing else.

I'm sure people participated in all those things when they wanted to. But I don't think that anybody was forced. I mean, you hear these stories about being called into an office, having the guy attack you and all of that.

Of course, Zanuck had a terrible reputation. I know that the secretaries' lives weren't worth a nickel in there, being chased around the desks and all sorts of things.

*Lynn poolside in late 1938. Bari was an avid swimmer, one whose lap workouts
helped to counteract the effects of the stressful situations in her life.*

The first two times Zanuck sent for me to talk about my "future" *(laughing)*, la-de-da, I had "bodyguards" with me. They were two friends, huge in size, who knew better. One was a production man named Ben. The other was Charlie Hall, an assistant director who later became involved in production. We went into Zanuck's office and they introduced me: "Okay, Darryl, this is Lynn Bari. You wanted to meet her. She's a *lovely lady*." They stood there with their arms folded the whole time I was there! When the conversation was over, they escorted me out.

When it came to the lascivious advances of Hollywood's power brokers, Lynn's best protection was her deeply-ingrained sense of right and wrong. She had learned from her stepfather a standard of ethics that would prevent her from falling victim to some of the seamier aspects of the movie industry.

What Bari had learned from her mother had been most harmful, however, ultimately denying her the opportunity to develop a healthy approach toward sex and conjugal relationships. Marge's wild accusations about her daughter's wantonness related directly to her own sexual repressions. She clearly had problems with intimacy. She also had little regard for men and did all she could to hold them at arm's length. The flirtatious manner she affected was more narcissistic than anything else. Her coquettishness did land her two husbands, but she seemed to deal with marriage coldly, as a societal obligation and financial pact.

Lynn's emotions were rarely romantic in nature; the attitudes of her "role model" provide a logical explanation for this. Bari did crave demonstrations of affection and approval but was only able to enjoy this type of attention in an unthreatening realm, outside of a primary relationship. Her more intimate involvements would replicate the twisted love she shared with her mother. The first such entanglement would be with Walter Kane, husband number one.

I got married so young because I'd have done anything to get away from my mother. I met Walter Kane at one of Billy Wilkerson's parties [in September 1938]. A few of us were on the lot one day when an agent at the studio, Joe Rivkin, came over and said, "I've got this tennis court and swimming pool you gals can go to." We said, "No, thanks." But he said, "This is a very nice man and he owns *The Hollywood Reporter*" — and that there would be pleasant people there and so forth. So another girl and I went over with our racquets. We got onto the courts. There was a very nice crowd of tennis players. Lana Turner was there. And Walter Kane was there.

Kane was a film agent who worked in his spare time as an assistant to Howard Hughes. Tall, facially nondescript and unctuous, he was nineteen years Lynn's senior and of the Jewish faith. His attraction to Bari was instant, displayed by the many compliments he showered upon her at Wilkerson's. Most of the bouquets thrown concerned her blossoming career. Kane claimed to have worked with some of the biggest names in the industry, and a duly-impressed Lynn gladly listened to the wealth of professional advice he seemed so eager to give.

This coaching would continue on a series of whirlwind dates at Hollywood's top night spots, where Kane would indeed introduce Bari to some of his more famous friends and associates.

The contrast between Lynn's miserable home life and the glittery social world of her new suitor was stark. Bari couldn't help but be drawn to all of the dazzle and, in doing so, fell under Kane's spell. What she didn't do was take a few steps

Lynn and Walter Kane, at the time of their March 1939 marriage. COURTESY OF PHOTOFEST, INC.

back to allow her perceptiveness to prevail; then, she would have come to the realization that her companion had been offering very little information about how he conducted his business affairs. Had she known then what she was later to find out, she might have spared herself from inviting one highly unstable individual into her life. Bari and Kane announced their engagement on December 7, 1938. The couple had known one another less than three months.

Out on the town: Walter Kane and Lynn at a Hollywood nightspot in February 1940. The couple is in the company of Bari's longtime pal, Elizabeth "Cookie" Gordon, wife of famed songwriter Mack Gordon. As Elizabeth Cook, "Cookie" had befriended Lynn while both were on the roster of Fox's Junior Stock Company.

Marge had actually encouraged their relationship. She had taken an immediate fancy to Kane who, at thirty-eight, was exactly seven years younger than she (the two shared a November 27 birthday). She liked the way he dressed and thought he behaved like a gentleman — a well-connected one at that. Her future son-in-law posed no threat to her; she felt he had a weak character, perceiving him to be a manipulable sort. The agent soon became something of Lynn's that she herself wanted to claim. She developed a schoolgirl crush on him, turning into the fluttery Southern belle whenever he came to call on her daughter. This amused everyone, including Bari. The lightheartedness at hand was abetted by the fact that Marge had chosen to limit her drinking while in Kane's presence.

Lynn and Kane were married in a civil ceremony, performed in Los Angeles, on March 5, 1939. The couple delayed their New York honeymoon until *The*

Return of the Cisco Kid had completed production (on March 27). They set up house in a modest Beverly Hills apartment and were joined there by Bari's pet dachshunds, Freddie and Frankie. The newlyweds could not have been characterized as a passionate pair, but they were certainly fond of one another. Their marriage got off to a relatively good start because their collective energies were focused on Lynn's career. Kane was very helpful to Bari in this respect. He bolstered her sense of professional self-worth and convinced her to pay greater notice to her publicity. Since her husband socialized with his illustrious business contacts, Bari became part of the Hollywood elite.

Walter Kane reveled in the excitement of Tinseltown nightlife. He was a champion table-hopper who could turn the pursuit of a deal into a party-like jaunt. His nocturnal excursions were frequent and they would soon become the first sore point in his marriage. Kane always wanted to paint the town on the arm of his glamorous wife. Depleted after a hectic day at the studio, Lynn generally preferred to stay at home. Arguments would follow, with Kane going off alone more often than not. Left in the company of her dogs, Bari would study her current script and muddle her way through phone conversations with Marge. She'd retire by 11 PM, only to arise not too many hours later for her regular early-morning call at Fox. Her husband, as usual, would be sleeping in late.

Walter never went into his office. He devised a trick where he had a switchboard hooked up from his office to his bedroom. He was an agent who lived from hand to mouth. He was also working for Howard Hughes and continued to be employed by his corporation until he died [in 1983]. He was paid by the Summa Corporation in Las Vegas. Eventually, he booked all the acts that came through the hotels that Hughes owned there.

In 1939 Kane was working for Hughes on a part-time basis. He had been telling Lynn he was Hughes's assistant, but would not elaborate on the meaning of this title. The billionaire playboy had been involved in movie production — so Bari had at first taken it for granted that he had employed her husband as a film agent. Hughes had, in fact, left filmmaking in 1932 to pursue his interests in aviation; however, it was being impressed upon Lynn that he had not lost his enthusiasm for the motion picture industry, to which he would apparently return. All of that was fine and dandy with Bari, but it didn't exactly explain her husband's present relationship to Hughes. She had now been in the company of both men on numerous occasions and had yet to learn anything concrete about their business association. This was becoming a cause of great concern to her.

Kane's slipshod work habits regarding his day-to-day agenting had provoked Lynn to annoyance, then anger — but she was sent into a state of disbelief when she finally discovered what her husband really did for Howard Hughes.

Costume designer Yvonne Wood provides some insight into Kane and his involvement with Hughes. Wood would frequently work with Bari at Fox, beginning in 1942. Prior to their association, she had been a sketch artist at RKO-Radio Pictures. RKO co-distributed *The Outlaw* (1943), the notorious Billy the Kid saga

that marked Hughes's reappearance on the film scene (in the capacity of both producer and co-director). The western was shot during 1940 and 1941, around the
time when Wood first met Kane — of whom her recollections are most pointed.

> YVONNE WOOD: "He was a son of a bitch. He was a wolf. I had
> the feeling that he was a procurer for his producer. He even put
> the make on *me* on two or three occasions! This was before I fig-
> ured out Kane or knew much about him. I first thought, 'Was Kane
> interested in me?' Hell no! The moment I even acted polite, boy, I
> was shoved right over on to the producer. 'Step over here' — you
> know. The producer was now in the conversation and Kane would
> disappear. Oh, I thought he was a bastard!"

Kane's pandering was something Lynn herself had tried to deny.

> All I knew was that I'd come home from work and Walter would say, "How-
> ard's coming over for dinner." And he always came in with a different girl or
> the girl would already be there. I really didn't know what was going on. I had a
> sneaking idea, and everybody said things. I think, perhaps, I kept telling myself,
> "It can't be true."
> It appears truer to me now because I can better understand Walter's ter-
> rible jealousy. It caused him to try to commit suicide a couple of times. Once,
> he damn near made it. I wouldn't go to Chasen's with him that night. I had to
> start a new picture in the morning. He accused me of all sorts of things when
> I never even looked at anybody else. He got loaded and took a bottle of pills. I
> took him to the hospital and they pumped him out. He was *insanely* jealous. I
> guess he was so filled up with the kind of women he got for Mr. Hughes that he
> projected them onto me…

Lynn would be permanently damaged by her husband's instability. Like her
mother, Walter Kane was jealous, possessive and sexually confused. Like her, he
was involved in the motion picture industry. Bari, despite her young years, had
long understood the necessity of maintaining an emotional boundary between
her personal and professional lives. Then she met Kane, married him, and that
line became erased once and for all.

You couldn't tell Howard Hughes anything. He pretended not to hear when
he didn't want to. He was interesting if you were talking to him about his field
of aviation. But I wouldn't know how to fly a kite. I spent as little time with him
as possible. However, he was very kind to me, I must say. When we would talk
he'd kind of laugh at me in a nice way. He liked to dance with me, too. I can't say
that there was anything wrong with him. There were things about him I observed
that I didn't agree with, but everybody to their own taste.

However, one unpleasant incident does stay in my mind. There was a pair of marvelous writers that Walter represented, Bella and Sam Spewack. They were wonderful people and I loved them. At the time, they had just come from their home in Connecticut to their place at the beach and were going to throw a big party for Mary Martin. They wanted us to bring Howard.

They asked us to tell Howard that this new English girl would be coming along with us as his date for the evening. They said that she was a very lovely person. So we said yes and got her name. Howard shows up and we get in our car and the driver takes us up to this place in Bel-Air. I said to Howard, "Well, this is where the girl lives." He said, "I'm not going in there. Why don't you go in there and get her?" Quite annoyed, I told him, "That's very rude." Finally, Walter goes in and he finds this lovely little thing sitting at the piano playing Chopin or something. Her mother's there. She asks, "Mr. Hughes?" Walter tells them who he is and escorts the girl outside. He introduces us: "This is Greer Garson." She had just come to Hollywood and she *was* lovely.

We got to the party. Howard ignored her *all* evening while he was talking to everybody else there. I've never seen anybody so really hurt as Greer was that night. I stayed by her and kept saying things like, "Please, wouldn't you like something to eat? They have this wonderful buffet." After getting her a couple of drinks, she finally said to me, "Mrs. Kane, do you mind if I take your driver and go home?" I said, "No. I'd like to go with you, but I can't. So please do. I'm so terribly sorry."

And this woman had just come to America. My God, everyone in the whole world was at the party and could see what was going on! And that was the way Howard could treat people.

But I had enough of my own problems with Walter. As I said, I merely married him to get away from my mother. I'm facing that. I kept saying, "Oh, I love him. We have a great association." But he *murdered* my career at this point. He went in, without my say-so, without even telling me, and wrote up a new contract for me. Then, when I divorced him in 1942, he insisted that I pay him ten percent of the whole seven-year contract, which I had to do.

Lew Schreiber, the head of casting at Fox at the time, told me that they were going to give me a much better contract anyway. He said, "Walter really loused you up. But he kept insisting on it." Oh, I was furious! He was not my agent. I never had an agent. Finally, the studio said, "Lynn, you'll have to get an agent so we can negotiate the different pictures, the money and everything else that's going on."

You see, at first I had a stock contract. So by the time I was playing leads in 'B's I was just earning peanuts. Then, in 1940, they gave me a new contract. I was making a couple of thousand dollars a week when I quit. In those days, that was a hell of a salary — especially for a contract player.

It was a seven-year contract, yearly options. It was *their* option whether to pick up your contract or not. If *you* said you didn't want to stay, they'd say, "That's great — we'll sue you and you won't work anywhere else."

The pay did not escalate that rapidly. You were only working forty weeks a year. You had three months' layoff, but not in big chunks. When you were off two days, they took those days out. So you never got thirty days to go anywhere or to do anything. I loved to go to Colorado Springs. But I'd be there three days and then I'd get a phone call and have to go home again. I was at the mercy of the studio. Jack Benny asked me to go to Germany with him when the Allies took over, but I couldn't. For God's sake, I never got to Europe till I was forty.

And when we were not working the studio usually had some publicity ideas for us. I remember there was a thing called "Market Week" and I was supposed to be "Queen of Market Week." Well *(laughing)*, it came out in the paper as "Queer of Market Week." I had *such* a time with that one!

I usually went along with these personal appearances but, in one instance, I did not.

At the time, Ed Sullivan was a little two-bit writer on a Hollywood paper. Get a load of this! He used to take a bunch of girls out to the movie theaters. After the picture was over, he'd parade them across the stage in *bathing suits* and introduce each one. He was planning to take this *show* on tour around the country. So, he approached Walter Kane and said he wanted me to go. Walter asked, "Well, how much are you going to pay her?" — *He* wanted the money! Ed said, "I don't pay them; this is publicity for the girls." Walter then told him what he could do with his offer. What Sullivan did was wait till everyone was on layoff and he picked them up; you had to go out and work for this guy for nothing. I didn't think this was right; so, I turned it down — and the bastard never spoke to me again.

Years later, I was in New York doing a live TV show. I had the same camera crew as Ed's show. They asked me if I would appear on his show one Sunday night. After being introduced, I was to walk out on stage and shake hands with Ed and then walk off. So, I get there and meet the camera crew; we're all buddy-buddy. Then they announced me and I walked across the stage. I put my hand out to Ed. He didn't take it; he let me stand there with egg on my face. He just said, "That way out." I wanted to die. He was a real son of a bitch. He was impossible and had none of the social graces. And people *fought* to get on *The Ed Sullivan Show!*

Although time would find her in a different frame of mind, Lynn had had good reason to feel that she had a "great association" with Walter Kane. It's hard to decipher the degree to which Kane had helped her in her quest for stardom; but helpful he had at first been — and Darryl F. Zanuck did begin to pay more attention to her career once she had married him.

Bari's association with Zanuck had had its origin on the set of 1935's *Metropolitan*. In the ensuing years she had bits and minor roles in many films personally produced by the production chief. These assignments might have been important to Lynn's development but they essentially went unnoticed by Zanuck, who was

March 1940; Lynn models a pantsuit for the Associated Apparel Manufacturers of Los Angeles. The organization had just named Bari "Queen of Market Week," issuing this photo to accompany a press release about the honor. Their announcement wound up being published with Lynn rendered greatly embarrassed.

making no attempt to guide her career in a forward direction. Things changed after Bari had established herself at Western Avenue. Pleased with her work there, Zanuck felt her ready to shine — albeit in support — in his own large-scale productions. He would cast her in four over the next two years: *Hotel for Women* (1939), *Hollywood Cavalcade* (1939), *Lillian Russell* (1940) and *Blood and Sand* (1941).

Standing on the sidelines in Hotel for Women *(1939); Lynn's mind is somewhere else, as she observes Ann Sothern, Jean Rogers and Linda Darnell engage in convivial conversation.*

Hotel for Women went before the cameras immediately after Bari had returned from her honeymoon. Also known as *Elsa Maxwell's Hotel for Women*, the film served as a debut showcase for fifteen-year-old Linda Darnell. It revolved around a group of aspiring young actresses and models at New York's Sherrington Hotel, a fictitious establishment patterned after the Barbizon Hotel in Manhattan. Darnell was Marcia Bromley, the innocent girl from upstate. Marcia had moved to the city to be near her hometown boyfriend, Jeff Buchanan (James Ellison). To her heartbreak, Buchanan ditches her for Melinda Craig (Katharine Aldridge), daughter of his employer, the noted architect John Craig (John Halliday). Craig is carrying on an affair with New York's top fashion model, the slinky Barbara Hunter (Bari). Marcia decides to become a model herself — and, overnight, replaces Barbara as the number-one mannequin in town. She also becomes the object of Craig's affection, leaving Barbara in a state of jealous fury. Not too many evenings later Craig entertains Marcia at his penthouse apartment. Barbara storms in and pulls out a revolver from her purse. She shoots her lover, seriously wounding him. Now thrown into hysterics, she is consoled by her victim — who, in turn, relinquishes Marcia to a repentant Buchanan.

Though saddled with a predictable plot, director Gregory Ratoff approached *Hotel for Women* with zest and its eighty-three minutes raced along. Welcome comedy relief was supplied by costars Ann Sothern, June Gale, Joyce Compton, and Elsa Maxwell — the society doyenne who played herself. Rounding out the large cast, in more dramatic roles, were Jean Rogers, Sidney Blackmer, Ruth Terry and Alan Dinehart. The entire acting ensemble went through their paces on the majestic Art Deco sets of Richard Day, Joseph C. Wright and Thomas Little. The work of these three designers and that of cinematographer J. Peverell Marley made *Hotel for Women* a truly lush and visually-arresting entertainment.

Hotel for Women **was a big production. I enjoyed working on it and had a lot of fun. I really got along with everyone — except Elsa Maxwell. She never spoke to me; I wasn't important. She only spoke to "God" or lovely ladies like Princess Grace, who banged every guy in Hollywood —** *(laughing)* **if you'll excuse the expression.**

Hotel for Women afforded Lynn the opportunity of being in the company of two dear friends, June Gale and Jean Rogers. Gale would soon (in December 1939) marry actor-musician Oscar Levant and move to New York. In her absence, Bari and Rogers would draw closer; their relationship would be a warm and long one, enduring over fifty years.

Jean Rogers and I had been friends before the film. Both of our husbands were agents and that's how we met.

Rogers, a former Universal Pictures feature player and serial queen (she was the original Dale Arden in the *Flash Gordon* series, which starred Buster Crabbe), had been put under to contract to Fox in 1938. The studio would stall her promising career, basically assigning her to inconsequential 'B' films for the better part of three years. *Hotel for Women* would, in fact, turn out to be the actress's only notable Fox appearance. Rogers would have somewhat better luck at MGM, to whom she'd be signed in 1941.

Jean Rogers was but one of many young Fox hopefuls featured in *Hotel for Women*. None of these players, though, would go on to attain stardom — with the exception of Bari and Linda Darnell. Darnell's rise was as swift as Lynn's was slow; her appearance as Marcia Bromley instantly made her a star of the first order. The exquisite beauty's thirteen-year career at Fox would involve several setbacks which would be countered by image alterations, ones that would encourage the actress's skills and allow her to remain in the vanguard throughout the 1940s.

Darnell's first incarnation, true to life, was as a shy, gentle and sweet Cinderella girl. She had only been a tenth-grader when she had left her Dallas classroom for *Hotel for Women's* soundstages, where she continued her schooling between takes. Almost always cast in adult roles, the actress was initially Zanuck's answer to Loretta Young, who had just exited Fox in great discontent. Darnell's successful build-up was witnessed firsthand by Bari, who would go on to appear with her in two other films.

I knew Linda pretty well. She was just a scared, sweet little girl. She bit her fingernails down to the quick and was nervous all the time. She had a family

Linda Darnell and Lynn rehearse a scene on the Hotel for Women *set. Director Gregory Ratoff is pictured crouching, at far left.*

like you wouldn't believe. The mother was really loose in the head; she gave a funeral at the studio for their pet rooster and invited Tyrone and a few others on the lot.

I think that Linda wanted very much to be an actress, but she didn't get a lot of help from her coworkers; they weren't too nice to her. I think they thought that she was just a beautiful face. She was very pretty, although she was never animated at any time. You looked at her face in fascination but it never changed. Later on, she started getting very tough and drinking and carrying on and found out, for herself, that that was the way to do it. Look at what she did in *A Letter to Three Wives* (1949); she was marvelous.

Darnell's performance in *Hotel for Women* wasn't exactly marvelous, but she came off winsomely. Although the spotlight seldom veered away from her throughout the picture, it did manage to beam on Lynn here and there. Barbara Hunter was a meaty, melodramatic role and Bari enacted it with vigor. One would have wished, though, that Lynn herself had looked better as she gave out so histrionically — for her physical appearance had been marred by a careless hairdresser during production.*

The hair department was a closed proposition at that time. They didn't allow men into their guild. The older women — which meant anything over ninety — could work. They got the first jobs that came up. Unless they were all busy making up the troops on some big picture, you got one of these darbs. But if you were little Alice Faye, you had a regular one all the time. She had a great hairdresser, Lillian, a very nice gal who worked with me later on.

We always had to test our hairstyles and clothes on camera for Mr. Zanuck; he was very particular about that. On *Hotel for Women*, I had already made the test scene for Mr. Zanuck and my hair really looked great. But I had had a fine hairdresser. Then the head of the department introduced me to her sister. She announced that she was going to do my hair. I said, "Oh, isn't that lovely." We went over to my dressing room and had lunch. I asked, "Have they told you how they want my hair?" She assured me that they did. I showed this lady the stills that were taken and she began cutting away.

Lloyd Nolan dropped in and we started talking. I wasn't paying much attention to what she was doing. Finally, I turned around and looked into the mirror. I cried, "Jimminy Christmas! What did you do to me?" She had cut all my hair off in the front, up to the hairline, to make a bang! I looked like one of The Three Stooges. She told me that she could fix it so it would look fine.

The head of the department came in and damn near fainted. She tried to placate me but I just got out of the chair and went home. My husband couldn't believe it when he saw me. He went right over to Lew Schreiber's office to tell him that my hair had been ruined. Oh, there was such a stink.

But that's the way they treated me. Everybody else got their own hairdresser and I got magnolia. Later on, they were nice; I guess you had to raise a little hell and have something terrible like this happen.

I did get Alice's hairdresser for the rest of the picture, but she had to paste on little pieces. I don't know how that other woman did it, but in three or four minutes she had scalped me. *(Laughing)* The next time I saw Lloyd, I told him, "Don't *ever* talk to me again when I'm having my hair done or getting made-up!"

Hair — or lack thereof — notwithstanding, Lynn's *Hotel for Women* appearance would rise head and shoulders above her next three ventures into the Zanuck big time. All would be personal disappointments, with *Hollywood Cavalcade* coming first. The lavish Technicolor saga of Tinseltown's pioneer days had The Keystone Kops, Buster Keaton, Ben Turpin and Chester Conklin recreating their hilarious contributions to the silent cinema, playing the discoveries

* In this regard, wearing a wig had not been an option for Bari. The makeup departments of Fox and other major studios were disinclined to employ hairpieces on their female stars (except on certain costume pictures), feeling their artificiality came through loud and clear on the big screen.

of the dynamic Michael Connors (Don Ameche). Connors was a fictional version of the comedians' real-life mentor, producer-director Mack Sennett (himself making a brief *Cavalcade* appearance). Alice Faye was Mabel Normand to Ameche's Sennett, cast as Molly Adair, a Connors find who became the queen of comedy shorts. J. Edward Bromberg co-starred as Connors' producing partner, the patient and kind Dave Spingold. Handsome Alan Curtis

Where did her hair go? Lynn, as Barbara Hunter, the peculiarly-coiffed supermodel of Hotel for Women.

The final cut of Hollywood Cavalcade *(1939) saw the virtual elimination of Lynn's character. This portrait reflects Bari's jettisoned scenes as a silent-screen vamp, in the mold of Theda Bara.*

portrayed Nicky Hayden, a gas station attendant in whom Connors had seen matinee-idol potential. Pre-release publicity saw Lynn receiving fifth billing for playing Connors' mistress, a silent screen vamp. However, by premiere time, Bari's name had been dropped from the credits, with her once-sizable role now whittled down to two seconds (in a flash, she can be spotted onstage in the opening scene).

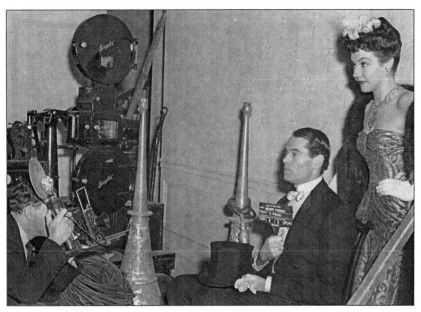

February 12, 1940; Henry Fonda and Lynn, in the midst of their make-up tests for Lillian Russell *(1940).*

I was supposed to be Florence Reed, Theda Bara — all those different silent movie sirens. They had me in a tent in a Turkish outfit with a headdress like Theda. There were a few scenes with Don Ameche but I don't remember them. I also did a scene from *The Shanghai Gesture*, which was the only thing left in the film. They said it was so long; that's why they cut it. I've made that picture leave my mind. I guess I've just willed it away. I was so sick about the whole thing.

My name was listed all the hell down in left field. The day after the premiere, I ran into Mickey Rooney driving down Wilshire Boulevard. We were going in opposite directions. He poked his head out the window and said, "Hey, Lynn, you were swell in that picture last night!" To which I replied, "Drop dead!"

I don't recall any other films where I was cut so severely. But you can't tell me that I'm not a smart lady. For the next few years, I sponsored the cutter's bowling team. *(Laughing)* They didn't *dare* cut me out!

Radical editing of another sort should have come into play with *Lillian Russell*, another Darryl Zanuck/Alice Faye epic. Laboriously and fictitiously, the biopic chronicled the career and romances of the singer who had risen to fame during the turn of the last century. Cast opposite Faye were Henry Fonda, Don Ameche, Warren William and Edward Arnold, as the men in Russell's life. Arnold was Diamond Jim Brady, repeating the role he had played five years earlier in the superior *Diamond Jim*. Lynn was on hand as Edna McCauley, a girlfriend of Brady's. Her part was minor and she received her lowest onscreen billing (twelfth) since *Lancer Spy*.

Warren William is greeted by Lynn and Edward Arnold in Lillian Russell.

I had a bit in that one. I looked forward at that time to having roles in 'A' pictures — but not little bits. I felt very funny about it, especially having come off a set where I'm the big cheese in a little pond.

Bari's role in *Blood and Sand* was somewhat larger, but wholly unsympathetic in nature. She played Encarnacion, the scheming, shrewish sister of toreador Juan Gallardo (Tyrone Power). The femme leads went to Linda Darnell and Rita Hayworth. Darnell was Carmen, Juan's long-suffering young bride. Hayworth played Dona Sol, the wicked temptress who led the bullfighter astray. Nazimova and Anthony Quinn co-starred, as Juan's saintly mother and his rival, Manola. All concerned benefited from the picture's exquisite Technicolor cinematography (which would be honored with an Academy Award). The classic Vicente Blasco Ibáñez story they enacted had first been filmed nearly twenty years earlier, with Rudolph Valentino in the lead. The tale seemed creakier this time around, but it was put forth in such a splendiferous manner that its inherent triteness became palatable. Moviegoers flocked in droves to see all the pageantry, making *Blood and Sand* one of the top-grossing films of 1941.

It was Zanuck's big picture that year. They offered me this little part in it and I had to take it. Practically everybody tested for the role of Dona Sol, but I tested for it two times. Everyone on the lot was so anxious for me to get it.

Lynn, cast as the sister of Tyrone Power (right) in Blood and Sand *(1941). Seated beside Bari is William Montague (aka Monty Banks), portraying her husband.*

The Westmores were making me up and all the right things were happening. In fact, a column came out in the *L.A. Times* with the headline, "Lynn Bari to play lead in *Blood and Sand.*" Somehow, they had gotten the names mixed up. I played the little bit part and they had hired Rita. Of course, she was a big star then.

My role was terrible and Rouben Mamoulian, the director, was such a bastard. Oh, God; he never introduced himself, never even spoke to me. When I first came over on the set to show him my costume, he snapped, "Tell her to turn around!" He was just awful. He would scream, "Get that actress in here!" In my first shot all they photographed were my hands poking pins into a pillow. He never gave me one bit of direction — not that I needed it, for God's sake. On a couple of other scenes, he just said, "Don't need that, we don't need that." Evidently, we had the wrong vibrations.

I had worked as a bit player on Tyrone Power's first picture, *Girls' Dormitory.** When I first saw him, I almost fainted and stabbed a girl! *(laughing)* He was darling and knew that I had a crush on him. He was always picking me up on the lot in his car and driving me wherever I had to go. We went bowling a couple of times and I'd giggle a lot. He knew I was just a kid.

Lynn was no longer a kid when she shared precious few moments of screen time with Tyrone Power in *Blood and Sand.* The part of Encarnacion — and her previous two assignments in Zanuck productions — had left her totally disheartened. Her self-confidence was jolted by the message her studio was sending her: after so much experience, she still was considered an unsafe bet as an 'A'-picture star. Paradoxically, though, Fox's awareness of her abilities and appeal had generated their belief that her name was a drawing card to a prestigious film — but that name had no place being above the title. The studio never entertained the thought that Bari might not accept such minor participation; they knew, as always, she'd come through as her old, reliable self.

Was I cooperative? You bet! I took any part they handed me.

Lynn's lackluster forays into the world of 'A' films were countered by a group of lower-budget efforts that served to advance her position at Fox. Although there were moments when she thought herself forever bound to the 'B' unit, she basically remained hopeful and gave her all to everything to which she was assigned.

Bari's sense of the melodramatic was put to good use in *Earthbound* (1940), an ambitious Sol Wurtzel production. Directed by Irving Pichel, the picture was one of Fox's rare ventures into the supernatural. Its script, written by John Howard Lawson and Samuel G. Engel, was full of rich dialogue that sometimes bordered on the poetic. These words were bolstered by Alfred Newman's splendid background music, which also underscored the story's fantasy element. Third-billed Bari played the sultry, high-strung Linda Reynolds. Linda had been involved in an adulterous affair with financier Nick Desborough (Warner Baxter — in his Fox swan song); the relationship had ended at Desborough's insistence. Heartsick, Linda tries to win her old lover back, but she is again rejected. Madness takes hold of her and she shoots Desborough dead. Nick's transparent ghost image emerges and becomes the unseen observer of his killer's activities. Linda allows her own husband (Henry Wilcoxon) to be imprisoned for her crime and ensnares Desborough's widow (Andrea Leeds) into her web of deception. She is later drawn to her comeuppance by the ghost, whose spirit will not ascend to Heaven until justice has been served.

* *Girls' Dormitory* was actually Power's third film, but it did account for his first billed screen appearance.

Stylishly executed, *Earthbound* was sent into release with an 'A'-picture pro-motion. It certainly had the look of a high-budget movie, thanks in great part to the deft cinematography of Lucien Andriot. Andriot photographed Lynn spec-tacularly (as he would do on several future occasions), giving her a "star aura." He also efficiently employed a matte technique that enabled Nick's ghost to go through its paces in a fascinating way.

Linda Reynolds (Lynn) guns down old flame Nick Desborough (Warner Baxter) in Earthbound *(1940).*

It was a very interesting new process and really quite innovative. We weren't told exactly what was going on as we filmed on this tremendous soundstage with mirrors. My scenes with Warner would be filmed without him. A script guy would be feeding his lines to me. Warner would be off on another set doing the same thing. Then they put the two shots together. I enjoyed *Earthbound* but, evidently, it didn't catch on at all.

Earthbound firmly established Lynn's "other woman" persona. Set in motion by *Always Goodbye* and *Hotel for Women,* this callous image was to become her Achilles' heel. Fox couldn't seem to make up their minds as to how they wanted Bari to be presented during the 1938-41 period, a most crucial time in her career evolution. On the 'B' level, she starred in sprightly, ingratiating roles. The reverse held true for her 'A' films where she was almost exclusively featured as a hardhearted secondary character, generally the femme fatale of the story. While not great in number, her siren turns eventually became the ones which left the greatest impression on filmgoers. Her "bad girl" reputation would become something difficult for her to eschew, undermining her bid for major stardom.

Yup, that's exactly what happened. I was always considered the heavy in the 'A's. In the 'B's, I was the heroine. I didn't like the heavies at all because anybody could do that. But the other things take concentration — especially comedy, which I had great fun doing.

From the destruction of one man to another: Earthbound's *evil Linda postures plaintively in the face of her unknowing husband (Henry Wilcoxon).*

Sol Wurtzel was aware of Lynn's talent for comedy. He would bring his star to her 'B'-picture peak in humorous films. Most would be spirited little entertainments, thoughtfully constructed and performed with finesse. Several cuts above the normal Western Avenue fare, they would garner Bari an increasing amount of favorable critical attention. An excerpt from *Variety's* review of *City of Chance* (1/24/40) highlights this positive mention:

> "City of Chance" unquestionably was put into the hopper as a program production, but it has turned out stronger than some of those intended as A films. ...Lynn Bari forwards her chances for stardom by a likeable portrayal of the scribe.

A smart comedy-drama, *City of Chance* had Lynn tracking down a gambling ring. C. Aubrey Smith, June Gale (her final film) and Donald Woods were also featured.

That set was terribly hot; something like one-hundred-and-ten degrees.

City of Chance was helmed by actor Ricardo Cortez, who for just one year would assume the director's chair, making films at Western Avenue. Cortez had previously guided Bari through *Chasing Danger,* and he would be doing so again in *Free, Blonde and 21* (1940), a quasi-sequel to *Hotel for Women.* This follow-up also took place at the Sherrington Hotel, but its protagonists were all new. Lynn

Lynn, Harry Shannon and June Gale in City of Chance *(1940).*

played a sympathetic character, that of an artist in love with a doctor (Henry Wilcoxon). Her sincere performance had its touching moments and it proved to be a steadying influence in a photoplay that alternated uncomfortably between the melodramatic and the zany.

Comedy and drama were more successfully blended in three other films Bari made during 1940: *Pier 13* (1940), *Charter Pilot* (1940) and *Sleepers West* (1941). All co-starred Lloyd Nolan and were directed by Eugene Forde. The first was a remake of Raoul Walsh's *Me and My Gal* (Fox, 1932), which had starred Joan Bennett and Spencer Tracy. The third had been filmed before as *Sleepers East* (Fox, 1934), directed by Kenneth McKenna, with Mona Barrie, Preston Foster and Wynne Gibson headlining. As for *Charter Pilot*, it beared more than a passing similarity to Allan Dwan's *High Tension* (1936), a Brian Donlevy-Glenda Farrell vehicle. Fox forever reworked their old, proven properties — and usually to positive effect. Such was certainly the case with *Pier 13, Charter Pilot* and

Lynn does a wardrobe test for an outfit she'd be wearing in Free, Blonde and 21 *(1940).*

Sleepers West, action romps made highly enjoyable by Lynn's chemistry with her leading man.

Lloyd Nolan had been contracted by Paramount for four years. He moved over to Fox in 1939, making three films there (including *Pier 13*) as a freelance actor. The studio signed him to a long-term contract in the summer of 1940 (*Charter Pilot* was his first film under this pact). Nolan's work at Fox paralleled

Attired in this ensemble, Bari shares a tense on-screen moment with her Free, Blonde and 21 *costar, Mary Beth Hughes.*

his tenure at Paramount, where the bulk of his assignments had consisted of star turns in 'B' pictures and second leads in 'A's. His background in movies was definitely akin to Bari's — as was his strong, unaffected acting style. The two players turned out to be a great match, always melding together brightly onscreen.

Lynn also benefited greatly by working with Eugene Forde, Fox's most competent 'B'-picture director. A former child actor, Forde had begun his directing career at the studio in 1928, helming some of the last Tom Mix westerns. His flair for action extended into the mystery series genre, where he had lensed five of the better *Charlie Chans* and would go on to film three *Michael Shayne* whodunits (of which *Sleepers West* is one). Forde's evolution at Fox had also brought to the fore his knack with swift comedies, like *Meet the Girls.* The director's various talents were very much in evidence in his Bari/Nolan pictures, where the stars' rough-and-tumble, wisecracking relationships added a luster to the excitement being presented.

Pier 13 was a New York waterfront adventure. **(Now, that was a good picture.)** Lynn played Sally Kelly, the gum-chewing cashier of a dockside coffee shop. Sally's sweetheart is patrolman Danny Dolan (Nolan). Dolan becomes embroiled in the capture of jewel robber Johnny Hale (Douglas Fowley). Sally discovers that Hale has been keeping company with her sister Helen (Joan Valerie). It turns out that Helen had been used as a pawn in Hale's heist. Sally

manages to extricate her from the clutches of the thief, who is then gunned down by Dolan. The cop's heroics net him a promotion, a reward, and a promise of marriage from his girl.

King Morgan (Nolan) was the title character of *Charter Pilot*. The flier's daring exploits provide the basis of a weekly radio show named after himself. The serial's announcer and scriptwriter is Morgan's fiancée, Marge Duncan (Bari). Though in love, Marge and King continually bicker. The couple squabbles their way down to Honduras, where Morgan meets up with his copilot, Charlie Crane (George Montgomery). The two men do battle in Central America with aerial saboteurs. Things come to a climax with Morgan and Marge on a perilous eighteen-thousand-foot rescue mission — broadcast to twenty million listeners as another thrilling installment of the *King Morgan* show. **(That was kind of funny.)**

Secrecy and protection were the prevalent components of *Sleepers West*. The mystery finds detective Mike Shayne (Nolan) in Denver, escorting Helen Carlson (Mary Beth Hughes) onto the *Comanche Limited*. Carlson, a hard-boiled blonde, is San Francisco-bound to testify as the star witness in a murder trial. Disguised as a brunette, she and Shayne settle into their respective compartments.

In this Pier 13 *(1940) wardrobe test, Lynn models one of the many costumes created for her by Herschel (McCoy), Western Avenue's fashion designer extraordinaire.*

They have barely done so when nosy newspaperwoman Kay Bentley (Bari) boards the train. Kay, a former girlfriend of Shayne's, is on her way to cover the trial. She runs into the detective and sparks fly. Immediately suspicious of Shayne's presence on the *Comanche*, the reporter sets out on her own investigation. Both she and her ex get into more trouble than they had bargained for, as the train becomes littered with shady passengers.

The affection displayed by Lloyd Nolan and Lynn in Charter Pilot *(1940) was very real.*

We tried to get as much humor into those things as possible. Lloyd and I did, all told, five pictures together. I was always delighted when I was going to be doing a film with him. He was a helluva actor. I know I was too tall for him — so I'd slop around in my flat heels all the time; just to make him look good. We used to get loaded with the crew at wrap-up parties and tell stories. We always had a barrel of fun.

Lynn's progress in films began to receive wider acknowledgement in 1940, resulting in her being considered for projects created outside of Fox. Independent producer Edward Small had seen a preview of *Earthbound* and had been impressed with Bari's performance. On the strength of it, he secured Lynn for a loanout for his fictionalized tale of a legendary frontier scout. *Kit Carson* was a sweeping western adventure, shot on location in Cayente, Arizona. Jon Hall played the title role and Dana Andrews, Army Captain John Fremont. Together, their characters escorted a group of wagon trains to California, through the Oregon Trail and Shoshone Indian territory. Both men fell in love with their lovely fellow traveler, the genteel Dolores Murphy (Bari). Dolores was heading back to her family's hacienda in Monterey. Her return home became imperiled by

The lighthearted conclusion of Sleepers West *(1941), with Lloyd Nolan, Mary Beth Hughes and Lynn.*

Indian uprisings (engendered by Mexicans) — and complicated by affairs of the heart. After encountering strife of all sorts, she wound up in the arms of Carson, who'd been instrumental in bringing everything to a state of calm.

Kit Carson was released through United Artists in August 1940. Under the direction of George B. Seitz, it proved to be a moneymaker. The oater gave second-billed Lynn a substantial part, one which she handled in a winning way. Playing heroine here also served to introduce her to Dana Andrews, who would go on to become a lifelong friend. (**Dana was an *awful* nice guy.**) The actor was also under long-term contract to Fox, working on loanout to Small.*

Dana Andrews had been but one of many additions to Fox's stable of players during 1939 and 1940. Included among the newly-signed were Betty Grable,

---

* Dana Andrews had actually been contracted by both Fox and the Goldwyn Studio in late 1939. His prodigious work at both companies would extend over a twelve-year period. Oddly, he would never work with Bari at their mutual home base.

Carmen Miranda, Laird Cregar, George Montgomery, John Payne and John Sutton. Then there was also the bevy of young actresses who had little, if any, experience before a camera. All were immediately assigned leading roles in 'A' pictures. With the exception of Linda Darnell, Gene Tierney and Anne Baxter, none of them would make the grade. Most (e.g., Virginia Gilmore, Mary Beth Hughes and Brenda Joyce) would quickly find themselves planted on Western

An on-location candid of Lynn and her Kit Carson *director, George B. Seitz.*

Avenue. After a two-year stretch in the 'B's, they'd be given their walking papers. This particular demotion process had been in effect at Fox for some time; practically every 'A' leading lady of the thirties had gone through it. Alice Faye, Sonja Henie and Darnell would, in fact, be the only women to bridge the decades as stars at The Hills.

Lynn's status at Fox during this period remained unchanged. Her situation, however, was a frustrating one. She wanted to star in 'A' pictures but her studio was content to keep her headlining at Western Avenue, where she was their chief box-office draw. In effect, she was left to witness a slew of newcomers receive the type of build-up she had come to feel she herself deserved.

George Montgomery was not among those who had been pushed by Fox from the outset. The tall, strapping and handsome Montanan had been signed by the studio in the autumn of 1939, at the age of twenty-three. His first two years at Fox saw him in minor roles. Then he starred opposite Mary Beth Hughes in *The Cowboy and the Blonde* (1941). The romantic comedy was a 'B', but it proved to be a sleeper, with Montgomery attracting a lot of attention — especially from the bobby-sox set. In no time, he would become Zanuck's answer to Clark Gable, playing the love interests of Ginger Rogers and Maureen O'Hara, in *Roxie Hart* (1942) and *Ten Gentlemen from West Point* (1942), respectively. Teenage girls would by now have come to envy his many glamorous leading ladies — including Lynn, his most frequent costar.

The three principals of Kit Carson: *Dana Andrews, Lynn and Jon Hall.*

GEORGE MONTGOMERY: "Lynn and I were in three films together: *Charter Pilot, Orchestra Wives* (1942) and *China Girl* (1943). I remember her as a very bright, beautiful person and a good actress. She must have been well-liked at the studio because, after all, she was there a long time."

Lynn and George Montgomery embrace one another in Charter Pilot, *as Arleen Whelan and Lloyd Nolan look on.*

Montgomery would be contracted by Fox six years less than Lynn. Like her, though, he had started out as an extra and had gone through the Western Avenue experience. Both would be promoted from Fox's 'B' unit during the production year of 1941-42.

GEORGE MONTGOMERY: "I think that, if you're going to break out of the 'B's, there are many factors — including your fan mail. That's what got me out of them very fast. My fan mail was sort of extraordinary during the first few years, maybe because of Ginger [Rogers] and Hedy [Lamarr], whom I went with; naturally, that induced a lot of press.

"The greatest mystery is how in the hell one got to be a star in films. When you're coming in off the farm, everything seems to happen in a fog. It was rather unbelievable to be in the folds of Hollywood and the picture business. It just seemed to happen so fast — as if you were on a rocket. The first few years, you really didn't know what the hell was going on. And, thirty years later, you say, 'Jeez, if I had known then what I know now!' *(laughing)*"

The type of disorientation experienced by Montgomery and others who shot to stardom had no relevance to Lynn. Her unfolding as a screen actress had included no short cuts, grand press-agentry or brainstorming by Fox's front office; she had just gone along slowly and surely. Her movement might have been steady, but it had involved a tremendous amount of activity. In her first three years as a featured player, Bari had amassed a staggering amount of credits — twenty-eight to be exact. All of these assignments had allowed her to refine her acting skills and had helped to make her one of Hollywood's most familiar faces. This had made her increasingly more popular, both with the public and the press. By 1941, her recognition factor paralleled that of an 'A' star. This was quite an achievement, considering she had had neither the publicity machine nor the top roles to back her up.

The day would finally come when Fox would realize the true extent of Lynn's popularity, something at which they would actually marvel. Accordingly, they would at last take decisive action on behalf of their erstwhile stockgirl — and Lynn Bari would become a star.

Lynn Bari, as Vivian Dawn, in Sun Valley Serenade *(1941).*

CHAPTER SEVEN

MOON OVER HER SHOULDER

Naturally, I felt things were really beginning to happen by this time. I could never understand why they didn't sooner. However, I'm reminded of something that Cesar Romero said about me in a recent TV interview. He said that I was the only star to rise through the ranks. And that's the way they treated me — "Oh, Lynn will do it … get Lynn." Also, I think a lot of it had to do with my mother; they were afraid of my being involved in a scandal. I've taken an awful rap because of her; people thought I'd done all these things. But the only person who actually ever said anything lousy about me was Louella Parsons. On the picture with Barbara Stanwyck, she said, "Lynn Bari is the new girl in the picture. I don't know what everybody's raving about." The old bitch; I couldn't stand her. She was about as subtle as a train wreck.

Not even Louella Parsons herself would have denied the fact that Bari was within close grasp of stardom during 1941. Lynn would reach this goal by virtue of two films released that fall, *Sun Valley Serenade* and *Moon Over Her Shoulder*. The costly *Sun Valley* turned out to be a smash hit, as had been expected. The modest *Moon Over Her Shoulder*, on the other hand, created no buzz prior to its release. Much to the delight of all concerned, it would prove to be a sleeper.

Bari's career had so far encompassed many breaks, but *Sun Valley Serenade* came to be her luckiest one. The fates were truly working in Lynn's favor here, for she was rushed into the film as a last-minute replacement for starlet Cobina Wright, Jr.* The role she took over was that of blues singer Vivian Dawn. The temperamental Vivian descends upon *Sun Valley* at its outset, during a session at a New York recording studio. This setting is where the songbird develops a crush on Ted Scott (John Payne), the pianist in Phil Corey's (Glenn Miller's) orchestra. Vivian goes on to hire Phil and his band to appear with her in Manhattan and Sun Valley, Idaho. Just before they all take off for the glamorous ski resort,

---

* Bari had at this point been slated to support as Connie Fentress in *Moon Over Miami* (1941). Quite ironically, this part would eventually be played by Cobina Wright, Jr.

Ted receives word that a refugee is about to be placed into his hands; a publicity stunt arranged by the band's manger (Milton Berle) is becoming all too true. Expecting to greet a little Norwegian girl, Ted and his fellow band members are startled to discover that the refugee is actually the very grown-up Karen Benson (Sonja Henie). Karen immediately falls for her guardian — and a rivalry between her and Vivian ensues. Against Ted's wishes, the persistent Karen winds up in

Lynn, Milton Berle and Glenn Miller in Sun Valley Serenade.

Sun Valley, where she takes to the ice rink and ski slopes, eventually landing her man and leaving Vivian out in the cold — literally!

The idea behind this story came from Darryl F. Zanuck himself, born of his imagination while he had been vacationing in Sun Valley. To flesh things out into a finished screenplay, Zanuck hired a battery of writers. One of them was Fox scenarist Milton Sperling, who would also serve as *Sun Valley's* producer, making his bow in this capacity. With mentor Zanuck always a phone call away, Sperling would perform his new task admirably.

Sonja Henie was another who would profit greatly from *Sun Valley*. The musical marked the Olympic skater's first screen appearance in two years and would serve to revive her movie career. Henie would actually never be more delightful on film, and the ski resort to which she ventured would provide a magnificent backdrop for her various pursuits to take hold.

Sun Valley had many positive components but head and shoulders above them all were its musical elements, in particular the dazzling contributions of Glenn

Miller. Miller and his orchestra were now riding their third year as *Billboard* magazine's number-one recording artists. The bandleader's rise to the top had been accomplished in just over ten years' time. Miller went on to be unequalled in the music industry; there is little argument that he led the most successful band during the swing era. Confident, brilliant and exacting, he hired only the best musicians and vocalists and expected nothing less than the best from each and every one of them.

Miller would also not let his orchestra be presented in circumstances that were anything less than optimal — and this encompassed the medium of motion pictures. He had seen other notable big bands perform in screen musicals and thought their appearances there rather demeaning. All had been featured as guest stars, basically incidental to storylines that were, for the most part, insipid. Miller correctly thought that Hollywood was cashing in on the big band craze, making a fast buck off of high-caliber musical talent in lower-grade entertainment fare.

Then he was given the script to *Sun Valley Serenade* — and an opportunity to participate in a major way in a film project with first-rate production values. In addition to his musical chores, Miller would be afforded the opportunity to leave the bandstand and interplay with other cast members. His role was undemanding but, nonetheless, he would evidence a quality of naturalness in his first-time-out as an actor.

In March 1941 Miller and company settled in Los Angeles for their ten weeks on *Sun Valley*. The picture was lensed mostly at The Hills, but cast and crew also went on location to Sun Valley and Salt Lake City. The aesthetics of both the outdoor scenery and the band in performance were heightened by the expert photography of Edward Cronjager, who would receive an Academy Award nomination for his work. Oscar nods would also go to musical director Emil Newman and songwriters Mack Gordon and Harry Warren, for the intoxicating "Chattanooga Choo Choo." Miller's Bluebird recording of "Chattanooga" charted about the same time *Sun Valley* went into release and it quickly rose to the number-one position.

Miller's musicians on *Sun Valley's* soundtrack and its Bluebird counterparts were essentially the same. However, substitutions and additions were made when it came to the vocalists. "Chattanooga Choo Choo," as heard on disc, featured the current Miller vocal lineup of saxophonist Tex Beneke, Paula Kelly and the Modernaires. The Nicholas Brothers and Dorothy Dandridge were added to this mix on film. Kelly waxed the Bluebird recording of the rapturous "I Know Why (And So Do You)," but the song went to Pat Friday in the movie. Friday was Lynn's singing voice double in both *Sun Valley* and *Orchestra Wives*. The twenty-year-old had first made a name for herself while a UCLA coed; a college talent contest had led to a radio guest spot on Bing Crosby's *Kraft Music Hall*. Another appearance there resulted in a contract with Crosby, and for two summers she was Bing's vocal replacement on his show. During this time Friday also recorded four sides with the Harry Sosnik Orchestra. Marriage put a finish to her association with the Crosby contingent, whom she claimed did their best to blackball her in the entertainment world. Most thankfully, she was then approached by Miller for *Sun Valley*. Friday signed with Fox, under the strict stipulation that she not reveal she was working on the picture. Studio publicists would then promote Lynn Bari's newfound — and extraordinary — vocal gifts.

Next to Glenn Miller, no one benefited more from appearing in *Sun Valley* than twenty-one-year-old Bari. Lushly captured by cinematographer Cronjager (a wizard) and sumptuously clothed by Travis Banton, she was finally being accorded the full movie-star "treatment" in this, the first 'A' picture in which

In this deleted Sun Valley Serenade *musical sequence, "At Last" is performed by Glenn Miller and his orchestra, with John Payne and Lynn taking to the mike.*

she had been so glamorously and prominently cast. Lynn would have had even more screen time here if Darryl Zanuck hadn't pared down the musical before its release. Out had gone three Gordon-Warren numbers. One of those jettisoned had featured the band at a New York club, with Lynn and John Payne at the mike. The song they'd performed was the superb "At Last." Instrumentals of the tune can be heard in *Sun Valley's* background, but "At Last" wouldn't be cast in the full light of day until the following year, when it would be more inventively filmed in *Orchestra Wives*, with the focus on Bari and Miller balladeer Ray Eberle.

After the two Glenn Miller movies, Lynn would go on to portray Benny Goodman's vocalist in *Sweet and Low-Down* (1944) — making her the only actor to have performed with both swing giants on film. By virtue of these appearances, she would become known as Hollywood's premiere band singer (with audiences still in the dark about her being dubbed). Bari's experiences as a pop-music songstress would account for a most happy interlude in her life, one she would enthusiastically recall decades later.

Listen, I would have *paid* them to be on those pictures at that time; that was The Big Band Era! Glenn and Benny were *real* musicians, in addition to being jazz musicians; they proved this with their arrangements. They were

Lynn, at home, sings along to a master recording of a Sun Valley Serenade *song she would soon be lip-synching before the cameras.*

two of a kind that way. As people they were completely different, but I liked them both.

Glenn was very quiet and a nice guy. Everybody said that he had no sense of humor. I thought he did. It was funny and dry. He was a Midwesterner, you know — certainly no frills or anything. He was just a genius with band music.

They say that *Sun Valley* and *Orchestra Wives* were seen by more military men during the war than any other pictures shown. I just adored being around Glenn and the band; it was so exciting. And those ballads I did were absolutely lovely; I had a feeling they would become standards. I had wanted to do my own singing. Harry Warren, a very good friend, was for it. But Mack Gordon was opposed to it. My voice wasn't bad; it recorded okay. I did sing [later] in a few pictures and I've sung on the stage. But at that point I was just too scared. I couldn't really cut it and go in with all those musicians and record. The studio knew it, so they got a girl, Pat Friday. Her voice was absolutely marvelous, but it didn't sound like me. Glenn liked my voice and told me that I sounded more like a band singer than Pat did.

As for the lip-synching, I took the songs home and worked with them like crazy all the time. It's very difficult to make it look real. The only way to do it is to sing really loud. When the film was rolling, I had them turn the music all the way up. I didn't care if people had to put cotton in their ears; I didn't want to miss a note. If I was flat or sharp, nobody would know.

Nor did anyone outside the studio know for sure it wasn't Bari's voice warbling "I Know Why" and "It Happened in Sun Valley" on the *Sun Valley Serenade* soundtrack. Lynn's adeptness at lip-synching even had most critics fooled — including *The Motion Picture Daily* (8/28/41), who wrote that she "sings enchantingly." Judging by their wording, however, *The Hollywood Reporter* (7/23/41) might have had their suspicions: "Lynn Bari appears to stunning advantage as the soloist."

By presenting her in such an alluring manner, *Sun Valley* highlighted the striking contrast between Lynn and the film's leading lady, Sonja Henie. Every time the two were framed together Bari's sexy, womanly qualities became more apparent — as did the diminutive Henie's coquettish and cloying tendencies. The skater did have her charming ways, but those faded in Lynn's presence. As Vivian Dawn, Bari punched up a formula "other woman" role with a special dynamism and shadings of vulnerability. Her performance would, in effect, make one question why a piano player would dump a woman of substance for a "Scandinavian Hillbilly" (as Vivian tagged her rival in a fit of pique).

Preview audiences reacted most favorably to Lynn's appearance as Vivian. So did Zanuck. He sent Bari out on her first multi-city promotional tour, coinciding with *Sun Valley*'s release. Lynn was accompanied by costar John Payne, her brother's childhood friend. The two gave countless radio and press interviews, in addition to attending local premieres of their film. Both experienced a moment of personal glory when they stopped off in Roanoke and were greeted by an ardent mob of hometown fans. All of the hoopla surrounding this coast-to-coast publicity junket excited Lynn, who was being presented by her studio as a lead attraction of the tour. Being cast in the limelight this way would be among the first of a rush of actions affected by Fox to forward Bari; she was now being handled with much greater attention, treatment befitting a rising star.

Sonja Henie, however, was being dealt with shabbily by Fox. The former box-office queen's previous few films had failed to ignite, making her studio

A rivalry in the making: John Payne introduces Lynn to Sonja Henie in Sun Valley Serenade.

increasingly more intolerant of her iron-will and unyielding monetary demands. Things came to a head on the *Sun Valley* set, where she was to suffer a great humiliation. Henie's skating finale, shot on dyed black ice, was an intricate number that required meticulous attention and gradual filming. Consequently, its production time kept expanding, pushing back the wrap-up date of the picture, which was now going way over budget. Director Bruce Humberstone thought he was finally completing the sequence when, on her last spin, Henie slipped and fell onto the ice. Because her outfit and body had become blackened with dye, production was halted for the day — and for good. Zanuck unleashed his animosity toward the star by refusing to have the number re-shot. The printed result is an ice ballet that never reaches a point of conclusion!

Sonja Henie's career at Fox was in deep trouble once *Sun Valley* was in the can; she was on the verge of being dropped. Things changed when the movie hit the screens and began racking up incredible grosses, with the studio rethinking

Henie's situation (even though Glenn Miller's music was the primary reason for the picture's success). Zanuck extended the Norwegian ice-twirler's contract for two more films. He did so most grudgingly; it was a well-known fact that he couldn't stand her.

I'm sure he couldn't but she had made so much money for Fox. Her last two pictures at the studio (*Iceland* [1942] and *Wintertime* [1943]) didn't do so well and they got rid of her. They didn't give a damn about their actresses. They had no heart at all. Nobody does at a studio when you start slipping at the box office.

I adored Sonja — but she was quite a character. I came on the set one day in this absolutely gorgeous white peau du soie dress, embroidered with bugle beads; it sounds garish, but it wasn't. Sonja's mother came out of her [Sonja's] dressing room, took one look at me and disappeared. Then Sonja came out. All of a sudden, there was deathly silence on the set.

It seemed that Sonja wanted to wear the dress. *(Laughing)* She was playing a peasant girl! Everything stopped on the set and now they're all talking about my dress. So Darryl Zanuck comes down. When Zanuck comes down on the set, something really terrible is happening; even the cameraman's death wouldn't bring him down! He said to her, "But, Sonja dear, you're playing a peasant girl. You've just come over from Norway. It would be ridiculous for you to wear this." She put her foot down, "I want that dress!" There's a pall, and finally the two of them go into her dressing room for a long talk.

Glenn says to me, "Jesus, we've got a date in an hour-and-a-half. What the hell is going on?" So they come out. Zanuck's evidently placated her and she sits down at the table. We go into the scene. I get up and walk over to the band-stand and do "At Last."

Well, PS, they cut the number from the film! They told me that this was done because the picture was too long. But I think it was because of that dress.

Later on, Sonja had us up to dinner when she was married to Bob Topping. They had rented Myrna Loy's old house, a beautiful place on the way to Hidden Valley. While the guys were all having a brandy she came over to me and said, "Come upstairs. I show you my bedroom." It's a big, elegant room. She opens the doors to this tremendous closet. And there's *that* dress! Miniature size! *(laughing)* She swings it out and says, "Vell, I had to do it. I had it made. Looks like hell on me!" She was a *very* persistent lady.

————

There is no question that the tide turned for Lynn once *Sun Valley Serenade* first previewed in July 1941. Fox had still been giving her relatively little consideration the previous month when they had thrown her into *We Go Fast* (1941), an inane comedy concerning two motorcycle cops (Alan Curtis and Don DeFore) who did battle over a sassy diner waitress (Bari). Lynn's energy had gone into high gear here, in a valiant attempt to uplift what was clearly a forgettable piece of nonsense. (**Oh, God.**) Her efforts, however, couldn't mask the fact that the film was a cheapie, one vastly inferior to most of her other second features. Sol Wurtzel served as *We Go Fast's* executive producer, with Lou Ostrow producing. Directing "honors" went to Paramount's William C. McGann, working on what would be a one-time-only loanout to Fox. *We Go Fast* would die in theaters during *Sun Valley's* initial phase of release.

We Go Fast notwithstanding, Bari's career at Fox most probably would have leaped ahead because of the reaction to *Sun Valley*. Thankfully, though, her promising situation was fortified by the late October release of *Moon Over Her Shoulder*, an unusual little gem from Fox's 'B' unit. The picture was a cerebral romantic comedy with a feminist slant. Lynn was the whole show here, playing an intelligent, spirited and assertive young woman who, in character, bore a remarkable resemblance to herself. Trade reviews and early public response would catapult *Moon* from the lower berth on the double bills to the top slot. Subsequently, Bari herself would be elevated — into the exhibitor's popularity charts. Lynn would never lose sight of the factors behind this ascent, especially her role in *Moon* — the type of assignment for which she had long waited.

I always felt that any part I got where I could *really* do something would effect a change.

Moon Over Her Shoulder's Susan Rossiter did, indeed, prove to be that part. Susan was the creation of two female scenarists, Helen Smith and Eve Golden. Written in a clever and urbane manner, *Moon* is centered on Rossiter's search for her own identity, a pursuit that evolves from matters of the heart. Susan is the neglected wife of Dr. Phillip Rossiter (John Sutton), a stuffy marital psychologist. The couple resides with their twin six-year-old daughters in the suburbs of LA. Playing the role of model homemaker leaves Susan unfulfilled, a feeling aggravated by her husband's obsession with his work. When the kids are sent off to Girl Scout camp, Susan becomes restless. A rather blasé Phillip suggests she might be settled by a return to an old hobby, painting. Susan halfheartedly follows through with this idea, as she sets out to explore what is meaningful to her life. Unexpectedly, she comes to experience her resurrection.

One day, while painting on a bridge (Pasadena's San Rafael Bridge), Susan is thrown together with Rex Gibson (Dan Dailey), a freewheeling fishing-yacht skipper who mistakes her point of placement for a suicide perch.* Rex "rescues" Susan and takes her aboard his boat.** A mutual attraction draws the two into a special daytime relationship. With both fascination and delight, Susan embraces Rex's eccentric lifestyle and undergoes a personal renewal. However, nightly she returns to the staid world of her unresponsive husband, trying to make sense of her marriage. An odd turn of events brings her dual existence to an end — and

---

* Dan Dailey was working on loanout from MGM. He would go under long-term contract to Fox in late 1946.

** The vessel, the Zoa III, was actually owned by Preston Foster.

she is finally forced to choose between the skipper and the shrink. She does so with her newfound sense of self-possession intact.

Although lighthearted in tone, *Moon* came across as a substantive relationship study with a well-etched protagonist. Susan was a most intriguing woman; sharp of mind and cultured yet frustrated and yearning for recognition. Her evolvement was something Lynn conveyed quite believably. The empathy she evoked lent

A musical moment from Moon Over Her Shoulder: *"The Girl with the Sugar Brown Hair" is sung with gusto by Dan Dailey (left), Lynn and Alan Mowbray.*

itself to good humor, and it was a joy to see her character gaily shed her repressions on the road to self-understanding. There was a delicacy to Bari's portrayal, even in moments of broad comedy. This fineness was enhanced by the care that had gone into her physical presentment. It is obvious that great attention had been paid to her hair, make-up and wardrobe — for she looked vastly appealing throughout, whether in stunning evening gowns or formless rain wear. She also captivated musically, huskily singing — *sans* voice double — the boisterous Alfred Newman-Walter Bullock tune, "The Girl with the Sugar Brown Hair."

In short, Lynn made a thoroughly smashing impression in *Moon*, a film that was also a feather in Western Avenue's cap.

> *Variety* (10/17/41): "It achieves its effect and purpose a good deal better than much higher-bracket films with the same weight and color. With the well written script, the complications make for brightly performed, smartly dialogued action against pleasing and

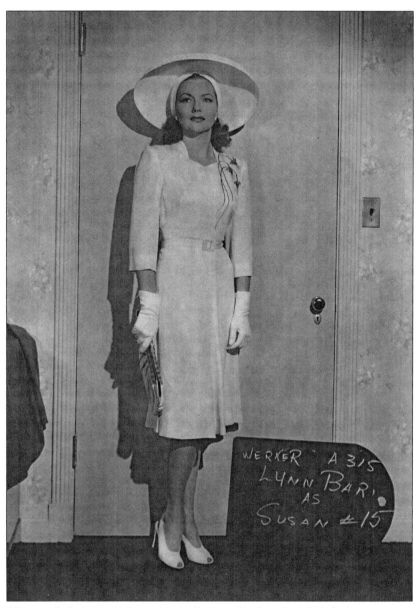

This wardrobe test served as a clear indication that Lynn would be looking spectacular in Moon Over Her Shoulder *(1941).*

varied backgrounds. Richard Day and Lew Creber's setting rate particular comment for effective good taste in a medium budget film. So do the Herschel gowns that adorn with pleasing variation the toothsome Lynn Bari. Alfred Werker directed well, for both pace and points, and Lucien Andriot's photography is excellent, the best Miss Bari has had to date."

The Hollywood Reporter (10/17/41): "Lynn Bari, a delightful example of a young matron, makes the best of a meaty role playing it with great charm and zest."

I loved that one. I really thought it was such a darling picture. It was a decent story that really had something to it. I had a good director, Alfred Werker. A lot of people didn't like him, but I did very much. He knew me and what I could do. I also had that wonderful designer, Herschel, with whom I had worked many times. And John Sutton was marvelous; we laughed a lot and had great fun.

Despite the above comments, Bari's *Moon Over Her Shoulder* recollections were also marked by unpleasantness. Many of her noteworthy achievements, such as this film, seemed to have been tainted by an injustice inflicted upon her by a family member or coworker (e.g., Peter Lorre on *Mr. Moto's Gamble* — her first lead, Sidney Lanfield on *Always Goodbye* — her first major role in an 'A'). These actions by others — more specifically, Lynn's *reactions* to them — denied her the chance to bask in the full glow of a fruitful endeavor. Forty-eight years after the fact, she vividly recalled what had brought her down on the *Moon* set:

Dan Dailey hated my guts. He was the only actor in the motion picture business who really hated me and I don't know why. From the first day on the set, he took off at me. I didn't know that his dog had died the night before, although I found out later. If somebody had only told me or if he had said something, I would have left him alone.

We had had such a good time in rehearsals. Then we started filming. We were doing this big scene at a bar in a country club. There were all these extras on the set. Dan was blowing his lines so dreadfully and I just pleasantly reached over to him and said, "Oh, come on, Dan, don't worry, you'll get it." He shouted, "Don't touch me, ever! Don't *ever* touch me!" I drew back and thought that he was kidding. But it went on from there. Then I finally broke into tears, ran off the set into my dressing room, and felt like a damned fool.

But he made me look and feel like a fool. Later, there was a knock on my dressing room door. Dan came in and said in muffled tones, "The director said I had to apologize to you or you won't come back on the set." I just looked at him. "Well…I apologize," he said — and, with that, he turned and walked out. From there on, I just ignored him, pretending he wasn't there. If you want to show that you feel something for somebody, try being in a smooch with someone who hates your guts!

Nonetheless, *Moon Over Her Shoulder* was a damned good picture. Even the great king Zanuck saw it. He never bothered to look at those lower-budget pictures. I think that film had an awful lot to do with my being promoted to bigger pictures because, soon after that, I was regularly in 'A' productions.

Bari's performances in *Sun Valley Serenade* and *Moon Over Her Shoulder* convinced her studio to once and for all promote her to the 'A' league. This decision engendered a problem, however. At the time Fox didn't have an appropriate script available to showcase Lynn's raise in rank. Dollars-and-cents concerns apparently took precedence over career strategies, because Bari was told that she was to report to the 'B' unit for an indeterminate period. Idle time was money wasted — especially where Lynn was concerned. Having renegotiated her contract the previous year, she was not only the highest-paid player on Western Avenue, but commanded more in salary than many of the young stars at The Hills.

The period between September 1941 and February 1942 would see Bari on the sets of four films of varying quality. The first in this quartet would have the highest budget and would come to bear the industry classification of a "shaky 'A.'" The others would be strictly 'B' affairs. Lynn would do all compliantly — and her longstanding back-and-forth activity between the 'A' and 'B' rungs would draw to a close.

Fox was in the nascent stage of phasing out their 'B' unit, as it presently existed, when Bari made *The Perfect Snob* (1941), one of the first films to reflect this change. The studio was now striving for a more streamlined look to their medium-budgeters. As for the lower-case 'B's, they would disappear from Fox's production schedules by 1943. Western Avenue supervisor Sol Wurtzel would be directly affected by all of this. Wurtzel had turned sixty in 1940, the year in which the volume of his individual producing assignments had begun to diminish. Things intensified, in this respect, as fresh blood began to define the product on Western Avenue. New among the producing personnel there were Walter Morosco and Ralph Dietrich, who had been contracted in 1940. They would be joined in 1942 by Bryan Foy, who had had a prolific career at Warners.

Walter Morosco produced both *Moon Over Her Shoulder* and *The Perfect Snob*. *Snob* was categorized as a "shaky 'A,'" unlike the similarly — if not more carefully — executed *Moon*. The earlier film had gone into release as a 'B' and had built steam after it had opened. *Snob*, on the other hand, would benefit from a promotion somewhere between the 'A' and 'B' levels. Most significantly, its four stars (Lynn, Cornel Wilde, Charlie Ruggles and Charlotte Greenwood) would be billed *above* the title, something that never happened in a Fox 'B' movie.

Publicity for *Snob* would virtually spell out the studio's intention to overhaul Western Avenue:

> "Said to be unusual in that the picture represents a grouping of top notch stars in a lower bracket film, 'The Perfect Snob' represents an

attempt to do away with the so-called 'B' pictures. It has been called first-rate entertainment and rates that on name power alone."

The Perfect Snob was lensed at both Western Avenue and The Hills, where it made use of the marshy sets that had been constructed for Jean Renoir's *Swamp Water* (1941). The film was an appealing bit of fluff, enhanced by some witty dia-

This charming scene from The Perfect Snob *(1941) established Chris Mason's (Lynn's) relationship with her protective father (Charlie Ruggles).*

logue that was delivered with zest by its attractive cast. Lynn was Chris Mason, daughter of veterinarian Edgar Mason (Ruggles) and his class-conscious wife, Martha (Greenwood). The family's story unfolds with Chris graduating from finishing school. Her diploma nets her a Hawaiian vacation with her mom. The two are joined out in the Pacific by Dr. Mason, who's grown very wary of the haughty Martha's influence over his impressionable daughter. He arrives just in time, as Chris finds herself on the verge of engagement to Freddie Browning

(Alan Mowbray), a rich old swain that Martha's been palming off on her. Enter Mike Lord (Wilde), the man Edgar has hired to break up Chris's courtship with Freddie. One triangle dissolves and another one is born, with the appearance of Mike's friend and business partner, Alex Moreno (Anthony Quinn). Chris's romantic dilemmas eventually come to an end, with true love taking precedence over monetary considerations.

Cornel Wilde and Lynn pose with Daisy, one of the four-legged players of The Perfect Snob.

Lynn was undeniably the focal point of *Snob*. Holding her own in the presence of scene-stealers Ruggles and Greenwood, she affected an air of youthful sophistication, at times tart-tongued but basically ingratiating in demeanor. She was given the chance to feign a quality of worldliness, something that went beyond her character's actual catalog of experiences. Playing Chris allowed her to create an interesting child-woman portrait. The deb's tender, girlish side came to the fore in a touching early moment, shared with the vet and a litter of puppies. Bari hadn't been presented so softly in quite some time, and *Snob* offered her what was perhaps her best ingénue turn — good preparation for an 'A' leading lady-in-waiting. The film itself was remembered by its star with affection.

I liked the cast in that one. Charlie was such a wonderful guy. So was Tony [Quinn]. And that was one of "Corey's" [Cornel's] first pictures. He was anything but wild; a very serious person. He was married to a real little Puritan girl then. Some of us were playing poker on location one day and he came up to me and said, "You *gamble?*"

The Perfect Snob was Cornel Wilde's debut film at Fox and his first lead assignment.* The picture's second lead, Anthony Quinn, would be signed by the studio once the film wrapped, remaining under contract for three years. Already

Anthony Quinn and Lynn, in a playful mood on The Perfect Snob *set. (Dialogue director Hal Yates stands in the background.)*

a veteran of 'B' pictures, Quinn's career rise would be even more protracted than Lynn's, encompassing tenures at five different studios over a period of sixteen years (1937-53). His long climb to international acclaim would entail over sixty stepping stones, two of which (*Blood and Sand* and *Snob*) he shared with Bari.

* Cornel Wilde would be simultaneously contracted by Columbia and Fox, to whom he would be signed for thirteen years.

ANTHONY QUINN: "We worked together in my early days in Hollywood. I did enjoy working with Lynn in *The Perfect Snob* and found her to be a lovely girl who seemed to have a wonderful sense of humor. I was very, very fond of her."

After playing romantic scenes with Quinn, Lynn drew close with a young actor recently signed by Fox. His name was Roddy McDowall. McDowall had

been a featured player in British films since 1938. The previous year he had evacuated London, a city engulfed in a blitz. Now a US resident, he was on the brink of attaining overnight stardom — at the age of thirteen — in Fox's prestige picture of 1941, *How Green Was My Valley*. Cast there in the pivotal role of Huw, he would be singled out for an astonishingly sensitive performance. Gifted with a quality of naturalism, McDowall would go on to give many a notable characterization during his four years at Fox. He became the first of several juvenile players at the studio with whom Bari would form a special friendship — the result of her great affection for children, on whom she always conferred respect.

Roddy McDowall, 1941.

RODDY McDOWALL: "Lynn was just *so* terrific to me. When I was thirteen, she was twenty-two — and, as far as I was concerned, she was a very sophisticated lady. But she treated me like an adult and was very kind. I *really* had a good time with her. She was funny and always hit the nail on the head about something, without being patronizing or put-down; she always hit the true value.

"My first year at Fox, I did five films. They realized that they had something. Then they gave me this piece of shit, *On the Sunny Side* (1942), which was my first starring role. We made part of it on the Western Avenue lot. Luckily, I got *The Pied Piper* (1942) as the next one. I didn't last in the garbage heap. *(laughing)* If you were exiled there, like Jane Withers was — because of Mrs. Temple [Shirley's mother], then I think that you really felt like you were being punished for something. Lynn used to say, 'You and I are friendly because we're on the whipping team.' That would mean that if you weren't 'in the moment,' you know, didn't have a hit film, then you were relegated to the boondocks. She had been in so many 'B' films and I could never understand why."

It's also hard to understand why Fox loaned Bari out for *The Falcon Takes Over* (1942), shot at RKO throughout November 1941. The whodunit was an installment in the *Falcon* series, which starred George Sanders as the suave sleuth,

Lynn and George Sanders in The Falcon Takes Over *(1942).*

Gay Lawrence (aka, "The Falcon"). The source of *The Falcon Takes Over* was the first-rate Raymond Chandler novel, *Farewell, My Lovely*. None of the bite of the Chandler work was, however, to be found in its *Falcon* incarnation, a lackluster hodgepodge of mystery and comedy. Lynn played reporter Ann Reardon, a role that was too vapid for her to mold into something interesting. She was not at all a dominant presence here but, nonetheless, she received star billing alongside Sanders.

I had worked on bits and small parts in George's films before this. We were very friendly. *The Falcon Takes Over* was remade as *Murder, My Sweet* (1944) right after that; it brought Dick Powell into the limelight again. RKO had asked for me for the *Falcon* picture. Fox said, "Sure, she'll go," whether I wanted to or not. The studio made the decision — you couldn't. You could have said, "I won't do it," but then you went on suspension immediately, with no salary. So once a loanout was agreed upon, you got a letter, delivered with a script that said, "You're expected at wardrobe at such and such a time."

Bari's next wardrobe date at Fox was on Monday, December 8, 1941 — the day after the bombing of Pearl Harbor. It was definitely not a normal Monday in the motion picture industry, which shared the shock, sadness and state of

confusion that had at once overwhelmed the country as a whole. Lynn spent hours before the still cameras, doing costume tests for *The Night Before the Divorce* (1942), which would take hold on the soundstages by week's end.

The Night Before the Divorce would prove to be a neat little tonic for moviegoers clamoring for escapist fare. The film was a comedy (based on a European play),

Mary Beth Hughes beams brightly at Lynn, whose birthday is being celebrated on the set of The Night Before the Divorce *(1942).*

well-directed by Robert Siodmak and carefully photographed by Peverell Marley. Both men helped to obfuscate the fact that this was a shoestring-budgeter — one which would turn out to be a very good vehicle for its leading lady. Bari played another Lynn (Nordyke), an archetypal emancipated woman who excels in all to which she applies herself. Mary Beth Hughes costarred as her kittenish rival.

That was cute. It wasn't a bad picture at all. I liked Robert Siodmak tremendously. He was a very interesting guy. Mary Beth was good in it, but the studio never gave her a fair shake.

Bari hadn't even finished shooting *The Night Before the Divorce* when she embarked upon what she considers her worst film, *Secret Agent of Japan* (1942).

Although laughably histrionic, the spy melodrama quickly became a bodacious footnote in the annals of American cinema. Its production was set into motion posthaste by Darryl Zanuck, who had wanted Fox to be the first studio to release a film dealing with the Pearl Harbor atrocity. This goal was indeed met with *Secret Agent*, which also became the first anti-Japanese picture of World War II. According to legend, Zanuck had commissioned its script on the night of the

bombing. Screenwriter John Larkin immediately went to work and completed draft one on December 10, 1941.

The story Larkin wrote concerned a gorgeous British agent named Kay Murdock (Bari). Kay is in Shanghai in early December 1941, planning to warn Naval Intelligence of an impending attack on a US military base. The plot thickens as she joins forces with a brash American solider-of-fortune, Roy Bonnell (Preston Foster), against a network of Axis spies. The evil Japanese and German agents the two encounter are defined by their peering eyes and sneers — not to mention their torturous acts. Accomplishing much of what they had set out to do, Kay and Roy manage to flee the clutches of the enemy, making a quick air escape to Chungking.

Secret Agent shot late at night because most of its cast and crew had already been committed to other projects. Many of the supporting players were Caucasian-Americans enacting European and Asian roles. However, approximately thirty actors were Japanese-Americans — a class of individuals who would soon be denied film work, as US involvement in the war rapidly escalated. These performers engendered a great amount of concern during the filming of *Secret Agent*, with Fox later issuing the following press release:

> "All were American citizens and all were checked with the FBI and Naval Intelligence. To make this check (the actors) were told that photographic tests of them with Lynn Bari had to be made. Copies of these tests were then passed on to the proper officials. Two uniformed policemen and two plain-clothesmen were stationed on the set at all times and the Japanese, many of whom were in Japanese army uniforms, were forbidden to leave the set unless escorted by a policeman. This was to prevent them from coming to any harm and also to prevent studio employees from becoming used to the sight of Japanese soldiers in case the real thing should one day appear."

An air of unreality permeated the *Secret Agent* set throughout. Things were made even more bizarre by the outlandish theatrics that were going on before the cameras. Kay's arrival at the fade-in, in fact, has to be one of the most unbelievable entrances in film history. She's first towed through the bustling streets of Shanghai in a rickshaw. Dismounting in a clinging evening gown, she projects smoldering allure as she cruises into the seedy, sweaty Dixie Café. The dress is very tight, but the agent manages to prop herself up on a bar stool, next to fellow spy Doris Poole (Janis Carter). For Doris's benefit, Kay lights a cigarette encoded with a secret message. Our heroine destroys the communiqué as she smokes away, surveying her mysterious surroundings with furtive glances.

Viewed in its entirety, *Secret Agent* is absurd kitsch. Critics of the day lambasted it as totally preposterous 'B'-picture propaganda. Ticket buyers, however, made it an unqualified hit. Its success was, of course, due in great part to its timely release — and the blazing promotion that accompanied it. The tag lines were memorable. Some of them: "SHE defied all danger for her country!" — "NOW! The Inside Story Behind 'The stab in the back!'" — "The first expose of the enemy's newest secret weapon! It's revolutionary!" — "What do they know about December 7, 1941?" — "Rips the lid of treacherous intrigue which led to the vicious attack on Pearl Harbor!" — "LOOK OUT! for the Secret Agent of Japan!"

Mention of the above exploitation provoked the secret agent herself to giggles. Bari's mirthful mood didn't change as she recalled *Secret Agent* — and the drama that had gone on behind the scenes.

It was a real quick picture and it was awful. At one point, around Christmas, we had to go out on the back lot at four in the morning and stand before a firing

squad. They had this big trench we were supposed to fall into. I was looking at all of these Japanese guys standing across from me. All of a sudden, it became very eerie. I looked at Preston and asked, "Are you *sure* they're using blanks?" Pres thought that I was being ridiculous. But I went over to the propman and asked him if he had loaded the guns. *(Laughing)* Oh, God, you get crazy at a time like that. The whole thing was just a mess.

Kay Murdock (Lynn) descends upon a nest of vipers, the Dixie Café, in Secret Agent of Japan *(1942).*

Secret Agent was in the can on January 26, 1942. Less than two weeks later came the trade preview for *The Night Before the Divorce.* Reviews were mixed, but Bari's notices were uniformly positive.

> *Variety* (2/7/42): "Lynn Bari, as the individualist wife, provides a strong performance to rise above the material at hand. Player displays abilities that rate better assignments in feature buildup."

Almost to the day of this critique, Lynn was handed that better assignment — the female lead in *The Magnificent Dope,* Fox's most important comedy of 1942.*

---

* Originally *The Magnificent Jerk,* the film's title would be changed prior to its release — at the insistence of the Hays Office, who had found the word "jerk" vulgar.

Coinciding with *The Magnificent Dope's* production (February-April 1942), Fox launched a campaign to establish Bari as a star of the first order. The studio was aware of the press's fondness for Lynn, and they knew they'd be more than willing to acknowledge her progress. Accordingly, a flood of publicity releases were issued with confidence.

Fox's latest promotion of Bari was similar to those of other actors for whom they had given the big push. Generally, the studio made it seem that they had been the first to recognize their up-and-comers' great potential. Lynn, though, had to be handled slightly differently because she had been so long under contract. This came into play in her current studio biography, which emphasized a well-planned, long-range development of her career — something for which Fox took total credit. Filtering out this and other puffery, one could read an accurate portrait of an amenable person with natural talent who had worked hard to earn her stardom.

Studio biographies were essentially ephemeral, constantly being rewritten for the exploitation of a star's next film. Bari's 1942 bio, however, contained a gimmicky slant that would have unexpectedly far-reaching consequences. To underscore her past achievements, the tag line, "Queen of the 'B's," was appended to her name. The "Queen of the 'B's" title caught on fire immediately but quickly faded from print, in a manner that was par for the course for throwaway lines. However, it would boldly resurface a year or two later, never burning out. Why this would happen is open to speculation — but it is clear that the label would gradually turn into a lifelong inhibitor for Lynn, beclouding virtually every other aspect of her forty-year career.

Ironically, Bari was linked up with this title at the moment when she was ostensibly leaving 'B' pictures behind. She would never be able to disassociate herself from the label — the thing for which she'd be most remembered. Truth be told, though, the moniker had validity. There were certainly other 'B' queens: Metro's Ann Sothern, Paramount's Ellen Drew, RKO's Lucille Ball, Universal's Evelyn Ankers, and Warners' Jane Wyman. Lynn, however, was not only Fox's 'B' queen — she was *the* "Queen of the 'B's;" her enormous output and popularity in such product (from 1938-41) back this up without question.

> ANTHONY QUINN: "I don't think that Lynn was particularly thrilled by her title, queen of the bees, but she should be, because it's nice to be the QUEEN of anything."

I'd like to catch the son of a bitch who called me "The Queen of the 'B's!" It's one of those terrible things. I begged the publicity man not to do it, and he went ahead anyway and used it. It really was absolutely terrible for my career. Everybody would say, "Who is this broad?" — "Oh, her name is Lynn Bari. She's a 'B'-picture actress." — "I don't want her in this picture." Or "'B' actress? Get somebody else!" At that time, it labeled me as being something inferior, although I don't know why. Most of the 'B' pictures were as good as the 'A' pictures. But it immediately said, "This is a minor actress." I still tell people who interview me, "Please do not use 'The Queen of the 'B's' as a tag line."

Who exactly defined this title as a label of inferiority? Perhaps it was no one but Lynn herself. She had immediately perceived the appellation to be a personal affront, and her insecurities would make it into an adversary. For years to come she would struggle with something that could have been a source of pride; she'd become defensive about the moniker and would try to justify her career in terms of it. Taking this needless stance, her interviewers would be inspired to pen such articles as "'Queen of the B's' Seeks Her Place in 'A' films." That one, a *Los Angeles Times* essay, would be written two years *after* her promotion to 'A' pictures!* By choosing to make an issue out of a harmless press blurb, Bari fostered the growth of an identity she detested. Had she accepted the title as the publicity tool for which it had been intended, the "Queen of the 'B's" tag line might be remembered today as a sidelight to a more important career.

That Fox publicity man — contrary to Lynn's belief — might very well have had her best interests at heart. Certainly, in 1942, his idea made for good copy. A slew of very flattering profiles on Bari were then being published, many with catchy headlines like "The Queen of the B's Rates an A" and "Hollywood Needs More 'B' Girls! Lynn Bari found a Million Dollar Future In Forty of Hollywood's 'B' Productions."** By playing up the "dreaded" 'B'-picture association, these articles would achieve their intended purpose — they would contribute to the forward movement of their subject, whose career had never before seemed so full of promise.

---

* Written by Edwin Shallert (4/25/44).

** The first headline accompanied a syndicated feature by John Chapman (3/15/42). The second led off an article on Bari in a 1942 issue of *Screen Guide* magazine.

The Lynn Bari publicity blitz of 1942 begins in the Fox photo gallery with this portrait.

CHAPTER EIGHT

HOLLYWOOD CAVALCADE

It was the public who made me a star. After I had left Western Avenue, I remember running into the girl from the fan mail department. She told me that I got the most fan mail — which they used to judge you by — that month. She said, "Maureen O'Hara was getting all the mail; you've even beat her." Everybody would tell me how popular I was and they'd also write about this in the papers and magazines. I felt, "Well, hell," and hired a press agent. The studio got sore about that. They didn't allow it.

What Fox did allow was yet another Lynn Bari publicity blitz, this one set in motion to herald the July 1942 release of *The Magnificent Dope* — and its leading lady's new career in 'A' pictures. Happily, for all concerned, the star and her film proved to be a winning combination.

Lynn owed her *Magnificent Dope* appearance to the perceptive casting of producer William Perlberg. Perlberg was then at the beginning of his long and fruitful partnership with screenwriter (and, later, director) George Seaton. Perlberg and Seaton would go on to create some of the freshest and most intelligent films of the postwar era. Before collaborating on more adult fare like Paramount's *The Country Girl* (1954) and *Teacher's Pet* (1958), the two focused on inspiring comedies that celebrated the American spirit in a homey manner, pictures like Fox's *Miracle On 34th Street* (1947) and *Apartment for Peggy* (1948). This quality had also evidenced itself in their earlier work; including *The Magnificent Dope*, which was their third joint venture at Fox. Seaton's well-knit script to *Dope* was based on an original story by Joseph Schrank, *Lazy Galahad*. It was a bright and lively adaptation, filled with witty dialogue and humorous situations. At its heart was a morality lesson, one that would be set forth in an undidactic and buoyant way by director Walter Lang.

Bari played publicity director Claire Harris, a sharp-sighted, warm New Yorker. Claire masterminds a nationwide contest to find the "perfect failure" — a gimmick that will promote the success school of her pompous fiancé, Dwight Dawson (Don Ameche). The dubious competition takes hold as a search for the "Ideal Subject." The winner turns out to be a Vermont rowboat renter, the

179

ingenuous and happy-go-lucky Tad Page (Henry Fonda). Having entered the contest to raise money for a truck for his local fire department, Page arrives in Manhattan to pick up his check. He is viewed as a piece of putty by Dawson, who impresses upon him that his prize comes with the bonus of an enrollment in a success course. The simple Tad finds no need for such instruction — much to Dawson's exasperation. To counter this resistance, Dawson encourages his betrothed to use her charms on Page — who is unaware of their engagement.

A poignant moment from The Magnificent Dope *(1942): Claire Harris (Lynn) realizes that Tad Page (Henry Fonda) has fallen in love with her.*

The Vermonter soon becomes enamored with Claire and decides to cooperate with the stunt, which will ultimately lead to a job in Gotham.

Claire develops a genuine affection for the lovesick Tad. She admires his easy-going, unaggressive demeanor and realizes that he is a sensitive fellow who has no place being in the cutthroat New York work force. Her courting of him has made her feel like a heel. Meanwhile, Page catches on to his exploitation and he becomes furious with both of his promoters. He ingeniously gets an upper hand on the success school — during which time Claire herself turns the tables on Dawson, whom she has come to despise. The huckster is left behind by his ex and Tad, who are headed for Vermont together — in a brand new fire engine.

Lynn received second billing — over Don Ameche — as Claire Harris. The part was her most multi-dimensional to date and she delivered a fine performance, something that was first noted in *The Magnificent Dope's* trade reviews:

Variety (5/29/42): "Lynn Bari finally has an opportunity to show her ability. How she does it will win her new fans and, undoubtedly, even better assignments in the future."

The Hollywood Reporter (5/29/42): "Lynn Bari displays handsome abilities to match her looks. It is her first leading part in a picture out of the low-budget classification, a promotion she has earned."

Lynn and Don Ameche enact the final confrontation between Claire and Dwight Dawson in The Magnificent Dope.

Despite the praise, Bari herself looked back on *Dope* with a self-critical eye.

I enjoyed *The Magnificent Dope* very much and I loved working with everybody in it; they were all just great. The only thing is that I think I tried too hard and I don't think my performance came off as I felt that it should. If you don't see it, well then, that's good; maybe it did what I wanted it to do. But, then, I felt so overwhelmed. I was just so tremendously excited about it. I was so afraid and tried so hard because it was my first really good script.

I was in awe of all these guys. I'd worked as extras on their pictures. They were all very kind and tried in every way to be helpful, but I still felt like an inadequate dope myself.

I had had a terrible crush on Henry. He was a very serious worker and fine to perform with. Like I did, he used to get the scripts from wardrobe first, so he could turn down a film if he didn't like it. He came in prepared. I never saw the "louse" come in with a script! Never took it home either. I asked him, "What do you do with the script?" "I learn it," he answered. He had everything in his head; it really was remarkable.

Don Ameche was the most professional man in the world, a lovely guy who couldn't have been nicer. My other co-star, Edward Everett Horton, was a favorite of mine; a very dear, kind man. He invited us to his house several times for dinner. Walter Lang did *The Baroness and the Butler* — where I had my bit part with William Powell — and a lot of other things I was in. It was always a pleasure working for him.

But I didn't think I was photographed too well there [in *Dope*]. Peverell Marley, the cameraman, would hang all these different things to make shadows on your face. He'd take so much time with that, and he worked very hard on me. Also, my hair was so awful in that. I didn't like it when they put it up — it looked like a washboard with bangs! I always preferred my hair down. Of course, in costume pictures, you had to have it up; but I liked the longer hair.

You know, I never felt I was beautiful in any way. No, I never did. I thought I was pretty. But beauty, to me, was somebody who had flawless features. Like Madeleine Carroll. My mother told me that I looked like a frog. Her favorite crack was, "If you'd had *my* nose you would have been Lana Turner!" And I thought, "*Oh*, mother dear, if you *only* knew!" *(laughing)*

If Marge wasn't around to undermine Lynn's self-confidence, Walter Kane would be there to do the job. Bari's marriage had by now disintegrated into a shaky business arrangement, but her husband's envy of her remained unchanged. This jealousy had been most cruelly expressed during the production of *The Magnificent Dope*.

Walter had told me that they had wanted Jean Arthur for the part of Claire, but she wouldn't do it and that's why they took me. And I just thought, "Oh God, they don't want me. I'm not right. I can't do what Jean Arthur does." I wish

I could! *(laughing)* So, finally I went to Bill Perlberg. He said, "Why, that son of a bitch! We *never, ever, ever* even thought of Jean Arthur. We asked for you from the very beginning." See what people can do to you?

The Magnificent Dope hadn't yet wrapped when Lynn began work on the film for which she is most remembered, *Orchestra Wives* (1942). Bari's second outing with Glenn Miller has had a fervent cheering section since day one. From start to finish, it lifts the spirits and delights the senses; it's fast-paced, witty, visually dynamic and musically sublime. The movie has come to be a veritable time-capsule representation of early 1940s Americana, depicting a period when this country's youth — always our trendsetters — were most enthralled by big band music. And it features the biggest of the big bands in an innovative manner, a way in which the musicians themselves are central to the film's narrative.

As Miller's vixenish blues vocalist, Bari's participation was similarly important to the storyline and musical aspects of the picture. Jaynie Stevens was a showy role, but it was not a bona-fide lead. George Montgomery and Ann Rutherford were the ones who were placed above the title here, with Bari earning second-lead status in a more complex part. Billed below Lynn were Carole Landis and Cesar Romero, who topped a large supporting cast that included Virginia Gilmore, Mary Beth Hughes, the Nicholas Brothers, Tamara Geva, Jackie Gleason, Harry Morgan, Dale Evans and Marion Hutton (Glenn Miller's hot singer). As for Miller, being the picture's biggest draw, he received special star billing for his appearance as bandleader Gene Morrison.

Glenn Miller had signed on to *Orchestra Wives* while he was still creating box-office magic with *Sun Valley Serenade*. Elated that his band would be the centerpiece to this second venture, he set aside six weeks in the spring of 1942 for another stay in Hollywood. *Orchestra Wives* would, in fact, ultimately take nine weeks to complete.

Lynn was the first actor cast. It had been assumed from the start that she would play Jaynie, who had no factual counterpart in the Miller band. Bari and Miller had benefited by one another's presence in *Sun Valley* and they had gotten along well offscreen; consequently, there was every reason to repeat this winning combination. With Lynn now onboard, her voice double Pat Friday wouldn't be far behind!

Orchestra Wives began with John Brahm in the director's chair. Brahm had evidenced a definite flair for ambiance and movement in smaller, more dramatic fare. Now his particular talents would be applied to a large-scale musical — something that seemed quite exciting to all parties concerned. Cameraman Lucien Ballard was met with equal anticipation. The cinematographer had come to be recognized for his adeptness with black-and-white interior photography — and *Orchestra Wives* would be shot almost entirely on soundstages. Overseeing everything would be William LeBaron, to whom Darryl Zanuck had assigned producing chores. LeBaron would work under the studio chief's aegis through pre-production.

Midway through filming, though, Zanuck would go on active duty overseas with the US Army Signal Corps. William Goetz, now temporarily in charge of production at Fox, would quarterback the movie through its release.

The story to *Orchestra Wives* was the conception of one James Prindle, who in all probability was Zanuck, writing under a pseudonym. The two scenarists of Prindle's tale were, however, very much extant. Karl Tunberg and Darrell Ware

An Orchestra Wives *(1942) cast portrait. Front row (left to right): Carole Landis, Mary Beth Hughes, Virginia Gilmore, Ann Rutherford, Lynn and Marion Hutton. Back row (left to right): Tex Beneke, Moe Purtill, Glenn Miller, George Montgomery, Jackie Gleason and Cesar Romero.*

had done their best work when paired together at Fox. Breezy musical comedies had become their forte and films such as 1941's *Week-End in Havana* and *Tall, Dark and Handsome* had displayed their particular talent for smart dialogue.

Cleverness was a key component to *Orchestra Wives'* script. In a totally unveiled manner, Fox had intended it to draw upon Clare Boothe Luce's sophisticated 1936 play, *The Women* (which went on to be memorably filmed by MGM in 1939). Exactly like its stage model, *Orchestra Wives* was directed on its twisty, amusing course by the theme of female cattiness. The fictional counterpart to Glenn Miller's orchestra provided the foundation to the narrative, with Miller assuming a lead and a number in his contingent enacting characters of varying importance — parts that were portrayed by both actors and Miller's own musicians (including drummer Moe Purtill and vocalist/saxophonist Tex Beneke). All played against the distaff side of the cast, complementing the lively and somewhat risqué situations among the women themselves.

The title characters of *Orchestra Wives* were the spouses of the musicians in Gene Morrison's band. These women endured certain hardships when the orchestra went on tour and they trailed their husbands from town to town. The stress of being on the road found them given to gossip, bickering and general troublemaking. All of this unpleasantness boldly evidences itself when Connie Ward Abbott (Rutherford) arrives on the scene. Connie is the bride of Gene's first trumpet, Bill Abbott (Montgomery). Starry-eyed and head-over-heels in love, she falls prey to the wives' viciousness when it is revealed to her that Bill

The introduction of Orchestra Wives' *attention-grabbing Jaynie Stevens (Lynn). Assuming the foreground with the vocalist are four boys in the band, played by (left to right) Glenn Miller, George Montgomery, Cesar Romero and Jackie Gleason.*

had had a year-long affair with songbird Stevens. Jaynie still carries a torch for Abbott — and the trumpeter's marriage and devotion to Connie haven't stopped her from trying to win him back. Having maneuvered a friendship with her rival, she goes in for the kill when the wives' gossip leads Connie to a hotel room where the singer and Bill are caught in a seemingly compromising position — one that has been whipped up by Jaynie herself. The trumpeter tries desperately to reason with his crestfallen bride, but she'll hear none of it. Shortly thereafter, however, she comes to realize the facts behind Jaynie's scheme — and the degree to which the wives had tried to disrupt her marriage. She lashes out at her confreres with some gossip of her own. The effects of this are disastrous, causing a major rift between her and Bill — and a break-up of the band itself. Happily, though, all is resolved by the fadeout, with Connie having helped to engineer a reunion of Gene's band — minus Jaynie.

Interspersed among these dramatic goings-on was a super musical score, largely composed by *Sun Valley* hit-makers Mack Gordon and Harry Warren. *Orchestra Wives* boasted such Gordon-Warren classics as "I've Got a Gal in Kalamazoo" (Oscar-nominated), "Serenade in Blue," and "At Last" (which had been slowed down and softened since its *Sun Valley* incarnation). These three songs were to reach high positions on the hit parade during the early months of *Orchestra Wives'* release. First up was Miller's RCA-Victor version of "Kalamazoo," which began its seven-week stay at the top of the charts as the film was opening in September. This achievement reflected the extraordinarily heavy promotion of *Orchestra Wives'* music, which equaled the massive exploitation that had been accorded to the movie itself.

As the female balladeer of the film's score, Lynn came across spectacularly. *The Hollywood Reporter* said it well when they wrote that she was "something extra special as the soloist." Bari was nothing short of luscious as Jaynie and, more significantly, she was at one with her character's songs, "Serenade in Blue" and "At Last."

"At Last" is arguably the best big band number recorded on film. Director Brahm approaches it in a sweeping yet thoughtful manner that complements the orchestra's lush intonations and the sprawling mise-en-scène of its performance at an outdoor arena. In an energizing way, the song interblends the musicians and their many adoring fans with an unfolding dynamic between Jaynie, Bill and Connie. The number ends magnificently as the camera focuses on the mouth of Bill's horn, a point from which it endlessly track out to an ultra-wide shot, revealing the entire populous environment.

Lynn dealt ably with Jaynie Stevens' dramatic rendering of "At Last." In her duet with Miller's Ray Eberle, she adroitly mouthed the song's emotional lyrics — and at the same time played off Connie's enraptured stares at Jaynie's lost love, Bill. Bari pulled this off with just the right amount of histrionics, thereby helping to introduce the romantic predicament of the movie in a clear-cut way. Looking fabulous, with the wind machines gently brushing her chestnut hair, Lynn truly seemed to be giving her all to "At Last." The musical sequence forever remained a favorite moment in the career of the star herself.

That was good, wasn't it? You know, I hate to talk about myself this way, but I have to say that I *really* liked that. I had wanted to do something different. I was so sick of seeing the girls amble up to the mike and stand there so stiffly, as they mouthed the words out. I was trying to think of all the things that would be going through my character's mind at the moment. The whole thing photographed so well; we had one helluva cameraman on that picture, Lucien Ballard.

Oh, yes *(giggling)*, on "At Last" my partner was Ray Eberle. He was so short. I was five-ten in heels. I took off the shoes and put on the old bedroom slippers.

Then they lined up a row of apple boxes and had Ray walk out on them. You never saw our feet. When we arrived at where we were to sing, he couldn't move because he was afraid that he was going to fall off — which was all right with me!

This reminiscence provoked Bari to gales of laughter, but her mood abruptly changed with mention of John Brahm's sudden dismissal from the film. Like the rest of the cast she had been perfectly happy with how things had been proceeding with the director. However, his intricate and elaborate handling of what had so far been shot — in particular the musical numbers ("At Last" and "People Like You and Me") — had not only placed the film behind schedule, but also way over budget. The disgruntled front office gave Brahm his walking papers, announcing that illness had caused him to leave *Orchestra Wives*.

It was *so* sad that they took Brahm off that. I went to visit him a couple of times in his bungalow. We weren't fast friends, but he liked me and, for years afterwards, sent me Christmas cards. Very few people did that.

Brahm was succeeded by Archie Mayo, a screen vet who had hit his stride at Warner Brothers, with *Bordertown* (1935), *The Petrified Forest* (1936) and *The Black Legion* (1936). Those were dramas, but Mayo had also competently handled other genre of film, infusing all of his projects with a certain brisk pulse. In 1940 he moved over to Fox, where his direction would unfortunately not distinguish itself. Short in stature, Mayo had increasingly evidenced a Napoleonic personality, creating varying degrees of enmity between himself and his stars. Lynn (who would work with him again on *Sweet and Low-Down*) certainly didn't count him among her favorites.

Archie Mayo couldn't direct traffic! As far as I'm concerned, that's about *all* he did: "Go in there. Come out. Say the line. Kiss her. Okay, back up," — you know, *nothing* about what you were feeling or what you should be thinking about. I mean, he was just that. But he was a highly-touted, well-paid man.

Bari may be a tad too harsh in her appraisal of Mayo. In the final analysis, he handled *Orchestra Wives* efficiently, keeping its dramatic elements moving along in a relatively spirited manner. His overall work here, however, was unquestionably less inspired than John Brahm's had been. In comparison to what Brahm had done with the music sequences, Mayo's lensing of the up-tempo "I've Got a Gal in Kalamazoo" and "Bugle Call Rag" seemed almost static. The fact that those two songs came off so well was largely due to the pyrotechnics of the musicians in both and the Nicholas Brothers in the latter. As for the beautiful "Serenade in Blue," it was the most unoriginally filmed of the lot. Most interestingly, the song had been recorded with Pat Friday and Ray Eberle singing lead vocals, then photographed with Lynn and Eberle at the mike. Somewhere along the way a decision was made to edit out Eberle's warbling. This made good sense in terms of integrating the haunting ballad into the plot, because its lyrics of lost love were solely applicable to Jaynie.

For entirely different reasons, a blues serenade would have been appropriate for Fox's Linda Darnell and Osa Massen. Both actresses had been cast in *Orchestra Wives* — and then dropped from the film early in its production. Tamara Geva replaced Massen as Becksie, the homespun orchestra wife. Beforehand, MGM's Ann Rutherford had stepped into Darnell's shoes as Connie.*

Originally recorded as a vocal duet, "Serenade in Blue" wound up in Orchestra Wives *as solo number for Jaynie (Lynn).*

We shot with Linda for a few days. She couldn't loosen up. Then they said, "She's too wooden; she's not hip." So I asked them, "Then, *who* the hell is?"

As for Ann Rutherford, she might not have been the hippest gal around, but she was certainly quite pert. Rutherford was also good at projecting sincerity — as was Tamara Geva. This quality suited both ideally for their roles of the two forthright orchestra wives. On the other hand, Carole Landis, Mary Beth Hughes and Virginia Gilmore were better at being saucy than sweet — and this helped to make them totally fitting as Rutherford and Geva's bitchy cohorts. This contrast in personalities came to the fore in a catty sequence that was set in a dressing compartment on a train. Amidst claustrophobic surroundings, the

---

* Darnell's dismissal had been unexpected, causing a scramble for a new Connie. All of Fox's suitable actresses (e.g., Gene Tierney, Brenda Joyce and Anne Baxter) had been in the midst of other projects, so it became apparent that someone would have to be hired on loanout. Rutherford was signed, actually seeing her Metro contract bought out by Fox during the course of filming.

witty lines were flying fast and furiously as Bari entered the picture, delivering a truckload of sarcasms to hilarious effect.

Lynn remembered well this scene and had fond recollections of the women in it — with the exception of Carole Landis, who played Natalie, *Orchestra Wives'* chief troublemaker.*

Orchestra Wives' bitchy dressing-compartment scene, focusing on the tensions between the characters portrayed by Lynn and Carole Landis. The discord here also extended into real life, with Mary Beth Hughes (left) bearing witness to it all.

Carole was a kind of brittle person. She got out of line with me on the set one day. I was doing a scene with all the wives in a train compartment. The lines were kind of funny. I was talking to one woman, then another. Then Carole was supposed to say something to which I was to answer. In replying, I took my time turning towards her because it required that; you don't turn your head quickly as you answer something that's quite involved. So I turned and she snapped her fingers in my face! The director, Archie Mayo, said, "Cut!" We started the scene over and Carole does the finger-in-the-face bit again. She keeps snapping it. She wants my lines faster. I said, "Don't you *ever* do that

---

* Voluptuous Carole Landis was certainly not without talent. A Zanuck protégée, Landis was under contract to Fox for five years (1941-46). During that time, she became an immense favorite with GIs, entertaining the troops on various fronts. For reasons that are open to speculation, her once-bright film career quickly died out. The actress would commit suicide in 1948, at the age of twenty-nine.

again!" She looked at me like I had hit her. But I would have, had she done it again. She must have known what was going on because we got along fine after that.

She was a strange gal. I guess they all were … *(laughing)* I was, I guess, too. I always thought that Carole was on something. Sometimes she was in such a deep sleep that you couldn't awaken her. I remember one incident when we were changing planes on a publicity trip to New York. In those days, we had sleepers so we had to make a stop. I think this particular time it was in Kansas City. We all started to get off the plane but nobody could awaken Carole. Someone said, "Just leave her alone. Don't wake her up because she goes *mad*." So they taxied the plane into the hangar and just waited until she woke up. Have you ever heard of anything like that? I thought she'd probably taken too many sleeping pills.

I think that in spite of her veneer, underneath Carole was quite emotional — things really got to her. Well, they must have, if she took her own life.

Landis's fate in *Orchestra Wives*, though, had been a better one than Bari's; she had made it to the penultimate reel. No such luck for Lynn, however. Two-thirds of the way through the film Jaynie warbled "Serenade in Blue," spoiled things between Bill and Connie, and then vanished.

Yes, I just disappeared from the picture. They used to get rid of the villain-esses — and you wouldn't hear from them again!

On paper, Jaynie Stevens might have appeared to be a setback for Lynn, being yet another "other woman" role — one that had come on the heels of her *Magnificent Dope* break. *Orchestra Wives*, however, was a musical comedy and bore little resemblance to most other films in which Bari had played a vamp. The one exception here had been *Sun Valley Serenade*, but Vivian Dawn had been far less humorous than Jaynie — a character whom moviegoers really didn't come to dislike. Audiences, in fact, seemed to delight in her antics. Lynn brought her own special brand of verve and spice to the role, punching up the comedy and adding glamour to the music. *Orchestra Wives* was, in short, a blessing rather than a comedown for Bari.

Time has not diminished *Orchestra Wives'* unique glow, in the mind of Lynn and countless others. In the annals of entertainment, the film has always stood out — initially because Glenn Miller and his Orchestra were no longer when the movie premiered. Miller was now a Captain in the US Army, soon to be leader of the Glenn Miller Army Air Force Band. This outfit, at Miller's request, would go overseas in June 1944. First stationed in England, they would prepare to leave for France that December. Paris was to be their next stop and Miller would journey there ahead of his unit, having taken off in a single-engine military aircraft on a very inclement day. The plane would disappear into a fog over the English Channel, never making its destination — and leaving the world without a supreme musical talent.

Orchestra Wives had, in effect, become a historic document upon its release. The disbandment of Glenn Miller's civilian band had made this highly engaging film something to be sentimentally savored by wartime audiences. Once Miller had been declared dead, it became something to be treasured.

———————————————————

Lynn was quick to admit that she'd made some bad career decisions. The first such misstep — one from which she would be rescued — had come while she was shooting *Orchestra Wives*. She had turned down Henry Hathaway's *China Girl* (1943), a costly espionage adventure in which she had been asked to portray "Captain" Fifi. Fifi was a lead; however, she was also a double-agent who worked for the Japanese. Having had her fill of playing bad girls, Bari got herself out of *China Girl* — much to Fox's annoyance. The studio threw her into *That Other Woman* (1942), a second-rate romantic comedy about an architect (James Ellison) and his ardent secretary (Lynn). Eight days into filming, production came to a halt and Bari found herself on the *China Girl* set, replacing Osa Massen as "Captain" Fifi. She would go on to give a compelling performance — becoming the actioner's main attraction and a critical darling. No one would be more surprised by these happy turn of events than Lynn, who vividly recalled the circuitous road that had led her to *China Girl*.

Charlie Hall, who was now in the production department, came over to me one day and said, "Lynn, I want you to come up and meet this director. You've *got* to play the heavy in it." I said, "I do not want to play heavies anymore, Charlie." He said, "Come with me. It's a big 'A' picture."

I read the thing and went up to Hathaway's office. I told him, "Mr. Hathaway, I'm having enough trouble getting a part in a picture where I'm a nice person. I really don't think I should play a Japanese spy right now, with the country at war." He said, "Okay. You don't want to play the part. To hell with it! I don't care. Charlie was the one who said you're so great."

I started shooting *That Other Woman*. The picture's going very poorly and running late. The director, Ray McCarey, is a client of Walter Kane's — and he has a drinking problem. I get a call: "Come over on the Hathaway set. We're closing your picture and you'll go into *China Girl*." At that point, I ran for it because I was not happy with the one I was doing — Virginia Gilmore eventually replaced me.

Anyway, I was immediately sent downtown to the old Bradbury Building which they were using for a Chinese hotel. Hathaway walks in and stares at me.

"What is *she* doing here? She doesn't want to play this part; then I don't want her here," he said.

"They just closed down the other picture and they told me to come over," I said.

"Okay, you want to do the part? You told me before you didn't want to do it. What the hell do you want to do now?"

"Mr. Hathaway, I'm ready to do the part."

"Okay. Fix her make-up. Fire and fall back everybody!"

You didn't know what had hit him! With the crew he'd always yell, "Fire and fall back!" Then he did this really horrible thing, which I hated: he'd fire a gun for "action." They were blanks, but it shook the hell out of you! Hathaway was such an unpredictable guy. But we got to be very good friends. I loved him.

Victor McLaglen and Lynn in China Girl *(1943).*

The tale Hathaway directed covered an astounding amount of ground. Centered in Japanese-occupied Burma, *China Girl* included these plot elements: spies, counterspies, mass executions, aerial attacks, detention camps, escapes, political neutrality and conversion, pro-Chinese and anti-fascist tracks, newsreel photography, nightclubs, education, miscegenation, a love triangle, and the Flying Tigers — all in 95 minutes! Things moved at such break-neck speed that one had not a second to attempt to contemplate the incredible goings-on — concocted by Mr. Darryl F. Zanuck himself, under the pseudonym Melville Crossman.

Zanuck had seen *China Girl* through its inception but, because he was now abroad with the Signal Corps, William Goetz shared executive producer credit on the film. Months before the studio chief had gone overseas his wild-and-wooly story had been turned into a script by Ben Hecht, the acclaimed screenwriter who would also serve as *China Girl's* producer.

Hecht's protagonists numbered four: "Captain" Fifi, American newsreel cameraman Johnny Williams (George Montgomery), Canada's Major Bull Weed (Victor McLaglen), and the film's title character, Haoli Young (Gene Tierney), the Vassar-educated daughter of a Chinese doctor (Philip Ahn). Fifi is first seen in November 1941, working in consort with Weed, a fellow spy. She changes her allegiances after she becomes smitten with the individualistic Williams. The photographer, however, has become preoccupied with romancing Haoli — when he's not been trying to outwit the enemy. Without going into further detail, it would be best to say that the exploits of each in Hecht's quartet were complexly interconnected. Everything, nevertheless, came together as good, pulpy entertainment — thanks in great part to Hathaway's blood-and-guts approach and Lynn's dynamic acting.

> *Variety* (12/8/42): "Henry Hathaway directed the colorful background in his usually okay style, while production values are sturdy throughout. Although Montgomery carries the footage as the loosely loving and living American adventurer, Miss Bari is spotlighted as the gal who falls for him in a big way, easily shunting efforts of Miss Tierney into the background. Latter is adequate, while McLaglen displays his usual rough-tough character."

Vic McLaglen was like Mount Olympus. He was a very nice guy, but you never knew whether he was really "with it" or not; it was kind of touch-and-go there. He was a quiet man; he kept to himself. However, he was very courteous and I worked well with him. In one scene, I was supposed to hit him. Henry said that I should really give it to him. So I did. I didn't mean to do it as hard as I did, but I damn near killed him! *(laughing)*

> GEORGE MONTGOMERY: "Lynn was billed above Victor McLaglen and that's pretty strong. Because a few years before that he had won the Academy Award for *The Informer* (1935). I must say that Victor was off by himself a lot. You can never get terribly close to guys like that because they've certainly gone through the great build-up and demise — and Victor was on the way down. You think about it years later and say, 'My God, how could that have been the situation when he was such a great actor.'
>
> "I naturally thought that *China Girl* was a very exciting film. But I had a heck of a time with Hathaway because I really didn't know what the hell I was doing in the acting department — so they brought in a coach for me, Phyllis Seaton, George Seaton's wife. Hathaway swore a lot and I'd swear back at him. I must say that he had his crude way of saying and doing things, but he was a very good director. We were very, very close friends in the years that followed."

While Hathaway behaved in a relatively unbridled manner toward both Montgomery and Bari, Gene Tierney was apparently treated with kid gloves. This situation came to light when Lynn's train of thought turned from Victor McLaglen to others in the *China Girl* cast.

George and I were friends. I bought his house when he went off to war. Bobby [Robert] Blake was also in *China Girl*. He was great, so well-behaved. He did

exactly what he was supposed to do. And Gene was a nice kid. I liked her very much. But she was sort of "out-of-it" all the time. I remember George, Gene and I were rehearsing a scene with Hathaway. He was giving very explicit directions. When he finished, we noticed that Gene was staring at his waist. She said, "Henry, that's the most adorable belt buckle! Wherever did you get it?" He responded very politely, saying that someone had sent it to him for his birth-

The hearts of two women go out to one man: Gene Tierney, George Montgomery and Lynn in China Girl.

day. He then turned around, looked at me, slapped his head and walked out the door. Isn't that funny? Gene didn't hear a goddamned thing that he had said to us; not a word…or *(laughing)*, maybe, she did.

Whatever her level of concentration, Gene Tierney wasn't able to breathe much life into her character. In all fairness, though, Haoli was a passive, one-note role. The opposite held true for the vital "Captain" Fifi, a part made more interesting by Bari's provocative portrayal. Lynn's performance here, in fact, has been considered by some to rank among her very best.

Oh, you're joking! I'll be damned. I tried hard, but I thought I went a little overboard. I did it the way Hathaway had told me to do it, which was much stronger than I had intended it to be.

Hathaway was right. Bari stole the show in *China Girl* because her director had been aware that she was an actress of great strength — and he capitalized on this. This is first demonstrated when Fifi is introduced. Outfitted in a trench coat and matching hat, she stalks into a hovel inhabited by a sequestered Johnny Williams and Bull Weed. She confronts them with a revolver and then aids in their escape, leading them to an awaiting plane. From there, the energy of Lynn's Fifi either keeps up with the action or sets its pace. Tierney's Haoli, on the other hand, is much more reactive. Her ethereal allure can cast spells, but she is generally in a mode of being objectified. Lynn's role is too commanding for that, yet it does have its sensitive side. This comes into focus with Fifi's affection for the hard-edged Williams. Bari projects her love with a note of world-weary sincerity. Her character is met with only a modicum of understanding by Johnny, whose treatment of her is basically cut-and-dried. With the genteel Haoli, however, he responds by letting down his guard. Although the China girl eventually dies, Johnny's love for her doesn't. Fifi may survive, but she's too bold a woman to have ever had a chance with the cameraman.

China Girl illustrates well a quality of assertiveness that had defined most of Bari's performances from *Meet the Girls* onward. The past four years had shown Lynn's aptitude for playing proactive women, ones who usually whipped things into shape or tore them asunder. Bari didn't just stand around; she appeared and the ambiance of a scene would be altered.

Although Lynn interacted fluidly with others onscreen, she was too powerful a presence to be cast in parts where she was primarily the source of someone else's attention. Bette Davis, Ida Lupino and Rosalind Russell had found themselves in a similar position, but they worked at studios where properties had been developed to complement their charged personalities. Things were different at The Hills, where the leading-lady characters tended toward the retiring or the unthreateningly perky. These sorts had become stock-in-trade for Tierney, Anne Baxter and Linda Darnell, narrowing Bari's casting opportunities. Happily, though, *China Girl* had come along — as had *Orchestra Wives* and *The Magnificent Dope*. During her first year at the 'A' unit, Bari had struck three home runs, playing forceful yet engaging women. These types of roles, however, would be in increasingly shorter supply at The Hills — and Lynn would come to realize that her talents could never be fully promoted by Fox.

Principal photography on *China Girl* had been completed in early August 1942, with Bari being called back to the project for retakes at the end of the month. The film finally wrapped and Lynn hopped onto the two-month Victory Tour — from which she returned home defeated. While unpacking her bags, she received a long-distance phone call.

It was Aunt Ellen. She said, "I don't understand your mother, Peggy. She calls up and tells me she's been on tour with Ronald Colman." "She told you

Autumn 1942; a Victory Tour whistle-stop. Virginia Gilmore assumes the center position, surrounded by (clockwise, from upper-left) Greer Garson, Lynn, Joan Leslie and Ann Rutherford.

that?" I asked. She says, "Yes! Was she lying?" I said, "No, she was on tour with him. So was I, Aunt Ellen." She said, "Well, she says he's just adorable and he just loves her!" And I thought, "Brother, I wish you'd been on that train!" If I had said it, she would have said that I was an ungrateful child. They were crazy people! *(laughing)*

I confronted my mother later on about what had happened on the tour and she told me that she didn't remember anything — when you knew damn well that she did. After anything like this happened she used to say, "I don't know what you're talking about!" It was an impossible situation.

The Victory Tour had been but the beginning of what was to be Lynn's latest round of troubles with Marge. Over the next two years — the period when Bari would be most ripe for major stardom — her stamina in dealing with her mother's alcoholism would be put to its severest test.

Marge had divorced Robert Bitzer during the first half of 1942. The split-up had left her with more time to meddle in her children's lives — primarily Lynn's, since John Fisher had recently enlisted in the Navy. From this point on Marge would be single, placing an interminable burden on her son and daughter.

After my mother divorced my stepfather, she never remarried. Who would marry her? Good God! My brother and I were the only ones who could really have taken responsibility for her. All of our other relatives were back East. But I don't think that they would have seen her had they been out here. She and Aunt Ellen *loathed* each other. The only time they talked was to fight on the phone.

John was now fifteen-hundred miles away, stationed in Corpus Christi, Texas. Commissioned as an ensign there, he would soon be sent to Grosse Pointe, Michigan, where he would enter a training school for flyers, from which he would graduate a lieutenant. Fisher would eventually serve in the South Pacific, a situation that would naturally cut him off from the affairs of his family. This was not entirely the case while he was still Stateside, however.

My mother was at her worst when John was in the service. In fact, she almost got my brother thrown out of the Navy! She went down to where he was stationed in Corpus Christi and hit the telephone operator on the head with a phone receiver because she wouldn't get her a number. They called John in. He went through hell. Thank God they sent him overseas to the Marshall Islands!

Before going abroad, John received another visit from his mother, this time at Grosse Pointe. Marge was accompanied by a handsome woman named Nan, who brought along her two small children. Fisher had dated Nan for a brief spell, prior to his enlistment. He had become acquainted with her kids and was fond of them. At thirty-seven, Nan was nine years John's senior. She affected a flashy bearing that contrasted somewhat with her cultured and wealthy background. Marge had liked her from the start and became taken with the idea of her son marrying into her family. Nan herself was eager to tie the knot with Fisher. John expressed to his mother his uncertainty about wedding Nan, mainly because he really didn't know her that well. The powers of persuasion, though, took over at a very vulnerable moment in Fisher's life — and he found himself marrying

Left: John Fisher (ca 1942–43), a Navy flying instructor at Grosse Pointe, Michigan. Right: Lt. Commander John Fisher, 1944.

Nan at Grosse Point. John's concern had been well-founded, however. Returning home from the war several years later, he would immediately be met with rumors about Nan's wild times during his absence. Fisher would promptly divorce his wife, before the two had ever established a home together. By this time Marge would have conveniently forgotten the imprudent role she had played in her son's marital misfire.

John took a lot more from my mother than I did. He's such a "Straight Gus." He won't even discuss her. If anybody said anything bad about her, he'd protest. We've always been close and he's a helluva nice guy.

Not a day went by when Lynn didn't pray for John's safety while he was in the South Pacific. She missed her brother terribly and was left without anyone to whom she could turn. Fisher was Bari's one true confidant. Despite her warm and caring nature, Lynn had great difficulty expressing her own troubles to another. John was almost identical to his sister in this respect. Both were sensitive, principled people who related to others in a dignified fashion — at any cost. Consequently, social propriety was always the order of the day and feelings of anger, hurt and fear became repressed. The two, in a sense, assumed a divided character, the direct result of their traumatic and fractured upbringing. Adopting a behavioral pattern that had been learned at home, they had learned to compartmentalize their emotions, as they related to the chaos in their lives and their many accomplishments.

In order to offset the personal upheavals that she had come to accept as a way of life, Bari strove for perfectionism. She applied herself to her career with utmost dedication. Her need to please people was almost as intense as her desire to prove herself as an actress. There was always a tremendous force behind Lynn's pursuit of her professional and social ideals, a power that carried her through her every waking moment.

As Lynn's aspirations were materializing in a big way, her mother's boozing heightened. Marge was now without a husband and could really drink as she pleased. This meant making frequent nighttime excursions to seedy bars in downtown Los Angeles. She would have a grand old time hanging out with the low-lifes who came into these dives. Sometimes, however, the socializing would get out of hand, with Marge being at the center of a brawl. The police would be summoned and off in the paddy wagon she'd go with her pals.

She'd been arrested something like seventeen times and put through the Beverly Hills jail. I'd send the chauffeur over with the money to bail her out — and two weeks later she'd be back in again. Harry Brand, who was the head of publicity at Fox, and some other people, had planned to frame her once, but that fell through. He wanted me to leave some booze in the house — which I couldn't do. He said, "Just leave it there and we'll have somebody go over around midnight with the police and just have her taken away; and we'll get her into a sanitarium." She was in about twenty.

I took her to this one place where they sober you up. She had agreed to go. So, we walked into the man's office and she said, "Well, hello, doctor. I'm so glad that my daughter has given up and is going to take your treatment." Of course, he knew what was going on, since I had already talked to him. He said to her, "Yes, isn't that lovely. Now, you just come with me."

At one point Marge's behavior became just too much for Bari to handle by herself. She sought out a psychiatrist for assistance.

I went to a doctor and said, "Please, Dr. Immerman, for God's sake, nobody will help me with my mother. I don't know what to do. She's driving everybody crazy. I'm going to quit pictures if she doesn't lay off." He said, "The only thing I can tell you is that the woman lives vicariously through you. She'll be up and down." I said, "I'm not down — except when she's giving me hell."

Lynn saw Dr. Immerman for a very short term. Their few sessions, at least temporarily, made her better able to cope with Marge and get on with her life.

She also dealt with Walter Kane, realizing that she finally had to take decisive steps in divorcing him. Having already disintegrated into nothing more than a professional alliance, their marriage had now turned into a one-sided business affair — with Kane coming out on the winning end. Bari was earning far more than her husband and the disparity in their wages was about to increase dramatically. The recently-released *Orchestra Wives* had greatly strengthened Lynn's box-office appeal. The front office at Fox had been cheered by this and they called Bari in to renegotiate her contact. Her fourth seven-year deal amounted to $500,000 in expected earnings.

That hefty sum came into play during Lynn's divorce proceedings. Walter Kane, having come to act as his wife's business manager, maintained that his agency was entitled to $50,000 — ten percent of Bari's new contract. Naturally, this didn't go over well with Lynn or her lawyers. The case reached the Los Angeles Superior Court on November 25, 1942, and it was announced that the couple had settled their financial differences. Reportedly, Bari had agreed to pay Kane $7,500 (that transaction had already, in fact, been made) and Kane waived all

Los Angeles Superior Court, November 25, 1942; newswire photo of Lynn, her marriage to Walter Kane coming to an end.

claim to the $8,500 in jewelry and furs he had given his wife. Lynn would always deny that these were the only terms involved, holding to her assertion that she *did* have to give Kane ten percent of her future earnings at Fox.

Marge Fisher (she had just reverted to her previous surname) had been present at the hearing, corroborating her daughter's testimony. According to *The Los Angeles Evening Herald* (11/25/42), Bari had stated the following to the court:

> "Mr. Kane acted like he didn't want to be married to me. Four or five times weekly he would not come home to dinner. Frequently he didn't get home until 3 A.M. And it wasn't business that kept him."

A decree of divorce was promptly awarded Lynn — who at once said goodbye to her husband and her manager.

Lynn, as Bernice Croft, in Hello, Frisco, Hello *(1943).*

In the spring of 1943 Bari received word that MGM production chief Louis B. Mayer wanted to speak with her. Mayer had just screened a print of Lynn's latest film, *Hello, Frisco, Hello* (1943), and her appearance in it had convinced him that she should join his stable of stars. Bari met with Mayer and heard him offer her a long-term contract. She was flattered by this, but her loyalties were with Fox — and the sense of security she felt there was something she was not yet ready to abandon. Bari also knew that her studio, now heavily invested in her promotion, would never consent to her release and/or a buyout of her contract. She politely turned Mayer down and the two left on friendly terms.

Exuding the majestic type of glamour to which Mayer was partial, Lynn had enacted the bitchy Bernice Croft in *Hello, Frisco, Hello*. The Technicolor musical was Bari's fourth consecutive box-office hit, one in which she received star billing alongside Alice Faye, John Payne and Jack Oakie. *Frisco* was actually a reworking of *King of Burlesque*, the 1936 songfest that had starred Warner Baxter, Faye, Oakie and Mona Barrie (in the counterpart to Lynn's role). The earlier film had been set in present day, while *Frisco's* action took place in the 19th century. Faye, Payne, Oakie and June Havoc played Barbary Coast song-and-dance troupers who journeyed through a series of ups-and-downs. Many of the downs were courtesy of Bari, as the fetching society woman who lured Payne away from Faye — before getting her just deserts.

The plot to *Hello, Frisco, Hello* was incredibly trite but the film itself was nonetheless highly entertaining and technically masterful, representing the Fox wartime musical at its peak. Charles Henderson and Emil Newman's arrangements injected freshness into a string of old chestnuts, most of which were performed to sensational effect by Alice Faye. Faye also sang the picture's one new tune, "You'll Never Know." Written by Gordon and Warren, "You'll Never Know" instantly became Alice's signature song and went on to win an Academy Award. *Frisco* cinematographers Charles G. Clarke and Allen M. Davey received well-deserved Oscar nominations, having given their film a rich visual luster. The musical's tableaux were also enhanced by the contributions of designer Helen Rose, whose period costumes were nothing short of exquisite. Benefiting most from Rose's handiwork was Bari, who looked splendid in a succession of stunning gowns.

Yvonne Wood was Rose's assistant on *Frisco*, working as her sketch designer. Over the past year Wood had been employed in a similar capacity on other films at Fox, including *Orchestra Wives*. The studio would promote her to a costume designer post by the end of 1943, with Wood remaining at Fox a total of four years. Throughout her tenure, Yvonne would maintain a harmonious professional relationship with Lynn.

> YVONNE WOOD: "I worked with Carmen Miranda, Alice Faye, Vivian Blaine, Linda Darnell and Lynn Bari. Lynn's attitude was different than other stars there because she was kind of 'family.' She really was. When she came into fitting, she was welcomed and liked. She'd go out into the workroom and greet the seamstresses and the fitters, saying, 'What have you been doing the last

few weeks? I haven't seen you!' I really liked Lynn. I never heard a *word* against that girl. She was marvelous and lovely and, of course, had a beautiful figure; just exactly all the right proportions. Boy, I don't know what a designer could ask for more than that gal. And, of course, she wore some of the best clothes, including all the beautiful, beautiful ones she did with Herschel in so many 'B'

Lynn stirred up a lot of trouble for Hello, Frisco, Hello's *John Payne and Alice Faye.*

pictures. Those films were often ten times better than the 'A's!

"On *Hello, Frisco, Hello* I sketched for Helen Rose, whom I'd worked with before. She was great and I learned so much from her. You don't take these opportunities without learning. We'd read the scripts and break them down for the wardrobe plot. Then we'd shop for the fabrics and did the sketches and all that. Sometimes they didn't give us the cast until fairly late. With *Hello, Frisco, Hello*, I did so many patterns for Helen, the seamstresses and the embroiderers. The eighteen-nineties-type dresses were made of about seventeen different long pieces. On certain dresses, I did the designs for the beaders to work on. I remember a low-cut one that Lynn wore the day the man from the Hays Office came to look down our backs. It was light pink satin and beaded in pearls and rhinestones, which came up to the top. When this guy would walk onto the set, Lynn would just sink down into this top! And when he walked off, then — boy — up she came and we'd be grinning from ear to ear! *(laughing)* Lynn was a real darling."

Bari's revealing décolletage wound up being glimpsed by many millions, for *Frisco* turned out to be a megahit, providing Lynn with her single greatest exposure to date.

That was a big 'A' picture, an Alice Faye musical. Ever since the day she had arrived at Fox, I had played an extra on Alice's sets. I did little bits and worked as a showgirl in her musical numbers. I loved Alice. Everybody did. She was very warm. Alice was a former showgirl herself and knew everybody by name. She was very clubby with all of us.

> ALICE FAYE: "Lynn was in all those pictures, going way back. I didn't know her well, but we all loved her. She was a great gal."

While working with Faye on the *Frisco* set had been something she thoroughly enjoyed, the film itself was shaded with disappointment for Lynn — because of the disagreeable nature of her character, Bernice Croft.

I was asked to play another heavy. That seemed to be the way Mr. Zanuck saw me. I've never had any desire to act like the snooty "other woman" parts that I played. That would be ridiculous. I'm terribly afraid of people like that.

I remember one of the few times I refused a role. The picture, *Strange Triangle* (1946), was being produced by Joe Schenck's nephew, Aubrey Schenck. Signe Hasso, a marvelous Swedish actress, eventually played the part. The script was really terrible. In one scene, my character was supposed to back her car into a garage — knowing full-well that her husband is inside, bending over a workbench. She squashes him. That's only one of the little things that she did. So I turned down the film. You know, I was trying to get a fan letter and all I got were threats on my life!

Did you ever see that picture, *The Fan*, with Lauren Bagel?* *(Laughing)* Jack Benny used to call her that. They ran it the other night and, about twenty minutes into it, I turned it off and thought, "I'll never sleep tonight." I've had so much trouble with those guys. They once had the police around my house in Westwood for days, when some jerk came up from Boston to marry me. They told him that I was already married, but it didn't make any difference to him! Listen, once at the opening of a picture in San Diego, a gal came up to me and screamed, "Why did you do that to Linda Darnell?" — Whom I was mistreating in some picture. She then spat on me! Isn't that awful? God, you don't know. Playing all those villainesses encouraged some people to write me these real hate letters saying, "How could you do those things?" Very few people can separate reality from illusion, my dear — that's why there are so many actors.

I guess I could also be considered a "fan." I had two favorite actresses then; I've got three now. I've already mentioned Greta Garbo and Jean Arthur — and

---

* The 1981 thriller cast Lauren Bacall as a stage and screen star who was being stalked by an obsessed fan.

I've added Glenda Jackson to the list. Every time there's a picture of theirs on, I glue myself to the set. I think that these three women are the epitome of professional acting.

You know, I never felt completely confident acting — but I don't think *anybody* does, honey. I really liked doing the comedy better than anything. It's the hardest thing to do; but if you make a damn fool of yourself, what are they going

San Francisco, March 11, 1943; the world premiere of Hello, Frisco, Hello *is attended by (left to right) starlet Gale Robbins, California Governor (and future US Supreme Court Justice) Earl Warren, Lynn, and her close chum, Linda Darnell.*

to say? I found that on the stage I did so much better. By the time rehearsals were over, I had discovered what I was going to be and yet still grew in the part while I was doing it, discovering other things. But in a movie, you walk in cold. Lots of times, on the first day of shooting, they wouldn't put film in the camera because some people were so nervous. This was especially so when you walked in and you were going to be in a picture with some *famous actor* whom you've adored for years, and you thought, "What am I doing?" Like when I was in *Always Goodbye* with Barbara Stanwyck; I was eighteen and so scared. I thought, "Barbara Stanwyck; this marvelous actress, this strong lady. And here I am; this big goof." I was terribly unsure of myself in the beginning. Well, of course, by the forties, I knew how to walk across the stage without falling on my fanny.

I think that you're always treading on eggs till you get going. You know, when you look at that typewritten page and you read it and say, "Oh, that's funny," or

"Gee, that's so sad," and then you think how do you take those words, put them in your mind and then act them. It's a helluva skip from that page into your head. They once asked Sir Ralph Richardson how he approached acting. He said, "Acting is the ability to dream on cue." I think that's what I did. I used to read the script a couple of times when I got home from work. I'd be so tired. They'd give us about twenty pages to learn. I'd read it over quickly and I'd think about it. Then I'd put it under the pillow and say, "I'm going to get this by osmosis." I'd get up in the morning, go to the studio and, by the time they'd finish with my hair and face, I knew it. And I also had a pretty good idea how to do it. They used to kid me and call me "One-Take Bari."

1943 saw Lynn experiencing a six-month break from filmmaking, from late January until late July. This was by far her longest time away from a soundstage since she had entered pictures. Now an 'A' star with selectively-chosen assignments, she came to understand motion-picture hiatuses firsthand. This by no means meant she wasn't working, however. In fact, she was busier than ever, having become one of the most frequently-employed screen stars on radio. Fox actually took great pleasure in this because all of Lynn's broadcasts made mention of her recent releases — and the studio didn't have to pay one cent for this advertising.

Bari had made her radio debut in 1938, on Walter Winchell's NBC show. That appearance had found Lynn trembling before the mike, with Winchell calming her down during the commercials. Things became slightly less tense for Bari when she played opposite her buddy Tyrone Power in "The Laughing Pirate," a 1939 installment of NBC's *Jergens' Hollywood Playhouse*. From there, Lynn quickly overcame her nerves and developed into an adept radio performer — and an audience favorite. Bari's clear and resonant voice seemed to lend itself to the medium's dramatic fare. Her intonations were subtle and radiated an air of spontaneity. She used them to clever advantage when called upon to modify a mood, something she did fluidly. Playing an equally important part in her success on radio was her deft sense of timing, a gift which had been cultivated in all those fast-moving 'B' pictures. Broadcast producers and directors had come to adore Lynn, marveling at how she could breeze through a show, always delivering a smart, nuanced turn.

Radio was easy and it was very lucrative. For a period there, I was making more money in radio than in the movies. I got between a thousand and fifteen-hundred per show. You'd just go in for a rehearsal or two and then do the show in front of an audience. I liked performing in front of people because it gave me a big *up* that I didn't ordinarily have in films. I also got the chance to work with some very fine people. At that time, we had to do two shows — one for the East Coast and one, later, for the West.

Her radio credits included multiple guest shots on numerous dramatic anthologies, ones like CBS's *Screen Guild Players*. That half-hour show usually presented bare-bones condensations of swiftly-paced film fare. For instance, it would slash down the Dorothy Parker-Alan Campbell script to Warners' *Weekend for Three* (1941), a zippy marital farce that had starred Dennis O'Keefe and Jane Wyatt. O'Keefe would repeat his role in *Screen Guild's* 1946 version, however this time he would be playing against Lynn. Together, the two would banter into their mikes in an engagingly rapid-fire way, making the most of what remained of the

Lynn, performing the role of Joyce in the Lux Radio Theatre *presentation of "Each Dawn I Die."* COURTESY OF PHOTOFEST, INC.

movie's saucy dialogue. O'Keefe would be one among dozens of male film stars with whom Bari would be paired on radio — but not on film. Prominent in this group would be Orson Welles, who would perform several very droll sketches with Lynn in a 1944 airing of his CBS series, *Orson Welles' Almanac*.

Of all the broadcast shows in which Lynn would appear, none would be more prestigious than Cecil B. DeMille's *Lux Radio Theatre*, which aired Monday nights on CBS — to an audience of thirty-million listeners.* DeMille hosted weekly a star-studded array of performers, all of whom had jumped at the chance to enact his series' well-written encapsulations of popular screenplays. Generally, *Lux's* hour-long format pared down film scripts by eliminating and/or coalescing supporting characters (and their corresponding storylines). The hearts of the original plots would suffer little damage in these radio translations.

A March 1943 *Lux Radio Theatre* airing found Bari costarring with George Raft and Franchot Tone in the show's version of *Each Dawn I Die* (Warners, 1939). The crime drama cast her as Joyce, a role that had been created on screen by Jane Bryan. Many times *Lux* would assign Lynn to parts that had been originated by others. On more than a few occasions she would find herself playing opposite the male lead of the film. Two 1946 broadcasts would illustrate this: she would replace Fox's Maureen O'Hara as John Payne's costar in the tearful "Sentimental Journey" and she would take over for Claire Trevor, as Pat O'Brien's leading lady in the twisty rendering of RKO's *Crack-Up*. Both of these shows would be aired on the heels of their cinematic model's release. The same had held true for Bari's debut on *Lux*, a downsizing of *The Magnificent Dope*, which had reunited her with Henry Fonda and Don Ameche.

While Lynn had done a bang-up job reenacting Claire Harris, her finest hour on *Lux* would come with "Grissly's Millions" (1945), a retelling of the recently-released Republic 'B', which had starred Virginia Grey. The radio version of this mystery-thriller would actually surpass its filmic counterpart, principally because its soft-spoken heroine, Katherine Bentley (Bari), would alternately project blind trust and confusion — two intangible qualities ideally suited to radio drama. Katherine was the granddaughter of Grissly Palmor, a cantankerous goldmine magnate. Upon Palmor's seemingly natural demise, the young woman is revealed to be the sole beneficiary of his vast estate. This bequest plunges her into a whirlpool of familial hatred, deceit and violence. Wherever she turns, Katherine becomes victim to a vulturous act: she's thrown down an embankment, framed for a double-murder, blackmailed, drugged and suffocated — all before being rescued by a police detective. Pat O'Brien would play the gumshoe, a role that had been originated by Paul Kelly. Elisabeth Risdon would be called upon to recreate the character of Katherine's kindly old Aunt Leona — who'd be discovered the killer in the story. Risdon and O'Brien would give nimble line readings, but both would stand in the shadows of Lynn, who'd

---

* DeMille's association with Lux had begun in 1936. It would end in 1945, amidst a petty labor dispute. Fellow film director William Keighley would take over as the show's permanent host in November 1945.

lead her audience through Katherine's tunnel of terror in a vivid and excruciatingly tense way.

Bari did, indeed, remember "Grissly's Millions" but not clearly enough to count it as her best turn on *Lux Radio Theatre*. Sharper in her mind were the more general aspects of the series — and the contributions of Cecil B. DeMille.

The *Lux Theatre* people were very nice to me. But, DeMille's show? — Oh, that was the biggest hoax in the world!

We did them in a theater with a large audience. We'd all come in to rehearsal in slacks, and drag a dress. Well *(laughing)*, the boys wore pants — although some of them stole my dresses, I'll tell you! Afterwards, we'd get all done up and sit in a circle on the stage. Just before the show, Mr. DeMille would enter from behind the velvet curtains and come up to each actor and talk with them a little bit. For instance, when he got to me he'd say, "And how is Miss Bari tonight? You are my favorite, my dear. You do not wear that ugly red nail polish. Thank you so much." Then he'd walk on to the next actor. Now, the audience thinks he's telling us how to do the show. He doesn't even know what the hell we're doing! And for his name, they paid him one helluva salary.*

Oh, speaking of which, Fox was pretty *cute* about our radio appearances; they took half of our salary! I found out how to get around this from Vincent Price, who was no dummy, believe me. We were doing a broadcast of *Shock* (1946), a picture we did together.** I told him that I didn't like doing this stuff at cut-rate. He said that I didn't have to and explained how to get around it. The next time the studio told me that I was to do a radio show, I told them, "No, I can't work for that kind of money. It's not worth it and, besides, I get too nervous." So they asked, "Will you be too nervous for the whole salary?" "No…" It all finally worked out and I did damned well."

———

Lynn's fame widened as World War II progressed. Her film and radio work contributed to making her more popular than ever — as did her sessions in the Fox photo gallery. No stranger to cheesecake, her poses in swimsuits and other clingy wear were now stepping up radically, bringing much delight to hundreds of thousands of GIs. Bari the pin-up would, in fact, poll second among the military by war's end. She came to be known as "The Woo-Woo Girl" and "The Girl with the Million-Dollar Figure."

I don't know about *that (laughing)*, but that's what they said I looked like. My figure wasn't bad and I thought my legs were quite straight. The designers liked to get me on a picture because they said that I showed off their clothes so well. I was tall — and we'll leave it at that *(laughing)*.

* *Lux Radio Theatre* was actually directed by Sanford Barnett (1936-45) and Fred MacKaye (1945-55).
** "Shock" aired on CBS's *Hollywood Startime,* February 3, 1946.

Winter 1943; Lynn, emerging as a top World War II pin-up girl.

Most fortunate were the serviceman who got to see Lynn in person. As many other stars did, Bari gave much of her time to the war effort and met with countless soldiers. Lynn was as touched to be in their presence as they were to be in hers.

The GIs seemed to like me. The Italian prisoners all assumed I was an Italian *(laughing)* and thought I was tremendous! Wherever we were, we got the hospital duty and that was the hardest. In fact, I was mostly sent out on hospital

Lynn reacts graciously to an enamored Air Force serviceman in 1943.

This cheesecake shot (dating from late 1943) makes evident the reasons why GIs crowned Lynn "The Girl with the Million-Dollar Figure."

tours. We went to burn units and various installations. It was awfully difficult to see the sights that you saw.

I went out with Ray Mayer, an ex-vaudevillian of the Evans-and-Mayer team. I had met Ray through Johnny Mercer and we later worked together on *Sweet and Low-Down*. While Ray played the piano, we asked the guys to pull out songs. And we all sang — that is, the ones who could. I'd do six-to-eight

Summer 1944; a picnic at a military base is made special by the presence of a lovely Hollywood foursome: (left to right) Grace MacDonald, Marilyn Maxwell, Lynn and Marsha Hunt.

weeks of that at a time and practically have a nervous breakdown when I got home. It was very draining emotionally and I went to pot.

I just got a letter from Roddy McDowall the other day. We had been on one of these tours together in 1943. One of our stops along the way was Washington, where we had the honor of being invited to the President's Birthday Ball. Roddy enclosed a picture of the two of us standing before President Roosevelt's birthday cake. Roddy's looking into the camera like he's on fire! He wrote: "Whatever is it you said to make me look like this, such a very long time ago — ay? Loving memories to dear you. Roddy."

The wartime years saw all film studios in a state of elevated activity. The production schedules at the majors were jammed with projects, causing the releases of some pictures to be indefinitely delayed. Fox was doing especially well, racking up immense profits with features that had received the go-ahead from Darryl Zanuck and his fill-in, William Goetz. Goetz was more than a titular production chief during Zanuck's absence, and he made some very decisive moves with regard to film properties and studio personnel. When Zanuck returned from the Signal Corps later in 1943, Goetz left Fox to create International Pictures. International would merge with Universal in 1945, with Goetz himself taking the reins of this new company, becoming one of the most powerful men in motion pictures.

The William Goetz substitution had been but one of three front-office reorganizations at Fox during the war. The other two had occurred in New York. Joe Schenck, whom Lynn remembered as "a nice guy," had been forced to temporarily relinquish his position as Chairman of the Board. This followed his 1941 conviction for tax evasion and labor-related mob payoffs. Schenck would serve four months of a one-year sentence in 1946, returning to his former post shortly thereafter. At this point he would be working with Spyros P. Skouras, Fox's current corporate president. Skouras succeeded Sidney R. Kent, upon the latter's death in 1942. Unlike Kent, he maintained a relationship with Zanuck that was anything but amicable. Despite the antipathy between the production chief and himself, he would remain president of Twentieth Century-Fox for twenty years.

The longevity of Skouras's tenure would reflect both his business acumen and his personable nature. Darryl Zanuck aside, he got along well with most everyone at Fox. Lynn grew to be quite fond of him, usually seeing him fleetingly as she breezed through the studio's Manhattan offices during a Gotham stopover. The two did, however, share more than a passing greeting sometime in 1943.

The one experience I had with Skouras was most embarrassing. He was the head of the office and a very kind man. I was in New York doing publicity and some war work. Skouras calls me: "Bevair of Greeks bearing gifts." With his heavy accent, I didn't understand what he was saying. I had to ask him to repeat himself three times. Finally, he just spelled it out for me. I said, "Oh, I'm sure I don't have to beware of you, Mr. Skouras." He then told me that he and Mrs. Skouras would like to take me to dinner at The Colony. I said, "Oh, that's wonderful. Thank you very much."

I thought, "This is going to be fine. I'm going to be wined and dined at The Colony!" I got all done up. Jean Pettybone, my publicity woman from the Henry Rogers Agency, was joining me. As we walked into the restaurant, I heard this voice say, "Hey, Bari!" I thought, "Oh no, God, don't let it be me." I didn't dare look at the Skourases. I just kept walking. Then, like over a bullhorn came, "Hey, Bari! Lynn Bari!" I said to Jean, "Oh, my God. What do I do?" I stopped and turned around. It was Harry Cohn.* That pig. He screamed, "Bari, call me. I'm at the Sherry [Netherland Hotel]! You hear?" I just waved my hand and walked on. I got to the table wondering if I should say anything. I looked at the Skourases and just said, "I'm terribly sorry." "Think nothing of it," he said. So I really was relieved because, by that, Skouras was saying to me, "I know that SOB, too."

---

* Harry Cohn was head of production at Columbia Pictures.

But can you imagine that? Cohn was terrible, horrible. I mean, I hadn't seen him in a hundred years and I wouldn't want to. He was a friend of Walter Kane's. My God, he was completely amoral. When Cohn died, everyone in town went to the funeral — they wanted to be sure he left!

You know, everything happened to *me*. Oh God, I had wanted that evening to be so perfect. Well, when you're young, those things faze you. Today, I would have walked over and poured a glass of water over his head! *(laughing)*

"On the slim and lovely shoulders of Lynn Bari will rest much of 20th Century-Fox's histrionic chores for the next season."

The above quote, written by *The Los Angeles Herald-Express* on October 5, 1943, had no doubt been culled from a Fox press release. Given that, it was still clear that Bari's studio had placed tremendous faith in her capabilities; they wouldn't have allowed such a grandiose statement to have been created if they hadn't. Lynn would, in fact, be treated to great consideration by Fox during the production year of 1943-44. With her in mind, they lined up one project after another. Most of these plans wouldn't materialize, however. Bari tested for Edith Wilson in *Wilson* and Laura Hunt in *Laura*. To her great dismay, those parts would go to Geraldine Fitzgerald and Gene Tierney, respectively. Lynn was announced to costar with Betty Grable in *Pin-Up Girl*, but her role was written out of the final script. She was also supposed to do *Bowery After Dark*, a Technicolor extravaganza with William Bendix and Perry Como. That film was shelved. So was *Rusty*, which would have had her paired with Randolph Scott. The one designated project that actually came to fruition was *Tampico* (1944), costarring Edward G. Robinson.

Then there were the phantom films for which Bari was announced. These were movies Fox never had any intention of making; they were just concoctions to keep Lynn's name in print.

Yes, those were just publicity blurbs. At one point they had me going into so many pictures with Michael Redgrave that I felt like I knew the man!

Bari would certainly get to know Edward G. Robinson, particularly in light of the fact that their film, *Tampico*, would be in production for the better part of four months. Partially lensed in the Mexican gulf port of Tampico, the espionage romance completed its eight weeks of principal photography in mid-September 1943. Zanuck was not satisfied with the final cut, however, and ordered script revisions. Additional sequences were added and *Tampico* went before the cameras again the third week of October, finally wrapping in mid-November.

Tampico's protracted shooting schedule had actually encompassed the intended eight-week production of Lynn's next assignment, United Artists' *The Bridge of San Luis Rey* (1944). Bari had been signed to the adaptation of the Thornton Wilder novel with a guarantee of solo star billing. There had been no guarantee, though, about *The Bridge's* end date — and, once again, Lynn would find herself returning to a project she had assumed had finished filming. Immediately after saying a second goodbye to *Tampico*, she went back to *The Bridge* set and newly-written scenes.

Having graduated *summa cum laude* from Western Avenue with a degree in back-and-forth filmmaking, Lynn had managed to juggle her two latest projects

Santa Monica, November 23, 1943; Lynn and Sid Luft are all aglow, moments after obtaining their marriage license.

with ease. She had been in especially high spirits throughout, even though she had had deep reservations about her casting in *The Bridge* and the quality of the picture itself. Normally, such concerns would have troubled her career-oriented mindset, sending her into a funk. But they hadn't, and this was because matters of the heart had been carrying her along of late.

The object of Bari's affection was a test pilot, one who would become her husband just days after her *Bridge* crossing — on November 28, 1943, to be exact. The pilot's name: Michael Sidney (Sid) Luft.

Lynn had met Sid Luft in the latter half of 1942 and they became a steady item during Bari's filmmaking hiatus. Luft was four years older, born November 2, 1915. The ruggedly attractive six-footer had an outgoing, enthusiastic personality that Lynn found appealing. A native New Yorker of the Jewish faith, he had relocated to the West Coast in the late thirties, apparently with show-business aspirations. War broke out and Luft joined the Royal Canadian Air Force, attending their bombing and gunnery school. He ended his two-year stint with the RCAF as a flying officer. From there, he headed to Southern California where he found work as a test pilot, first for Lockheed, then Douglas Aircraft. Most all of the vehicles he tested would one day be used in Air Force combat missions.

One Douglas flight turned near-fatal for Luft. It was winter 1943 and he was testing a single-seater A-20 over the desert. The craft suddenly burst into flames. Sid managed to guide it to earth, but the plane looped before it landed. This movement evidently entangled Luft's parachute leg strap, causing him to be thrown further back into the fiery plane when he tried to open the hatch. He miraculously escaped with his life, but suffered burns on his face, arms and legs.

The accident had coincided with Lynn's stay in the East Coast and the President's Birthday Ball. Bari rushed back to Los Angeles and Luft's hospital bedside. The two drew extremely close during Sid's lengthy convalescence — this, according to press reports and Lynn's own statements at the time. Luft rebounded in due course and healed in relatively fine fashion, although his injuries would preclude him from serving in the US military.

Not too long after being discharged from the hospital, Sid began to be seen about town with Lynn, his facial area free of bandages. The two were all smiles as they announced their engagement and November marriage, coming three days after the finalization of Bari's divorce from Walter Kane.

As with Lynn, this would not be Luft's first walk down the aisle. Shedding some light on the circumstances surrounding his previous marriage is forties teen actress Barbara Whiting. Born in 1931, Barbara was a true child of Hollywood. Her late father, composer Richard Whiting, had written dozens of noteworthy film scores. Whiting had also been a beloved fixture in the movie world. Together with his wife Eleanor, he had frequently opened his home up to screenland's glitterati for evenings of music and good times. Eleanor Whiting carried on hosting these festive gatherings after her husband's 1938 death. In the early forties her older daughter, pop-singer Margaret Whiting, brought aboard a younger generation of guests. Starstruck little Barbara had the time of her life at these events. Sunny and vivacious, she never failed to charm those who were in attendance — sometimes among them, Sid Luft and Lynn, whom Barbara would support in *Home Sweet Homicide* (1946).

BARBARA WHITING: "I knew Lynn before I went to the Fox lot. She knew the Whiting family. She was always so friendly. With Sid, she probably was at the house. I certainly knew Sid well before the year they married. When I was a *very* little girl, before I ever went over to Fox as a fat teenager, Sid spent a lot of time around our house. My sister Margaret had done a lot of shows entertaining the troops around the California area. She met a lot of the guys that were flying, the pilots. Sid had been, as I recall, a test pilot. So, he was around the house a lot. I used to have a mad crush on him. Of course, I think I was six! *(laughing)* One of his wives, I think it was his first; she was named Mary Lou or something. One night about twelve-thirty or one o'clock in the morning, under my mother's window, comes, 'Eleanor! Eleanor! Get up!' And it's Luft and this gal he's going to marry. He says, 'We're going to Las Vegas to get married!' My mother says, 'Well, so?' *(laughing)* He says, 'Can I borrow some money? And I need a ring.' By this time my father had passed. So, she threw down her wedding ring and said, 'Well, I want it back.' So, she threw some money for him and a ring — and then off he went and got married. I don't think that lasted very long.

"I just thought he was a test pilot and very good looking. And my mother did take a liking to him. But who knew what went on in the back room? So, that was sort of an association for me, knowing Sid, probably before he knew Lynn."

Barbara Whiting says she wasn't at the Bari-Luft wedding, but she can't remember whether her mother was present. The affair was small, by Hollywood standards, taking place at the Bel Air home of Lynn's *Magnificent Dope* producer, William Perlberg, and his wife, Bobbe. Guests included the Harry Brands and the Mack Gordons (Mrs. Gordon, "Cookie," was an old stockgirl chum of Bari's). The marriage ceremony was nondenominational, performed by Judge Edward Brand (brother of Fox's publicity chief) in the Perlberg living room. Lynn and Sid said their "I dos" in front of a specially-created altar, comprised of an arrangement of pink chrysanthemums and a majestic candelabra. The bride's wedding gown was the work of designer Howard Greer. The form-fitting costume was made of beige crepe, with cardigan sleeves and a neckline edged in French gold beads. Complementing the dress were Lynn's brown velvet halo-hat and her bouquet of white camellias and Talisman roses. Other than her rings, Bari wore no jewelry — with the exception of a wrist adornment that had been a wedding gift from Sid. Press reports would claim it was either a platinum wristwatch or a gold mesh bracelet, set with diamonds and rubies. Overall, Lynn's appearance was elegant and subdued. She harmonized well with the groom, who was outfitted in a conservative dark suit.

It had been obvious to all that Bari had wanted a traditional wedding the second time around — and she got it; down to the corsage of green orchids (also from Sid) she wore after the service was over. Following the reception the Lufts left for their honeymoon in Palm Springs. They traveled by bus rather than auto, reportedly because of wartime gas shortages. The press refrained from hounding them at the popular resort community but Harry Brand's team had certainly been at work at the Perlbergs', resulting in dozens of published photos of the nuptials. These pictures showed Sid looking uncharacteristically restrained, sometimes cracking a smile. Perhaps he just seemed to be low-key since he stood in contrast to Lynn, who was beaming broadly — when she wasn't swooning. The photos left little doubt about the bride's state of mind; she was in love.

Time does often change one's sentiments — especially when it comes to romantic relationships. The day would come when the mere mention of Sid Luft's name would stir Bari to anger.

You know, a man called me a couple of months ago and told me that he had run into Sid at this very fancy delicatessen down in Hollywood, Spago. He said to him, "I'd like to see Lynn Bari. Do you have any idea where she's living?" And Sid told him some horrible little town, like a border town out here; nothing but two-bit hookers. *(Laughing)* So the next time anyone asks me if I know where *he* lives, I'm going to say, "I hear he has a lovely little townhouse in West Covina and he just has more fun bowling," — there's a bowling alley on every corner there. I mean, he's a dirty bastard. Why would he say a thing like that?

I had met Sid through Bill Goodwin, an actor, and his wife, Phillippa Hilber. Bill was with Bob Hope; he was his announcer for years. She was a dancer [and former Fox stockgirl] whom I'd known ever since the days of MGM. They were a nice couple. They had a house in the valley with four kids. Phillippa calls and says she wants me to meet this very nice guy who was a pilot for the RCAF. And I said, "Gee; that sounds interesting." She told me that he was just a couple of years older than I, and was not "ancient" like I had been married to. It sounded nice. So I met him. Then they came over to the apartment one night and the four of us had dinner. At the time, Sid was working at an airplane factory. He was one of the pilots they hired to ferry the planes to a place called Dagget, out in the desert. The Army, not able to fly the planes directly out of the factory themselves, picked them up there.

I went away for a couple of months, first to New York for some publicity work and then to do hospital tours. When I came back, we went out. I thought he was a bit of a hero when I met him. I never met anybody else after my divorce. And he was *so* persistent — you know; we were going to get married and all this. I had filed for divorce from Walter Kane in November 1942. But it took a year to go through. So I wasn't legally divorced from him until November 1943. The next day, like a damn fool, I married "dear" Sid. Oh God.

Bari had been a year into her latest contract with Fox when she wed Luft. Her combined film and radio earnings were netting her substantial money. Some of her income went to the support of her mother, another part to paying off Walter Kane. Still, even after taxes, Lynn was in extremely comfortable financial shape and had accumulated quite a nest egg. She had recently drawn from her savings to purchase her first home, one she had bought from George Montgomery.

> GEORGE MONTGOMERY: "I was going into the service and I sold the house to Lynn and Sid. It was right back of the Chevy [Cheviot] Hills, a short way from the studio. The back of it was on a golf course. It was a damned nice location. Wish I had it now! *(laughing)*"

The Lufts returned from their honeymoon and set up housekeeping in Cheviot Hills, with Lynn's schnauzer Kim joining them there. It was December and the couple couldn't have appeared any happier, so looking forward to celebrating holidays in their beautiful home. New Year's came and went and, before long, that very home became a rather disquieting environment for Bari, as she began piecing together bits of information she had been discovering about her new mate.

Eleanor Powell's mother and Sid's mother, who was a character, were very good friends. Sid's mother used to sell her clothes back in New York, where she was working in the Waldorf dress shop as a saleslady. Later, Sid was *called* Eleanor's secretary and he came out to Hollywood with them [MGM star Powell and her mother]. He was on salary from Eleanor.

When I met him, he had just gotten a divorce from a very wealthy gal whose family lived in Bel Air — the father paid him off and got rid of him. Oh, God. I'd run into people who knew him from his hometown and everything and they'd say, "How *did* you?" I couldn't believe it, the things that he's done.

When I went to New York, he was going to come and join me. But he burned up in this plane — through his own carelessness — delivering it down to Dagget from Santa Monica, where they took off. He was in the hospital for a long, long time. When he got back, he would just slough around with his work and they fired him.

I tell ya, this man — you *cannot* believe! He was thrown off the MGM lot when he was there because he had a floating crap game on the back lot. They just said, "Out of the studio. We just don't allow this." No good. And he got in bad with Billy Wilkerson, who ran *The Reporter*. I wish to God Billy, whom I knew very well, had *told* me about it. *Nobody* told me anything about him. They'd just say, "Well, don't rush into anything, Lynn."

Lynn Bari, 1944.

CHAPTER NINE
THE BARI BOOM

"Lynn is highly recognized for her genuineness, her utter lack of pretense. People react warmly to that sort of sincerity in Miss Bari's case, because she holds to her opinions."

So wrote Edwin Schallert in a *Los Angeles Times* piece (4/25/44) that explored Lynn's desire to be cast in more challenging roles, ones that would move her forward in the hierarchy of 'A'-picture actresses and bring to her the film career of which she had always dreamed. Schallert was convinced Bari's days of screen glory would soon be upon her. His subject, however, wasn't placing bets on this. Lynn, mindful of the proclivities and machinations of her studio, examined her current status with caution:

"My present problem is to try and keep away from the heavies, adventuresses and the like. I don't object to playing these characters, but I don't want them exclusively.

Probably because I worked in so many melodramas during the 'B' days, and acquired a certain rugged experience and technique in cops-and-robbers films, I seem to be thought of in that light, despite the change to 'A' pictures."

Bari's concerns were more involved than she had cared to state to Schallert. What had gone unspoken was the fact that she had been bracing herself for the fallout from *The Bridge of San Luis Rey*, the biggest misfire of her career.

If Lynn had had her way, *The Bridge* would have slipped in and out of theaters barely noticed. That was not to be the case, though, for the drama had a publicity campaign befitting a four-star spectacle — courtesy of its producer, Benedict Bogeaus. Bogeaus, 39, was a Hollywood neophyte who had amassed a fortune as a real estate broker in Chicago. Having decided to give the movies a try, he had formed Benedict Bogeaus Productions. His company would work as an independent and release through United Artists. Bogeaus, it seemed, had the fancies of a seasoned showman; this would be reflected in the extraordinary attention he'd pay to the promotion of his product. It would be rather presumptuous to pin down the

producer's artistic vision but, for the most part, it appeared that he wanted to entertain moviegoers in a somewhat cerebral manner. To affect his purpose, he would
often draw upon literary properties. Two of Bogeaus's more successful endeavors
in this vein would be Jean Renoir's *The Diary of a Chambermaid* (1946, based on

the Octave Mirbeau novel) and Zoltan Korda's *The Macomber Affair* (1947, from
a Hemingway story). Those films would come after *The Bridge* — and by that time
Bogeaus had been better schooled in what it took to make a solid picture.

One could not have argued with the source of Bogeaus's inaugural presentation. The novel, *The Bridge of San Luis Rey*, had earned Thornton Wilder a

Pulitzer Prize in 1928. The book was philosophical in an altogether human way. It concerned an 18th-century priest who searched for a divine meaning in the accidental deaths of five people who had toppled off a creaky bridge in Lima, Peru. At the center of the story was the fiery Camila, called by some the "Perichole," meaning half-breed. As exotic as she was enticing, Camila had somehow touched the lives of those who had perished on the ill-fated bridge. A former street entertainer, she had become a noted stage actress by virtue of her association with "Uncle Pio," a theatrical impresario. Camila's fame and beauty eventually led her to the palace of Peru's viceroy, but her heart always belonged to a lusty adventurer named Manuel.

Filled with romance, intrigue and inspiration, *The Bridge of San Luis Rey* had been a natural for film. Its first screen version came a year after the Pulitzer. Released as a part-talkie by MGM, *The Bridge of San Luis Rey* (1929) starred Lili Damita as Camila. The picture was a big hit, going on to win an Oscar for Cedric Gibbons' art direction.

The 1930s saw *The Bridge of San Luis Rey* become one of the most widely-read novels of all time. Curiously, though, no movie studio endeavored to lens the property in this, the first decade of the sound era. One explanation for this might have been that Thornton Wilder's representatives had been asking an exorbitant amount for the screen rights to the story. The book certainly didn't come cheap to Benedict Bogeaus, who outlaid $50,000 for it in 1943.

Bogeaus began trumpeting *The Bridge of San Luis Rey* as soon as the story rights were his. He gave forth with some rather specious statements, proclamations that would not bode well for the prospects of his picture-making debut. He announced the film would be shot in Technicolor. It wouldn't be. Either Rouben Mamoulian or Fritz Lang was supposed to direct. Neither would. The man who wound up helming *The Bridge* was the far less illustrious Rowland V. Lee. Lee's work had long been erratic and, of late, he had only distinguished himself with Universal's *Son of Frankenstein* (1939) and *The Tower of London* (1939) — but those were horror films.

Bogeaus had originally chosen John Mescall to photograph *The Bridge*. Mescall had shot *Kit Carson*, where his work had been quite flattering to Lynn. The cinematographer had just received an Academy Award nomination for *Take a Letter, Darling* (Paramount, 1942). He then reported to *The Bridge* but, for some reason, parted ways with Bogeaus during the first week of production. In Mescall's place came John W. Boyle. Boyle had some noteworthy achievements to his credit — way back in the silent days. He had presently been spending most of his time on Universal quickies. As for the rest of *The Bridge's* technical staff, the majority were as new to filmmaking as Bogeaus himself. The one notable exception was composer Dimitri Tiomkin, who would earn an Academy Award nomination for *The Bridge's* extravagant score.

The Bridge had one other name of any consequence behind the cameras, that of screenwriter Howard Estabrook. Estabrook had just come off MGM's *The Human Comedy* (1943), for which he had received glowing notices. No such luck with his rendering of the Wilder story, which would be called ponderous and

verbose. Quite possibly he would have been met with an entirely different critical reception had his script been carried out by a more proficient crew.

The cast of *The Bridge* would be similarly undermined. All the actors involved
were talented, some with decades of film and theatrical experience behind them.
Akim Tamiroff was Uncle Pio, while Louis Calhern enacted The Viceroy. Donald
Woods played Brother Juniper, the questioning pastor. Francis Lederer had dual

*Hot Peruvian love: Lynn (as Michaela, the Perichole) and Francis Lederer (in the
role of Manuel) in* The Bridge of San Luis Rey *(1944).*

roles: the gallant Manuel and his sullen twin brother, Esteban. The great (Alla)
Nazimova, then in her mid-sixties, had the second female lead, portraying the
Perichole's nemesis. Blanche Yurka, another mature and celebrated performer,
was cast in support, as were the up-and-coming Joan Lorring and character players Abner Biberman, Barton Hepburn and Emma Dunn.

The Bridge's publicity machine stated that Benedict Bogeaus had considered countless young actresses for Wilder's heroine of Camila — now renamed
Michaela (Villegas). Besides Bari, the Mexico-born Margo is the only one whose
name can be verified in this regard. Why, exactly, Bogeaus's search had ended
with Lynn remains a mystery. The producer's press agents later claimed she had
possessed the right qualities for the "alluring" and "passionate" Perichole — "the
role of a lifetime."

The Bridge of San Luis Rey first previewed in February 1944, with a running
time of 108 minutes. The film ran 87 minutes when it opened in New York the

following month. Gone were scenes that had helped to clarify Michaela's actions and motivations, principally as they had related to The Viceroy — and her having taken up residence in his palace.* No ingenuity had gone into this editing, and a plodding film became a jumbled, plodding film. The effects of these cuts also served to underscore the movie's amateurish aspects.

The Bridge was a slapdash affair to which critics of the day responded, at best, tepidly. Forty-five years later Bari came to display little enthusiasm for the film, as she recalled its production and explained why everything had gone awry.

I know it was the direction, plus I was not right for it. In fact, I was just awful. I told them from the beginning that I was miscast. I felt that I didn't look it and I was certainly not a wild street singer and dancer by any stretch of the imagination. I think she should have been played by a hot-blooded South-American type, like Lupe Velez, or some really crazy lady.

The book itself is a classic; required reading. It is one of the best I ever read. My agent, MCA, had come to me with the script. It was something of a coveted part. They said that Benedict Bogeaus had asked for me. At first, I thought, "Oh, boy!" But then, feeling that I was not right for it, I told them no. They came back to me again, twice. Finally, I was told by the studio [Fox] that Mr. Schenck — who was very friendly with Ben Bogeaus — had said yes to them.

Rowland V. Lee? Oh, God! His idea of drama was to throw your cape over your face and rush out. He didn't know anything about human beings. A lot of superficial gestures do not indicate that the people had brains and hearts and could feel things. The whole thing was unreal. Much of it was shot interiorly, with papier-mâché rocks. It was very heavy-handed and flat. There was comedy, there was melodrama — and it all came off as nothing. You never had a moment when you thought that anything was *really* happening.

I never once felt, "Gee, I did that okay," or, "that was real for me." It was only by the grace of God that I didn't look the worse.

It was a great cast but we were all walking in and out of the set in a daze. Since the director had nothing going for him, everyone was trying to help each other. Akim Tamiroff would come to me and say, "Oooh baby, you've got to do it this way. That guy stinks; don't do what he tells you."

The scenes with Akim and Louis Calhern seemed interminable. They were both wonderful actors, but they appeared pedestrian. Louis was one of the finest men I'd ever met but he was sore as hell all the time. On the first day of shooting, his satin pants split! I mean, they were sweeping up the floor to make my wig!

Nazimova could read the phonebook and look good. Nothing would throw her. Nobody could tell her what to do. They wouldn't want to. She was just great.

Dimitri Tiomkin, a very talented guy, did the music on it. I talk-sang ["New Words to an Old Melody"] at the piano in the scene at the palace. Evidently,

---

* Thanks to The UCLA Film and Television Archive, *The Bridge of San Luis Rey* would be restored to its original 108-minute length in 1999.

that's how they did their poetry then. My other number was "The Donkey Song." We worked very hard on it. But, the day I was supposed to record, I lost my voice. I was sick for a few days and couldn't open my yap. I don't know if it was nerves; I've never quite been able to figure that one out. So they got some woman to record the song whose voice was *nothing* like mine.

Shortly after mouthing "The Donkey Song," Lynn had been paid an on-set visit by writer Erskine Johnson. The syndicated columnist had been one of but many who had interviewed Bari during filming. To all, she'd put on a brave face and talked up *The Bridge*. Nothing too special resulted — with the exception of the Johnson piece, which had found both parties involved getting a bit carried away:

> "Found, a beautiful young lady who says she's a ham. One of the biggest hams in Hollywood. In fact, she's glad the producer of her current picture owns the studio. 'Because,' she says, 'I'm eating up all the scenery.'
>
> The lady's name is Lynn Bari. After 10 years in motion pictures, playing just about everything except a potted palm, she's won the right to put a star on her dressing room door. She has the most coveted feminine role of the year in the film version of Thornton Wilder's 'The Bridge of San Luis Rey.' 'It's a wonderful role for a ham,' she said. 'About 50 wardrobe changes, dancing, fencing, singing, heavy drama, light comedy — everything in the book.'
>
> If the star on her dressing room isn't enough to prove Lynn Bari's new status in Hollywood, all you have to do for further proof is to visit Los Angeles' Main Street. A burlesque house there is featuring a strip teaser who calls herself Lana Barri. You've arrived in Hollywood when strip teasers start adopting your name."

(Laughing) Oh, God. But they did spend a lot of money publicizing the film and I had a publicist, too. Mr. Zanuck took note of all the mention. One night, I was sitting next to him at a private party at Chasen's. He said to me, "I understand your picture is doing very well." I said, "Oh, yes, we're working very hard; it's an interesting story." I'm not going to tell him that I'm miserable. So he said, "I'm going to get a cut of it and run it. If I think we can do something with it, I'll buy it from them," which meant it would have a Twentieth Century-Fox release. Obviously, he didn't like it because it turned out as a United Artists release. I don't know if it made or lost money.

Years later, I made a commercial for Ovaltine [the nutritional chocolate drink mix] where I said, "This is the dress I wore fifteen years ago in *The Bridge of San Luis Rey* and I can still get into it because I drink Ovaltine." That one played for years. So I guess people do remember me from that picture. It's certainly better than *Sleepers West* or *East* or whatever they call it.

Various manner of recognition would come Bari's way because of *The Bridge*. The most unusual had been related to her loanout agreement, with Fox paying her tribute in the form of a piece of machinery — a gigantic boom. This particular boom was a camera platform attached to a long metal arm which could hover over actors at great distances. The breadth of this apparatus came in very handy with extensive, complicated setups. And Lynn herself had come in very handy with regard to her studio acquiring this desirable gear.

That's when Fox loaned me for "The Bari Boom." When you're loaned from one studio to another, your studio was usually paid double your salary. Bogeaus was low on cash, although he had a lot of equipment. One piece he had was this tremendous boom which Fox wanted. It was during the war and you couldn't buy any contraption of that sort made of metal. It was agreed that Fox would take the boom for my services. It was nicknamed "The Bari Boom." It has always been called that and they still have it. Since it can really sweep out, they've used it in pictures where they've photographed big parades and large-scale city scenes. I must say *(laughing)*, "The Bari Boom" is quite a footnote to my career!

Ticket-buyers didn't find *The Bridge of San Luis Rey* all that objectionable and the movie would be reissued more than once over the years. Nevertheless, it had been deemed a grand turkey by the press and Hollywood insiders. Lynn, thankfully, had somehow escaped a personal razzing by *The Bridge's* detractors and her career wasn't set back. Playing into her good fortune was the fact that her previous assignment, *Tampico*, was released just *after* the Bogeaus film. *Tampico* turned out to be a minor triumph for Bari; she made the most of a provocative role and the picture itself went on to score well at the box office.

Tampico had been intended as a vehicle for Gene Tierney, but the actress became pregnant and bowed out of the espionage drama well before filming had commenced. Enter Lynn, who seemed ideal for the part of the enigmatic Kathie Hall, a sweet-tempered yet world-weary woman. Kathie is introduced as a newfound castaway on a Merchant Marine tanker. Her entrance is striking, displaying nothing more than her shapely legs dangling from the bunk-bed curtains of Captain Bart Manson (Edward G. Robinson). The drapery is obfuscating her nakedness and she is provided a sweatshirt and skirt. From there, she undergoes intensive interrogation by Manson and his crew because a nearby freighter has just been torpedoed by a German submarine. The young woman is barraged with accusations. In a plea to negate them, she tells her questioners she had been on record as a legitimate passenger of the downed ship, but her passport and luggage are now lost at sea.

Kathie describes herself as a showgirl who has been all over. Her current destination is uncertain; she's just searching for a place where her two feet can firmly land. Having nothing more detailed to impart, she becomes a chief suspect in the bombing. The lonely Manson volunteers to watch over her for the

remainder of the voyage. He does indeed become her guardian, despite the protestations of his burly first mate, Fred Adamson (Victor McLaglen). Adamson has made it known to Bart that he's certain Kathie's a Nazi spy, one who'll try to dupe his comrade with lovemaking tactics. The captain pays him little mind and falls for his charge in a big way. After docking in Tampico, he marries Kathie in haste. More incriminating evidence about the bride then begins to surface. Further intrigue, action and angst ensue. Kathie is eventually vindicated when the identity of the real saboteur is revealed, leaving her and Bart looking forward to calm seas ahead.

Tampico was one of the better wartime mysteries, fast-moving and lean. The performances of Bari and Robinson were convincing, helping to balance a movie that could have easily given way to melodramatics in less capable hands.

I liked *Tampico*. Now that director, Lothar Mendes, was terribly gifted. He would tell me what to do, and I would do so without any qualms. I always listened to the directors. That's why I was so disappointed with the man on *The Bridge*. Mendes was just fine, however, and liked by everyone.

The *Tampico* set was one of Lynn's happiest, reuniting her with Victor McLaglen and affording her the opportunity to play opposite Edward G. Robinson. Pitted against these two rugged foils, she added a gentle earthiness to the film. The romantic interplay between her and Robinson was quite believable, despite their vast difference in age (he was fifty; she, twenty-four).* The disparity between the two was furthered by the fact that Bari stood about three inches taller than the diminutive superstar. It was certainly an unlikely pairing but they did come off effectively together — with Lynn giving her leading man a little more dimension in the love department.

I thought our romance mustn't be played mushy. There were no histrionics. So it was a natural thing that came about between us. Eddie Robinson and I got along great — although he was worried about my height all through the picture. I remember the day we first met, when we were doing the wardrobe tests — which, as I had mentioned, we always had to do for Zanuck. I was leaning up against my trailer. He [Robinson] came over and said, "Hi, there ... Jesus, you're a tall one!" I said, "Wait until I unwind!" So I stood up straight and he shrieked, "Oy, My God!" Throughout much of the picture I would wear bedroom slippers; they would cut my feet out in most shots. If I had to walk in high heels in a scene with Eddie, they'd arrange it so I walked ahead of him, while using a camera angle that made it look like we were the same height.

I was kind of in awe of Eddie. So he pretended to be frightened of me! He killed himself trying to break me down and make me feel at ease. The first day of shooting came and he plastered my dressing room with his pictures from the still sessions. On them, he wrote things like, "Love, from Your Bully-Boy." God, at one point, he would say my lines with me because he was afraid I was going to do it wrong. Then he'd start to kid me and bring me a present. He was very nice.

* During this time Edward G. Robinson and several other "mature" screen actors (e.g., Charles Boyer and Ronald Colman) experienced career resurgences. With so many younger name actors in the service, choice leading-man roles were now more frequently being assigned to Hollywood's old guard.

As for Victor McLaglen, I don't think the poor man ever forgave me for swatting him in *China Girl! (laughing)*

McLaglen and Robinson were very well-respected actors but definitely not the matinee-idol type. Their plainness worked to good effect in *Tampico*, making its virile story line all the more plausible. Correspondingly, the role of

Lynn and Edward G. Robinson were a rather offbeat romantic twosome in Tampico *(1944); however, they carried off their characters' love story believably.*

Kathie Hall was sexy yet lacking in glamour. Lynn had had no problem with this. She had wanted to appear as natural as possible — especially in her first scenes.

I begged them, "Please don't make me wear any makeup. I want to look like I'm a shipwrecked person." They said, "No, it's not that easy because Eddie's wearing it and Victor's wearing it, too." I asked, "Why would they have to wear it?" They said, "They *want* to wear it." But for those early scenes, I wasn't wearing any except a little on my eyes, and my hair was just washed and towel-dried. When I went to the rushes, I was pleased with the way I looked. I told the cameraman, "I wish I didn't have to wear makeup again," — this aside from the fact that it took an hour to put on every morning.

Pictures from those days sometimes date terribly because of how we looked. There's nothing natural about a girl who's just walked out of the bath with long

eyelashes and full makeup. That's crazy, and so are those ridiculously dark lip-
sticks we wore.

Most of the time, however, I liked the way I was made up. After Sonja Henie
left Fox, I got her hairdresser, Nan. Yvonne Wood was my wardrobe designer at this
point and Bud and Wally Westmore usually did my makeup. The Westmores were
all so great. God, they all died so young; every one of them — I can't believe it.

> YVONNE WOOD: "On *Tampico*, I remember Edward G. Robinson
> being so short. The day we were testing Lynn's wardrobe, Maureen
> O'Hara was also on the set doing her tests with Eddie Stevenson.
> I had not yet worked with Maureen but later made five pictures
> with her. She had just done *The Fallen Sparrow* (1943) with John
> Garfield, who was also small in stature. Eddie introduced the girls,
> who were working on stages side-by-side, and they got along just
> fine — 'Yappity yap, quack quack,' as they were waiting for the lights
> to be finished and all that. They stepped forward and did their bits.
> Afterwards, they talked about those green apple boxes they have in
> different heights that a guy would be put up on. Anyhow, when the
> two were all finished talking and had to go to camera, they didn't
> kneel down; they kind of squatted down and reached out and shook
> hands — just as if they were on cue. *(Laughing)* It was so funny!
>
> "Lynn was just as witty as can be. Just yesterday, I used a phrase
> of hers I'd never heard anyone else say. I've never forgotten it. It was
> a crack she made about something she had to wear in some picture.
> She said, 'I looked like the side entrance to a beer parlor!'"

Adept at dressing Bari in smart suits and skirts, Yvonne Wood also possessed
a tasteful flair for the theatrical. This orchidaceous quality evidenced itself in the
musical sequences of Lynn's next film, *Sweet and Low-Down* (1944). Bari returned
to the bandstand in this picture, playing Pat Stirling, the lead vocalist in Benny
Goodman's orchestra. Pat was not a shrew like Glenn Miller's Vivian Dawn and
Jaynie Stevens. In fact, she even made the fadeout, after helping to weave together
the trite elements of *Low-Down's* seriocomic script. The story to the movie spun off
from a fictionalized take on clarinetist Goodman's Chicago childhood. From there,
it basically centered on a diamond-in-the-rough trumpeter (James Cardwell) who
was taken under Benny's protective wing. Goodman played himself here, heading
a cast that also included Jack Oakie, Allyn Joslyn, Dickie Moore and a very young
Terry Moore (then billed as Helen Koford). Linda Darnell was the ingénue of
Low-Down, for once presented as an ally of Bari's. The actresses had about the same
amount of screen time, though Darnell's role was far less showy than Lynn's.

Compared to the Glenn Miller films, *Sweet and Low-Down* was a weak sister.
The movie had no pizzazz — save for Bari and her numbers with the Goodman
troupe. A reed-thin Lynn lit up the screen as she lip-synched to Lorraine Elliot's
voice, performing four songs written by Mack Gordon and James V. Monaco.
Their titles: "I'm Making Believe," "Chug Chug Choo-Choo Chug," "Hey Bub!

Let's Have a Ball" and "Ten Days with Baby." Bari's participation added charm to the lilting "Ten Days" and she seemed to be having great fun with the scatting "Hey Bub!" However, it would be "I'm Making Believe" for which she and *Low-Down* would be remembered. The tune became a wartime anthem for those whose loves were stationed far from home. Ella Fitzgerald and the Ink Spots went on to cover the song for Decca. Their version entered the charts in Novem-

Back to the bandstand; Lynn, dressed to the nines by Yvonne Wood, swings out in Sweet and Low-Down *(1944).*

ber 1944, several weeks after *Low-Down's* national release. The recording rose to the number-one position in December and remained on the hit parade through March 1945. By that time, its original incarnation had received an Academy Award nomination for Best Song (losing out to "Swinging on a Star").

Whatever its deficiencies, *Sweet and Low-Down* had been a sure thing because of the colossal appeal of Benny Goodman, "The King of Swing." The fact that it had a pleasant score with a standout song added to its drawing power. The film was lambasted by the critics, but audiences of the day ate it up, relishing the music, the shtick of the beloved Jack Oakie, and the loveliness of Darnell and Bari.

I enjoyed working on *Sweet and Low-Down*. That also was not my voice. They recorded the numbers before I was on the picture. Benny Goodman was a nice guy to be around. I liked him tremendously. He and his wife used to come over to my bungalow. We'd yak and then go out for dinner.

I had worked with Jack Oakie before and knew him socially. He was always kind to me. Jack was a typical comic of his time. Did you know that he was almost totally deaf? He didn't want anyone to know, but he couldn't hear a thing. He read lips. When you were talking to him, you'd have to be looking directly at him. If somebody said, "Jack, what's the matter? Can't you hear me?" he'd fly into a rage. Otherwise, he was a very jolly guy, always *on* and very giving.

Lynn and director Archie Mayo appear to be enjoying one another's company between takes on Sweet and Low-Down.

Lynn had no impending film assignments once *Sweet and Low-Down* was in the can. Fox took advantage of her situation by making her part of their star-studded *Wilson* (1944) promotional tour. Sid Luft accompanied Bari on this junket, the biggest of its kind since war had been declared. Traveling throughout the US in the late summer, it touted in every way possible Darryl Zanuck's meticulously-filmed Technicolor biography of President Woodrow S. Wilson. The studio chief had spared no expense on his pet project, a critical hit that would catch no fire among moviegoers. Directed by Henry King, *Wilson* starred Canada's Alexander Knox in the title role. Charles Coburn, Geraldine Fitzgerald and Thomas Mitchell also headlined, with Mary Anderson, Vincent Price and Sir Cedric Hardwicke in support. The fact that Lynn hadn't appeared in this epic was of no concern to Fox with relation to her participation in the tour. She was available, and her presence would guarantee greater attention being paid to the product at hand. The same held true for other studio players currently at liberty — including Bari's pal, Roddy McDowall.

> RODDY McDOWALL: "It was at the height of the war and was all integrated with going to hospitals and doing war-bond shows. But it was primarily to promote *Wilson*. That was Zanuck's huge

New York, July 1944; fresh from a bond-selling tour, Lynn finds herself happily reunited with Sid Luft at the Players Club.

film, so they poured money into this tour and we went everywhere; I can't tell you how many cities. Carmen Miranda, John Payne, George Jessel, Gracie Fields, Dana Andrews and Mary Anderson also went with us.

"Being on tour with someone, you really get to know them — and Lynn was always just terrific.

"This is a funny story. I was about fifteen but I was small in stature and looked much younger. At all of the functions that we participated in, I would always make a beeline to Lynn because she was very gemütlich; so good to me, and very funny and sweet. I remember at one point Lynn was sitting on a chair and I was seated on the arm of this chair, looking down at her. We were just talking as pictures were being taken. As always, we were all very highly policed by the publicity department. Well, the next day I was called down to the suite of this publicity man who shall remain nameless. He was a real drunk. I was really read the riot act and told that I was an ingrate and terrible. He claimed that I was looking down in Lynn's cleavage as we were talking! He said that this was such a disgrace for the studio since I was the idol of young America! I was told that I must never do that again. I was so sheltered; *(laughing)* I didn't even know what the fuck he was talking about!"

While Lynn and Roddy McDowall were out on the road plugging *Wilson*, Darryl Zanuck was wrapping *Winged Victory* (1944). The boss's latest personal production was the film version of the Broadway hit by Moss Hart. Playwright Hart had also been responsible for *Winged Victory's* screenplay, having been brought to Hollywood by Zanuck. His story movingly addressed an average progression of those who had been called to serve in the Air Force. George Cukor directed this tale on-screen. The movie, like the play, featured servicemen on leave from active duty, a number of whom were professional actors (e.g., Lon McCallister, Edmond O'Brien and Don Taylor). These men were complemented by a handful of Fox's more talented starlets, playing their wives and girlfriends. Nineteen-year-old Jeanne Crain was the most prominent in this group. The delicate beauty had just shot to fame in *Home in Indiana* (1944) and was fast on her way to becoming a major star. The camera brought out Crain's sweet and wholesome qualities to captivating effect — something that was not being lost on Zanuck. The studio chief was now assigning her to the lead in his next project, a comedy-drama called *Bon Voyage*. Based on a recently-published literary property, *Bon Voyage* was to be directed by a renowned name from the New York stage. Cinematographer Glen MacWilliams was also on board, slated to capture the film's predominantly female cast. Crain was scheduled to share stellar billing with two far more experienced actresses — Joan Blondell and Lynn.

Bari and company reported for work on *Bon Voyage* in late September 1944, doing wardrobe tests and the like. The cameras started to roll on October 2. One week later the picture had been canceled.

Oh, that was a very sad experience. They had the script and we were told that Lee Strasberg was going to direct it. He was the founder of the Actors Studio and this would be his first film. Jeanne Crain was going to be the leading lady in it. She was going through her phase then; she had this real long hair that she wore down her back, and she'd walk and the hair would bounce. I don't know *(laughing)*, I've got only one word for this girl — but I wouldn't want to mention it! Well, she came in one day and she's got a couple of *dolls* with her! Children's dolls! And somebody said, "Oh, those are so cute. Who are they for?" And she said (in baby talk), "They're *my* baby dolls." And I thought, "Oh, God; not right after breakfast, kid!" She was a grown woman, you know. Dolls were out with me after seven…o'clock! *(Laughing)* Anyhow, she was going through her *new* personality thing and we were told we were going to do the picture and I thought, "Oh boy, this is going to be a real pain in the butt!"

The Fox directors were mostly good directors and worked fast — and I had never worked for somebody like *this* [Strasberg]; we get on the set and he doesn't know what the hell's going on. Here's this little guy and he keeps hoisting up his pants on the side, like a lumberjack or something. And Joan Blondell looks at me and says, "*That's* the director?" *(laughing)*

And they give him this *terrible* cameraman. He [MacWilliams] did a picture [with me later] called *Shock* — I wanted to kill him. *(laughing)* This guy had just done *Lifeboat* with Tallulah Bankhead — and he made her look great. So, I guess Mr. Zanuck thought he could do the same with all the women that were going to be on this show. He was actually a very good cameraman, but he was the *slowest* in the whole world. I mean, he took six hours to light a shot! He used a lot of gobos, black lights, eye lights, and other special things requiring that you had to hit the marks just-so and not move. It's very confining when you get a guy like that. And he's got a lot of women — I keep repeating that because they all have personalities and all have their own minds about what's going to happen.

Anyway, we're all working in this law office. Jeanne is Bonnie Voyage — that's her name! I'm supposed to be the ugly lady in the office. They've got me made up with the bun in the hair and the dark-rimmed glasses and this crummy-looking outfit. And, of course, I turn into this raving gorgeous lady. *(Laughing)* This is all very new, of course.

C. Aubrey Smith is my boss. We shot with him the first day. I'm supposed to come in through the door and hand him a letter. Now, C. Aubrey Smith I'd worked with I don't know how many times — the man is stone deaf; he can't hear a word. So here is the guy from the fancy theater, the Russian expert Strasberg, and he's saying, "Now, Sir Aubrey, we'll do it this way…" and C. Aubrey's saying, "What? What? What? Yes, yes; I pick up the pen." And the cameraman's going crazy — and I'm supposed to come in the door.

Studio portrait of Lynn, taken in conjunction with the ill-fated Bon Voyage
(1944).

I bet Strasberg made me come in the door ten times! How many ways can you open the goddamned door and bring a letter in? I don't know anything about what's in the letter; I don't know what it means. I just thought you came in the room. Finally, I turned to Strasberg and said, "How many ways can you come in a door?" I guess he wanted my motivation for coming in the door. Well, he had motivated me; he had told me I'm bringing in a letter to the boss. What am I supposed to be thinking of — Mount Vesuvius? *(laughing)*

I gotta do this cockamamie thing and now Joan is openly hitching up her trousers — in front of everybody — and everybody's making fun of the guy. It *was* terrible; it was an awful thing to do. But, anyway, about the fourth day we got a notice: "Pull the plug on the camera." And they just closed the picture down and he [Strasberg] went back to New York — and *(laughing)*, I think Jeanne put her dolls away for good!

> RODDY McDOWALL: "These types of films, when they started, had an aura about them on the lot. With Kazan, who had come from New York to do *A Tree Grows in Brooklyn* (1945), and with Strasberg, there was all of this cachet. I can remember when Strasberg arrived. I always thought he was full of shit, but there was this great hush over everything because he had come. And then came these stories that all they did was rehearse! It was the laughing stock of the lot."

Bon Voyage was permanently shelved and Lynn breathed a big sigh of relief, for she had come to feel strongly about the consequences of completing such a picture.

It would have been *death* for everybody concerned, I'm sure!

One in a series of sensual portraits for which Lynn sat during the production of Captain Eddie *(1945).*

CHAPTER TEN

SHOCK

The ill-fated *Bon Voyage* had no lingering effect on Lynn because she moved directly into an eagerly-anticipated assignment, the feminine lead in the lavish Fox biopic, *Captain Eddie* (1945). The captain was Eddie Rickenbacker (1890-1973), a pioneer in the development of automobile and air travel in America. Rickenbacker had achieved heroic status as a World War I flying ace, having received the Congressional Medal of Honor for downing an unparalleled number of enemy aircraft. His exploits would be dramatized on screen in the person of Fred MacMurray.* Bari was set to play Eddie's wife, Adelaide, a role that would require her to age some thirty years.

Captain Eddie was told in flashback, as Rickenbacker reminisced from a life raft during World War II. He had actually been on a worldwide goodwill tour of air bases and had wound up in this precarious state after the plane in which he had been traveling had made a crash landing in the South Pacific. Six service-men had also been aboard. All, save one, would pull through with Rickenbacker a grueling three weeks lost at sea. Their much-heralded November 1942 rescue renewed public interest in the survivor from the previous war. Soon thereafter the illustrious vet detailed this perilous journey in book form. As the tome was building steam, an Eddie Rickenbacker bio began looming large in many Hollywood minds. Rickenbacker was deluged with offers — some astronomical — as payment for his assent in this regard. Producer David O. Selznick was apparently among those who had tried to make a deal with Eddie. The flyer, however, hadn't made things easy for these parties; he wanted the film's story, cast, crew and final edit to be under his sanction.

Rickenbacker's demands were expressed by his close friend, sports agent Christy Walsh. Walsh had worked with Babe Ruth, Lou Gehrig and the New York Yankees baseball team. A number of his clients had been featured in a series of film shorts he had produced in the early thirties. Somewhere along the way Walsh had come to know Fox's then-production chief, Winfield Sheehan. Sheehan had almost totally absented himself from filmmaking after being deposed in the Twentieth Century-Fox merger. Zanuck would, however, keep him on at the

---

* Fred MacMurray had recently ended his longtime association with Paramount Pictures. Now a freelancer, he had signed a lucrative multi-picture deal with Fox.

studio in an emeritus-type position. In the spring of 1943 the fifty-nine-year-old screen veteran suddenly sprang back into action after successful meetings with Walsh about the Rickenbacker saga. Sheehan would produce *Captain Eddie*, with Walsh being billed as his associate. John Tucker Battle went on to receive screenplay credit, although many (uncredited) writers had collaborated on the story — as had Eddie, his wife, and his mother.

Eddie Rickenbacker (center) visits with Lynn and Fred MacMurray on the Captain Eddie *set.*

Sheehan and Walsh spent well over a year in preparation for *Captain Eddie's* four-month shoot. Lloyd Bacon was in the director's chair when the cameras started rolling in late November 1944. MacMurray and Lynn were supported by a large and distinguished group of actors, including Thomas Mitchell, Charles Bickford, Lloyd Nolan, James Gleason, Spring Byington, Mary Philips, Darryl Hickman and Richard Conte.

Captain Eddie came off best on a visual level. It was clear that considerable attention had been paid to period detail, and the unfolding of the 20th century was made arresting by the rich texture of Joe MacDonald's cinematography. Rickenbacker's derring-do also benefited greatly from MacDonald's work — and the special effects of Fred Sersen, which would earn a well-deserved Oscar nomination. The Academy wouldn't, however, give the film a nod in any other area.

Although eye-pleasing and sincerely performed, *Captain Eddie* was marred in no small measure by its hackneyed, sentimental storyline. The captain himself had insisted that his life be depicted as "warm and wholesome" — and this directive seems to have been overly-stressed, making much of the movie anti-septic and humdrum. Nonetheless, the picture would garner generally positive critical notices. Moviegoers, however, would not be as responsive; *Captain Eddie* would open to lukewarm business in the summer of 1945. Its release would coin-cide with the end of the war, marking a time when the public had already begun to tire of flag-waving epics.

A most wholesome romantic pair; Lynn and Fred MacMurray, as Captain Eddie's *Adelaide Frost and Eddie Rickenbacker.*

The eventual box-office failure of *Captain Eddie* would not take away from the movie's noble intentions — and those of its producer, Winfield Sheehan. Most unfortunately, Sheehan died of complications from surgery on July 25, 1945 — exactly one week before his comeback film's world premiere in Columbus, Ohio (Eddie Rickenbacker's birthplace). Lynn herself was greatly saddened by his death. Sheehan had not only been one of her earliest advocates, he had followed her career closely, finally seeing to it that she play a large part in his creative renaissance. Bari would always be grateful to him, with *Captain Eddie* being the icing on the cake.

That film I loved. It was an expensive picture, produced by Winfield Sheehan, who still had a production office at Fox. Sheehan was *always* a very decent guy to me. And I enjoyed working with Fred so much — and I liked my part.

Mrs. Rickenbacker, née Adelaide Frost, was introduced as the personification of virginal innocence. She wore dirndl dresses, tied her hair back in ponytails and rode bicycles in ladylike fashion. She had just been perched at a soda fountain when she met Eddie. The two courted in gracious fashion; they went on carriage rides, picnicked together and attended dance-academy socials, with "Moonlight and Roses" being their song.

Adelaide Frost Rickenbacker was Bari's favorite 'A' role. One might think this a rather curious choice since Adelaide presented no dramatic challenge, being little more than a typical, soppy movie heroine. Her limitations were obvious, but they apparently didn't concern Lynn — for she had finally been afforded the chance to be the sweet-and-demure leading lady of an 'A' picture.

Bari had pinned great hopes on this role for a somewhat inapplicable reason: actresses with Adelaide-type images had the best chance of becoming big stars at Fox. Jeanne Crain had been one of them, but she had been groomed to play the gentle heroine. Lynn most certainly hadn't, and it appears doubtful that Fox would have ever considered fixing her into this mold so late into her career. In any event, the studio already had enough "nice girls" on their payroll who were ideal for the saccharine parts.

It wasn't really a question as to whether Bari could be believable in a nice-girl role. She, in fact, projected more warmth than most of her contemporaries. But, unlike them, she was a forties star who had been trained in the thirties; she had come from a different school, one that was out-of-vogue by 1945. Leading ladies of the previous decade had tended to play forcefully positive characters. They also had more of an intimate and easygoing on-screen connection with their leading men. Like thirties stars Jean Arthur, Claudette Colbert and Myrna Loy, Lynn appeared most comfortable in a knockabout yet soulful relationship with a man.

Fox's preference for passive beauties and girl-next-door types had left Bari with an eclectic list of credits. Now the chilly *film noir* dames were also on the scene — and Lynn's career course was in dire need of a focus. She had thought that her *Captain Eddie* assignment would give it one. Time would prove otherwise.

The images of women introduced onto the screen during the postwar period were reflective of broader transformations within the film industry itself. At Fox, significant personnel changes had already taken hold, affecting things in both a creative and financial respect. The studio was without half of its old directorial staff by the summer of 1945.* It would be Fox's new directors, Elia Kazan and Joseph L. Mankiewicz, who'd be making the striking impressions — both in form and with content. Equally successful would be the more mainstream George Seaton, the *Magnificent Dope* scenarist who'd embarked on a directorial career with *Billy Rose's Diamond Horseshoe* (1945), a Betty Grable blockbuster. With Grable's follow-up, *The Dolly Sisters* (1945), entertainer George Jessel hit the jackpot in his initial outing as a Fox producer.

The studio was investing much energy into the careers of Gregory Peck, William Eythe, Cornel Wilde, Dick Haymes, Richard Conte, Clifton Webb, June Haver and Jeanne Crain. The expectancy of these rising actors was in direct contrast to the marked dissatisfaction of three established names who had recently exited Fox — Don Ameche, Alice Faye and Roddy McDowall.

> RODDY MCDOWALL: "I was at Fox from 1941 until 1945. In the middle of my sixth year, my mother thought that I would go to MGM, and so I asked for my release. Well, Fox was only too happy. I looked so much younger than I was; they didn't know what to do with me. They had no imagination. God knows what would have happened had I stayed at Twentieth. Nothing! I don't think that they would have had the foresight to have guided me into anything. So they gave *Green Grass of Wyoming* (1947), which would have been my next film, to Robert Arthur."

The cherubic Robert Arthur would sign with Fox in 1946, after two uneventful years at Warners. At his new studio, the twenty-one-year-old would quickly become as popular as Lon McCallister with those all-important ticket buyers, the bobby-soxers.

> ROBERT ARTHUR: "I was under contract to Fox for five years and became friends with the Zanuck family for years. So I had kind of an inside look at Fox. I liked Darryl Zanuck. He did rule that studio. I always thought that he was a hard man. Then again, he was running a business and all the businessmen that I've ever known were hard. I don't think that he particularly liked babying actors. However, he always treated me nicely. You could appeal to him.
> "Lynn Bari, as you know, quite often played the second banana. Zanuck, I'm sure, cast her this way for business reasons — and she continued to work all the time. They pigeonholed me, too. I worked

---

* Fritz Lang, Rouben Mamoulian, Archie Mayo and Allan Dwan were among those who had left Fox by this point. The towering John Ford would soon join the studio's departed, finishing off his long-term contract with *My Darling Clementine* (1946).

as a juvenile for fifteen years! I was always the boy who said, 'Golly, Marge!' — and then turned around and ate a hamburger.

"Lynn was something of an icon to me. She was one of the pillars of our business. When I was growing up in Aberdeen, Washington, I was a great movie fan. Everybody was in those days. We all went to the movies twice a week; double bills. It seems that I saw Lynn every week of my life because she appeared to be in every film! She was a marvelous person to look at, kind of an 'Adrian model.' She had a beautiful figure and was always smartly dressed, coiffed and groomed. Lynn stood straight up, tall and proud.

"Lynn and I made *On the Loose* at RKO in 1951, but I never had the privilege of working with her at Fox. However, I do remember that she was never any trouble to anybody at the studio — and that's saying *a lot*. She was always professional and perfect for every part they gave her."

Bari's rapport with Fox's players, directors and technicians would be as strong as ever throughout 1945. Her familial connection to her studio was helping her to weather the many changes occurring on the lot. She now held a unique position at her company — the result of Alice Faye's fury at Darryl Zanuck. Zanuck had recently downsized Faye's footage in *Fallen Angel* (1945), to play up costar Linda Darnell. Having come to realize this in a screening room, Alice stormed out and said good-bye to Fox — where she'd left Lynn as the sole contract performer from the merger days. One couldn't say that Bari was lonely without Faye, but no more would there be another at hand as conversant with the ins and outs of being an actor at the studio. With Alice gone, Lynn went unchallenged as the company mascot; her longevity as a Fox star was something insiders had come to admire with affection. This durability, combined with her appearance in the prestigious *Captain Eddie*, reinforced the long-standing assumption that Bari was destined for the top. In actuality, though, Lynn's life had already begun to unravel — both at her studio and at home.

Bari's second marriage had created for her yet another disruptive personal bond, one that was causing her to play an active role in the subversion of her career. Lynn failed to realize this undermining at the time, in part because Sid Luft was meeting her needs — to a certain degree. Youthful, brash and full of big ideas, Luft had been injecting a new excitement into his wife's life. Lynn was now twelve years under contract to Fox and she had grown tired of the way the front office had been treating her, feeling that her position at the studio had stalled. Sid had been encouraging her to face her discontent head-on, expressing that she deserved better. His influence on Lynn was, however, ultimately self-serving — and, in turn, the conflicts engendered by his clout were forceful enough to move Marge, Bari's primary champion and destroyer, into the backseat. Marge herself had no use for Luft, perceiving him to be a snake-in-the-grass who was exploiting her daughter.

Sid had been described by Louella Parsons as being "one of our successful movie agents."* Lynn would offer a differing account of his activities during this period.

I got him a job when I was working on the Fred MacMurray picture — with my agent Zeppo Marx, one of the Marx Brothers. Zeppo gave him a job run-

New York, October 1944; Sid Luft and Lynn making the scene at Manhattan's hottest nightspot, the Stork Club.

ning errands and everything. He worked for two months. And then Zep called me and said, "I'm sorry, it's not going to work out because he goes out and plays golf every day. He's never been in the office." So, I said, "Sid, what the *hell* are you doing?" I mean, he wasn't making any money. I was paying them $150 a week [to employ him] and they were paying him [a salary of] $135. *(Laughing)* So, it was just my money going to him. He said, "Why the hell should I go in the office? Zep's out playing golf every day; I see him there." I said, "Of course you do, you damn fool. How do you think he saw you?" Can you imagine that?

The Lufts were now quarreling often. According to Lynn, the main topics of their battles concerned her career, which Sid seemed intent on orchestrating, and his inability to secure work. The former subject had come to be a hot-button issue for Bari — yet she did give some credence to what Luft was saying, his control tactics notwithstanding. With this and other matters, there was no one

---

* *The Los Angeles Herald-Examiner* (4/10/45).

else to whom she was turning for counsel. Marge had been temporarily edged out, John Fisher was overseas and Dr. Bitzer had been excommunicated from the family by her mother. Consequently, Lynn's perspective narrowed and frequently aligned itself with Sid's way of thinking.

The attention she and Sid were paying to Fox's executive branch had come to be intense. Lynn was certainly within reason to perceive them as indifferent since they had been failing to structure a plan of film assignments that would truly advance her career. Frustrated, she had begun to assert herself in an uncharacteristic manner, marked by demanding and resistive behavior that had been advocated by Luft.

Sid was just obnoxious about what I could do and what I couldn't do. He had me turning down pictures and giving me lousy advice and getting me agents. He told MCA that if they gave him ten-thousand bucks he'd have me sign with them. One of their agents came over to the house to see me one day — he was a *friend*. He said, "You know, Sid wants that ten-thousand upfront before he makes a contract." I said, "*What* ten-thousand?" When he told me I said, "That's the most ridiculous thing I've ever heard. If there's going to be any money paid out, you're going to give it to *me*." I said, "I don't want any *money*; I want you to *represent* me. Let *me* make the money." *

The front office's patience with Bari and her self-destructive associations was now wearing thinner by the day. She had come to be viewed in a negative light by Fox's production end, the very people who had been rather protective of her in the past. In retrospect, Lynn could trace the beginnings of this discordant situation to the summer of 1944 and her refusal to play a handpicked role.

It was a miserable thing. Around the same time as *Captain Eddie*, I was offered another picture with Fred, *Where Do We Go From Here?* (1945). It was a musical, but I was to be the heavy.** Bill Perlberg had specifically asked for me to do it. He was a very good producer and a swell guy. I had worked with him on *The Magnificent Dope*. My husband said, "Oh, you can't do that." My agent said, "Don't do it." Here Bill had just given us our wedding. Sid said, "Oh, you don't owe him a thing. Just tell him no." I alienated him, his wife and everyone at the studio by turning the damn picture down. But, you know, when you're a kid and you've got nine different people talking to you...

From there on in, nobody trusted me anymore. They thought I was erratic, certainly ungrateful. However, that's life. And I always say that Fred never would have gotten married because the girl who replaced me [in *Where Do We Go From Here?*] was June Haver, whom he eventually did marry.

---

* Bari would be intermittently signed with MCA over the next ten years.

** Producer William Perlberg had wanted Bari to play Lucilla in his musical-fantasy about a 4-F who travels through time with a genie. While not an out-and-out heavy, Lucilla was both a vain and capricious character. *Where Do We Go From Here?* was filmed in Technicolor and featured an original Kurt Weill-Ira Gershwin score. The film would go on to bomb at the box office.

Later, I became pregnant and lost out on a couple of great pictures. Walter Wanger wanted me for *Canyon Passage* (1946) at Universal; Susan Hayward got it and her career skyrocketed. And I was supposed to do *Smoky* (1946), also with Fred.

Smoky began production at Fox in July 1945, with Anne Baxter in the part that had been intended for Lynn. The touching Technicolor horse saga would go on to become one of the highest-grossers of 1946. The fact that Bari had been considered for this important film points up what had become the mercurial nature of her relationship with her studio; one minute she was in their good graces; the next, she wasn't. Turning down *Where Do We Go From Here?* had resulted in the planned *Bon Voyage* — and playing second fiddle to Jeanne Crain. Then Winfield Sheehan had come to her rescue with *Captain Eddie*. Her spirits were boosted by making the movie, but she became disgruntled when she was without a screen assignment for two months. Good advance word on the Rickenbacker biopic started to surface and she was offered *Smoky* in late April. At that point her pregnancy was made public and a hold was put on her film work until after her baby's August arrival. It was understood she wouldn't be on straight salary during this period. Despite this, it appeared to Lynn that a cordial alliance between herself and her studio had been reestablished.

Bari's general mood became increasingly more upbeat as her due date drew nearer. Not wanting to rock the boat with Zanuck and company, she made herself available for any Los Angeles-based publicity work. Most of this would center on the upcoming *Captain Eddie* and tie-ins involving the product endorsements to which she was currently signed (e.g., Royal Crown Cola, Deltah Pearls and Wadsworth Compacts).

Lynn went on to give numerous interviews during her final trimester, none particularly noteworthy. Something far more fascinating — and revelatory — was an article she herself had written for a summer issue of *Movie Mirror* magazine. Under the title, "How I Feel About Hollywood," Bari penned the following:

> When I first went into pictures, I was a 13-year-old youngster fresh from Roanoke, Va. And I was terrified. After working in pictures for more than 10 years, I'm still frightened.
>
> Every day brings a new problem, a new experience. I don't think an actress is ever truly happy. The ambition that drives us all may bring us to sheer ecstasy one moment — and make us miserable the next. But I'm used to the roller-coaster feeling by this time. I've never been sorry that I chose this career. I've never been bored with my life in Hollywood. So many people find themselves in a rut. They become complacent and contented with their narrow outlook on life. Maybe they are happier than we are — if you call that happiness.

Spring 1945; Lynn, pregnant, full of good cheer, and about to hit the airwaves on an NBC radio show.

But our lives are cut to a pattern, and I guess my pattern has emphasized excitement — excitement over meeting different people, over intense competition for important roles. I've missed out on some big chances, being doomed to play good girls in 'B' pictures and bad girls in 'A' pictures. Then along comes the chance to play the heroine of 'Captain Eddie,' and I'm riding high again.

A dozen illustrations accompanied the above, all with captions by Bari. The first three were taken from Lynn's family albums. Beneath these photos was her teasing headline, "Producers Would Never Have Picked Me to Play the Angel Child." The trio was introduced with this comment: "I've learned to take the Hollywood jitters lightly. But when I was Marjorie Bitzer of Roanoke, Va., life was real, life was earnest." Picture number one was a baby portrait in which Bari's sporting, of all things, a rifle ("At the age of 7 months, I was already hunting for a man"). The second had her dressed in a coat and cap and carrying schoolbooks ("As a 6-year-old, off to school, I must have been smart — I certainly wasn't beautiful. The outfit was definitely not designed by Adrian"). The third illustration was an arm-in-arm shot

The "Hitler's Children" photo, dating from 1927 and set in Melrose, Massachusetts.

of her and Johnny appearing menacingly robust in their Sunday best ("Brother John and I look like 'Hitler's Children,' all set to bop some innocent bystander. But I'm right proud of him now. He's a lieutenant in the Navy Air Forces").

Interestingly, Lynn provided no other personal photos for this article; totally absent were Sid Luft, her parents and Reverend Bitzer. Bari also led the reader to believe she was Marjorie *Bitzer* from Roanoke; she had been given to this bit of subterfuge for some time, not wanting anyone to explore the facts behind her natural father and his death. Other than that, her text for *Movie Mirror* was marked by genuineness. The piece drew to a close with a still of Lynn and Fred MacMurray from their impending release. Below it, the headline, "I Learn to Grow Old Gracefully in 'Captain Eddie'," and the concluding caption:

In the early scenes of 'Captain Eddie,' I'm a 20-year-old Cleveland girl who meets her future husband, Eddie Rickenbacker, when he runs over her bicycle. Fred MacMurray, playing Eddie, is a good friend of my friend Lloyd Nolan. They enjoyed working together, though they suffer convincingly in the scenes on the raft. As the story goes on, I age to about 48 or 50. I'll be curious to see whether the make-up man has made an accurate picture of the Lynn Bari of 1970. But no matter what the lady looks like, I'm sure she'll be in there trying for the best character parts, still on that roller-coaster, scared and excited by life in Hollywood.

Bari was dead-on in characterizing her life in Hollywood as a roller-coaster; it always had been — and forever would be. Little did she know then her up-and-down ride was about to take her to an emotional low-point.

A grave misfortune descended upon Lynn on August 14, 1945. That was the day her baby both entered and left this world. Most tragically, her child had been born with an enlarged heart and survived no more than a few hours. Thoughts of her great loss would always move Bari to tears. Her voice was alternately sub-dued and agitated as she forty-four years later recalled a very dark time.

We were living in a two-story house. I had a *nice* house when I met him [Sid] and, "Oh, it wasn't good enough…prestige…you gotta have a better one." While I was working with Fred, he goes out and buys a house! I said, "I don't *need* it." Well, all right. So, I looked at the place; it was *very* nice. Mr. Zanuck had owned it at one time; a very pretty house in Westwood. So, we bought it.

It was the war — you know, full blast. I was about ready to come forth with the baby and I had a girlfriend over for dinner. We were in blackouts then and she had to get home before it got dark. She lived way down in the Pacific Palisades. She left. I had a maid then, which *nobody* did, and her husband was home on leave. She was going home to her place. I'm left in this house. He [Sid] says he's going out to play gin rummy with [script supervisor and future producer] Jules Levy and I could get him there in case I needed him. And I said, "I wish you wouldn't go." He says, "Oh, for God's sake. Everything's fine." Imagine. He never stayed home with me all the time I was pregnant. He left and, of course, the baby was coming.

I called my doctor who lived in Malibu. He said, "Time the things." I tried to get him back but his phone was busy. So, I called my sister-in-law. My broth-er's over in the South Pacific — I think. And I said, "Nan, you'll have to come and help me." She said, "Guess what — John just walked in the door!" They'd sent my brother home. She didn't know he was coming. I said, "You won't be able to get in. I can't walk down the stairs right now. Just knock in the glass on the kitchen door and reach in and open the door." So, the two of them came over. They come upstairs to get me. And just as we're getting downstairs with the suitcases and all the paraphernalia, Sid comes running up with this Jules Levy. I could see he [Sid] was loaded. I said, "No, my brother's gonna take me."

He said, "You get in the car!" So, he and Jules drive me to the hospital. I get in — the doctor's not there. It was a breach birth. The doctor showed up at the last minute.

Evidently, they had given me something that knocked me out. I woke up the next morning. I kept asking to see the child and they wouldn't bring her in. They told me I had a little girl — that was it. So I said, "Where's my husband?" [The hospital staff said,] "Well, we haven't seen him." He had gone over to Mack Gordon's, the songwriter's, house and stayed there all night. About twelve o'clock he walked in and he had the *nun* come in and tell me about it.

After the baby died, I was in terrible shape. I asked if I could have some time off. I went off to the Broadmoor in Colorado Springs for what would have been two or three weeks, just to get out of town. After about four days, I got a call from the studio. They were going to start a new picture, *Shock*, in six days and I'd have to be back for fittings in three. I really didn't feel up to working.

The month following her daughter's death would remain a blur to Lynn. By all accounts, she'd pretty much secluded herself at home. The press provided few details about her postpartum period but dealt with her in an extremely sympathetic manner. One report had her first venturing about to attend a friend's baby shower, trying her best to put on a sunny face for all who were there. What had been tantamount to a maternity leave actually came to an end for Bari in mid-September 1945. The additional time she'd been requesting hadn't been officially approved by Fox, for she wouldn't have been called back to the lot as she was.

Shock had a start date of September 26. Fox had planned the film with Bari and Vincent Price in mind for the leads. The thirty-four-year-old Price had been at the studio since 1940, usually grabbing attention in demanding supporting roles of the sinister-yet-urbane variety. The actor would play the same type of character in *Shock*, his first star turn at Fox. The picture would also return Lynn to the alluring villainess persona she had for so long been trying to eschew; she would portray Elaine Jordan, a scheming nurse who takes psychiatrist Richard Cross (Price) down an adulterous and murderous path. Despite this casting regression, the story Bari and Price were set to enact would be rather intriguing — and part of Hollywood's first wave of narratives that combined suspense with the subject of psychotherapy. Psychoanalysis itself had come to the fore in the US during World War II, as a significant number of returning servicemen were diagnosed with mental disorders, the result of their traumatic experiences overseas.

Sordid and bleak, the story to *Shock* had been the creation of prolific 'B'-picture writer Albert deMond, who was at the time employed by Republic. Somehow, though, deMond had been encouraged to develop his tale of the nefarious Dr. Cross for Aubrey Schenck, nephew of Joseph Schenck. The younger Schenck was then a lawyer working at Fox's legal department in New York. *Shock* would come to be his initial venture as a film producer, although it is questionable as to whether he had been the one originally assigned to oversee the movie.

According to Lynn, he assumed this duty once it had been decided to scale down the project's budget. The same had evidently held true for *Shock's* director, Bari favorite Alfred Werker.

It was first going to be a big Henry Hathaway production. We released it as an 'A-minus', but we made it on Western Avenue.

Elaine Jordan (Lynn) and Richard Cross (Vincent Price), the licentious lovers of Shock *(1946).*

Vincent Price recalled the following to writer Wheeler Winston Dixon, in a 1992 interview for *Classic Images:*

> VINCENT PRICE: "*Shock* was an experiment, actually. The studio was spending too much money on films and taking too long to make them. Something had to be done to boost output and cut down on costs. So they asked me and Lynn Bari if we could make a film in twenty days and still have it look like a first-class production. I read the script and thought it was pretty good. I said, 'Certainly, we can do it, if you don't change the script and louse it up for us.' And so they agreed, and we went ahead and shot it, in exactly twenty days. The film did very well at the box office, so Twentieth was very pleased."

Fox had decided to release *Shock* with an 'A' promotion, the result of surprisingly positive trade reviews. *Variety* (1/16/46): "Put out unpretentiously as one for the supporting feature brackets, the show is nevertheless good enough for top billing in many spots and should contribute strongly to box-office draw." The movie's notices would grow more glowing with its nationwide opening in March 1946. *The Los Angeles Herald-Examiner* (3/7/46) would comment, "Here's one of

the best of the season — and I'm referring to 'Shock,' a terrific little picture that, without any particular ballyhoo, steps into the same category as 'Lost Weekend' and 'Spellbound' for intelligent, engrossing entertainment."

Shock's unassuming production values had come to work in its favor, adding a shrill yet riveting quality to a progression of startling events that were fresh in their day. The picture's boldfaced luridness played into the more prurient tastes of the movie-going public. Strengthening this appeal was reaction of the psychiatric community, who were up in arms over their depiction in the film, bringing to *Shock* a groundswell of free publicity — including a feature article in *The New York Times*. Another boost had come from the aforementioned radio version of the thriller, broadcast on CBS's *Hollywood Startime* in February 1946. Headlining Price and Bari, it had presented a condensed and considerably altered rendition of the screenplay where Lynn — who had been slain by her costar on film — survived the fadeout.

Its unexpected success notwithstanding, *Shock* signaled the beginning of Lynn's decline at Fox. Its merits couldn't obfuscate the fact that it was a decidedly bare-bones affair — not the type of film to which a star in good standing would be assigned. In all probability Bari would never have been considered for the picture had *Captain Eddie* fared well commercially. Going from the genteel Adelaide Rickenbacker to the diabolical Elaine Jordan had amounted to a slap in the face for Lynn. Elaine was, in truth, her most blatantly evil role. Unflatteringly one-note, it had not only thrown her back into the kind of casting that had become anathema to her, it had devalued her worth as a serious actress. Making matters all the worse had been the fact that she had to cavort about in such a nasty way so soon after a devastating personal event. Her troubles came to display themselves onscreen; minus her usual crispness, Bari looked somewhat at sea throughout *Shock*.

Can you believe why? I read the script and thought, "This is really depressing." But I knew I'd have to go back to work. Because there was no money, and I was married to *Mr. Luft* then — who never made a dime in his life and had spent all of mine at that time. I couldn't have gone on suspension. Fox might have had me out on that for a year or more if they had wanted to. Already, when it had been announced that I was pregnant — boom! I was suspended with no pay.

When I found out that Vincent Price was going to do it, I felt better about it. He was one of the most intelligent men I've ever met, such a funny guy. *(Laughing)* I got loaded at his house one night and insulted one of his art pieces. I was *so stupid!* Oh God, the things I did then. But I had the time of my life with him. He's a tremendous person. While Sid was constantly talking about his Cadillacs and his house and had to have "Champagne for *everybody*," Vincent could sit in front a beautiful picture for three weeks and have a great time.

However, *Shock* didn't make up for my career. The picture stunk. It could have been so good, but it was done in a quick manner.

Lynn's antipathy for *Shock* had been longstanding. At the time of its release she was particularly revulsed by the publicity surrounding her appearance in the film. Somewhat perversely, the Fox flacks had pigeon-holed her in a way that she would obviously find distasteful. The following illustrates this in no uncertain terms:

[Lynn] has played a meanie in almost every picture she has appeared in. [That's not true!] She appreciates the honor and does not feel at all bad about playing baddie parts in pictures. Many screen stars, she points out, have heightened their successes in this type of role.

You know that's a good quote from me! Are you kidding???

The *Shock* ballyhoo gave clear indication that Bari's studio had lost interest in promoting her as a leading lady. Lynn had been made aware of this turn in the tide in November 1945, shortly after *Shock* had wrapped. Her pal Henry Hathaway was then about to start *The Dark Corner* (1946), a taut murder mystery

Lynn became a more problematic photographic subject after the death of her daughter. This Shock *portrait illustrates the degree to which Bari's visage could be adversely affected by her personal troubles.*

centered on a private eye and his nimble secretary. The latter character, Kathleen Stuart, had originally been planned for Warners' Ida Lupino. Lupino had to bow out at the eleventh hour when her home studio insisted she report to the set of *Escape Me Never*.* Hathaway now wanted Bari to play Kathleen. Lynn would have been perfect for the part — an assignment that assuredly would have energized her career. However, Fox's front office threw an obstacle in Hathaway's path; questioning his choice, they demanded that Bari screen-test for Kathleen. This formality somehow caused Lynn to lose out, and MGM's Lucille Ball was rushed into *The Dark Corner*. Ball would go on deliver a fine performance as the secretary.

Bari's *Dark Corner* experience had cast a large shadow of uncertainty over her future at Fox. It's doubtful that anyone but Darryl Zanuck could have overridden the formidable Henry Hathaway, in what was obviously a move to demote Lynn. Zanuck had put Bari in her place — and he would do so again imminently.

---

* *Escape Me Never* began its two-month shoot at Warners in November 1945, but it would not be released until November 1947.

Lynn, as Isabel Palmer, in Margie *(1946).*

CHAPTER ELEVEN
SERENADE IN BLUE

Lynn was still smarting from *The Dark Corner* matter when she was offered a different crime drama, the infinitely more modest *Strange Triangle*. She turned down the picture in anger and spent the 1945 holiday season on suspension. As Bari had mentioned, *Strange Triangle* would have presented her as yet another villainess. However, she would have been the focal point of the film, in the very showy role of the murderous seductress, Francine Matthews. Lynn would have also had the opportunity to play opposite her old buddy Preston Foster in the thriller, whose production values would be on a par with those of *Shock* — if not better. Darryl Zanuck went on to cast the talented Signe Hasso as Francine and she had a field day with her part.

For many reasons, Lynn had made a serious blunder by refusing *Strange Triangle* — not the least of which was engendering additional strain on her relationship with Zanuck. The production chief had indeed grown rather exasperated with Bari, who'd rejected several film assignments since saying no to *Where Do We Go From Here?* Most notably, she had nixed *Do You Love Me* (1946), a glossy musical in which she would have costarred with crooner Dick Haymes and swing king Harry James. The Technicolor songfest had, in fact, been developed as a vehicle for Lynn, who had become closely associated with big-band fare. Perhaps she and Sid Luft had felt it was time for her to leave the hit parade or they hadn't liked the script — or both. *Do You Love Me* would turn out to be a mediocre film, but it would make money — and it wouldn't hurt Maureen O'Hara, who had eventually come to play its femme lead. Lynn, on the other hand, had been hurt by not doing the picture; refusing it had accounted for her two-month idle stretch after *Captain Eddie*. The *Smoky* offer that followed had given Bari a false sense of security as far as the front office was concerned; for once *Captain Eddie* bombed, Zanuck would never again entertain the thought of starring her in an 'A' picture. Bari may still have been Miss Congeniality on her sets and in the Fox commissary, but the boss had had enough of her personal baggage and how it had manifested itself with casting decisions.

Despite it all, Zanuck liked Lynn and wasn't about to let her go. He did, however, know her long and all too well, realizing the effects of her private life were something with which he no longer wanted to contend. Consequently, she'd once again be handled as a contract player — not a star — making her

263

less of a thorn in his side. There was never a formal edict issued about Bari's demotion. Lynn was a smart cookie, this Zanuck knew, and she'd have no problem coming to an understanding about the situation — and in the process she could perhaps console herself with the fact that she'd still be taking home a very large salary.

Bari received Zanuck's message loud and clear when she was offered a small role in *Margie* (1946), the production chief's latest project — and a solo starring vehicle for Jeanne Crain. Lynn swallowed her pride, signed on to the film, and went off suspension. *Margie's* director Henry King, not Zanuck himself, had been the one who had approached her with this subordinate assignment.

Henry King.

Margie was a pastel slice of America, shot in Technicolor. Based on several of writer Ruth McKenney's works, its charming story centered on an endearingly awkward teenager of the 1920s, Margie McDuff (Crain). Scenarist F. Hugh Herbert gently balanced elements of humor and pathos in his exposition of the girl's experiences, which allowed for the inclusion of many jazz-age standards. The Roaring Twenties and the attitudes of the period's adolescents were evoked by King in a masterful way. This accomplishment would be responsible for bringing major stardom to Crain, who was on-camera throughout.

Lynn would receive third-billing in *Margie;* her supporting part was not at all central to the narrative. She portrayed Isabel Palmer, the librarian of Central High. Isabel was introduced as Margie's confidante. Later on, though, she became the girl's unspoken rival for Central's handsome French teacher, Ralph Fontayne (Glenn Langan). The librarian went on to find herself on the losing end of this triangle at a school prom to which Fontayne was escorting her. This was depicted symbolically, as Isabel chided the teacher about his being remiss in not having presented her with a corsage — an arrangement that had instead gone to Margie, via a diverting series of events.

Margie had had a ten-week production schedule, from late January to early April 1946. The picture's cameras had begun rolling in a snowy Reno, Nevada, the site of exterior footage. Bari had come aboard once shooting had resumed on the Fox soundstages. Her participation had been minimal, for her role had amounted to a four-scene appearance.

Needless to say, *Margie* was a loaded subject for Lynn. She first recalled a lighter moment that had occurred during filming — which, in turn, inspired the memories of cast member Conrad Janis, who had been featured as Johnny Green, the Romeo of Central High.

An early moment from Margie; *in the presence of French teacher Ralph Fontayne (Glenn Langan), Central High librarian Isabel (Lynn) bestows praise upon student Margie McDuff (Jeanne Crain).*

I remember one funny thing that happened. Conrad Janis, the guy who played Mindy's father on [the ABC-TV sitcom] *Mork and Mindy*, was a young kid then, about sixteen. One day, I was standing on the sidelines waiting to go on the cafeteria set. He was sitting at a table talking to the other kids. He stared at me and then said to them, "Gee, she's got great legs!" And I just looked at this little twerp! I told him about it a few years ago: "You were cute; you were such a little smartass. I wanted to kill you!"

> CONRAD JANIS: "Well *(laughing)*, most people felt that way about me in those days. You see, I had just come out from New York and had gotten great notices on Broadway. I was a seventeen-year-old hotshot, all full of myself and arrogant. What did I know? But, of course, Lynn did have great legs and I was flirting with her outrageously.

"I knew exactly who Lynn was. I had seen many, many of her films, both the 'A's and the 'B's. I was not starstruck, but I was quite aware that she was a major name and was very popular on the lot.

"We had an extremely happy set on *Margie*. Mr. King was doing something he really loved. And we all loved Henry King. We called him 'Mr. King,' not because he said to, but because he was a Southern gentleman with an aura about him that said to us all, 'This is a man we should respect.' He was one of the legends. The rap on him, apparently, is that he did not have an *auteur's* style. In other words, you couldn't look at a movie and say, 'That's a Henry King movie.' But what places him in the pantheon was his ability to always be true to the script. He shot *Margie* in a very subtle Technicolor — not the 1950s cartoon-Technicolor of MGM, where everyone never had a hair out-of-place. Even the music comes in legitimately. King directed us very simply, wanting us to be as natural as possible.

"The cast was very professional — that's one of the things that I admired about Lynn. Jeanne Crain, at the age of twenty, was powerful enough to carry that film with her name above the title. Lynn was very well-known, so her name lent a cachet to the picture. She was wonderful in it.

"Zanuck presented only about four films a year. He was totally involved with the picture — but not on the floor, where Henry King had complete control. I remember, when we finished the film, I could not leave Hollywood to do a Broadway play until Zanuck had OK'd every frame.

"*Margie* turned out to be a big success, grossing a lot of money for Fox. Because of that, I went under contract. I was signed with Fox for several years. It later appeared that they didn't want an actor who had overtones of the street or the dark side; so I left in 1948, when there was a tremendous weeding out of the contract players.

"Now we cut to thirty-nine years later; 1985. My wife and I decide to throw a *Margie* reunion party. We call up the man who was the second assistant director, Howard W. Koch, who's now one of the biggest producers in Hollywood, and has been for years. The third assistant was Stanley Hough, who also turned out to be an important producer and later married Jean Peters, who was a contract player at Fox. Maria, my wife, who is nothing if not intrepid, got a hold of Jeanne Crain, Glenn Langan, Alan Young and Barbara Lawrence, who happened to be living in Caracas, Venezuela; she flew in for the party. We then called up Lynn in Santa Barbara. I gathered she wasn't feeling well. However, we chinned and chatted and reminisced about the film — mostly about Mr. King. But the thing that I love is that, thirty-nine years later, she remembered that I said that she had great legs! I thought that was awfully sweet. Lynn told me she was going to try to make the party. She was very sorry when she couldn't. [**I had the flu and was so sick I couldn't move.**] If she had come down, we would really have had the entire cast.

"Of all my films, *Margie* is my favorite. It's really a sweet movie and I'm proud to have made it."

Margie was truly one movie that had everything going for it. Fox knew they had something special on their hands and they delayed the film's release so it would open wide during the 1946 holiday season. This move would pay off spectacularly, with *Margie* going on to become the studio's sixth highest-grosser of the 1940s. The picture was an unquestionable triumph for Jeanne Crain, who would never be more enchanting. The young actors who were prominently cast as Margie's classmates would also be well-served by the comedy; screen newcomers all, Conrad Janis, Barbara Lawrence and Alan Young would see their stock take an immediate rise as a result of their delightful turns in the film.

For Lynn, though, *Margie* was a striking comedown. The clock seemed to be turning backwards as she once again found herself supporting the latest sensation on the Fox lot. Truth be told, she hadn't been featured in such a secondary way since *Blood and Sand*.

It was a very tiny role. I was only on it a few days and I was not good in it. Mr. King had asked for me in *Margie* and I couldn't say no. As I mentioned, he was always so terribly, terribly nice to me. He said, "Hope you don't mind doing such a little part." "Oh, not at all, Mr. King," I told him. I would have pushed a peanut across the floor for him — with my nose! He was one of the really fine directors at the studio. Everyone liked him. They were scared of him, too. He appeared to be a tyrant because he was a perfectionist. But everybody respected him. Mr. Zanuck did, I know.

Zanuck was sort of filled up with me and Sid Luft, mostly, at this point. I knew that the boat had sailed over there. Everything had gone wrong.

I agreed to do *Margie*. I knew that I'd have to do the picture or they'd say that I was through or suspended. As I've said, if they put you on suspension they could keep you there as long as they damn well pleased until you accepted another picture — and that could be one *dog* followed by another. *Margie* was going to go on location, but they did whatever I had to do at the studio. I'm glad I did it, but I was lousy in it. I was also uneasy. I had absolutely nothing to do. That was it.

Lynn's compliance on *Margie* put her in slightly better standing with her boss. Zanuck was then steeped in preparations for his prestige production of the year, *The Razor's Edge* (1946). The adaptation of W. Somerset Maugham's sweeping novel featured a character Bari desperately wanted to enact, the tragic alcoholic Sophie. Betty Grable, Judy Garland and Susan Hayward had already turned down this choice part. The field had narrowed down to just Bonita Granville when Zanuck allowed Lynn to screen-test for Sophie (this occurred after she had completed her work on *Margie*). The results of the test seemed to work in Bari's favor, but Anne Baxter suddenly came into play and she was cast in the role — one for which she'd win a Supporting Actress Oscar.

The Razor's Edge misfire dispirited Bari greatly; she felt Zanuck was about to send her off into oblivion. Such was not the case, however, for a solid assignment soon came her way; she was cast as the fictional counterpart to famed mystery novelist Craig Rice (pseudonym of Georgiana Ann Randolph Craig) in *Home Sweet Homicide* (1946). The picture was based on Rice's 1944 bestseller of the same name, a semi-autobiographical work concerning a whodunit authoress and her three young children. The book had charmed its readers with its engaging mix of fast-paced mystery and humor — a combination of elements that had come to define Rice's literary approach. Her writing style had won Rice a legion of fans and great acclaim, culminating with a January 1946 *Time* magazine cover story (which had made her the first mystery novelist so honored by the publication). Fox had been thrilled by this mention, having just purchased the screen rights to *Home Sweet Homicide*.

Craig Rice was a hard-living, brilliant and funny woman whose quick wit had been transferred into many of the offbeat characters about whom she wrote. A rather handsome brunette, Rice bore more than a passing resemblance to Lynn. The qualities the two shared had no doubt been behind Bari's casting in *Home Sweet Homicide*. The role she would play, Marian Carstairs, would approximate the age of Rice herself, thirty-seven. Lynn was only twenty-six at the time yet her physical appearance and general comportment bespoke of an older person. Bari's maturity would lend credence to her performance as the war-widowed Marian — but it would go on to work against her in that youth-obsessed place called Hollywood.

Lynn did, however, look younger than Craig Rice and she was far more attractive — making the author herself more than happy to see her as her filmic alter ego. Rice held high hopes for *Home Sweet Homicide*. She had been assured by Fox that they would handle her work respectfully and in a first-class manner — something that had not occurred with earlier screen adaptations of her novels. The studio would deliver on its promise and Rice would be quite satisfied with the finished product.

Margie scenarist F. Hugh Herbert was responsible for *Home Sweet Homicide's* buoyant script. Herbert placed great emphasis on the warm and snappy camaraderie that existed between Marian and her children, Dinah (Peggy Ann Garner), Archie (Dean Stockwell) and April (Connie Marshall). Expert second-guessers — as far as their mom's mysteries were concerned — the kids had longed to be real-life crime-solvers. They got their wish when an actor's agent was murdered in their quiet Southern Californian community. With the help of Dinah's best friend, Jo-Ella (Barbara Whiting), the precocious three utilized their mother's plot devices to seek out the killer. Their attempts to accomplish this had them shielding a wrongly-accused man (John Shepperd) and bringing grief to the lives of the homicide investigators assigned to the case, Lt. Bill Smith (Randolph Scott) and Sgt. Dan O'Hare (James Gleason). The Carstairs kids eventually earned the admiration of the gumshoes, as their sleuthing had helped to lead them to an accurate arrest. Things came to a close with the children

Romance blooms between the characters portrayed by Randolph Scott and Lynn in Home Sweet Homicide *(1946).*

having reason to be doubly-proud, for their efforts had also led their mom directly into Lt. Smith's arms.

Home Sweet Homicide was lensed from mid-March through mid-May 1946. Its producer, Louis D. Lighton, had just wrapped *Anna and the King of Siam* (1946). Previous to this, Lighton had been responsible for *A Tree Grows in Brooklyn* (1945). That memorable drama had made a star out of thirteen-year-old

Mystery novelist Marian Carstairs (Lynn), enjoying the company of the junior sleuths of Home Sweet Homicide. *Beside Bari are (left to right) Peggy Ann Garner, Dean Stockwell and Barbara Whiting. Connie Marshall is also featured here, back to camera.*

Peggy Ann Garner. The gifted youngster had gone on to make another tremendous impression with *Junior Miss* (1945), Fox's sparkling adaptation of the 1941 Broadway hit. A comedy, it had also featured Barbara Whiting, making her film debut as Garner's wisecracking confidante, Fuffy Adams. Barbara's notices for *Junior Miss* had been almost as glowing as Peggy Ann's and she was promptly signed by Fox. *Home Sweet Homicide* re-teamed the girls and featured another of Fox's juvenile players, Connie Marshall, then thirteen. The film's youngest cast member, ten-year-old Dean Stockwell, was working on loanout from MGM. Randolph Scott had also been borrowed for the picture, from RKO. The handsome star was not known for having a light touch and he would turn out to be *Homicide's* one acting disappointment; his performance would be wooden, totally out of sync with the movie's sprightliness.

Scott and company were steered through *Homicide* by Lloyd Bacon, a master of crackling comedy. Bacon basically treated his actors as an ensemble, with no one dominating the spotlight. What resulted was a consistently amusing film where most everyone appeared to be enjoying themselves. Lynn certainly did. She added vim to a good role and her interplay with the children was delightful. However, her best moment actually came with Scott, in a poignant sequence where she described the rewards of being a mother.

That was a cute script. I had met with Craig Rice during filming. Randy was a big fellow. I think he was uncomfortable; he just came on the set and stood there, seeming to think, "Well, am I in the right place?" He played like that in every picture. But the kids were great. I liked them all. Oh, I shouldn't say it but that other kid, Connie — she was a little *bastard*, I swear. None of the kids liked her; she'd do terrible things. The kids wouldn't even talk to her. I mean, kids know one another and they just left her alone. But she did some nasty things to get attention — she really did. *Really* nasty — I won't tell you even!

However, I was just nuts about Peggy Ann, Barbara and Dean. I get such a kick out of seeing Dean now. He never made a peep on the set; you never knew he was there. He'd be out in the back throwing balls with his stand-in. He was very polite. So was his mother, a sweet little lady.

Peggy Ann was a poor, tragic kid. She had a mama, too. Boy. But she was so protective of her — you never could say anything about "Mama." She was a wonderful actress. She could break your heart — and she was *really* like that.

One night, I brought Peggy Ann and Barbara home for dinner and some strawberry shortcake. We went to the movies afterwards. I said, "It's so dark in here. I can hardly see the screen." Finally, I told them, "I'd better go wash my face off; my eyes feel funny." They assured me not to worry, that I'd be fine. So the picture's over and we go to the ladies' room. I have half-tennis balls all over my body! I'd had a penicillin shot earlier that day. I found out then that I was allergic to it. You should have seen them getting me home! I damn near died.

Barbara Whiting is amazed by Lynn's recollection of this incident, having long forgotten it herself. She does, however, remember with great affection her friendships with Bari and Garner and the film in which the three of them had been featured.

> BARBARA WHITING: "*Home Sweet Homicide* was fun. I thought I'd be out on my ear already, after just doing *Junior Miss*.*
>
> "I loved Lynn very much. I had known her before I went to the Fox lot and she knew the Whiting family. This helped to give us a nice younger sister-type relationship when I was at the studio. At home, she was always so friendly, just a perfectly wonderful woman.

* "They kept me at Fox for two years and finally said, 'This is not God's answer to Jane Withers.' I never met with Zanuck. See, I wasn't his type, let's face it — fourteen and fat. Of course, I left there before I was sixteen so he was at least smart enough not to attack young children!"

"Lynn was a very nice part of my life. Of course, there was an age difference; but we were pals. Some of the other girls [at Fox] were a little snotty to the young kid-types coming around, but Lynn was always charming. It was very nice for me to get a chance to work with her; when you've met somebody at your home and you've known their husbands, it gives you a whole different attitude. Lon McCallister, who was also on the lot, is one of my close, close friends. He, too, remembers Lynn fondly and said to me, about her, 'Just tell the truth!' Everybody on the lot just loved her; no one ever had a bad word to say about her — absolutely!"

Barbara Whiting was fourteen at the time of *Home Sweet Homicide*, as was Peggy Ann Garner. Lynn was older by about a dozen years and found herself portraying Garner's mother; not the first — and certainly not the last — time she was anachronistically cast in a maternal role. Did this bother her?

No! You know, I was thinking about that the other day. I was looking at this thing about Joan Evans, who played my daughter in a picture with Melvyn Douglas [*On the Loose*]. There was actually something like ten years' difference in our ages. When I was in *Moon Over Her Shoulder*, I was about twenty-one but I was supposed to be the mother of twin girls, aged six. The same thing happened with the kids in *Home Sweet Homicide*. I've had very good experiences working with children. I love them and I like being around them. And, as it went on, I kept playing "mother." So, if the part was good, it [the close age disparity] didn't bother me. I think others were surprised by this, but I didn't mind at all.

BARBARA WHITING: "It wouldn't have bothered Lynn because she was good — that's good acting."

Bari's affinity for maternal characters set her apart from the majority of actresses her age, women who didn't want to be perceived in a matronly light.

During the production of *Home Sweet Homicide* Lynn's services had been secured by RKO for the femme lead in *Nocturne* (1947), a mystery set in Hollywood. She began the film as soon as *Homicide* had wrapped, playing opposite George Raft and working under Edwin L. Marin's direction. *Nocturne* was produced by Joan Harrison, the longtime assistant to Alfred Hitchcock. Harrison's first solo project, *Phantom Lady* (1944), is regarded as one of the finest *film noirs*. *Nocturne* also fell into the *noir* genre and was almost as good.

Nocturne's title refers to the composition of a playboy songwriter who is shot dead at the whodunit's opening. The tune becomes a key clue in solving the murder of the musician who, by all accounts, was an out-and-out cad. LA police detective Joe Warne (Raft) is out to find the killer and twelve movie starlets come under his suspicion. Chief among them is Frances Ransom (Bari), a gorgeous bit player who is hounded by Warne. The cop's investigating tactics are quite aggressive and they get him into big trouble. Trouble of another kind comes his way when he and Frances fall for one another. The lives of each become further complicated, with more violence and deception taking hold. Things reach a somewhat satisfying conclusion, and Joe and Frances are left to pursue their romance.

George Raft and Lynn in Nocturne *(1947).*

Nocturne's employment of music was all-encompassing and rather unique to *noir*. The movie also evidenced another uncommon characteristic, its on-location photography, which created a virtual tour of Hollywood — particularly of Tinseltown at night. Never before had a crime drama made such abundant and realistic use of the film capital. Scenes were filmed on Hollywood and Vine Street, at the Brown Derby and Gotham restaurants, inside actual photography studios and nightclubs, at the Pantages Theatre, and up-and-down the Sunset Strip. Most remarkably, a sequence involving Frances was shot on the *Sinbad the Sailor* (1947) soundstage at RKO, while the adventure epic was being filmed. The iconographic settings utilized in *Nocturne* were indeed many, bolstering the mystery with a special atmospheric charge.

Alfred Hitchcock's influence on Joan Harrison is strongly reflected in *Nocturne's* overall dynamic, which combines suspense with believable character portraits. This is one *noir* where the intrepid detective is not entirely tight-lipped or hardboiled; Joe Warne, as played by George Raft, is a man possessed of a normal array of human foibles. Joe's softer, more vulnerable side is brought to light by his love of music, his relationship with his mother (Mabel Paige) and his enmeshment with Frances. The byplay between Warne and his prime suspect is sharp and to the point, in the best *noir* tradition. Although exhibiting a brusqueness commonplace to heroines of the genre, Lynn's delineation of Frances is also infused with elements of warmth and intelligence. Her performance serves to melt down Raft's traditionally steely screen persona (as had happened with the gruff Edward G. Robinson in *Tampico*). The pair's sexual chemistry is heightened by the contributions of cinematographer Harry J. Wild, who captured Bari to stunning effect. There is much about Lynn's Frances that makes her an attractive and interesting person — and *Nocturne* was, without question, Bari's best loan-out assignment.

I very much enjoyed *Nocturne*. RKO made pictures written particularly for women; they had a mess of them. I had a lady producer, Joan Harrison, who had worked with Alfred Hitchcock. She was a very talented woman. And she had great taste. She was with me for every pin they put in my suits. A man says, "Oh, you know, put her in something gray." Many of them don't give a damn. But a woman knows what a woman needs for a part, whether it's going to photograph or not. Gee, I wish there were more women producers — especially for women!

And George was fine. I had known him for a long time. He was very, very professional. He did the scenes, never ruffled or angry. He didn't exert himself other than in the acting thing, though; he had a girl comb his hair, a valet brushed his suits and put on his coat, and somebody drove his car home for him.

Both Raft and his leading lady would take great pleasure in the response to *Nocturne*; the January 1947 release would become an unqualified hit, in both critical and financial terms.

Fresh from a rewarding interlude at RKO, Bari reported back to Fox and was struck indignant by a script that was handed her. The screenplay was to *I Wonder*

Who's Kissing Her Now (1947), which was set to start in three weeks, on July 18, 1946. The studio told her she would be playing stage star Fritzi Barrington in the musical biography of 1900s' songwriter Joe Howard. Up-and-comers Mark Stevens and June Haver would be headlining, as Howard and Katie McCullem, the impish hometown girl who champions the composer. Reading through the script, Lynn quickly realized that Fritzi was clearly of secondary importance to the film and yet another "other woman" role — and not the only such character in the movie; the other vamp would be enacted by Martha Stewart (no, not *that* Martha Stewart). The thought of strutting around as one of the perky young Haver's nemeses was more than Bari could bear and she demanded to be taken off the film. Fox acceded — and put her on suspension, for a period lasting eight weeks.

Refusing to do *I Wonder Who's Kissing Her Now* would amount to Bari's worst career move. The film itself was a handsomely-mounted Technicolor production, directed by Lloyd Bacon — the man with whom Lynn had happily worked on both *Captain Eddie* and *Home Sweet Homicide*. *Kissing Her Now* would reap huge profits for Fox, providing wonderful exposure for all in its cast — including Lenore Aubert, who had replaced Bari as Fritzi. Fritzi may not have been a lead, but she was an arresting presence who flirted about and warbled away in eye-catching period costumes. The role had also offered far more screen time than Isabel Palmer of *Margie*. Had Lynn played her cards right and portrayed Fritzi, Fox might very well have treated her with benevolence. They'd certainly done so after she had signed on to *Margie* — when *Homicide* came her way. The studio at this point would never have accorded to Bari the promotion of a June Haver or a Jeanne Crain, but there were certainly choice roles at Fox that could have gone to her, like the one that would shortly be handed to freelancer Jane Wyatt in Elia Kazan's *Boomerang!* (1947). However, opportunities such as these would no longer be presented to Lynn once she had failed to play ball by turning down *I Wonder Who's Kissing Her Now*.

Bari did her penance and was back on the Fox payroll in late August 1946. The studio had nothing planned for her film-wise but she kept working on radio, where the shows in which she appeared plugged the forthcoming *Homicide*. First came the aforementioned "Weekend for Three," on *Screen Guild Players*, and "Sentimental Journey," on *Lux Radio Theatre*. Both were broadcast by CBS. Lynn returned to that network in October for one of her most memorable on-air turns, *The Hollywood Players* version of Clifford Odets' Broadway smash, *Golden Boy*. Bari starred here with John Garfield, the two creating much electricity as Lorna Moon and boxer Joe Bonaparte (roles that had been enacted on film in 1939 by Barbara Stanwyck and William Holden).*

---

* *The Hollywood Players* show was but one of John Garfield's several associations with *Golden Boy*. The first had been in the original 1937 Broadway production, where he had been featured in support. Being teamed with Bari would turn out to be a nice warm-up for Garfield, for he would go on to recreate Joe Bonaparte in a 1952 New York stage revival, directed by Clifford Odets himself — and ending its run only weeks before the actor's untimely death.

Margie opened and Lynn ended her year costarring with Pat O'Brien in *Lux's* December 30 broadcast of "Crack-Up." Still, no film projects were in the offing. Equally ominous was the situation concerning Bari's official studio portrait. This type of photo had previously been updated every few weeks for Lynn's fans. No longer was this so, as Fox was now in their sixth month of recycling a pose Bari had struck for *Homicide*. Without any new pictures to autograph or lines to memorize, Lynn came to terms with an unpleasant fact: Fox was just about finished with her. She began to seriously entertain the thought of breaking with her studio before the inevitable pink-slip. Uncertainty about this prevailed, though, and she chose to wait things out. Bari had never felt so unsettled — and, years later, she would look back on this time with extremely mixed emotions.

People were steaming me up that I wasn't going anywhere at Fox and, if I was going to move, I'd better do it then. This seemed to be the case. I think Mr. Zanuck had had it with me and Sid and the whole thing. I was discontented more because I really *loved* it there — it was like my home.

Unfortunately, at this time, I also had a small personal run-in with Mr. Zanuck at a party. I took affront to something he had said about a mutual friend. I didn't know Mrs. Zanuck was listening in on my conversation about this with someone else — *(laughing)* you never *do* know! She went and told Zanuck and there was a big brou-ha. But he was very nice about it. He said, "No, I shouldn't have said what I did, Lynn, and I apologize." I didn't know why I was so jerky about it to begin with. Even if that had not happened, the handwriting was on the wall because many of the contracts were dissolved within the next year. I was just about the first to go.

The motion-picture industry had grossed record high box-office receipts in 1946. However, this postwar boom also translated into an inflation which caused most film companies to pare down in all departments. Further cutbacks appeared later in light of television's rapid growth and the precarious state of studio-owned theater chains.* Scrupulous budgeting became the order of the day in Hollywood, even with regard to prestige 'A' films. As for the 'B' units at the larger studios, most of them had become a thing of the past by war's end.** Production was now becoming leaner on every front — particularly as it applied to acting talent. Studios just couldn't afford to retain high-salaried stars that weren't bankable to the max. The process of eliminating costly long-term actors took hold and would continue in waves over the years, eventually spelling an end to the contract system.

* The locked-in method of a studio block-booking its product into company-owned theaters would be banned by the government in 1948. Later, federal antitrust laws would force the studios to relinquish their theaters completely. Fox would do so in 1952.

** Fox had been among the first to begin phasing out a lower-budget production department, with many stalwart 'B' players and technicians being terminated by the studio in 1943.

The contract terminations at Fox to which Lynn was referring had actually begun in the summer of 1946. It was then that the Brazilian bombshell, Carmen Miranda, had been let go by the studio. On the heels of this had come the departure of Carole Landis. George Montgomery had been the next popular star to exit, breaking with Fox in December. He would be followed in 1947 by Lynn, John Payne and Henry Fonda. Fonda would leave by choice, most happy to be free of the obligations of a contract player. Payne would be less exultant parting with Fox, but he'd say goodbye amiably. Carmen Miranda and Carole Landis's splits, on the other hand, had been tinged with disappointment because the performers had been treated with a noticeable lack of deference during their final year at the studio.

George Montgomery's Fox termination had had somewhat devious overtones. In a sense, one could say Montgomery had been manipulated into asking for his release. The way in which he'd been maneuvered had illustrated the iron-fisted rule of studio front offices, where challenges by a star could be met with power plays engineered to cut one down to size. These measures would have one of two results: the targeted actor would either fall into line or resign. The latter had certainly been the case with Montgomery — as it would be with his friend Lynn some months later.

> GEORGE MONTGOMERY: "I think I have a situation that differs from most of the people because I was signed by Fox at seventy-five dollars a week, did sixteen films there and earned, over the seven years, only twenty-one-thousand dollars! I was one of the top film personalities there when I went into the service [in 1943] and I think I was getting three-hundred-and-fifty dollars a week! By the time I was discharged, Fox had already announced they were putting me into *Three Little Girls in Blue* (1946), replacing Victor Mature.* So my agent said, 'We're going to stick 'em!' So he went in and got me thirty-seven-hundred-and-fifty dollars a week.
>
> "Zanuck said, 'I'm going to kill that son of a bitch in the business.' And on *Three Little Girls in Blue*, I didn't have *one* close-up! They never even filmed them! When I had asked about this, Zanuck said, 'Just know your lines and don't worry about it.' Also, everything I did was printed on the first take whether it was good, bad or indifferent. The next picture I did was *The Brasher Doubloon* (1947) and right after that I told my agent, 'Hey, look; I'm being treated shitty here and I want to get out of the contract.' So we broke it."

Lynn, needless to say, had also been experiencing a mounting frustration with her employers — and her final conflicts with them would smack of an insidiousness that would be comparable in character to what had transpired

---

* *Three Little Girls in Blue* was a lavish Technicolor musical that had shot from November 1945 through February 1946. George Montgomery's casting in the picture had come at no small expense to Fox, for a number of scenes with Victor Mature had already been filmed.

with Montgomery. In January and February 1947 there was a period of uneasy silence, with Bari collecting her paychecks but sitting idly by. On March 3 she returned to work for *Lux Radio Theatre's* "Somewhere in the Night." The show was a condensation of the 1946 Fox mystery that had starred John Hodiak and Nancy Guild. Hodiak repeated his role of amnesiac George Taylor for the broadcast, with Lynn stepping into Guild's shoes as nightclub singer Christy Smith. Bari delivered a solid performance in what was to be her very last acting turn as a Fox contract star. Soon she'd be handing in her resignation to her studio.

It was my decision to leave but it was also a big mix-up. I actually asked for my release at this point because I was misinformed by this schmuck who was the casting director; to think I left the studio because the guy gave me the wrong information. Mr. Schreiber had been kicked upstairs and Ben Lyon was the new casting director. Lyon told me to come over and work on a picture of Betty Grable's called *Mother Wore Tights* (1947). He said the studio wanted to use my voice to help the cutters with their editing. He also told me that Miss Grable was going to Del Mar to watch her horses run and didn't have time to come in and use her own voice.

Lyon told me two wrong things. First of all, this was intended for the *soundtrack* of the picture. Secondly, Betty didn't do the narration on it. It was supposed to be the recollections of her daughter when she was grown up — Anne Baxter eventually did this [the narration]. But he had said that I was to be the nice girl who'd come in and help the cutters out, narrating it so they'd know where to edit the scenes.

Now one other thing Lyon had neglected to mention was that Walter Lang, the director of *Mother Wore Tights*, had specifically asked for me to do this. Walter was always telling me that I had the loveliest voice in pictures. If Lyon had mentioned this, I would have said, "Well, of course, I'll be right there — as soon as I go to the dentist." What the hell…I had a doctor's appointment.

(Laughing) I had a terrible tooth, but I did agree to do it. I went into Lyon's office to see where I was to go. He kept me waiting for an hour-and-a-half. I told his secretary that I was going to the dentist. So I get in the chair and the guy's giving me the Novocain. The phone rings and it's Ben Lyon; he has to talk to me immediately:

> "You get right back over here," he screamed.
> "Listen, Mr. Lyon, I waited for you for an hour-and-a-half,"
> I explained.
> "I was with Lew Schreiber and he has precedence over everyone at the studio — *certainly* over you."
> "But I'm having a tooth filled."
> "You get over here right away!"

Lyon then ordered me to come over and pick up my lines and be on the stage at nine o'clock the following morning. I told him to stuff it. I really did. I said, "I'm sorry, I'm not going to do it." And I slammed the phone down. He called back and I said, "Look, I want to quit. I'm not going to come back again if I have to work like this. You won't give me a part and you won't do anything that I ask you to do. I'm just sick of it and I want to quit." So I did.

I guess if I'd stayed on I could have done another couple of little parts and then they would have let me go.

When I called Mr. Zanuck to say goodbye, his secretary put me on hold. She came back and said, "Mr. Zanuck does not speak to actresses." He would not talk to me. But I can see now where he thought that I was an ungrateful person.

Darryl Zanuck had been uncharacteristically understanding of Lynn during the greater part of their twelve-year association. In many ways he had treated her as a friend; he had admired her intelligence, spirit and wit and he had socialized with her in a manner he hadn't with most of his players. Zanuck had also long recognized Bari's abilities as an actress, not to mention her career stick-to-itiveness. Her tenacity, however, was both complex and confounding, born of a need to prove oneself amidst difficult circumstances. This particular drive had been what had propelled a faceless extra to stardom — but it had also led to Lynn's undoing at Fox.

Bari's rise through the ranks had seen a heightening of antagonism and disquiet in her personal relationships. These involvements and their effects eventually spilled over into her professional affairs to a harmful degree. The front office was to find itself extremely aggravated by the disruptive forces in Lynn's life — and her inability to put them in check. Consequently, Bari lost Zanuck's support.

Had Lynn freed herself of her negative attachments, she still would have had a hard time reaching the top at Fox. The matter of casting had always seemed to get in her way; she had a distinct persona, but one that hadn't rested easily into her company's star mold. The studio could have taken Bari's special qualities and built upon them, but they didn't invest the energy. With the exception of *The Magnificent Dope* (and the declined *Do You Love Me*), Fox hadn't cultivated a vehicle for Lynn on the 'A' level; essentially, she had been treated as a standby.

Bari's career as a featured player at Fox was as remarkable as it was unfocused. She didn't remain at Western Avenue, as every other 'B' actress did — nor was she heralded in a few 'A's and then sent on her way. She couldn't be compared with those who worked steadily in 'A' pictures either, her "other woman" assignments making her an atypical star. On those few occasions when she was cast as a heroine in a top-shelf film, she brought to her characters the geniality she had fine-tuned in her 'B' roles. This distinguished her from the more successful Jeanne Crain, Linda Darnell and Gene Tierney — all of whom had been groomed to project an ethereal, 'A'-star aura.

Lynn Bari was Fox's ultimate contract actor — and their most enigmatic star. Her term at the studio was exceptional yet marked by disappointment; there was never that big payoff for those fourteen years of hard work.

I went to Fox with great awe and wonderment about the business, and came out learning a little something about it. But that's life, kid.

Lynn Bari's very last official studio portrait as a Twentieth Century-Fox contract star, photographed in 1946.

RODDY MCDOWALL: "I never could understand why Lynn never made it into the first rank. You can think of a lot of people whose careers just didn't orbit, and you don't know why. Like Tuesday Weld. She's one of the best actresses and should be one of the biggest stars in the business. Why she isn't, I don't know.

"The strange thing was that all the fun and warmth and gaiety that Lynn projected in life didn't transfer into film. She was a very adept comedienne but she was always given that 'second woman's' role, playing the rich bitch — like in *Hello, Frisco, Hello*. Loretta Young used to say that Zanuck always categorized the women: you were either a whore or a librarian. It's strange how he classified. There were women on the lot who were the ladies: Loretta (it drove her crazy), O'Hara and Jeanne Crain. Betty Grable, like Lynn, was a terrific woman and tough, in a good sense; a very ballsy lady. But on the screen there was this wonderful vulnerability about her. One thing that made Betty Grable irresistible is that she didn't seem narcissistic; just a really adorable creature. Lynn, however, was never given roles that were warm parts — and I could never figure out why. I was amazed at this because she was *such fun*.

"There was one film, though, in which I thought she was enchanting, *Moon Over Her Shoulder*. She's charming, just fabulous, in that film. That was more of the Lynn that I knew around the lot. That had more of her in it, as a person, than other films.

"Lynn was a 'Good Joe' and there seemed to be no temperament. I don't know if she ever did have a power base at the studio. She certainly was the longest running of the group on the lot — which, in itself, says a lot. She was there a long time without any particular 'sponsor' — I never heard that she was anyone's girlfriend. I don't remember anyone saying a bad word about Lynn. She was wonderful. I did care for her a lot."

GEORGE MONTGOMERY: "I always thought that Lynn was a wonderful gal and a very good actress. But she was always sort of the second lead, which was proven out in her career. She never climbed above Linda Darnell or Gene Tierney. Although she did play the lead in *Charter Pilot* and some other things, maybe Zanuck and the other producers and executives didn't see her as the lead personality. With John Sutton they didn't — and he was a damned good actor. When we made *Ten Gentlemen from West Point*, I kept thinking, 'Jesus, here's a guy that's so bloody clever and *good* — and here I'm playing the lead and he's the second lead, or heavy, in it.' It's difficult to say why this happens; there are so many things that go into it.

"It was a different time, the forties and fifties. That was the 'pretty period' of people. Lynn was strong. That's why she took the lead in *China Girl*. She was a good lead heavy. That was a good position to be in because, my God, look at all the kids who went through the leads at Fox during the time that Lynn was there. Some of these film personalities that went into the lead never made it into the character lead, or heavy, which had a far greater staying power."

BARBARA WHITING: "Lynn was the type of person whom you knew you could count on to do the 'kitchen work,' while you brought in the flashy little [breaking into song] da-da-da-da-da-da.

"Some people came along with obvious star quality, the kind they call 'quicksilver.' There's just something there. Gene Tierney and a lot of those kinds of girls did come up and do those star roles after Lynn had already been there. What put them in the parts against someone like Lynn — who was so credible that you could count on her to give a fine performance every time? Maybe if she'd left the studio [earlier] she would have had a [better] chance someplace else. But in those days you didn't walk out on a contract.

"Lynn was never what you would call a 'starlet' — you know; couches and stuff like that. I never have heard a detrimental word about Lynn Bari."

CONRAD JANIS: "Lynn had an edge to her which, in some sense, made her more interesting. Because in those days, most actors were — on the surface — very bland. It doesn't mean that they weren't wonderful actors. Jeanne Crain was terrific in *Margie* but there was no edge or hint of darkness in her performance whatsoever. Today, we want to see that there is some darkness and shade in a person's performance because we know that we all have those things. It's more believable and it creates a verisimilitude about film.

"Lynn Bari had a feeling about her that she was a real woman. With that comes a certain sexuality. What probably prompted my wiseass remark about her legs was that she had an edge of sexuality that was more real. That isn't to say that Jeanne Crain, Alice Faye and June Haver weren't sexy, but they had a certain wholesomeness about them. Lynn had that, but she was a little more knowing; she knew about life and knew that it didn't hold any shocks for her. I think that's why Zanuck put her in those 'other woman' parts. Because, in the first place, it wasn't popular to have intelligence. That wasn't a commodity they wanted to see on the screen. Lynn always projected intelligence out of her wonderful eyes. There was also a secret smile in her performances. She used it with Glenn Langan in *Margie*, when she gave him a little zutz about the corsage.

"Lynn was really quite something. She was a perfectly beautiful woman who was considered to be a top pro, a top actress and a real 'member of the family.' But I don't think that Zanuck knew quite what to make of her. It might have been that her edge of intelligence and womanliness was a little bit too much — that we were a little too naïve to handle that in those days."

Lynn Bari, 1948. PORTRAIT BY JOHN ALTON, FOR EAGLE-LION STUDIOS.

CHAPTER TWELVE
ON THE LOOSE

Lynn was thrown into a state of anxiety by her break-up with Fox. Gone was her creative, financial and emotional support system. For the first time in her life, she was truly on her own. This independence would be something to which Bari would have great trouble adjusting — and what should have been a period of thoughtful redirection would instead turn into a time of rash decisions.

Just weeks after her release, Lynn made up her mind to divorce Sid Luft. There were three credible explanations for this decision, all marked by a sense of urgency: one, she felt the need to make a clean break from a destructive relationship; two, she was seeking greater financial security; three, she wanted the industry to know she was ending a marriage that had contributed significantly to her downfall at Fox.

Bari had come to be immensely irritated with her husband and equally annoyed with herself for having gone along with many of Luft's ideas for each of them. While Sid had been dispensing her career advice, he'd also been talking up his own professional aspirations, to which Lynn had generally responded favorably. The early part of their marriage had seen her bankrolling his attempts at movie-agenting. After all that had come to naught, Luft's attentions became focused on film producing — and Bari was again there with her pocketbook. Things had actually materialized on this end in the fall of 1946, with Sid becoming half of Dick Hyland-Sid Luft Productions, Inc. During Lynn's final month at Fox, Hyland-Luft had gone ahead with their plans to lens *Kilroy Was Here* (1947), a campus comedy starring Jackie Cooper and Jackie Coogan as two young vets. *Kilroy* had shot in three weeks and went on to be distributed by the low-rent Monogram Pictures.

The degree to which Bari had invested in Hyland-Luft remains unclear, but it is certain that she wasn't in the most solvent situation once *Kilroy* had wrapped. Lynn was very stressed by this because she knew that Darryl Zanuck's ire at her had become common knowledge in Hollywood, making her unwelcome at the major studios. Aware that her employment options were limited, she hastily accepted the first offer that came her way — a multi-picture deal with the recently-formed Eagle-Lion Studios. She had signed on to this at the behest of Bryan Foy, an old friend from Fox who was now in charge of production at

Eagle-Lion. Foy had promised her lucrative compensation but Bari knew all too well that the pictures she'd be making for his company would be double-bill filler, doing nothing to help her professional standing.

At least Lynn could console herself with the fact that Eagle-Lion wasn't a poverty row outfit. In its short-lived existence, the company would produce many glossy medium-budgeters, some rather ambitious in nature. Most of these efforts

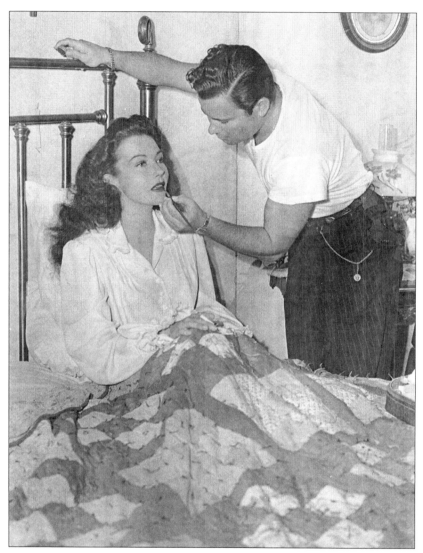

May 1947; with able assist from make-up artist Frank Westmore, Lynn returns to filmmaking as a freelance player in Eagle-Lion's The Man from Texas *(1948).*

would headline capable players of the second rank (e.g., Joan Leslie and Diana Lynn) or deposed glamour queens (e.g., Paulette Goddard and Hedy Lamarr). The eventual failure of Eagle-Lion would center not on its actors or scripts but on the studio's weak distribution network. This deficiency would cause the vast majority of their product to fall by the wayside — leaving stars such as Lynn out of the movie-going mainstream.

Lynn and James Craig, portraying the troubled young marrieds of The Man from Texas.

So, with a wary eye, Lynn embarked on her freelance career on May 5, 1947, replacing Carole Landis in Eagle-Lion's *The Man From Texas* (1948). Being back on a movie set proved emboldening for Bari, helping her to disengage from Sid Luft. Ten days into filming she moved out of their home, with her collie Champion in tow. About two weeks later the public became aware of her marital troubles. The *Los Angeles Times* reported the following on May 28:

> "Actress Lynn Bari, suing under her legal name of Marjorie Luft, yesterday filed a divorce action against her husband, Michael S. Luft, film producer and onetime test pilot for Douglas Aircraft Corp.
>
> In her Superior Court complaint the actress set forth that Luft had treated her with 'extreme cruelty' since shortly after their marriage in Bel-Air Nov. 28, 1943. The couple separated last May 15.

Miss Bari disclosed that she expects opening of negotiations for a property settlement soon. If not she will file an amended action delineating all community holdings, she added. There are no children."

Lynn was in constant contact with her divorce lawyers during *The Man from Texas* shoot. Her personal concerns were of utmost importance, but they didn't distract her from her work. Unfortunately, though, the vehicle to which she was applying her talents was turning out to be a weak affair. Things had looked slightly more promising to her when production on *Texas* had begun. The movie, a moralistic western, was actually solid in origin. It was based on *The Missouri Legend*, a critically-acclaimed 1938 Broadway play starring Dorothy Gish and Dean Jagger. James Craig, who had been featured in the show, enacted Jagger's role on screen. He was *Texas's* title character, a repentant outlaw who went by the name of Tobias Simms. Bari was Zee (Gish's role), Tobias's noble and long-suffering wife. Also suffering would be those who went to see *The Man from Texas*; the picture would come together as a crashing bore, dying out at the box office soon after its March 1948 release.

It was a very good play; a quasi-comedy based on Billy the Kid. But, in the movie, they put in all this action to liven it up. They ruined it.

Luckily, Lynn had little time to ponder her *Texas* experience because she and Pat O'Brien were set to star in *The Rexall Summer Theater*, an upcoming radio series for NBC. The weekly show debuted in late June 1947.

Yes, I had my own series, with Pat. Pat was lovely; I got a big kick out of him. We did the show for the Rexall drugstores which were owned by our radio boss, Justin Dart. He was the fellow who married Jane Bryan, that really good actress down at Warner Brothers. The show took place in a drugstore. Pat was a pharmacist and I was a nurse. Our conversations were about the various people who would come into the store. The series ran just thirteen weeks — we signed for that. They thought that it would run longer but, evidently, we didn't draw too big an audience. What we needed was some comedy; they played it too straight.

Bari did attract a large audience on another network, when she electrified in "Murder by an Expert," an episode of CBS's *Suspense* series. Broadcast July 24, 1947, the show would come to be her favorite radio credit.

I did a solo thing on *Suspense*. Kay Thompson's husband [William Spier] was the director. Hans Conreid did one line at the beginning. And then I had to do the whole show. The entire script had me thinking about murdering my husband. Then I finally do it. There was no audience present because it would have interfered with the stream of consciousness that had been established; it was all in my character's head. I was pretty shrewd knowing what to do with my voice. That one got an awful lot of recognition.

Two weeks later Lynn was receiving recognition of another sort, as her divorce action continued to play itself out in the papers. Beneath the headline, "'I Was Only Breadwinner' — Lynn Bari's Reply to Sid Luft," *The Los Angeles Examiner* (8/7/47) wrote:

> "Strongly challenging alleged claims of her husband, Sid Luft, to a share of her large film earnings, Actress Lynn Bari yesterday informed Superior Court:
>
> 'During our marriage I was the only bread winner in the family.'
>
> Her claim was made in an amended divorce complaint in which Miss Bari asked the local court to award her as separate property certain assets.
>
> Since recently filing her first suit, Miss Bari contends Luft has laid claim to a half share of:
>
> The $18,000 home and furnishings, an $8656 note payable to both of them, two cars, a bank account and other assets.
>
> She contends she owned considerable property before their marriage and only placed the assets in their joint names because he pleaded with her to be 'a man of property.'
>
> The new suit contends Miss Bari 'trusted' her husband and never intended the transfers should be outright gifts.
>
> The only community property is an interest in Hyland-Luft Productions and the film, 'Kilroy Was Here,' she contends."

Reports such as the above were to come out fast and furiously over the following month. However, when Lynn ended her *Rexall* stint, one could find little mention of her conflicts with Luft in the dailies and trades. Fan magazines were still keeping Bari's marital difficulties alive, but these periodicals had had early deadlines to meet. Soon, though, publications like *Photoplay* and *Movie Mirror* would be giving a new slant to their articles about Lynn — focusing on her newfound happiness with Sid.

Bari and Luft reconciled in October. What had provoked this unexpected turn of events? Lynn herself offered a vague, yet dramatic, explanation:

Let's just say that she [I] tried to divorce him at one period and he pursued her to come back — and she foolishly did. *(laughing)*…I tried like *hell* to get a divorce from him. He followed me around. He always had a gun. I was living at the Bel Air Hotel. One night, I had dinner with this nice couple whom I knew. I came home. The man had left me in the lobby; I told him not to bother to walk me to my room. You know the Bel Air Hotel — *nothing* could go on there. I walk into the room and he's [Sid's] standing there. He'd been through my papers on my desk. And he had a gun. I took the gun away from him. Finally, I said, "I won't talk to you." And I went in and threw the gun down the linen shaft in the bathroom. And then, finally, I said, "You've *got* to get out of here. You just have to go. I won't talk to you." It was just a mess.

It went on and on and on. And, of course, I wound up absolutely broke again. Then I got a couple of pictures to do and I got some money and I was all right.

But then he was out on my balcony on the fire escape one night when I came home with somebody. The guy left and then I took my dog out for a walk and he [Sid] was out front. I had to talk to him. So I went out with him and we talked and talked and talked. And, I don't know, I just thought, "Well, I don't know what I'm going to do." And I just said, "*All right*, we'll try it again."

January 1948; three months after their reconciliation, Sid Luft and Lynn engage in some serious conversation at a Hollywood nightspot.

It would be safe to say that Bari was in a despondent mood when she buried the hatchet with Sid Luft. Six months away from Fox, she felt lost. The *Rexall* series had ended, no assignments at Eagle-Lion were pending and her career had come to an abrupt halt. There was a tremendous void in Lynn's life that she couldn't seem to ride out on her own, so she embraced the familiar and rejoined with Luft. As much as she didn't want to admit it, she knew Sid's presence would boost her adrenaline, enabling her to carry on in a more energized way.

Bari's impulsive divorce action and subsequent reconciliation would work to the further detriment of her career. Quite likely, she would have gained a better foothold in Hollywood had she thought things out more cogently. This did not happen and she'd find herself stalled in minor productions at a time when she could have been flourishing in films once more. It became glaringly apparent to Lynn that the major studios turned their backs on her completely when she again complicated her life by inviting Luft back into it.

Nobody was about to offer me anything.

Thankfully, Eagle-Lion came through for Bari as best they could. The studio secured her some advertising tie-ins for the forthcoming *The Man from Texas*. The most notable of these was a huge campaign for Sinclair Motor Oil. Running through spring 1948, it featured Lynn astride a broomstick, outfitted in a witch's hat and a swimsuit with a flowing train. "Like Magic — Premium Sinclair Oil gives your car more power," went the tag line. Beneath it: "Witches, especially beautiful ones like Lynn Bari, may find plenty of power in a magic broomstick. But you'll find you get more power from your car with the modern magic of *premium* Sinclair Opaline Motor Oil."

Magic — or, rather, hocus-pocus — would be central to Bari's second Eagle-Lion venture, *The Spiritualist* (1948). The picture began production shortly after her twenty-eighth birthday, in January 1948. Lynn assumed the role of Christine Faber, a ravishing young heiress who resides in a mansion along the California coastline. It is on the beach where Chris first becomes haunted by her supposedly-deceased husband, Paul (Donald Curtis). Paul is actually alive and well — and plotting to send Chris to an early grave. His scam comes to involve the services of a phony seer named Alexis (Turhan Bey). Alexis has already been utilizing aspects of the occult on Chris and her sister Janet (Cathy O'Donnell), swindling them both in the process. The mendacious medium is not totally indecent, however. His conscience ultimately prevails, helping to thwart the murderous intentions of Chris's not-so-dead hubby.

A gothic chestnut if there ever was one, *The Spiritualist* proves to be quite enjoyable, in its own nonsensical way. The chiller, in fact, has now gained a certain cult status — as *The Amazing Mr. X*, the title by which it has been known (in the US) since its second wave of release.

(Laughing) I don't know why they changed it; either one of those names were terrible. I mean, they could have called it anything — *The Falcon's Lair* or

something. The only thing *really* great on that picture was the photography [by John Alton].

They rented J. Paul Getty's house. It's an old, old house, way up on a cliff over the beach. The view is beautiful. Getty wouldn't let us go inside, so we had trailers parked on the estate. He wasn't living there, but his caretakers were. I think it's now the home of the Getty Museum.

Christine Faber (Lynn) encounters the mysterious Alexis (Turhan Bey) in The Spiritualist *(1948).*

Cathy O'Donnell was so sweet; she was lovely. And I liked Turhan Bey very much. People say, "Oh, Turhan Bey," and make fun of him. But he was a very smart guy and a real gentleman. I think that's what killed him, career-wise, because he was a *gentle* man. He also had a great sense of humor, read everything in the world and knew a great deal about music and drama. And he did okay with the girls, too!

Bey, O'Donnell and Bari herself would be pictorially referenced by cinematographer John Alton throughout his groundbreaking book, *Painting with Light*. Published by Macmillan in 1949, *Painting with Light* would quickly become a seminal resource for those interested in motion-picture camerawork and lighting design. The volume would be reprinted numerous times, being appreciated by both professional and amateur filmmakers. Alton had begun writing *Painting with Light* while he was under contract to Eagle-Lion and shooting *The Spiritualist*. Consequently, many images from the movie would be featured in the book. Alton would also employ a variety of publicity shots he had taken of Lynn, to illustrate his discussions on still portraiture. Bari would wind up being a most prominent presence in *Painting with Light* — something by which she'd be extremely flattered.

Painting with Light would turn out to be Lynn's last link with Eagle-Lion Studios. She had thought she'd be making three films for the company, but the association came to an end with *The Spiritualist*. Nevertheless, that picture and *The Man from Texas* had helped greatly to put her finances back in order. Her monetary situation was also bettered — momentarily — by her husband's employment situation. Sid Luft was then completing work on *French Leave* (1948), his second producing endeavor. Shot over two weeks at Monogram, *French Leave* was a quasi-sequel to *Kilroy Was Here* that reteamed Jackie Cooper and Jackie Coogan. Luft oversaw the project solo, his partnership with Dick Hyland having bitten the dust. Lynn's "contributions" to this movie are open to question. However, she maintained that past experiences had by now taught her to invest her funds more cautiously. This new approach had come into play while she was at Eagle-Lion.

I managed to save *all* the money on those two [films] — hid it away! *(laughing)*

Lynn's spirits soared in the spring of 1948. Great happiness had entered her life because she was awaiting the birth of a child in September. Impending motherhood gave her a fresh outlook on everything. For once, her career didn't seem so all-important. She put any thoughts of work on hold and went about her days restfully. More than anything, she wanted a healthy baby, one whose delivery would be normal.

Bari learned that life away from the cameras could be quite pleasant. As she relaxed, she began to nest and became more at peace. Her new frame of mind caused her to be introspective and clear-sighted. She realized she'd have to do some fence-mending if her child were to grow up in a secure environment. This made her a conciliatory force in her marriage, and the situation with Sid improved in a number of areas, including those not associated with the baby. Lynn also reached out to her mother with goodwill. The two women had maintained only minimal contact over the past several years. Now, thanks to Bari's initiative, the ice between them was beginning to melt.

Marge was in the midst of one of her better periods. She was presently living in Laguna Beach, CA with John Fisher, now thirty-three. John had been discharged from the Navy in 1945. Shortly afterwards he had gone into the automobile business — his father's profession. He eventually moved from LA to

April 1948; with a strategically-placed LP in hand, a pregnant Lynn strikes a pose in her living room.

Laguna Beach, where he purchased a Lincoln Mercury dealership and rented a home by the water. He set up house there with his mother. Marge took an instant liking to her new environment. Her mind away from the Hollywood scene, she began to pursue some of her long-dormant interests. Her days were spent at the beach, writing short stories and reading the doctrines of Religious Science. Much to everyone's surprise, she started embracing her faith with a heretofore

Above: December 1948; Sid Luft assists Lynn in weighing their three-month-old son, John.

Right: Proud grandmother Marge Fisher lovingly holds Johnny Luft in late 1948.

unrealized fervor. Her increased sense of spirituality enabled her to cut back on her drinking and get more pleasure out of life. She was still an unbalanced and contentious woman, but she was no longer so volatile. There were even those moments when she appeared to be receptive to the needs of others.

Lynn was totally heartened by her mother's apparent transformation. She began seeing her regularly and the two shared in the excitement surrounding Bari's pregnancy. The prospect of becoming a grandmother thrilled Marge — and she conveyed this to her daughter on a near-daily basis.

On September 18, 1948, Lynn gave birth to John Michael Luft at California Lutheran Hospital in Los Angeles. The blessed event received extensive reportage, with print articles featuring photos of tiny Johnny and his beaming parents.

Bari was calmed by Johnny's arrival. Holding her little one in her arms, she experienced a feeling of unqualified love and was, for the moment, untroubled. She had little desire to work, choosing instead to stay at home with her son. The two were not often alone, for Lynn welcomed visitors — and the chance to show off her baby. Her mother and brother were among those who dropped by most frequently. John began to come in the company of an effervescent young woman named Eugenie Ediss. Eugenie would later become his wife — and the unifier of the entire Fisher family.

Born in Yugoslavia in 1924, Eugenie Ediss was the second child of two Russian refugees. Her mother, a baroness, had trained as a nurse during the Revolution. Her father had been a mathematics teacher who'd served as a colonel in the Czar's army. When Eugenie was nine months old, her family immigrated to the US. Mr. Ediss, also a talented artist, found work in New York as a muralist. His home became a place where one's creativity was lovingly nurtured. Eugenie responded to this, pursuing formal art training during the early 1940s. Her parents relocated to Los Angeles while she was in school. She joined them there once she had completed her course of studies. Her first contact with Lynn Bari came soon after her move west.

> EUGENIE FISHER: "My father, Theodore Ediss, was a set designer at Twentieth Century-Fox. When I came to California, he arranged for me to have an interview at the studio, for a job in their costume design department. I showed up for the appointment with my portfolio and sat there, waiting to be called. Joan Bennett breezed by and went into a little fitting room. They were fitting her for underwear, putting zippers in. In the midst of all this, this gorgeous woman in a beautiful full-length fur coat came striding by. People were saying, 'Good morning, Miss Bari.' And I looked and I thought, '*That's* Lynn Bari?' I had seen her in pictures with Edward G. Robinson and I had imagined her to be this sultry brunette — and here she is this real Anglo-Saxon beauty. This was my first encounter with Lynn Bari. Of course, I never dreamed I'd marry her brother."

Three years later Eugenie bought a ceramics studio in Laguna. She was then introduced to John by a mutual friend. The two began to date and, before long, Eugenie became acquainted with Lynn and Marge. Both women took to her right away, calling her by her nickname, "Genie." Quite fortuitously, Genie came to know the Fishers when family relations were relatively tranquil.

EUGENIE FISHER: "I was absolutely thunderstruck when I first met John, because I thought I was going to meet this slick city type. This very sensitive, kind person was there, not what I thought a 'car man' should be. He was such a gentleman, an extremely courtly man. He was also strong; a man's man, most definitely; very masculine. Other men always set him up as an ideal. He was the type of man that other people leaned on. He never said anything unkind about anybody. He was good with people. As long as you were straight with him, and told him the truth, he would do anything for you. Peggy [Lynn] was the same way. They both had a lot of integrity.

"John and Peggy were extraordinarily disciplined people. They were so disciplined about getting up at the right time, exercising, maintaining themselves. Unfortunately, both of them were really hooked on cigarettes. I think that they were born with nicotine in their systems, because their mother was a heavy smoker. Nevertheless, they were very orderly, clean, clean people; always so tidy and beautifully dressed. So the training must have been there in the beginning.

"John had a really deep affection for his sister. In a sense, he was her father image. He was very paternal towards Peggy, so reliable and kind. Of course, the two of them didn't always get along — siblings do fight. But he always loved her. He was also very proud of her success.

"Peggy was a handsome-looking girl; slim, long-legged, with fair skin and chestnut hair. She was much more spontaneous than John, who could be rather shy. She really projected a lot of charisma — and people would react. I asked her once, 'How do you feel about people recognizing you?' And she said, 'Oh, it's a lot of fun!'

"At times, Peggy could be very direct. I think, in a way, that was 'family.' They all sort of told it like it was, without making it sound tough. There was a kind of sweet frankness about them. Marge had that, too.

"The first time I saw Marge was when John brought me home for dinner. I remember driving up to the house. She was standing outside; looking very, very slim. She had gorgeous, short, curly, silver hair. She was the most attractive person and *totally* warm. I thought that she was the most engaging, lovely person. It was hard for me to believe that this woman could be anything but that..."

In January 1949 Lynn related to the press that her husband was about to produce *Man O' War*, the bio of the legendary thoroughbred racehorse who had shot to fame in 1919. Man o' War had been foaled in Lexington, KY — and it was in Lexington where Sid Luft was planning to shoot his third film project, an independent production. Bari told reporters Luft would soon be heading east to scout locations. She said she'd be accompanying him on this trip, which would also include a visit to her hometown of Roanoke. No sentimental journey would, in fact, take place because *Man O' War* never managed to reach the starting gate, falling through during its conception stage.

The reasons behind *Man O' War's* failure are open to speculation — but somewhere along the way Lynn had again found herself financially overextended and greatly displeased with her mate. Had *Man O' War* come to fruition, Bari would have very happily remained at home with Johnny throughout his first year. She instead had to resume her career at once.

My intentions were that, I figured, if I quit and I wasn't making any money, then Sid would be *forced* to go to work; I mean, he'd have nothing to live on. Do you think *that* was the case?

Bari contacted her agent at MCA, impressing upon him her urgent need to secure work. No film assignments were immediately available, so she settled for a radio stint on *NBC University Theater of the Air*. A Peabody Award-winning series, *University Theater* presented hour-long adaptations of classic novels. Lynn starred in their March 20 broadcast of Nathanial Hawthorne's "The Marble Fawn." She played the ethereal Miriam and gave a flawless performance.

"The Marble Fawn" brought Bari critical acclaim, but it didn't lead to more substantial or remunerative offers. Frustrated by this, Lynn broke with MCA and signed with the Manning O'Connor agency in May 1949. Manning O'Connor was a relatively small concern, far less prestigious than MCA. Its client roster was by no means top-heavy with major stars — something that Bari knew would work in her favor. She was now a big fish in a little pond, with her new representation poised to put in overtime on her behalf.

Manning O'Connor came through straightway, landing Lynn a lead in *The Kid from Cleveland* (1949), an independent distributed by Republic. The film was a domestic drama with a sports slant. It was made noteworthy by the presence of The Cleveland Indians baseball team, winner of the 1948 World Series. Satchell Paige, Hank Greenberg and their fellow Indians helped weave together the story of a troubled teen (Russ Tamblyn) who aspired to become a ballplayer. Off the field, the boy found guidance in the form of sports writer Mike Jackson (George Brent) and Jackson's patient wife, Katherine (Bari). Hackneyed was the only way to describe *The Kid from Cleveland's* syrupy plotline — and Lynn's equally maudlin role. Bari did, however, manage to breathe a bit of life into her banal lines, all the while looking quite the trim young matron, complete with a trendy bob. Lynn's loveliness here triggered a flood of admiring fan letters — most of them written by males who had yet to reach puberty.

(Laughing) Oh God, yes. But I'll tell you, I did have fun on that — meeting all the ballplayers. We shot it in Cleveland during the summer, and it was very hot. We went to the night games to cool off. You know, I understand that George [Brent] was Bette Davis's heartthrob — he couldn't make me even waver!

The Kid from Cleveland holds a minor place in Bari's catalogue of credits but, nonetheless, it came to represent yet another turning point in her life. Her post-Fox

Lynn displays motherly concern for the confused Russ Tamblyn in The Kid from Cleveland *(1949).*

doldrums were now no longer, thanks to the picture and her new agents. Manning O'Connor would continue to find Lynn work, their efforts helping to broaden her acting skills and marketability. In short order her career would be placed back on the fast track, with Bari being recharged by the whirlwind. All of this activity would come with an inevitable price, though — for Lynn was not fueled by creative juices alone; to advance herself professionally, she also needed to be embroiled in any manner of personal turmoil.

By the summer of 1949, there were negative factors aplenty to keep Lynn forging ahead. Sharing center stage with new career strategies were Bari's mounting marital problems and an ongoing feeling of financial insecurity. Mother troubles had also started to reemerge. Marge had somehow regressed in the year since she had come back into the picture. The current hubbub in her daughter's life seemed to incite her meddlesomeness — and soon she and Lynn would once again be at each other's throats.

Bari's season of serenity had come to a definite end.

Lynn's approach to her career always stood in direct contrast to how she handled her personal affairs. Volatility had not marked her sixteen years in show business. For the most part, she had dealt with her professional life pragmatically. Her sensibilities in this regard now brought her to the conclusion that she was never going to be among the pantheon of screen legends. Studio politics at Fox and her recent experiences as a freelancer had made this clear. However, her commitment to her craft was as strong as ever and she wanted to grow as an actress. The movie world had come to be an inappropriate place for her to expand, given her uncertain standing within the industry. The theater, unexplored territory, held more promise. So did television, a medium that was alien to most everyone.

The stage and home screen would, in fact, be quite kind to Bari. Over the next quarter-century, she'd find steady employment in both entertainment venues, playing the types of roles for which she had seldom been considered in films.

Lynn made her theatrical debut in autumn 1949, starring in the national tour of Moss Hart's *Light Up the Sky*. The play, a comedy, had closed on Broadway that May, after a seven-month run. Hart himself had directed the original company. Actor Sam Levene performed this chore for the road version. Levene had been featured in the New York production, as Sidney Black — a part he continued to play on tour. Bari took over for Virginia Field, in the role of actress Irene Livingston.* The flamboyant Irene presented a great challenge to Lynn, for she dominated *Light Up the Sky*. Bari made the most of her task, though, and came through with flying colors in her first stage outing. Interestingly, this achievement wouldn't have come about without Sid Luft.

I got the job because Sid had hooked up with this writer named Freddie Finklehoff — a real jerk. He knew Moss Hart's agent, who was Swifty Lazar. I went over to meet Lazar and he offered me the lead in the play. On Johnny's first birthday, I went to New York to rehearse at the Maylin Studio. They used that place for everything I ever rehearsed for in New York, both on the stage and TV. In *Light Up the Sky*, I was supposed to be several of the great actresses wrapped up into one. Sam Levene was a marvelous actor but, *Jesus;* he really took it big on the directing thing!

I met two of my very dearest friends on that show — Tom Coley, who died recently, and William Roerick, who now appears on *The Guiding Light* [the CBS-TV soap opera]. They were both in the original production of *Our Town*. If it hadn't been for those two guys, I'd have dropped dead! Never having been

---

* Virginia Field had been under contract to Fox in the late thirties, during which time she had headlined in *Lancer Spy* — the film that had given Lynn Bari her first onscreen credit.

on the stage before, I was scared to death. Also, the producers didn't tell us that we were going to play split-weeks and one-nighters. It toured one-hundred cities in six months. It was an experience! And I learned so much.

WILLIAM ROERICK: "The first interesting thing that I noted about Lynn was that she was early for rehearsal. Then, the minute we were on our feet and started blocking the play, she did not give

January 1950; publicity photo for Light Up the Sky's engagement at Chicago's Studebaker Theatre. Pictured are the show's four principals (left to right): Sam Levene, Lynn, Glenn Anders and Margie Hart.

a room-temperature 'film performance.' She was taking stage. She instinctively knew how to do all of that. She had great presence. Right off, I admired her. I've worked with a couple of other Hollywood actresses who either wore inappropriate jewelry, because their friends were in the audience; or just faced front, even though they were told to turn to the people they were speaking to; or were just plain horses' asses. So, to have somebody come on and behave with discipline and authority made you instantly like Lynn.

"The producers of the play were sort of amateurs and had little money. They gave us a contract with a sliding scale; in addition to a guarantee, we got more if they grossed more. There must have been some confusion about the booking when we ended up playing a split-week in Zanesville, Ohio. Well … *Light Up the Sky* in Zanesville, Ohio! The matinee came and there was practically no one out front. You could use the old theatrical cliché, 'Don't be frightened dears, we've got them outnumbered!' *(laughing)* Sammy Levene was furious because he wasn't going to get his extra money for the week. And through the first act he just schlepped, rattled and didn't try to make any points. The curtain came down. Lynn, who was bigger than he was, went over and grabbed him by the collar. Almost lifting him off the floor, she said, 'Listen, you son of a bitch! Don't take it out on the ones who came. Now let me see you get out there and give a performance!' She dropped him and he went scurrying out. This was perfect theatrical ethics; she knew what she should do. Quite correctly, Lynn made the point in front of the whole company. That is *real stardom*. Fake stardom is the people who think that stardom is a privilege. The good stars know that they are responsible for the morale of the company, for setting an example, being on time and knowing their lines. Lynn seemed to know all of this right off, *instinctively*, without any theater background.

"Tom and I always called Lynn 'The Brain.' It came about when she had done something that she had considered idiotic. She hit her forehead with her palm and said, 'This is big brain!' At some point, Tom said, 'Oh, come on, Brain, what do you expect? We're just a couple of slobs.' So she called us 'Slob One' and 'Slob Two.' It was a running, affectionate thing.

"Lynn had great wit. She was full of expressions like, 'Do you want a knuckle sandwich?' I remember there was a snowstorm when we played Utica. Tom and I were walking down a street when along came The Brain, on her way to the Laundromat. Holding a bundle of laundry — and through the snow — she sighed, 'Gotta get a room tonight.' *(laughing)*

"We all had immense respect for Lynn's humor, her talents, her generosity and everything else about her. She was a very beautiful woman — great stature, beautiful legs. She was just stylish, chic. Politically, she was a liberal. She was always vindictive about crooked politics.

"She was also a vulnerable person. She wasn't self-confident. Many of my friends aren't. Mostly, untalented people are self-confident."

William Roerick and Tom Coley exchanged heartfelt au revoirs with Lynn when their company disbanded in the spring of 1950. No small thanks to her friends, *Light Up the Sky* had proven to be a deeply rewarding experience for Bari. She wasn't, however, displeased by saying goodbye to the play. Throughout her run in it, she had been weighed down by a longing to be back home with Johnny. The tour had allowed her only a few layoffs, all brief; precious little time to spend with her son. In her absence, she had placed him into the caring hands of her mother. Lynn's trust in Marge was unfaltering — as far as young children were concerned.

1951 portrait of Lynn Bari, taken in conjunction with her appearance in I Dream
of Jeanie *(1952).*

CHAPTER THIRTEEN
BOSS LADY

On June 2, 1950, Lynn attended the wedding of John Fisher and Eugenie Ediss. Both Bari and Marge knew that John had found for himself a gem, and they welcomed Eugenie into their family with open arms. John's relationship with Genie would prove to be thoroughly rewarding — standing in great counterpoint to the marital unions of his mother and sister.

EUGENIE FISHER: "I'm glad I can say this — I think I brought out more in John than any human being ever did.

"When I first met him, I used to ask him questions and he would answer them. I remember once we were driving, and I asked him *normal* questions like, 'What did you do after that,' et cetera. All of a sudden, he stopped and said, 'You know, you're the first person I've ever *talked* to.' And I looked at this guy, thirty-four years old, and he's saying this!

"I don't think that that family ever *really* communicated. To a certain extent they did, but not on a level that was really satisfying. John was truly affectionate and he would answer anything, if you asked him. But he had that reserve that ran all through the family. I think it came from the absence of a family structure; with the love between two parents that was handed down to their children; with the tacit understanding that the parents really loved each other. I think that the children understood that the father was over here and the mother was over there. It wasn't a 'together thing,' and they grew up with that missing link.

"John and I shared the same values and motivations. We started out as entrepreneurs with no money. He had everything sunk into his agency and I was eking out a living, trying to keep my ceramics studio afloat. Peggy was *extremely* generous to us both. She'd give me her clothes, wonderful designer dresses. And when we got married, she practically furnished our entire house."

The newlyweds had moved into a home with an ocean view, in the Temple Hills section of Laguna. Marge went to live with them there, residing in a separate wing. For several years, this arrangement would be marked by harmony. Being under the same roof would afford Eugenie the chance to observe the many aspects of her mother-in-law's personality. The knowledge she'd gain from this would help her to clarify the dynamics of her husband's family, which would, in turn, contribute to the solidity of her marriage.

EUGENIE FISHER: "Marge could be disarming. She was a rather ingenuous person. I thought she was kind of flighty, frothy. She adored horseracing. We always took her to the races on her birthday. She also played the horses on the telephone. John would get these surreptitious phone calls from the 'deese, dem and dose' guys saying, 'I think ya betta take care of ya mudda's debts here — she owes about six-hundred bucks.' *(Laughing)* It was funny that she associated with these people because she was very socially-conscious; she had a pride in her background and thought she was of good stock. She *really* was a lady. But when she would get on the booze, she was transformed. The things that would come out of her mouth were like Mickey Spillane — I mean, unbelievable!

"Of course, I had heard that she had made trouble for herself through drinking. John would wince when he'd tell me how he'd have to go down to some squalid jail in Los Angeles, to pick his mother up. His humiliation must have been profound. Not that anyone was watching, except him.

"Some of the traumas that Peggy and John experienced, because of their mother, made an awful impression. And yet I really don't think that Marge had a mean bone in her body. It's just that her cogs would get out of sync when she'd drink and she'd be totally irresponsible. She was diseased. You're looking at an alcoholic personality. The problems are not the drinking; it's that whole make-up.

"For the most part, Marge was excited and pleased by Peggy's success. Her focus was always on keeping Peggy moving. Peggy, of course, had an active career at that point. Marge was supportive of her doing things and made sure that little Johnny was okay, while his mother got the show on the road.

"She really loved kids. When Peggy was on tour, I noticed what a good grandmother she was. I would catch her sitting with child-like candor, talking to Johnny and gazing at him, absolutely at peace and happy; relaxed like she never was around adults.

"She didn't believe in discussing illness. She thought that you only gave it validity by talking about it; so you made it go away by not discussing it. About a year after I married John, she was talking to me, bemoaning the fact that Peggy was not treating her kindly. There was some kind of squabble going on and Marge was upset. She said, 'She wouldn't talk to me like that if she knew how sick I was.' I said,

'What are you talking about?' With that, she pulled her blouse open. She had the most hideous inflammation on her breast. It looked like a terrible carbuncle or boil. I said, 'My God!' So I quickly got a hold of John and we got her to the doctor's that day. It turned out that she had cancer. They performed surgery on her the next day.

"But had she not gotten upset with Peggy, she wouldn't have said anything. I think that she was trying to heal herself because she would say, 'Day by day, in every way, I get better and better.' When I went to see her in the hospital, she was sitting up in bed — bright blue eyes, white hair, big smile, lipstick on. She had pretty much indicated that it was a piece of cake; that she was going to have some treatments and that was it. And we *never* discussed it!

"When I think of all the garbage that John had to carry, it's amazing that he was so darling; a nice, nice man. Into his life, I brought him family — because that was important to me. And he was embraced by my family. He adored my father and appreciated him for all the things that he had never experienced with a father. My father was totally devoted to my mother and to his children. Both of my parents' interests were completely focused on the family — certainly not on Hollywood and Ronald Colman! *(laughing)*"

John and Eugenie's wedding day brought Lynn's return home to an end. In the month prior she had committed herself to two projects that would keep her on the East Coast from June through September 1950. Bari knew that hectic times were ahead, but she embarked on this latest cross-country sojourn a more self-assured performer. *Light Up the Sky* had been a tremendous confidence-builder, her success in the show also making very real the notion that she could prosper at her craft independently. New vistas were open to her and, at age thirty, she looked forward to taking professional risks.

The 1950s would see Lynn become an actress of increasingly greater depth. Unfortunately, though, her creative evolution wouldn't play itself out on film. She was already on shaky ground at the beginning of the decade, being one among dozens of former contract stars who were now freelancing. The going was tough for these players at the major studios, where the plum roles were being handed to those under contract. The unaffiliated were soon to multiply in number, making this situation worse. Actresses who had gloried in the forties would be at a particular disadvantage because of Hollywood's everlasting obsession with youthful beauties. The onset of time would find these women scrambling for any type of decent screen work. Such assignments would come Bari's way, but most would cast her in a matronly light. Joan Bennett, Betty Field, Ruth Hussey and Teresa Wright were among those who'd be similarly pigeonholed. Many of these women, like Lynn, would only be in their thirties when they'd shift from the leading-lady spot into character parts. Although not exactly welcoming this transition, these stars would at least secure respectable employment in an industry known for its shabby treatment of mature women. The majority of their contemporaries wouldn't be so lucky, drifting off into minor roles, grade 'Z' pictures and obscurity.

Bari would make ten movies in the 1950s. Eight of these would bear a major-studio logo. Only two in this group, however, would be deemed artistically excellent. The rest, medium-budget affairs, would turn out to be routine entertainment and no more.

Alexander Hall's *Louisa* (1950), a delightful family comedy, had been offered to Bari during her *Light Up the Sky* tour. Her commitment to the play had resulted in her turning down the movie, which was to begin production at Universal in February 1950. Ruth Hussey stepped in, going on to receive third-billing as *Louisa's* mother figure, Meg Norton.*

Lynn's fifties film career instead began on a more prestigious note, with the Technicolor drama *I'd Climb the Highest Mountain* (1951). *Mountain* was a Twentieth Century-Fox production, shot on-location in Georgia during the late spring and summer of 1950. Directing the picture was Bari's old friend, Henry King. For King, *Mountain* was something of a pet project — and he had wanted Lynn to be a part of it from the start. He had thought she would be perfect for the "other-woman" role of Mrs. Billywith. Playing this type of character didn't thrill Bari — nor did prospect of having to return to Fox. The chance to work with her favorite director made up for this, however, and she agreed to do the movie.

Henry King, sensitive to her situation, had originally intended to offer Lynn *Mountain* in a personal way, by phoning her at home. Bari was then on the road with *Light Up the Sky*, so Sid Luft wound up speaking with the director. Immediately afterwards, Luft placed a call to Lynn, detailing to her his conversation with King.

I asked Sid, "Do I have to go back to the studio?" He said, "You only have to go back there to get your clothes fitted. You don't have to work there." I did not want to go back there. But I did. By then, they had fired [Ben] Lyon and gotten a guy who was worse. I went into his office with the producer, Lamar Trotti, an erudite gentleman. The casting director had his feet up on the desk, was reading *Variety*, and didn't bother to stand up to say hello. He said, "She doesn't look right for the part. Her hair's too short." Lamar said, "Well, she'll wear a wig." The guy then said, "She's no good for this part. She's too tall." He was like a character out of *Guys and Dolls* — a real jerk. So we settled his hash and I went over to the wardrobe department. And, my gosh, they met me there with roses! Everyone in the sewing room came out. Then Charlie Le Maire [Fox's wardrobe director] came over. It was like homecoming. So I felt better about it.

But I was glad to get out of there. Even by then, it had all changed. Almost everybody else had left. I wish I could have gone out with a nicer feeling about everything, because I did have a sentimental feeling about the place.

---

*Meg Norton's husband, Hal, was portrayed by Ronald Reagan. [The president we just kicked out! *(laughing)*]

Shortly after this return, Bari boarded a plane to Atlanta to begin work on *I'd Climb the Highest Mountain*. The picture had already been in production for two weeks. Lynn got into costume and was warmly greeted by Henry King. The director then introduced her to the film's stars, Susan Hayward and William Lundigan. Both Hayward and Lundigan had been around Hollywood since 1937. Each had been contracted by Fox in 1949. The studio was furthering Lundigan to some

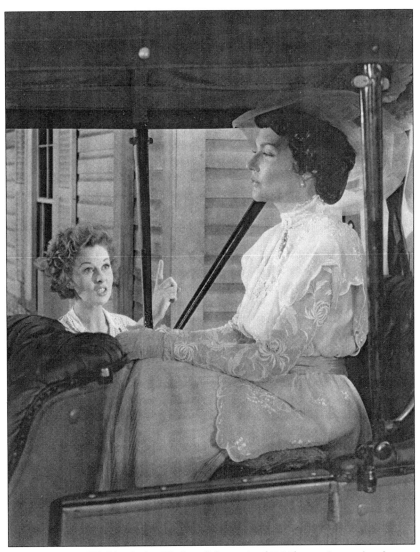

A moment from I'd Climb the Highest Mountain *(1951), one that makes clear the relationship between Susan Hayward's and Lynn's characters.*

310 FOXY LADY: THE AUTHORIZED BIOGRAPHY OF LYNN BARI

extent, but he was not a particularly dynamic actor and his screen career would go under in 1954. Nevertheless, his turn in *Mountain* would be fine, with King making the most of his retiring qualities. No one had to draw Susan Hayward out, though; she was a totally vital performer. Fox would capitalize on Hayward's energy and very real talent, along the way helping to make her a superstar.

I'd Climb the Highest Mountain was a poignant illustration of rural America at the turn of the 20th century. Set in the North Hills of Georgia, it chronicled the loving marriage of a dedicated country preacher (Lundigan) and his city-bred bride (Hayward). Giving focus to the couple's relationship were a handful of subplots involving parishioners of the minister's church. Bari was Mrs. Billywith, the drama's lone outsider — the Atlanta society woman who tried to lure the reverend away from his wife. Lynn's sequence was forthrightly told, in a manner that reflected *Mountain's* overall presentation. King possessed a profound appreciation of American culture, past and present. This latter quality certainly evidenced itself in *Mountain*, a picture that was at once patriotic, nostalgic and intimate in tone. The sensitivities at hand held great sway in May 1951, when the movie opened to an especially warm critical reception. In the ensuing years, *Mountain* would become widely recognized by film scholars. It is now considered to be King's quintessential screen work — with the director himself having thought it his best.

None of the above acknowledgement impressed Bari, however. Beyond her gratitude to Henry King, she had nothing good to say about *I'd Climb the Highest Mountain.*

God, I thought it was the worst I'd ever seen. I hated that movie. Being on location with Miss Hayward was like being in a room with a piranha. She was not dear to anybody, I'll tell you. She was the *staahr.* She thought she was pretty beautiful. And most of the girls who really were didn't give a damn about it; they were just natural and nice. She *worked* at it. But she was an awful good actress. ...Oh, yes, I did get along with her — well, listen, I get along with anybody.

Here had been Lynn, supporting someone who'd been treating her with disdain — an actress who, like herself, had been named a Star of Tomorrow in 1942 — a woman who was rising to screen heights that were now well out of Lynn's reach. On the surface, this might appear to be the reason behind Bari's condemnation of a movie that has long been highly-regarded. There is, though, another — far more profound — explanation as to why Lynn detested *Mountain*. It comes to light in comments made to her at a Hollywood party, following the film's premiere.

Gary Cooper's wife, Rocky, said to me, "Boy, I just got through with that picture. You were lovely, love (you know all that junk they give you), but that dead baby lying on the table! Ooh. It's the worst picture I've ever seen."

Sandra "Rocky" Cooper had been referring to the premature birth and immediate death of the son of Hayward and Lundigan's characters. The infant's body was seen covered by a sheet, resting on a table in the couple's bedroom — where the minister then performed a baptism. Clearly, this heartbreaking aspect to *Mountain's* story resonated deep within Bari, triggering thoughts of her own daughter's death. The movie had also featured two other incidents that surely must have contributed to Lynn's upset: the funeral of a baby during a devastating flu epidemic and the accidental drowning of a young boy at a Sunday school picnic.

I'd Climb the Highest Mountain has touched many over the years. Perhaps no one had been more affected by it than Lynn herself.

Bari completed her work on *Mountain* and the next day jetted to New York. She began setting up house in a Manhattan apartment she'd soon be sharing with Johnny and a governess. Her relocation would be temporary, covering the period in which she'd be starring in *The Detective's Wife*, a CBS television series. The half-hour sitcom was scheduled to be broadcast live on Friday nights during July-September 1950. Episode one was set to air on July 7, leaving Lynn little more than a week to familiarize herself with a completely new work routine.

Arriving at CBS, Bari was escorted by the network brass into a conference room where she became acquainted with the staff of her show. Also present was actor Donald Curtis, late of *The Spiritualist*. Curtis was to be the only other regular on *The Detective's Wife*, playing private investigator Adam Conway. The breakdown of the series had Adam getting his own detective agency off the ground in the opener, "Our First Murder." Notoriety comes to him in this episode, by virtue of his solving an important murder case. From there on, homicide would be his beat and each show would find him trying to track down a different killer. Complicating matters straight through would be Adam's live-wire wife, the bewitchingly beautiful Connie Conway (Bari). Connie has trouble staying out of other peoples' business — especially her husband's. Thinking herself the more perceptive one in her family, she'd be embroiling herself in Adam's dangerous exploits, often using her feminine charms to entrap a guilty party. Connie's ongoing shenanigans were going to deliver laughs aplenty — at least this is what series producer Charles Irving was conveying to Lynn and company at their initial meeting.

Charles Irving had little trouble generating publicity for *The Detective's Wife* — mainly because Bari would be headlining the show. Television was something from which most Hollywood luminaries were shying away — particularly when it came to having a series. With *The Detective's Wife*, Lynn would become one of the very first film stars to grace the home screen weekly. Her trailblazing was duly noted by CBS, who issued the following Bari quote:

> "I knew that both Don [Curtis] and I were pioneering in the
> up-and-coming medium and that we would both have to discover
> the differences between picture-making and television simultane-
> ously. Frankly, it wasn't as tough as I thought it would be."

Lynn made the above statement *before The Detective's Wife* premiered. The going would be getting rougher for her after the series was in full swing. Remarkably, though, there was one aspect of the sitcom by which she would remain unperturbed — its live presentation.

I had done single live TV shows before. After the first couple of them, I wasn't afraid. You see, most people panicked on the set. I was just so numb by the time they got around to shooting it; I'd be icy cold — no nerves at all. As soon as I found the secret of it, I didn't mind doing it in the least. But a lot of people wouldn't touch it.

Donald Curtis was apparently also unfazed by the rigors of performing live and he clicked airily with Bari in "Our First Murder." Both garnered much critical praise for the episode, which was thought to be well-produced. Reviewers, however, dismissed the show's script, by head writer Milton Lewis — the man who had penned *The Thin Man* radio series. Lewis, it seemed, had tried to inject too many stock elements of sophisticated comedy into "Our First Murder," with none of his lines or bits coming off as truly witty. It was generally hoped by the press that his work would improve on *The Detective's Wife.*

The detective's wife herself made the cover of *TV Guide's* July 22, 1950, issue, with the magazine featuring a relatively lengthy essay about Lynn and her show. Entitled "She's the Apple of His Private Eye," the article ended, "It's going to be pleasant these Friday nights to watch Lynn Bari decorating the TV tube." This comment delighted Bari, who was then anticipating an extension in the run of her series. Two weeks later, though, everything would be up in the air — leading to an abrupt defection by Lynn. Bari would try to make sense of this turn-of-events, as she'd look back on *The Detective's Wife:*

I could write a whole book about that show. It was supposed to be like the William Powell-Myrna Loy [*Thin Man*] movies — but wound up absolutely nothing like them. It was live only on the East Coast. Out here [in California], they had snowy-looking Kinescopes.

At first, we had fun doing it. But by the fifth or sixth week, CBS had not yet paid me. I called my management and told them that I was going home if they didn't give me a check. They said they were sending some "killer agent"

over. Little David Susskind showed up. He managed to get my money for me. They were paying me "fifty-cents-and-some-change," you know. Those big concerns, none of them paid you; they figured that you were lucky to be working for them.

The show ran thirteen weeks and I quit after the eleventh. I said to David, "I'm going to have to leave this show or I'm going to kill myself. I'm losing my mind." I weighed about three pounds. Sid was driving me nuts. I was trying to get a divorce from him. He was going all over the country, betting on the horses. I was paying for a house in California, the apartment in New York — on Fifth Avenue yet, I had a little baby to support, plus a nurse to take care of him. I just couldn't stand it anymore. It wasn't any one thing, just a combination of everything.

Lynn bade Manhattan farewell, returned to Los Angeles and found herself revitalized by the thought of terminating her marriage to Sid Luft. She took concrete steps in this direction immediately, once again consulting with her lawyers. By mid-autumn, she had initiated a Superior Court divorce suit against her wandering husband. Bari was asking for custody of John and $1,000 a month in alimony and child support. Her complaint, charging cruelty, had also made a request of the court to issue an order restraining Luft from disposing of any property — pending trial of the suit.

Lynn's legal actions were cheered on by her family — all of whom had been waiting for the day when she'd truly proceed with her divorce plans. It would be an understatement to say that they weren't fond of Sid Luft.

EUGENIE FISHER: "John couldn't abide Sid because he didn't think he lived his life honestly. He [John] hated devious moochers.

"Marge didn't like any man that I know of. *(laughing)* With good reason, she had no use for Luft at all. Oh, she hated him.

"I met Sid just a couple of times. I was never impressed by him. I was appalled that any nice gal like Peggy would go out with him. *(Laughing)* I'm certainly not Lynn Bari, but I thought, 'Why do these gorgeous women get fouled up with these men who aren't worth two cents?' I think of the attractive, eligible bachelors who were interested in her — and there were lots of them — who would have loved to have courted her. But that kind of relationship would have taken some work on her part. People like Sid could move in and take over. Somehow, women like Peggy were susceptible to that kind of domination because they lived in a world where people always did things for them; their lives were pretty well managed for them. Normal relationships between couples don't necessarily start with someone coming in aggressively. They take time."

Lynn's perceptions and interactions had long been unduly influenced by Hollywood and her star status. Moreover, her behavior toward men had always seemed predicated on how her career was progressing. Things were no different in 1950, a year in which she was again working steadily, and in a more meaningful way, having conquered the stage. Her recent professional activity, and the commotion it had engendered, had helped Bari to assume she was a better position

December 1950; the stressful situations in Lynn's life evidence themselves to a startlingly unflattering degree on the set of Sunny Side of the Street *(1951). Bari is seen here with star Terry Moore and Fred Sears, the musical's dialogue director.*

to deal with her inner conflicts — but, in actuality, she wasn't led to a more introspective way of thinking. Consequently, Sid Luft would continue to loom large in her life for years to come. The day would then finally arrive when she'd come to an important realization: her personal problems had a life of their own.

Needing work, Bari hastily agreed to play a second lead in Columbia's *Sunny Side of the Street* (1951). Her snap decision would cost her dearly in two respects. First, she hadn't bothered with negotiating her billing and would wind up eighth on the credit scrolls, behind the likes of Dick Wesson and Audrey Long. Worse, in the short run, was the fact that she hadn't paid attention to *Sunny Side's* production calendar, which would commence in December 1950 — smack in the middle of various legal conferences and the Superior Court trial.

December began relatively peacefully, with Lynn and Johnny ensconced in their Beverly Hills home. Sid Luft had settled himself elsewhere, with Bari knowing full well he had been keeping company with Judy Garland. Sid's contact with Lynn had been minimal of late; basically, they had spoken only of Johnny and his schedule of prearranged visits with his father. These appointments had so far gone off without a hitch, with both parents rising to the occasion for the sake of their son. Then, on December 24 — two days before the trial — all hell broke loose. America was treated to news of what had occurred on Christmas morning. Under the headline, "Lynn Bari's Child Taken, Returned," the *Los Angeles Examiner's* Louella Parsons related the following to her holiday readership:

> "Lynn Bari, after one of the most harrowing experiences she has ever undergone, ended up with a happy Christmas Eve after all.
>
> For eight hours yesterday Lynn was almost hysterical with worry over her 2-year, 3-month old son, Johnny, who was carried away from her house by the child's father, Sid Luft.
>
> Taken about noon little Johnny was not returned to Lynn's attorney until after 8 p.m.
>
> Lynn said:
>
> 'I had told Sid that he could see Johnny at 10 o'clock Sunday morning. I got my son up and dressed him and we waited for his daddy. At 12 o'clock he came to the door.'
>
> 'I said the baby was asleep and could not be disturbed then. He went outside, kicked the window in, rushed into the house, knocked my mother down, struck me, grabbed Johnny and ran with him.'
>
> 'A spokesman for Sid telephoned to say if I would promise not to prefer charges against Sid for striking my mother, breaking into the house and taking the baby he would return Johnny to me.'
>
> 'My lawyer, Robert Rohe, who has been here all day, refused to permit me to agree to any such proposition.'
>
> 'However, I was so overcome with anxiety I would do anything to get my son back.'
>
> "Luft, a former test pilot, whom Lynn is divorcing, has been at night spots with Judy Garland."

Bari and Luft remained a hot topic on December 26 — the day Lynn was awarded an interlocutory decree of divorce. The next morning *The Los Angeles Daily News* had this report:

> "Actress Lynn Bari today won a divorce after testifying her husband would go out at night 'to get the morning papers' and not bring them back until morning.
>
> "The 31-year-old film player severed her marital ties with Sid Luft, 34, former test pilot, whom she once before sued for divorce in 1947. That suit was dropped because of a reconciliation.
>
> "Miss Bari obtained custody of the couple's child, John Michael, 2; alimony and child support of $500 a month for the first year,

316 FOXY LADY: THE AUTHORIZED BIOGRAPHY OF LYNN BARI

$300 a month thereafter; $1500 cash; a two-acre lot in Coldwater Canyon, and 10 percent of Luft's net income.

"Under the property settlement agreement, she gave up her interest in a motion picture Luft is planning to produce.

"The actress testified before Superior Judge Thurmond Clarke that Luft was not interested in maintaining a home, but wanted to spend his time in night clubs.

"'If I didn't want to go out with him in the evening, he would say he was going out to get the morning papers. He would stay out all night and not bring them back until 6 in the morning,' she related.

"Her corroborating witness, Mrs. Harriet Furst, said Luft ridiculed his wife's appearance on television which caused her to become nervous and ill.

"Attorneys Robert A. Rohe for Miss Bari and Robert B. Agins for Luft said a recent altercation over Luft's right to visit the child was 'all a misunderstanding' and had been ironed out."

Sunny Side of the Street had been lumbering along in December, with Bari and her problems at home not helping out. However, Lynn rose to the occasion once her trial was over, injecting some sorely-need pep into the musical. Shot in SupercineColor, *Sunny Side* feebly strung together the performances of three popular singers of the day: Frankie Laine, Billy Daniels and Toni Arden. The main backdrop of its story was a television station where Bari worked with girl-friend Terry Moore. Moore was the picture's nominal leading lady and Lynn filled the prerequisite wisecracking-broad slot. Although her part was cookie-cutter, Bari herself wasn't; she somehow managed to punch up her impossibly one-note lines, looking quite fetching as she did so. Her efforts went virtually unnoticed, as *Sunny Side* rested but briefly on the bottom half of the double bills.

That one was strictly for the money. However, I did like our director, Richard Quine. The last time I saw him was at a party at André Previn's. We talked about this screwball girl who was in the picture. He seemed so up — he was the last man in the world I'd think who'd commit suicide [Quine would take his own life in June 1989].

Leaving Terry Moore and the banal *Sunny Side of the Street* behind her, Lynn sought more rewarding work on the stage. She found it at the Pasadena Playhouse, California's official state theater. The Playhouse was one of the most prestigious theatrical venues in the nation, the launching pad for many a celebrated play. Its location appealed to dramatists and invited the participation of Hollywood-based film stars who enjoyed the stage. Bari would be happily associated with the Playhouse for fifteen years, acting there on a regular basis. Her credits at the theater would encompass dramas, comedies and musicals of the tried-and-true variety, plus a number of original works. Lynn recalled that she made her Pasadena debut sometime in the spring of 1951 — in a show whose name escaped her.

It was a comedy I did with Nancy Walker. I got great reviews in *The Reporter* and *Variety*. The day after the notices came out, I got a call from Charlie Lederer and Collier Young — they were doing a picture at RKO, *On the Loose*.

Terry Moore and Lynn in Sunny Side of the Street.

The two men cast Bari as Alice Bradley in *On the Loose* (1951), which was being directed by Lederer and produced by Young. The latter also served as co-author of the film's story, a somber tale about Jill Bradley (Joan Evans), an emotionally neglected teenager who went down a wayward path. Melvyn Douglas played Jill's father Frank, a businessman totally absorbed in his work. Frank's wife Alice was also quite self-involved, but her interests were focused on her physical appearance and whirling social life. The couple did battle with one another — and Jill — before seeing the error of their ways. In typical fashion, their point of self-confrontation had come when their daughter was suffering through a life-and-death crisis.

Lynn, as the vain and feckless mother of On the Loose *(1951).*

On the Loose was saved from total dreariness by the all-out performances of Douglas and Bari. Rather perversely, the two made child abuse entertaining to watch. Lynn's Alice would be considered camp today; however, she did play a woman obsessed with facials and hairdryers with much conviction — being upped to above-the-title billing while enacting her juicy character.

It was a good role, and we made up a lot of it on the set. I didn't have that big a part when we started. They added two whole scenes after shooting began.

On the Loose *reaches a melodramatic highpoint, with neglectful parents Alice and Frank Bradley (Lynn and Melvyn Douglas) having rushed to the aid of their hospitalized daughter, Jill (Joan Evans).*

So much other stuff was written while we were working. I remember the scene at the end, where I'm confronting the neighbors about my daughter — I had to learn that about three seconds before the camera started rolling.

I enjoyed *On the Loose* very much. It was a nice atmosphere, with nobody on their high horse. Charlie Lederer directed it and, to a point, he let you do whatever you damn well pleased.

Melvyn Douglas was a hero to me, a very fine actor. While we were working together, he said, "I don't understand it; you're being lost in Hollywood. Why don't you go to New York? They're crying for women of your talent and looks. You have such a great stage presence. The movies have never seen that side of you." Unfortunately, I could not take John with me if I went back to New York. That jerk [Sid Luft] had put this terrible clause in the divorce agreement that I

320 FOXY LADY: THE AUTHORIZED BIOGRAPHY OF LYNN BARI

could not take him out of the state [California]. God, I got offers for pictures in Italy and quite a few [Broadway] plays, including one Mel Ferrer had asked me to do with him.

While I was working at RKO, my first husband, Walter Kane, was running the studio for Howard Hughes.* At this point [in 1951] things had cooled off and we were on good terms. I went to him with a project I had in mind.

When I was in New York, doing *The Detective's Wife*, this writer friend and I were planning another television series for me. It was to be about airplane flight attendants. We wanted to have an assortment of funny women, with two leads. We were talking about Lucille Ball and me. This was before Lucille started doing *I Love Lucy*. If Lucy did not want to do it, we thought Nancy Walker, a very funny girl, would be great.

I told Walter about our idea and asked him if he could interest Howard in it. We thought we could also use the show to promote TWA [Trans World Airlines, another of Hughes's companies]. Walter said, "Oh, it sounds great. We'll have to look into it."

I told my agent at MCA, Alan Miller, what had gone on.** He said he and Jennings Lang would go over to RKO and talk with them. Now, these were two important men — they were running MCA. Walter kept them waiting for over an hour in his offices! This was his favorite trick with everybody; let 'em stew — to show what a *big shot* he was. They left, but did go back again and finally met with Walter. He told them, "Well, I gave the idea to Mr. Hughes and he thought it was very funny. However, he doesn't believe that there's any future in television. But he'd be very happy to loan you a mock-up of the plane for shooting." Isn't that something? It all would have been so easy to do and here was this great brain, Hughes, saying that there's no future in something that's new! And he was the one who was always shouting, "Nobody believes in me."

Lynn gave up on her series idea after her agents' meeting with Kane. MCA had redirected her attentions, having lined up for her a number of TV appearances. The first two would be broadcast live from New York in June, necessitating Johnny's being left in Marge's care for most of that month.

On June 11, Bari costarred with Lee Bowman and Butterfly McQueen in "The Weather for Today." The lighthearted show, directed by Fielder Cook, was an episode of CBS's *Lux Video Theatre*. It marked Lynn's initial foray into television's anthology-series format. Bari would find herself inspired by this type of programming, its fast production pace and the talent involved. She'd go on to guest-star on practically every major anthology series of TV's golden age — a slew of one-shot appearances that would make her most identifiable to home-screen audiences.

Lynn's second anthology outing was aired by ABC-TV on June 29, 1951. That evening she played opposite James Dunn in "The Big Break," the first-

---

* Howard Hughes had gained controlling interest in RKO in 1948.

** Bari rejoined with MCA in 1951, after terminating her agreement with the Manning O'Connor agency.

season windup to *Pulitzer Prize Playhouse*. The hour-long telecast told of the 1929 prison riot in Auburn, NY. Based on a story that had won a 1930 Pulitzer Journalism Award, "The Big Break" was live TV at its finest, well-written and bursting with excitement.

Far less stimulating for Bari was *I Dream of Jeanie* (1952), the mawkish Stephen Foster biopic she made at Republic during early autumn 1951. The Trucolor songfest cast Bill Shirley as the 19th-century composer. Twenty-four-year-old Eileen Christy was Foster's sweetheart, the film's title character. Thirty-one-year-old Lynn played Christy's mother, a part that was large in size, if not in scope. Despite her screen time, Bari was poorly billed in *Jeanie*, one of the last musicals produced by Republic.

Allan Dwan was the director on that. Now, Mr. Dwan was one of the first directors I had worked with. I liked him. He was a hardboiled sort of guy — you know; rough-talking, giving orders on the set. But he was a real gentleman. He had started out in pictures as a kid. I think he was about ninety then [Dwan was actually sixty-six]. He knew more about movies than anybody in the world. He used to laugh at me when the cameraman would say, "Oh, wait a minute; I want to get a light on Miss Bari." He'd say, "Don't worry; she'll find it." A funny guy.

I Dream of Jeanie wrapped and Lynn was back in New York working on television. "Agent from Scotland Yard" was her final home-screen credit for 1951. The show, an episode of *The Bigelow Theatre*, was broadcast live by the DuMont network on November 22. Bari starred as a sultry beauty who tried her very best to cover up a crime she'd committed. Much to her distress, she was eventually found out by the Scotland Yard detective whom she'd been vamping.

"Agent from Scotland Yard" illustrated the fact that Lynn was allowed to portray age-appropriate characters on television. The field was wide open for her in the new medium and she had her pick of all types of roles. The reverse held true in films, where her options were becoming increasingly more limited. Bari was now facing this situation head-on. She didn't intend to thumb her nose at movie offers, but she knew such undertakings weren't likely to prove artistically gratifying. It had become glaringly apparent to her that she'd have to throw her energies toward television and the stage for creative fulfillment.

Lynn's divorce from Sid Luft went into effect on December 30, 1951. The next day the *Los Angeles Times* covered this milestone. Under the headline, "Lynn Bari's Marriage Ties Finally Dissolved," the newspaper stated:

"Lynn Bari, 32-year-old screen actress, made sure yesterday that she would start the New Year free from the last vestige of matrimonial ties.

"Her attorneys, S.S. Hahn and Saul Ross, brought about entry in Superior Court of her final decree of divorce from Sid Luft, 35, theatrical agent and one-time test pilot. The interlocutory decree was granted her by Judge Thurmond Clarke on Dec. 26, 1950.

"In recent months Luft has been reported engaged to Film Actress Judy Garland, whose own final divorce decree from Vincente Minnelli, motion-picture director, will be entered the last week of March.

"Miss Bari testified in winning the interlocutory decree that Luft often left the house early in the evening 'to get the morning papers' and would not return until 6 a.m. The court gave her custody of a son John, now 3, and approved a settlement giving her $500 a month for a year and 10% of Luft's earnings thereafter, with the minimum set at $300 a month."

The finalization of her divorce had left Bari in a celebratory mood, and her spirits would remain high for several months. Entering into a new life phase, everything seemed to be falling in place. 1952 did indeed unfold well for Lynn. She was committed to several TV guest shots that winter and had just signed on to a major film that would be shot at Universal in the spring. Theater offers were also being presented to her. Realizing the importance of making a fresh start, Bari decided to let go of the home she had shared with Luft. It sold immediately. Lynn's bank account swelled and she leased a very comfortable Beverly Hills apartment for Johnny and herself. Marge helped her decorate it, much to Bari's pleasure. The two women were engaged in a truce, with neither questioning why they had arrived at a point of amicability. The calmness in Lynn's personal life enabled her to be more receptive to the opposite sex. She began to date and had fun being the object of her companions' attentions. For the present, though, there were no thoughts of developing a serious relationship. Bari wanted instead to cultivate her sense of independence and revel in the joys of motherhood, devoting as much time as possible to her son. On so many counts, it appeared Lynn had arrived at a place where she was most contented.

Unfortunately, however, times of good fortune always turned out to be difficult for Bari to handle; they weren't in agreement with her overriding feeling of inadequacy — something that needed to be validated on a periodic basis. Consequently, she'd latch on to something that would put a halt to her streak of enjoyment. She would do this by enmeshing herself with Sid Luft once again — just four months after she had been granted her freedom from him.

Luft had become engaged to Judy Garland, whose career he was now managing. The couple's relationship had begun in 1950, a year that had seen Garland hit rock bottom. During this time Judy had serious health problems, had made a suicide attempt and had been fired by her studio, MGM. Sid had helped her to rebound from these crises, proving to be a stabilizing force in both her emotional and professional lives. Garland had made a return to the live stage in 1951 at Luft's behest. Her triumphant concert appearances at the London Palladium and New York's Palace Theatre had been the result of Sid's encouragement. The comeback of Judy Garland had been nothing short of astonishing, justifiably earning her recognition as a living legend.

Perhaps Bari was stung by Garland's recent success — or, more specifically, Luft's success with Garland. In any event, Lynn still harbored ill feelings toward Sid and she used his relationship with Judy to act out her latest self-destructive urge.

A foreshadowing of what was about to transpire had been surfacing in Hollywood, with the press making allusions about Bari's having contacted Garland with warnings about Sid. The source of this information remains open to question, but it wouldn't be hard to believe that Lynn herself had been behind it. Bari did, however, certainly come into play in sensationalistic articles written about Judy and Luft in the months prior to their June 1952 marriage. One fan magazine dredged up an old photo of Lynn and Sid with the headline, "Sid Luft is dead wrong for Judy!" The caption beneath the picture explained

A heartwarming 1952 snapshot of John Luft and his adoring mother.

this proclamation: "Ex-wife Lynn Bari said Sid was associated with a horseracing enterprise. His history reveals he is an ex-pilot, ex-sportsman, and ex-participant in nightclub brawls. Well-tailored and witty, he's hardly the ideal husband."

April 1952 saw Lynn firmly entrenched in the tabloids, albeit as a sidelight to the current gossip about Judy Garland. The month was kinder to her professionally, for she was at Universal, enacting a plum part in *Has Anybody Seen My Gal* (1952). The movie was a big-budget affair that required much of Bari. Somehow, though, she found the time to initiate legal action against Sid Luft, with regard to child support; she wanted his $500 monthly payments to extend beyond the agreed first year. It became clear to those who knew her well that Lynn was stirring things up unnecessarily because she was well-heeled at the time. Confounding matters was the fact that she had professed enormous relief at having rid herself of Sid.

A court hearing was set for May 15. Garland was summoned by Bari's lawyers to reveal her financial arrangements with Luft. The trial opened with Lynn and Sid in attendance. Judy was nowhere in sight. The Associated Press related:

"Judy Garland was ordered arrested today for failing to answer a court summons, and a few minutes later put in a belated appearance.

"She had been subpoenaed in the suit of actress Lynn Bari against her ex-husband, Sid Luft, for support of their son. Judy is engaged to Luft, film producer.

"Miss Bari wants payments for their son, Joseph [sic] Michael Luft, 3, boosted from $200 [sic] a month to $500. Miss Bari's attorney, S.S. Hahn, charged Luft was contributing more to the support of his racehorses than he was to his son's care.

"Hahn introduced an income tax record for 1951 which showed a total of $4,392 for operating Rainbow Stables, including the cost of feed and grooming the horses …"

Bari's lawsuit would drag on for more than a year — with Lynn already getting what she really needed: the emotional turmoil that kept her going.

Has Anybody Seen My Gal was unquestionably Bari's best film assignment during her freelance years, even though it served to promote two Universal neophytes, Rock Hudson and Piper Laurie. A Technicolor confection directed by Douglas Sirk, the comedy took place in 1928 and dealt with the Blaisdells, an ordinary middle-class family who became unhinged by an unexpected inheritance of $100,000. The windfall most affected Harriet Blaisdell (Lynn), who had been introduced as a relatively sedate housewife, the mother of three (Piper Laurie, Gigi Perreau and William Reynolds). The greenbacks had their way with Harriet by turning her into a social-climbing, spendthrift flapper. Bari made the most of this amusing transformation and her snazzy, featherbrained comportment was a delight to behold.

Lynn's imprint on *Has Anybody Seen My Gal* was significant, for Harriet was a lead character. Oddly, though, she didn't receive commensurate billing; her name came after the title. Listed above it were Charles Coburn (as the old flame of Harriet's deceased mother — and the Blaisdells' anonymous benefactor) and a trio of young Universal contract actors: Laurie, Perreau and Hudson (as Laurie's boyfriend). Lynn's role was at least equal in size to those of the juveniles — and the subject of her crediting was something she was quick to mention.

Listen, you know I got billed down with "Lassie." Mr. Goetz [William Goetz, late of Fox, now Universal's production chief] was as sore as hell at me — and I don't blame him. I don't know how I even got the part. I wasn't a contract player. They didn't give a damn for freelance players coming in — unless you were Gable or something.

But I love *Has Anybody Seen My Gal.* It was a real laugh! And Douglas Sirk was a very good director. But, *oh God*, he worked us hard! We worked our fannies off; awful hours. We rehearsed *a lot*, and that's what wears you out. If you rehearse *too* much, then you've got nothing left for the film. Mr. Sirk did have a temper — which I don't blame him for. But he liked me very much and came to me with good ideas. We got along great.

Lynn reacts most unfavorably to a second reversal-of-fortune in Has Anybody Seen My Gal *(1952). Comforting Bari are (left to right) Larry Gates, Piper Laurie and Charles Coburn.*

Weren't the clothes marvelous? I'll never forget the day when Bud Westmore first made me up; he really *did* it. I said, "Listen, I'm supposed to be this kid's [Laurie's] mother and I'm ten years older." So he dulled it down and I walked out onto the set, wearing a white satin dress and a tiara. Sirk took one look at me and screamed, "Oh my God, no! No! No! No! Take that dress off and remove all that makeup from her face!" He threw such a tantrum.

Then we went over to the recording stage, where I sang "The Red Red Robin:"

> "Don't be sexy, Lynn; you're the mother," they kept saying.
> "I'm not being sexy. This is my voice — this is it," I said.
> "Well, can't you make it a little higher?"
> "Impossible!"

Real creeps. You know, they cast me as the mother and I was thirty-two. Piper told me she was twenty-two and Rock was twenty-seven. Rock was very nice, very sweet — but not exciting conversationally. As for Charles Coburn, what a dirty old man! *(laughing)* But he was such a funny actor and wonderful to work with. I liked him *very* much. James Dean was also in the picture. He had a little bit part. I don't remember him at all. Everybody asks me if I do. So I say, "Oh, sure!" to make them happy. *(laughing)*

Has Anybody Seen My Gal's *Blaisdell clan bids adieu to their anonymous benefactor. The farewell is enacted by (left to right) William Reynolds, Larry Gates, Rock Hudson, Lynn, Piper Laurie, Gigi Perreau and Charles Coburn.*

Bari returned to playing someone her own age in "The Other Woman," an episode of *Schaefer Century Theatre*, the NBC-TV anthology. The show filmed in June 1952, going on to be aired September 9. Much to Lynn's relief, she had not been cast as the title character; instead she portrayed a wife who suspected her husband (Douglas Kennedy) of infidelity.

The title role did go to Bari in *Boss Lady*, her second television series. The NBC sitcom was lensed in Hollywood during the summer of 1952 by Jack Wrather Productions. Lynn was Gwendolyn Allen, the gorgeous CEO of Hillendale Homes. Second-banana chores went to Lee Patrick, as Gwen's gal Friday. The stolid Glenn Langan (Bari's *Margie* costar) played Hillendale's amorous general manager, Jeff Standish. Much was made of Jeff's having to take orders from Gwen. Sexist humor of the day surfaced everywhere in each episode — involving Jeff, Gwen's clients and her doddering father (Nicholas Joy), the titular head of Hillendale. Against an onslaught of macho bravado, Ms. Allen carried on in an efficient and assertive manner. Most of her productivity, though, seemed to be based in her ability to zing barbs at her doubters. Needless to say, *Boss Lady* was more typical than topical. The show, a summer replacement for *Fireside Theatre*, premiered July 1, 1952. No ratings sensation, it would not be picked up as a thirty-nine week series. Lynn wouldn't be disheartened by this — something that reflected itself in her recollections of the sitcom.

The woman I played was the head of a big construction company. She was always reading the *Wall Street Journal* and talking to her stockbrokers. She was doing everything that women usually weren't, at the time. Other than that, there was no point to it. It lasted thirteen weeks. *(laughing)* I was amazed when they hired Glenn; I thought they were going to get a comic. His character was supposed to be a brash guy, a young Bob Hope. But they had very funny ideas about what was correct.

They made it on the same lot as *My Little Margie*. We shared our stage with another show. Each of us was to use it for three-and-a-half days. Well, the other company bowed out and we had to work the full week — doing *two* shows! I want to tell you, if I've ever worked hard, that was it. They worked our asses off. It was a real mess.

Jack Wrather, bless him, and his wife, Bonita Granville, produced *Boss Lady*. She was about to have a baby and came in every day saying, "If it wasn't for this stomach, *I'd* be playing the part." I once said to her, "Bonita, I wish to God *you* were!" She was furious. Mr. Wrather, the great moneybags, was such a miser! I told him that he had to publicize this thing. He'd say to me, "Oh, yes," and we'd have only one little snippet in *The Hollywood Reporter*. He was even charging us for the phone calls we made home when we had to say, "We won't be home for dinner; we're working late." My God! His mother used to come in with this big, black bagful of dough at the end of the week and pay everybody. Isn't that fun? He was a Texas millionaire. Boy *(laughing)*, have they got class!

Boss Lady would end Lynn's days as a television-series star. However, her association with the home screen was far from over. Dozens of TV appearances were to come, the next one being on NBC's *Ford Theatre*. The anthology show reunited

Bari with Cesar Romero in the comic "All's Fair in Love." Lynn played an attractive young mom and Romero, a dashing yet madcap artist. Shot at Columbia in
late 1952, "All's Fair in Love" aired February 26, 1953. Its broadcast prompted
Variety to tag Bari as "one of tele's best actresses."

The ephemeral nature of television — particularly with respect to fare of its
golden age — has made one lose sight of the high regard in which Lynn had

The stars of Ford Theatre's *"All's Fair in Love" (1953): Cesar Romero, June
Vincent and Lynn.*

been held by the medium's critics and general viewership. Tangible proof of this
does exist, though — on the Hollywood Walk of Fame. There, one will come
upon two stars for Lynn Bari: one, honoring her film achievements; the other,
her long-forgotten contributions to TV.

Lynn would spend little time performing in 1953; there would only be a short-term theatrical engagement *(Goodbye, My Fancy)* and her last star turn on radio ("The Third Mother," on CBS's *Stars Over Hollywood)*. She could have been more professionally active — but she'd instead chose to devote the better part of the year to dwelling on her protracted court case against Sid Luft.

Bari had come to further question her ex's earnings, in light of his affiliation with Judy Garland, now his wife. Luft and Garland had recently formed Transcona Enterprises, a company that was planning an extravagant musical remake of *A Star Is Born* (1937). The film would be made in conjunction with Warner Brothers, with whom Transcona had entered into a multi-picture deal. Judy was set to play Hollywood hopeful Esther Blodgett and James Mason, falling star Norman Maine. George Cukor would be signed on as director, with Sid himself in the producer's chair. *A Star Is Born* held an enormous amount of promise, creating tremendous buzz in Tinseltown long before its production.

Lynn was all too aware of Luft's latest project as she expanded her Superior Court suit, which charged that Sid had allocated the bulk of his community earnings to Garland. Bari's lawyers, S.S. Hahn and Lloyd Saunders, termed this action a "double shuffle." Specifically, they were voicing Lynn's claim that Luft, as Garland's personal manager and business partner, was already "much richer" as a result of Transcona's agreement with Warners. Taking everything into account, Bari reasoned he was entitled to half of his wife's income, as community property. Lynn estimated Sid's yearly income at $100,000.

Bari's revised lawsuit sought the establishment of a $50,000 trust fund for Johnny, to insure his "support and college education." Lynn alleged that Luft had agreed to set up such a fund in the wake of their divorce but, afterwards, "he refused and still refuses to do so." She charged that Sid would "dissipate" his money by "reckless spending on horses and living." Bari also asked for retroactive payment of alimony, based on Luft's perceived income. This amendment related to a stipulation in their 1951 divorce decree, which entitled Lynn to ten percent of Luft's net income.

The suit was in and out of the courts for months. During this time Bari, Luft and Garland were recalled to the stand to give additional testimony. All three appeared in Domestic Relations Court on September 11, 1953 — the final day of the trial.

In his closing argument, Luft's attorney claimed his client had lost more than he had earned the previous year, due to certain business ventures. He then stated, "Ten per cent of nothing is nothing."

Superior Judge Elmer Doyle said the only legal question was whether Lynn was receiving ten percent of Luft's income — in addition to the monthly $500 alimony and child-support payments Sid had been ordered to make. Weighing the evidence, Doyle voided Bari's action and dismissed the case.

Judge Doyle's decision was a crushing blow to Lynn. The amount of time, thought and money she had invested in the trial had been disproportionate, leaving her financially strapped and completely enervated. The only thing her legal actions had netted her was a stack of unflattering press clippings. Bari was sickened by the entire experience and became depressed. Out of this sadness, however, came a new awareness about her ever-present, self-destructive need for personal friction. This realization somehow caught her short and she responded to it frenetically. Wanting to stamp out all the discord in her life, she abruptly put an end to her relationship with her mother.

September 11, 1953; Lynn confers with her lawyer, S.S. Hahn, in Los Angeles'
Domestic Relations Court. COURTESY OF PHOTOFEST, INC.

Lynn and Marge had gone through countless ups and downs the past several years. Bari had found an ally in her mother during her divorce. From there, Marge once again became a dominant presence in her life. Lynn hadn't been overly bothered by this at first. Her mother had been very supportive of her career aspirations and she'd treated Johnny in an exemplary manner. She had also been given to sprightliness, smoothing out disconcerting moments with an upbeat spin on things. There had, however, been times when Marge's controlling and intrusive nature led to minor blowups between mother and daughter. Gradually, the arguments became more heated, with Marge now greeting Lynn with suspicion and contempt. It was obvious to Bari that a return to boozing had been the cause of her mother's change in behavior. She was soon losing patience with Marge almost every time they had contact, which was all too often. Tensions were flying everywhere when Lynn initiated her alimony suit and the two women came to be at constant loggerheads. Quite irrationally, they both went on to use the devastating verdict as a vehicle for further antagonism. Their situation reached a point of no return on Christmas Day, 1953.

Bari would acknowledge that a final break with her mother had occurred on this day, but she preferred to keep its specifics to herself. However, Eugenie Fisher offers this recollection:

> EUGENIE FISHER: "It was Christmastime and our son Jay was a baby. Marge had made plans to spend some time with Peggy in Beverly Hills. She had been living with us for over three years; and, in all that time, I had never seen any of the bad things about her.
>
> "John had been given this cachet of booze as presents — you know, a man in business always gets these glitzy packages of booze for the holidays. I placed them under our tree. Later, I noticed they were gone! I knew the background enough to forewarn John, because he was about to bundle his mother up in the car and take her into town to see Peggy. *(Laughing)* I said, 'John, I think some of those packages are gone under the tree.' He went back into Marge's quarters. I could hear him talking to her.
>
> "And she came out like a wrath! That was the *first time* I had seen that part of her. She had been nipping, and she had enough there to get her started. She came at me, because she knew who the source was of this accusation. She went into this diatribe of the most *foul* language. *(Laughing)* She had concocted this story about what I was and where I had been. And that I had been a streetwalker in Long Beach — she knew all about that. And I used to hang out at the bars there. *(Laughing)* Well, the whole thing was so ludicrous that I started to laugh. Well, that wasn't good either. So, with that, John got her into the car. When he came home, I said to him, 'We've got a child to raise; and if this is what he's

going to be subjected to — I don't want this. I just will not have this in my house.'

"I don't think that more than a day or so had passed when Peggy called and asked John to remove his mother from her house. Apparently, all hell had broken loose over there.

"So, John and Peggy put their heads together and decided that it was time that Marge should be responsible for herself. She had had her day and she wasn't making life any better for herself or for us."

Within weeks, John found his mother an apartment in Manhattan Beach, CA. Marge would live in it the rest of her life. Lynn would never visit her there.

Bari professed she was at peace with how she had dealt with Marge. However, her malaise continued and her career was marked by inactivity during the early months of 1954. She finally got her act together in the spring, looking fit and raring to go.

Nearly two years had passed since Lynn had worked at Universal on *Has Anybody Seen My Gal*. Her contributions to the film had not been forgotten by the studio, who were now interested in engaging her on a consistent basis. Bari was very pleased by this attention and made this known. Universal responded with a film offer, the first of many acting jobs to which they would assign her. Lynn's association with the company would be an enduring one, lasting through 1961.

I did an awful lot with Universal. They asked me to go under contract at the same time Anne Baxter and Lana [Turner] were there [in the mid-to-late 1950s]. I should have; but the shrink I was married to was taking care of somebody who just had a nervous breakdown from working there. So he said, "I'd advise you not to do it. From what they've told me, it's really gruesome." I was mad at Lew Wasserman [the head of MCA, who'd purchase Universal in 1958] anyway. He was my agent when I left Fox. He told me that if I left the studio, he'd have me making a hundred-and-fifty 'G's a picture, which was *a lot* of money then. And I said, "Fine." So when I *did* leave, I phoned him immediately — and he wouldn't take my call! He was a crazy man. He would have gone to bed with the devil; it didn't matter to him. He really was *quite* a man.

Anyway, I was out at Universal *all* the time, doing hour and half-hour television shows. They would send you a script and ask, "Do you want to do it?" And, naturally, you'd say, "Yes."

In the early days, you had to furnish your own costumes! The first show they gave me to do was a half-hour one where I had *seventeen* wardrobe changes! *(laughing)* I asked, "Where do I go for the clothes?" They said, "Wear your own." I said, "Oh, my God … will somebody help me get them over?" All they said was, "Well, the wardrobe girl will meet you at the set."

I played a very rich woman who was only interested in her home and ignores her husband. Finally, the walls began to talk to her. With seventeen changes, I'd be on one set where I had to open a door; then they'd say, "Cut!" — and now it's supposed to be the next day. I'd have to change my clothes and come through the door in another dress. My God, I was so tired by the time I got home from that thing. I told them the next time I either wanted to be in a bathing suit or on an island where there were no stores! *(laughing)*

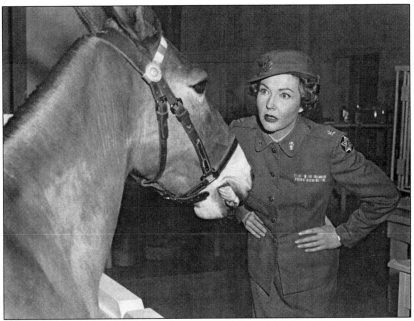

Major Louise Simpson (Lynn) goes head-to-head with Frances the Talking Mule in Francis Joins the WACS *(1954).*

Bari certainly didn't have trouble keeping track of her wardrobe in *Francis Joins the WACS* (1954); the Universal feature saw her practically glued into a starched military uniform. She portrayed Major Louise Simpson in this, the fifth entry in the popular comedy series about Francis the Talking Mule. Donald O'Connor played Francis's two-legged chum, the naïve Peter Stirling, and Chill Wills' voice anthropomorphized the mule into a decidedly salty being. *Francis Joins the WACS* had ex-soldier Peter recalled to active duty and mistakenly assigned to a WAC base, where the talking one got him into much hot water. Broad and predictable, the comedy was nonetheless merrily paced, with a few good laughs along the way. A fair share of the humor was at the expense of the strident Major Simpson. Somehow, Lynn managed to keep a straight face as she interacted with the mule and issued directives to a very odd group of *WACS*. Her underlings: Julie Adams, Mamie Van Doren, ZaSu Pitts, Mara Corday, Joan Shawlee and Allison Hayes. These six actresses appeared to have been quite a handful for Bari.

When you're working with a bunch of women *(laughing)*, it's kind of rough at times.

An infinitely more sober experience came to Lynn with a documentary on Israel that she and Lloyd Nolan narrated. The Universal release was a short subject, directed by Frederick de Cordova and made about the time the *Francis*

Lynn performs a charade on a 1954 episode of Pantomime Quiz. *Seated on couch are (left to right) Jeff Donnell, Richard Erdman and James Lydon. Behind them is series host Mike Stokey.*

movie was in production. Both Bari and Nolan donated their salaries for this project to an Israeli charity.

Lynn was then cast in an episode of *Viceroy Star Theatre*, an upcoming anthology series being produced for CBS-TV by the MCA subsidiary, Revue Studios. *Viceroy* presented Bari in the suspenseful original teleplay, "I'll Never Know When" (aired July 30, 1954). The show was all hers. She played Millie Karns, a young widow afflicted with a disease that was assumed to be not only incurable but terminal. Despondent, Millie hires a hit man to put her out of her misery at an unsuspecting moment. Hysteria sets in when her doctors tell her a new serum has been developed — and she will live after all. Abetted by an ingenious story, Lynn made "I'll Never Know When" exceptional television viewing.

Less remarkable — but ultimately more remunerative — was Bari's semi-regular gig on *Pantomime Quiz*, also for CBS. Lynn began with the game show that summer, playing something akin to charades with other celebrities. Her sharp mind and quick wit were clearly in evidence here and she came off vivaciously.

Bari's élan helped see her through the wacky *Abbott and Costello Meet the Keystone Kops* (1955), made at Universal during August-September 1954. The picture was a slapstick Hollywood satire set in 1912. It featured, in cameos, three men associated with the Keystone Kops silent comedies: producer-director Mack Sennett and actors Hank Mann and Heinie Conklin. Lynn was silent-screen vamp Leota Van Cleef. A real shady lady, Leota was in cahoots with conman

A tense yet humorous scene involving Abbott and Costello Meet the Keystone Kops' *four principals (left to right: Bud Abbott, Lou Costello, Fred Clark and Bari).*

Joseph Gorman (Fred Clark) — aka filmmaker Sergei Toumanoff — in the bamboozling of two knuckleheads (Bud Abbott and Lou Costello). The chicanery at hand found Bari playing straight woman to her three male costars. However, she interacted with them in a campy way, with extravagant line readings complementing her overly-theatrical wardrobe.

Lynn had previously worked with Abbott and Costello on a 1943 broadcast of their radio show. This first teaming had left Bari with warm feelings toward the duo. *Keystone Kops* changed her take on Bud and Lou, but she did enjoy making the film.

I loved the clothes in that one. *(Laughing)* Wasn't I elegant? I hung out with Fred Clark, who was a lovely man. Although they were very nice, Abbott and Costello hardly ever spoke to us. They played gin rummy all the time. It was very serious, and they were playing for an awful lot of money; thousands of dollars,

Lynn, as the underhanded Leota Van Cleef, in Abbott and Costello Meet the Keystone Kops *(1955).*

every day. They never spoke or suggested bits. The director [Charles Lamont] would tell them what to do and they'd do it — of course, improvising a little. I thought they'd be pals, laughing and joking around. But they had absolutely nothing in common with each other — except the gin game.

Bari bade the card sharks farewell and went on to costar with the genteel Ann Harding in "A Visit from Evelyn," a *Lux Video Theatre* drama, aired October 14. *Lux* had undergone numerous changes since Lynn had last been on the anthology. No longer live, it had relocated to Hollywood, switched networks (CBS to NBC) and was now a sixty-minute show. The extended format certainly worked in Bari and Harding's favor, allowing them to flesh out their complicated relationship in "A Visit from Evelyn." Lynn played the title character, a woman possessed with a hatred for a fellow college alumna (Harding) who'd become a best-selling author.

Bari had made a decision to recharge her batteries once her visit to *Lux* was over. Her workload lessened substantially during the final months of 1954, as she devoted more time to Johnny and her recreational interests, which included tennis, swimming and painting.

There was much pleasantness in Lynn's life when autumn drew to a close. She was, however, growing restless. Rambling about her flat, she came in touch with something about herself: her loneliness. Bari hadn't been involved with anyone since divorcing Sid Luft. None of the men she'd dated had seemed to satisfy her needs. All had ultimately been dismissed by her as "jerks." The majority of them probably hadn't been, instead being nice guys in pursuit of a sound relationship — not Lynn's speed, in other words.

Bari's estrangement from her mother had also contributed to her sense of aloneness. Still, she steadfastly refused to communicate with her. Marge was disheartened by this, although she herself would dare not make a move toward reconciliation. The two women would maintain second-hand contact through conversations with Eugenie and John Fisher. There was also a financial connection, with Lynn and her brother sharing in their mother's support.

Bari would never resolve her feelings about Marge. Had she been able to fully confront her own fears and motivations, she might have learned to accept her mother for whom she was and moved beyond negative people and situations. This wouldn't happen. So, by banishing Marge from her life, Lynn only freed herself up to play victim to yet another tormentor.

March 1956; CBS-TV issues this portrait of Lynn Bari to promote her appearance in the Climax! *series presentation of "An Episode of Sparrows."*

CHAPTER FOURTEEN

ENTER: THE SHRINK

1954 came to an end with Lynn at a New Year's Eve party. The event was hosted by actress Anne Shirley and her screenwriter husband, Charles Lederer. The Lederers were close friends of Bari's. Both felt she needed a man in her life and they used their fete as a means to introduce her to someone whom they thought might interest her. His name was Nathan K. Rickles. Psychiatry was his profession and he worked out of Beverly Hills, where he treated many of the film colony's A-list families. A tall and slender man, Dr. Rickles was fifteen years Lynn's senior. Bari was taken with him immediately.

> EUGENIE FISHER: "I'll never forget…Peggy called me and said, 'I have met the kindest, nicest man I've ever met in my whole life.' That's what she felt. And Rick [Rickles] came across to her as that kind of person: educated, established and respectable; not a 'Hollywood person.' And he had that demeanor — plus a kind of unctuous professional voice. I was impressed that he was a psychiatrist and, as the eldest son, had helped to put his brothers through college."

A mutual attraction existed between Lynn and Nathan Rickles, one which quickly bonded them into a serious relationship. The two were intellectual equals who appeared to have much to offer one another. Rickles, unlike Bari's previous husbands, was a man of means. His wealth negated any chance that he might use her as a meal ticket. Additionally, it represented something which Lynn herself had found to be appealing. She also admired the fact that the psychiatrist, like herself, was rearing a child on his own; he had custody of his daughter, Rena, who was a few years older than John Luft. Rickles raised the girl protectively and with devotion — mirroring the ways in which he was now treating Bari. The doctor was captivated by Lynn's beauty, intelligence and no-nonsense take on the entertainment world. While squiring her about town, it became apparent to him that she knew practically everyone in Hollywood and was well-liked by most in her industry.

In the spring of 1955, Rickles proposed marriage to Lynn — an offer which she readily accepted. She was soon walking on air, made happy by the thought of sharing her life with an estimable gentleman who could provide her with a sense of security.

EUGENIE FISHER: "I think that Rick did love her. I think they were both in love, in their own way."

The two planned a summer wedding. Bari had to fulfill a slew of television commitments before the event. Her TV work had been nonstop since January, encompassing more than a half-dozen guest shots on various series. In May

William Bishop and Lynn in "Hour of Nightmare," a July 1955 episode of television's Science Fiction Theatre. *The show was one among a cluster of home-screen entertainments on which Bari worked in the months preceding her third walk down the aisle.*

alone, she'd appear on three shows. Two of these would rank among her best home-screen appearances. The first would have her pulling out all the stops as a grasping wife in "Stake My Life," the May 5 episode of ABC's *Pepsi-Cola Playhouse* anthology. Two weeks later, she'd make the most of another unflattering role, that of the selfish daughter-in-law in the *Lux Video Theatre* presentation of "Make Way for Tomorrow." The drama, a remake of the classic 1937 Paramount tearjerker, would find real-life husband and wife Ernest Truex and Sylvia Field playing Lynn's neglected elders and her old Fox costar, Michael Whalen, in the part of her misguided husband.

Bari continued performing without a break up until her nuptials, now set for August 30. After filming TV shows that would air in the autumn, she returned to the stage. A brief Midwest tour was followed by a Pasadena Playhouse engagement, in the witty *King of Hearts*. Lynn starred as Dunreath Henry, a role Cloris Leachman had originated on Broadway the previous year. Bari very much enjoyed doing the show, its comedy in keeping with her currently light-hearted disposition.

Lynn was seemingly all aglow for her marriage ceremony, which took place at the Beverly Hills home of the bridegroom's brother, Dr. George Rickles (also a psychiatrist). Municipal Judge Sidney Kaufman performed the nondenominational service (Nathan Rickles was Jewish, as were Bari's two former husbands). Louella Parsons covered the wedding in the August 31 edition of the *Los Angeles Examiner:*

> "In the presence of a few close friends, Lynn Bari, well-known actress, last night became the bride of Dr. Nathan Rickles, Beverly Hills psychiatrist, whom she met last New Year's Eve at the home of Mr. and Mrs. Charles Lederer.
>
> "Lynn, a statuesque beauty who has played young character parts, received considerable publicity during her legal entanglements with Sid Luft, Judy Garland's husband, to whom she was once married. She has a son, John, 6½, by Luft.
>
> "Friends of Lynn, who has been unhappy for so long, are delighted over this marriage, and all those who have met the bridegroom speak highly of him.
>
> "After a brief honeymoon, Dr. and Mrs. Rickles will make their home in Beverly Hills."

Bari would be wedded to Rickles for seventeen years — a long union, by Hollywood standards. The duration of their togetherness wouldn't, however, have any bearing on the quality of the couple's relationship — and it was with great displeasure upon which Bari looked back at her third marriage. Apparently, the doctor had caused her annoyance from the time of their engagement.

He insisted that we marry, but he could never make up his mind about where. First, we were going to get married in Chicago when I was doing something there. Then, he wanted to go down to Florida and get married at his brother's house. Then, no, we wouldn't go there; we'd go to Seattle and do it at his family's house. We finally got back to Beverly Hills. I was putting all of my furniture in storage, but he had it sent over to his house instead. He'd put the leftovers in his garage — and had *given* half of it away to his ex-stepdaughter or something. I was never so furious in my life! And here I am ... so, we got married there.

Beverly Hills, August 30, 1955; Lynn and Nathan Rickles, minutes after the couple had become united in wedlock.

> I had had an apartment in Beverly Hills with Johnny. He [Rickles] lived nearby, with his daughter, in a little broken-down bungalow; it was one of the first ones built there. Johnny and I moved in with them. Then we took an apartment. And later we bought a beautiful home in Beverly Hills.

Lynn voluntarily took a hiatus from her career at the outset of the marriage. It was then her husband's hope that she would make acting a secondary concern. Rickles did, though, revel in Bari's celebrity and he was proud of her professional achievements. Lynn felt she was receiving mixed messages from the psychiatrist but she wasn't particularly bothered by this when she decided to go on a work sabbatical. Late 1955 found her busying herself with setting up the new apartment, a capacious and sunny dwelling. During this time she also became embedded in Beverly Hills social scene — a sphere of activity to which she hadn't previously wanted to belong.

1956 dawned with Lynn fast tiring of her rich young hausfrau role. She longed to be performing and made it clear to her husband that she was going back to work. This decision was the source of considerable dissension between the couple; but Bari had made up her mind and that was that. To show who was boss, Rickles countered in a way that would diminish his wife's independence; he apparently insisted she should place her future earnings aside, using only the money he would give her for her personal needs. A very reluctant Lynn went along with this arrangement.

Bari resumed her career with vehemence. She was now being represented by the Milt Rosner agency, who threw themselves into finding her work. Much would come her way. Leading things off were several television gigs, the most notable airing on March 29. Lynn starred in "An Episode of Sparrows," a live broadcast of the CBS suspense/mystery anthology, *Climax!* "Sparrows" brought the hour-long series into a particularly affecting realm, telling the story of Love-joy Mason, a poverty-stricken girl headed for delinquency. The youngster was portrayed by ten-year-old Patty McCormack, who was about to recreate her Broadway turn as the demonic Rhoda Penmark in the film version of *The Bad Seed* (1956). "Sparrows" also featured Brandon de Wilde, J. Carrol Naish and Jesse Royce Landis. Bari was cast as Mrs. Combie, the woman who changed Love-joy's life for the better, showering her with tenderness and enlightening her to the beauty of nature. Lynn loved enacting this sympathetic character and "An Episode of Sparrows" would come to be her favorite TV credit.

Perhaps Patty McCormack herself had proved to be enlightening to Bari on the "Sparrows" set, for Lynn would soon be heading the East Coast tour of *The Bad Seed*; she'd be stepping into the Tony Award-winning shoes of Nancy Kelly, as Rhoda's distraught mother, Christine Penmark. Kelly, like McCormack, had had to curtail her stretch in the play's national tour because she was due to repeat her role on film. So, as one erstwhile Fox star would become increasingly more hysterical before the Warner Brothers' cameras, another would be doing exactly the same on stage.

Bari hit the road with *The Bad Seed*, reaching the Northeast in the summer of 1956. She went on to be joined there by Nathan Rickles, who'd set aside his August vacation to be with her. The doctor was in Lynn's company when her show played upstate New York. Bari's dear friend, William Roerick, lived in the vicinity and he invited her and Rickles to a day at his farmhouse.

> WILLIAM ROERICK: "Lynn had first visited me there shortly after we did *Light Up the Sky*. It's the oldest house in the [Hudson] Valley, built in 1736. I'd lived there for years without running water, electricity or a telephone. And I lived in a *total* mess — as I still do! *(laughing)* Some people approve of my style, but then, thinking of Rick, I tidied up the kitchen-dining room. The room has a big Shaker counter to work at and a sofa. The real kitchen is a galley and has a fridge, stove and sink. By this time, I think I had running water. *(laughing)*
>
> "Well, the moment Lynn and Rick came in, I saw the look on Rick's face as he glanced around at the peeling ceiling, the huge fireplace with ashes a foot deep in them, and piles of stuff all over the place. After having been traumatized by the look of everything, he was finally able to open his mouth and speak without nervously looking around. He began to pour a little liquor when my old neighbor-friend Annette dropped by. She said, 'Why, Bill, you've tidied up the room!' *(Laughing)* I could see Lynn amused and Rick thrown back into astonishment.
>
> "I always thought that Rick was a little common and pretentious. He was always being the 'successful doctor' with us. He was probably from a very simple background. But he had made it. And making it consisted of having the right car, belonging to the right club, having the right clothes and a big, handsome home.
>
> "Rick was not strong on humor, which is always hard, but he was very bright and pulled himself up and made a fortune. Beverly Hills was certainly the right town for him to practice in."

Barbara Whiting, Lynn's *Home Sweet Homicide* costar, also knew Rickles. The perspective she maintains on him differs from William Roerick's.

> BARBARA WHITING: "He was a charming man — to me. But I was a client. At that point I was twenty or twenty-one and thought that I needed a little psychiatric help. *(laughing)* So, on a lark, I went to another of Lynn's husbands, Dr. Rickles. I saw him twice at his office on Wilshire Boulevard. I didn't tell my mother. I wanted to say [in therapy] how abused I was as a child and everything, which was not true at all; I had the most wonderful upbringing! I said to him, 'I've just got to get my life in order!' *(laughing)* He said, 'That's the silliest thing I've ever heard of!' He said, 'You just have to say,

'I want to be on my own." So, finally, my mother let me move out of the house — after meeting him.

"As I say, I only saw him two or three times professionally. He figured I was cured. I finally was able to say a few nasty things about life and then he said, 'Now, just get on with it! There's nothing wrong with you.'

"Then I used to see him over at the Beverly Hills Tennis Club all the time. He knew I knew Lynn. I'd go to the tennis club and see Dr. Rickles playing tennis and she'd be there with him. I didn't see Lynn socially because there was an age difference between us. But I could count on her being wonderful to me. You always could."

Bari had concluded her run with *The Bad Seed* by Labor Day. She remained on the East Coast for a short engagement in *A Roomful of Roses*, another play centered on a troubled mother-daughter relationship. From there, it was back to Los Angeles and *The Women of Pitcairn Island* (1957) — a film Lynn would soon want to put out of her mind. The widescreen 20th Century-Fox release was an incredibly far-fetched saga about the widows and children of the crew who'd been immortalized on screen in *Mutiny on the Bounty* (1935). Bari had the dubious leading-lady honors, portraying the wife of the late Fletcher Christian, Queen Maimiti Christian. How Maimiti had come to be a queen was anybody's guess, but she did rule the island on which those famous mutineers had become shipwrecked. Her chief concern seemed to be keeping Pitcairn's frisky teens in line. However, she did become more challenged when a band of unsavory sailors wound up beached on her isle. Playing the leader of this corrupt lot was Lynn's *Man from Texas* costar, James Craig. Former Fox ingénue Arleen Whelan supported as Maimiti's nemesis, the provocative Hutia. The role of the queen's son, Thursday October Christian, went to hunky John Smith.

Lynn, making a striking impression — of sorts — as the sovereign figure of The Women of Pitcairn Island.

Bari's appearance in *The Women of Pitcairn Island* was ludicrous, to say the very least. She was dressed throughout in a sarong, her head topped with an unflatteringly long black wig, adorned with flowers. Stomping about in this wardrobe, she resembled a leonine, over-the-hill pin-up girl. At least her comportment was in keeping with *Pitcairn Island's* unique cinematic tone — which could best be described as a beach party-women's prison hybrid. The film is, arguably, one of the worst ever made. Lynn herself saw justification for this.

Oh God. And, of course, this dear "friend" of mine — a terrible lady who shall remain nameless — made it into a cult movie by showing it around at

Queen Maimiti Christian (Lynn) admonishes her teenage subjects in The Women of Pitcairn Island *(1957). Standing next to the queen is her strapping blond son, Thursday October (John Smith).*

private parties. There were even little snips about this in the papers.

I was sent the script and thought it was good for a quick picture — three weeks. I asked my husband to read it. He said, "I think it's very good. You've got the lead and they'll probably take you on a nice location. You can also get my daughter a part in it." *That's* what he was *really* thinking about. So I had to wangle a role for his daughter — and one for Johnny, too; I couldn't leave him out.

We were supposed to go on location. I pictured Catalina *(laughing)*, with the water around us. Instead, we went to a place called Bronson Canyon, in Hollywood! Nothing but hot, dirty bushes and rocks — God, an awful place. We worked from early sunshine until it got dark. The box lunches were dreadful. I don't even remember who the director was. I just remember that the production man was the most *lecherous* old *bum* I've ever met in my life.

I was Fletcher Christian's wife, whom he had left on the island. My son was played by John Smith. I think he was about four years younger than I was — *(laughing)* oh God, you can't imagine. Jimmy Craig was a very handsome guy. But, after the first day, he always had a hangover. *(laughing)* He said, "I hate this crap!" He was fooled, too. We both gave a performance that's as good as you can give under the circumstances.

I couldn't believe what was happening. I had the last shot: we're all going to be killed and I'm sitting by myself, writing the book for everyone to see after we're dead. As I'm winding up the picture, these guys start moving out all the furniture around me! I mean, they're folding tents while the scene is going on! Finally, I put my pen down and said, "We might as well turn the camera on the people who are removing this stuff — it will give the audience a better idea of what we're going through." I've never seen such a thing!

Going from the ridiculous to the sublime, Lynn costarred with Ruth Hussey in the television adaptation of John Van Druten's stage hit, *Old Acquaintance*. The show was broadcast by *Lux Video Theatre* on November 29, 1956. Bari was quite amusing as the volatile dime-store novelist, Millie Drake. Her role had been played on film in 1943 by Miriam Hopkins. In turn, Hussey was Bette Davis's successor in the part of the placid Kit Marlowe, a renowned authoress — and the object of Millie's intense jealousy. *Lux's* hour-long format necessitated a scissoring of Van Druten's original work, specifically the elimination of several subordinate characters. However, nearly all of Millie and Kit's scenes together remained intact — as did the subplot involving the former's daughter, Deirdre (Joan Evans).

Lynn was left immensely satisfied by "Old Acquaintance," an assignment that capped ten straight months of work. At this point she was a bit worn-out and eagerly anticipating some downtime. The holidays came and went, with Nathan Rickles delighted to have his wife at home.

Long periods of repose were not to Bari's liking, though, and by February she was in frequent communication with her agents. Rickles was very disconcerted by this. He had married Lynn under the assumption that she would build her life around him, only working on a sporadic basis. Things had not evolved this way and Bari had once again become a full-time actress — one whose mounting work schedule had made her increasingly less available to her new husband. Lynn was aware her professional choices had brought with them negative marital consequences. However, she also realized that Rickles had been benefiting by her remaining in the spotlight; she sensed herself having come into play as a showpiece in his social and medical aspirations.

Lynn claimed the psychiatrist was at once presenting her on a pedestal and putting forth great effort to undermine her self-worth. She said he belittled her talent and questioned her attachment to her craft, which he deemed to be neurotic. Demeaning remarks, however, had no ill effect on Bari's creative ambitions.

Her career drive would continue to frustrate Rickles — leading to a mega-show-down in Beverly Hills.

The fabric of Lynn's marriage would change dramatically in 1957. The shift began in the early spring, when the doctor found out his wife had signed on to Universal's *Damn Citizen!* (1958). The film was a brutal, fact-based drama about political corruption in Louisiana. Bari was set to play Pat Noble, a society gal with very questionable affiliations. Lynn liked her part and thought Stirling

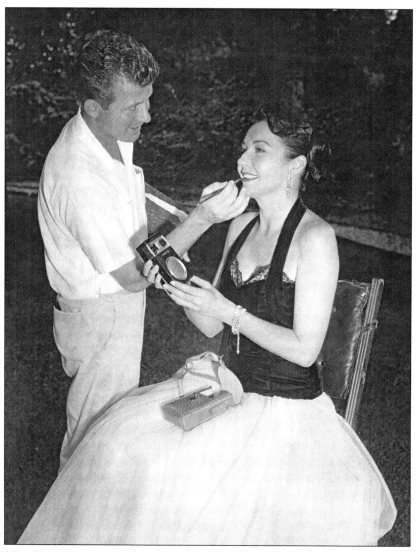

New Orleans, 1957; make-up artist Bud Westmore and Lynn, in high spirits during the on-location shoot of Damn Citizen! *(1958).*

Silliphant's script first-rate. Also appealing to her was the fact that *Damn Citizen!* would be shot on location. Her husband was not nearly as pleased by this — in truth, he hit the roof; possibly with good reason, he took Lynn's far-away movie commitment as a personal rejection. Mollifying Rickles was not uppermost in Bari's mind at this point, but her picture's imminent start date was — so she hurriedly packed her bags and got out of town. *Damn Citizen!* would turn out to be a most agreeable experience for her.

That was fun because we did it in New Orleans.

Lynn developed an easy camaraderie with costars Keith Andes, Maggie Hayes, Ed Platt and Gene Evans. The thirty-four-year-old Evans palled around with Bari off-set; the two whooped it up in the French Quarter and hit all the hot jazz clubs on Basin Street.

All the fun-and-games came to an abrupt end as soon as Lynn returned to her husband in Los Angeles. Already angered by her Southern sojourn, Rickles grew apoplectic when Bari walked through the door and informed him that she was about to begin a stage tour of *A Clearing in the Woods*. The scene was not a pretty one. A climactic moment had the doctor presenting to Lynn an ultimatum: she would either quit show business or their marriage was over. Thinking fast — and not wanting to forgo her cushy lifestyle — Bari admitted that her priorities had been out-of-kilter. She then promised to drastically reduce her workload. Her words seemed to appease Rickles. After much intense discussion it was agreed she could follow through with *A Clearing in the Woods*, to which she had already made a summer commitment.

The play, an adult drama with music, was proving to be a successful road attraction after its brief run on Broadway earlier in the year. Its original company had starred Kim Stanley as Virginia, the role Bari was now portraying on the West Coast.

Lynn was rewarded by *A Clearing in the Woods*. It would have been her preference to have segued into another show; however, that was not to be. There was now a marital obligation that had to be fulfilled: her fall and winter were to be reserved for housewifely activities. Bari would press on with this, not working at all for six months. The half-year ahead would be but the first of several extended periods in which her career would be placed on the back burner for the sake of placating her husband. Lynn would shudder at the mention of this.

It makes me ill to even talk about it.

Lynn's initial foray into enforced domesticity was centered more on her husband than her nine-year-old son. John Luft was not residing with her during the week, for he was enrolled at Chadwick, an exclusive California boarding school.

[Chadwick was] a *beautiful* school down in the Palos Verdes, where the kids stay for the week and you pick them up on the weekends.

According to Bari, she had sent Johnny to Chadwick the previous year because he had not been doing particularly well in the local public school he had then been attending. She hated being separated from her son, but he was flourishing at Chadwick and she saw no good reason to transfer him to a day school.

For Lynn, Johnny's absence only served to intensify the effects of the "house-bound" arrangement she had struck with Rickles. The four walls closed in on her quickly, making very clear how hard it was for her to carry on without the stimulation of performing. This problem would be an ongoing one for Bari, reflecting her inefficiency in dealing with free time constructively.

So, after attending to her household concerns, Lynn spent her days stewing about one thing or another. "Doing lunch" held little interest for her, as did gossiping and shopping for clothes. In short, the daily life of a Beverly Hills matron was something she abhorred. Her evenings often saw her out-and-about as Lynn Bari, wife of Dr. Nathan Rickles. In this guise she proved to be an enlivening presence at many star-studded parties — affairs she could have easily done without. Bari had plenty of old friends and didn't need these gatherings to make new ones. She also wasn't looking to network with people — unlike her husband, who made her his calling card at social events.

Lynn kept in regular phone contact with her girlfriends, but she saw them only intermittently. Most were busy raising families, the majority having long since left the Los Angeles area. Their inaccessibility heightened Bari's longing for the good-fellowship that went with an acting career. Deprived of this interaction, she became something of a loner.

In her solitude, Lynn placed a greater focus on her painting. She took private art lessons and was heartened by her improving work, manifested in brightly-colored landscapes. It was pleasant for her to have a creative outlet but nothing could substitute for acting, which satisfied her soul. Now several months away from performing, she found herself restless, dispirited and lonely.

Bari continued to be estranged from her mother during this period. Any thoughts of reestablishing contact with her — and there were some — were quashed by Rickles. The shrink was unequivocal in his opinion that Marge influenced his wife in a strongly negative way. Lynn couldn't argue with him there.

Bari still harbored tremendous hostility toward Marge — and emulating her was the furthest thing from her mind. However her emotional makeup was a near replication to that of her mother's; low self-esteem and a need for conflict had certainly been handed down from one to the other. And now Lynn would begin to assume another of Marge's characteristics: she'd become a problem drinker.

Bari and liquor had never been a good match. It had always taken very little to make her drunk. When inebriated, she could be a radically different person. Booze tended to unleash her repressed rage — and then the grand people-pleaser could be brutally direct, full of barbed put-downs. Because Lynn had trouble dealing with those who were really injuring her, her boozy anger would frequently be directed at an innocent party. Many had been the time she'd later been remorseful, at the very least realizing she had put her foot in her mouth while drinking. Consequently, she'd tried very hard to curb her liquor consumption and be on her best behavior when in contact with others. She had been, until this point, a controlled drinker, one who'd viewed her mother's alcoholism as a potent reminder of what booze could do to a person.

Marge used alcohol to escape from personal matters she was both unwilling and unable to confront. To a certain degree, Lynn had used her career for this purpose — all the while maintaining the traits of a social drinker who'd occasionally make a fool of herself by imbibing too much. Things were changing now that Bari was without the discipline of work. She began to drink in private — something she'd never done before. The long-range effects of this would prove to be devastating. For the moment, though, Lynn thought she could handle liquor; so she'd occasionally turn to it in her aloneness, as a means of dulling her present pains and disappointments.

Bari's first "retirement" was unwelcome to her, but it was by no means entirely downbeat. Weekends and school vacations revolved around the children (Johnny and Rickles' Rena) and were generally pleasurable. So were her intimate get-togethers with John and Eugenie Fisher. She saw the couple regularly and doted on their little Jay. Lynn also took delight in the children of the girlfriends with whom she sometimes rendezvoused. Her socializing included the company of another old chum, ex-husband Walter Kane. Kane would frequently invite her to be his guest at Las Vegas' Flamingo Hotel, which was owned by his boss, Howard Hughes. Bari would merrily go there, often bringing Eugenie with her.

> EUGENIE FISHER: "Peggy liked Kane and they stayed friends. He was a nice guy. He'd give us a suite at the Flamingo, with champagne. We'd arrive and Peggy would breeze over to the [slot] machines. She'd come back and throw forty dollars on my lap. Money came so easily to her — *(laughing)* she was amazing! She was a lot of fun. Oh, I really treasure those earlier days."

Not as cherished are Eugenie's recollections of Lynn's third husband. She would never become especially close to Rickles, but she'd get along with him well enough. There were, however, certain aspects of her brother-in-law's personality that turned her off — and he'd become less appealing to her with the passage of time.

> EUGENIE FISHER: "I remember he and his brother George would get together and always be talking about investments and real estate. I thought, 'My God, these are psychiatrists and all they do is talk about money!'

"Once, I went over to Rick's house with a girlfriend. He was all over Peggy. It was sort of disgusting — you know, kissing her arms and rubbing her and on and on. He was so unctuous; petting his wife, letting his sister-in-law know that she was being taken care of and adored. After this demonstration, I walked out. The girl I was with had been a model; she was a beautiful, big blonde girl. We got into her Ferrari, and Rick came over to her side and he made a pass at her! And I thought, 'My God, here's this guy with this big show of affection for Peggy!' But he couldn't resist that pass. That absolutely stunned me."

March 1958; Universal Pictures distributes this portrait of Lynn Bari, to coincide with the release of Damn Citizen!

CHAPTER FIFTEEN
TRAUMA

Marital harmony, such as it was, had been restored to the Rickles' home. This had come at no small sacrifice to Lynn, whose conciliatory gestures had made her husband a bit more sympathetic to her professional desires; pleased that Bari had honored her six-month no-work commitment, he saw no reason why she couldn't return to acting on a periodic basis. Not wanting to rock the boat, Lynn proceeded gingerly by taking on but a few short-term assignments in spring 1958.

Bari did a guest stint on *The Red Skelton Show*, broadcast by CBS on April 8. She clowned around with the series' carrottopped star, in one sketch playing Clara Appleby, the henpecking wife of Skelton's recurring George Appleby character. Lynn had a ball working with the comedian, greatly appreciating his good nature and sharp sense of timing. The laughter of Red's studio audience also meant much to her, helping to make her participation on his show an altogether uplifting experience.

June found Bari headlining a limited run of *The World of Robert Burns* in Los Angeles. The theatrical effort assembled numerous works by Burns, the iconic poet of 18th-century Scotland. Lynn took to the stage with a leather-bound script and read Burns' verse with heartfelt emphasis; the poet's romanticism and liberal bent struck a most responsive chord within her.

Bari's association *with The World of Robert Burns* lasted no more than a few weeks, but it left her artistically satiated and better able to go easy on her career for the good of her marriage. Nevertheless, she very much looked forward to the moment being right for her to plunge back into acting — without some of the personal constraints that were currently working against her.

That moment, as it would turn out, wouldn't come anytime soon. Nor were there to be those occasions when Lynn would even fantasize about her career. The dictums of Dr. Rickles would play a part in none of this. Rather, it would be the actions of a former husband — Sid Luft — that would make thoughts of playacting leave Bari's mind for an interminable period.

In the summer of 1958 Lynn became embroiled in a bitter child custody battle that turned her world upside-down. Her December 1950 divorce had granted her sole custody of Johnny — an arrangement that had met with no protests from Luft over the ensuing seven-and-one-half years. Now, however,

Sid was challenging this guardianship decision and taking Bari to court. Lynn would almost be pushed over the edge by thoughts of Luft actually winning his case. The fear was overwhelming but, despite it, she'd be able to summon every ounce of her strength in her attempts to quell her ex and hold on to her son. Five tormented months would be ahead for Bari, finding her in and out of court-rooms — and tabloid headlines.

At this point the financial situations of Bari and Luft were diametric: Lynn's lifestyle was marked by comfort and luxury, while Sid and wife Judy Garland were heavily in debt. Garland had ridden a wave of incredible professional suc-cess since her 1951 comeback; she had firmly reestablished herself as the nation's top female entertainer by virtue of a series of stunning live performances, hit records, a memorable television special, and her electric turn in *A Star Is Born*. There was no denying that Judy's curriculum vitae looked quite impressive on paper — but her career had been sent into a tailspin. Behind this decline had been her constant abuse of prescription drugs and booze; physically and emotionally, she had been in a precarious state several years running. Her various employers had responded to her instability with growing impatience and things began to slip away from her; a TV contract had been broken (resulting in a lawsuit that was still in litigation), recording sessions had been put on hold, and numerous live engagements had been cancelled midway or not even attempted.

Compounding matters was the fact that Garland was currently persona non grata in the motion picture business. *A Star Is Born* had contributed to this. Although Judy and her movie had met with enthusiastic critical approval, the film itself had gone way over budget and had proved to be a box-office disap-pointment. Warner Brothers had been partly to blame for this, but Hollywood had seemed to focus on Garland's troubles — including her producer husband — and what they had perceived to be her unreliability during filming. Taking the Lufts to task, Warners had put an abrupt end to the multi-picture deal they'd entered into with the couple's Transcona Enterprises.

Transcona was a nonentity in 1958, a year that saw Judy and Sid in horren-dous fiscal shape. Back taxes were mounting, as were lawyers' fees and agents' commissions. Also having to be met were household expenses, which involved the upbringing of the couple's young children, Lorna and Joey Luft. Faced with a barrage of monetary responsibilities, an exhausted, overweight and frequently-ill Garland continued performing as best she could. The work was certainly there for her; however, it always remained questionable whether she would be up to fulfilling any given obligation.

Luft was, in many ways, Judy's right arm. In this capacity, he'd expend great effort trying to keep her from completely self-destructing, hoping she might be restored to a condition that would enable her to work. These attempts on his wife's behalf would many times lead to violent quarreling between the two. The tenor of their lives was often frantic, always stressful. The couple's impecuniousness had caused their situation to be extremely pressured, with Sid frequently scrambling for money. To pay the bills, he'd sometimes secure loans from banks or friends. Other occasions would find him gambling on the horses or in crap games.

Luft's maneuverings for cash made possible Garland's July 1958 opening at the Coconut Grove nightclub in Los Angeles. Her two-week engagement there began with Sid arranging a last-minute loan to retrieve her stage wardrobe, costumes that had been in the hands of her creditors. Properly outfitted, Judy went on to play to capacity crowds. Her Coconut Grove gig would be followed by appearances at other major venues, including ones in Las Vegas, Chicago and Miami. These bookings would keep her busy until year's end.

Somewhere in the midst of this activity, Sid Luft had been able to focus his energies on bringing Lynn to court. Bari was a nervous wreck by the time his child custody motion went to trial on Monday, September 29. As her ex's grounds were being presented in Los Angeles Superior Court, she clung to Nathan Rickles, reacting in total disbelief. Luft was claiming that Lynn had shown little affection toward her son, demonstrated by her keeping him enrolled at Chadwick — a boarding school where he was supposedly very unhappy. Allusions about Bari's drinking habits were also being brought forward.

Luft said he saw Johnny once a month and six weeks over each summer. If the ten-year-old were to be entrusted into his overall care, he contended he'd be reared in a healthy environment by both Garland (who was not present at this trial) and himself. Sid said that his and Judy's plan was to place Johnny in a well-regarded day school, his attendance there allowing him more free time — time to be shared with the Lufts and their family (which included twelve-year-old Liza Minnelli, Judy's daughter by director Vincente Minnelli).

Lynn's turn came and she told Superior Judge Wallace L. Ware that she loved her son dearly. She went on to explain why she had chosen to send Johnny to Chadwick two-and-one-half years earlier. She claimed she had discussed the boarding school with Luft well before their son had been transferred there. According to Bari, Sid had been pleased by her selection of Chadwick.

> "So pleased," she added, "that he convinced Miss Garland to send her oldest daughter, Liza, there...which she did...and which school the girl is still attending." *

Lynn's lawyer, Stuart Fischer, stated that the atmosphere of the Luft household was not a particularly serene one in which to raise a child, citing the fact that Garland had recently sued her husband for a divorce. This was dismissed by Sid, who said that there had been an altercation that'd been "just one of those things that could happen to any couple, and we were only separated two weeks." **

The trial had been moving forward quickly. It drew to a close with Judge Ware weighing the custody matter without having consulted the child whose future hung in the balance. Bari wasn't especially disturbed by this, for the evidence

---

* Excerpted from "How to tear apart a little boy," a February 1959 *Modern Screen* article by Hugh Burrell, based on newspaper files, court records and personal discussions with Lynn Bari.

** The *Los Angeles Mirror-News*, September 29, 1958.

presented had left her feeling confident about the outcome of the case. In fact, despite her general upset, she had come to be so certain of a victory that she had decided to refrain from countering with more damaging charges against Luft, relating to his level of concern for their son.*

So, it was with anxious optimism that Lynn awaited Ware's decree. Her ordeal would soon be behind her — she thought.

Then came the verdict: Johnny would be placed into his father's care the following Monday. Bari was at once shocked and grief-stricken.

> "They'll just kill my little boy! They'll ruin him," she cried in a sudden courtroom outburst.**

> "She thinks I eat children for breakfast," Luft laughed to the press shortly afterwards. "He's been in a boarding school ever since he was seven years old and it isn't fair. He doesn't know what a home is like. That's all right for orphans but he's not an orphan. Those people out there [at Chadwick] are merely his custodians. Instead of a mother, he has a house mother. It just isn't fair. I'm going to try to give him a stable, normal life." **

Still in the Superior Court building, Lynn ordered her attorney to file an appeal. Stuart Fischer emerged outside minutes later, in the company of his visibly distraught client and her husband. Bari remained silent as Fisher responded to reporters about the bewildering upshot of the trial:

> "If the judge wasn't satisfied with having the boy in the Chadwick School I think he should have offered the mother the chance of taking the boy into her home and sending him to a nearby school. He didn't even make that offer to her although she testified she would do that if the court so ordered it." **

Bari returned home with Rickles, completely frazzled. She didn't go to her liquor cabinet for solace because, when informed of Luft's action against her, she had made a pact with herself to abstain from drinking entirely. Steadfastly, Lynn would keep to this resolution for some time to come. She had, however, become increasingly more dependent on cigarettes over these past troubled months and was now a full-fledged chain-smoker.

Nothing, though, could pacify Bari in the aftermath of the trial; the fact that she'd be losing custody of her child in seven days left her inconsolable. On Friday, October 3, she drove with Rickles to Chadwick to bring Johnny home for the weekend. With her husband behind the wheel, Bari tried to assume a semblance of composure as they reached the school. She alighted from their car and

* Referred to in the February 1959 *Modern Screen* article, "How to tear apart a little boy."
** The *Los Angeles Mirror-News,* September 29, 1958.

a mask of cheerfulness was there to greet her son. In his dorm room the innocent and perplexed child heard his soft-spoken mother gently break the news to
him. Sometimes her words came haltingly, for she, too, was in a state of confusion about what was transpiring. Fighting back tears, Lynn took Johnny by the
hand as they said their goodbyes to his classmates and teachers. The two then
returned to the dorm, where Bari packed up her boy's belongings. The drive home
was marked by warm conversation and tenderness, the beginning of a weekend
that Lynn and Rickles were determined to make a happy one for Johnny. Lynn
would relate the following to *Modern Screen* (February 1959):

> "It was hard, my heart was breaking inside me, and Rick — who
> has always adored Johnny — was terribly sad, too. But we tried not
> to show it. We never mentioned Monday and what would happen
> then — not Rick, not Johnny, not I. Instead we got up early Satur-
> day and spent all day at the Beverly Hills Club and played tennis
> and had lunch.
>
> "That night we went to a movie. Then the next day, Sunday, we
> took a drive in the morning and then we came back to the apart-
> ment and I prepared dinner. I made all of Johnny's favorites. We
> had an awful lot of fun, laughing, talking — almost forgetting about
> what had happened and what was going to happen.
>
> "After dinner, though, the day seemed to slow down. We went
> into the living room and watched television for a couple of hours.
> And then, before we knew it, it was nighttime. I made a light supper.
> Then I could see Johnny was tired. And I told him it was time to
> get ready for bed.
>
> "He was in bed a little while later, ready to be tucked in, when
> I went into his room to say good night. I noticed, as I walked in,
> that he was looking around the room, almost as though he were
> seeing it for the first time. … Johnny's room was very simple —
> with red Early American wallpaper, rock maple furniture and plain
> twin beds.
>
> "But it must have been very beautiful to Johnny at that moment,
> because he said suddenly, 'Gee, Mom, this is a knockout room. I
> love it.'"

On the morning of Monday, October 6, Bari and Rickles drove Johnny to the
Lufts'. Lynn and her son were met at Judy and Sid's front door by a maid. "Mr.
Luft isn't in right now," the woman told them. "I see…may I see Miss Garland?"
Bari asked. "She isn't up," the servant responded. Lynn had one more question:
"Didn't she know my boy was coming this morning — to live with her and Mr.
Luft?" The maid was silent.*

---

* Incidents and quotes relating to October 6-7, 1958, are derived from the February 1959 *Modern
Screen* article, "How to tear apart a little boy."

Mother and son shared a tearful goodbye: Lynn bent down to kiss Johnny; the two exchanged a few loving words and then clutched one another. After drawing apart, Bari turned around and bolted toward Rickles, awaiting her in their car. She was beside herself during the short trip home, her body trembling and her heart in her throat. Utterly dejected but now not despairing, she vowed to herself then and there that she would get her son back.

The following evening Lynn was with her husband in their living room when the telephone rang. Rickles answered the call, and Bari would later remember:

> "Then he smiled and turned to me and said it was Johnny. I grabbed the phone. But before I could say anything more than hello, I heard my son's voice say, 'I'm so lonely, Mom.' 'What's the matter, Johnny?' I asked. He told me that Judy and his father had left for Las Vegas that day, that Judy had a singing engagement there, that they'd be gone for a few weeks. 'Who's with you, now?' I asked Johnny. 'Just the maids,' Johnny said.
>
> "I tried to talk him into the fact that everything was going to be all right. I told him to do his homework and then watch some television and then, when he got tired, to go to bed.
>
> "'Can you and Daddy Rick come over and watch TV with me at least?' he asked. 'I miss you both. And I miss everybody at school. And I thought that at least maybe you and Daddy Rick could come over and stay with me for a while.'
>
> "I told him no, that we couldn't, that we weren't allowed to do anything like that. Johnny began to cry. He cried so hard that after a while he couldn't talk anymore and he hung up."

Seconds later Lynn was overcome by a desire to head straight over to the Lufts' and take Johnny home with her. Common sense then took hold, with Bari reminding herself that such an action would be in violation of the court order. Instead, she tried to phone her son back. A maid's voice came over the receiver, and Lynn would recall:

> "I asked to speak to my son. 'Is this Mrs. Rickles?' the maid asked. I said, yes, it was. 'I'm sorry,' she said, 'but the boy can't talk to you.' I told her that we'd been talking together only a few minutes earlier. The maid was blunt. 'I have orders,' she said, 'that no calls from you can be put through to the boy — and that he must not call you.' 'What was that?' I asked. 'I have my orders,' the maid said. 'I'm sorry ma'am — truly I am. But that's the way it's got to be.' A few moments later, she hung up. And I stood there now, shocked."

Bari became energized by the unpleasantness of the past two days — specifically, what was going on at the Garland-Luft home and the evidentiary strength it could give to her planned court appeal. She set out to have the custody ruling reviewed straightway, and a second trial was arranged for early November. Working on all cylinders, Lynn sought help wherever she could find it.

I even went to Walter [Kane] and asked him to get Howard [Hughes] to help me. Howard had a whole list of people I was to use.

Autumn 1958; Nathan Rickles appears to be a consoling influence on Lynn, deep in the midst of her custody ordeal.

Howard Hughes and Walter Kane were among the many friends who were extending themselves to Bari during her custody crisis. Her husband, however, was apparently being less supportive — although Lynn was portraying him to the press as a loving and generous man who was holding his wife's hand throughout her ordeal. Rickles' indifference toward Lynn and her situation went on to exhibit itself when she sought additional legal counsel.

> EUGENIE FISHER: "My husband John helped to get her an attorney, Bruce Sumner. Rick didn't want to pay him — and my John was left holding the bag. Rick really was a fink. He looked at himself as far superior to Luft, and went through the motions of appearing the dutiful husband."

Meanwhile, in Manhattan Beach, Marge Fisher was fuming. She was both angered and hurt that Lynn had not called upon her in her moment of need — though she herself hadn't made any attempts at reaching out. Nevertheless, she was keeping track of her daughter's plight as it was playing out in the tabloids and on local TV news programs. Being relegated to viewing Bari's custody drama second-hand miffed Marge to no end; she really wanted to figure into the thunderstorm of publicity generated by Lynn's current problems.

Then, in the most vengeful of ways, Marge went ahead and wedged herself into the picture.

> EUGENIE FISHER: "She was so *destructive* to Peggy — she called Hedda Hopper and told her that Peggy was a drug addict! Now, can you imagine a mother saying that about her daughter? And Peggy was trying *so* hard to provide for Johnny, to keep him; she loved him so much. And to have her own mother throw a monkey wrench in it! Hedda Hopper had enough sense to know where all this was coming from; she didn't use any of Marge's material. But it could have been devastating. It's all so sad to me."

Unlike her mother-in-law, Eugenie was completely repelled by the manner in which a private family matter had been unfolding in the public eye.

> EUGENE FISHER: "It seemed so unreal to me. I didn't know that people behaved that way. I never heard so many diatribes and so much badmouthing — on every side."

The negativity snowballed when the custody case reopened the first week of November. Outside Los Angeles Superior Court, a growing throng of curious spectators waited eagerly to get their glimpse of the participants in the sensational goings-on. Most wished Lynn well as she entered the building with Rickles and her lawyers. Sid Luft showed up shortly thereafter. He was without Judy Garland, who had been subpoenaed by Bari's attorneys to appear as a witness at the trial.

Luft took the stand before Lynn. He calmly told the court that he and Garland loved Johnny very much, and that the couple was certain that this love was reciprocated. Sid then said he and Judy felt the boy was very happy to be living with them.*

Bari was about to shed a different light on things. Her fury at Luft had been mounting since the earlier trial, where she had comported herself with a relative amount of restraint. She was now changing her tactics — and her anger became unleashed in her testimony:

> "In ten years, he has barely gone out of his way to see, write to or inquire about his son, let alone keep up with proper payments for his son's support! Just a month earlier [before the September 29 trial], he stood before this same judge and asked to have his support

---

* Incidents and quotes relating to this court session and the week following are derived from the February 1959 *Modern Screen* article, "How to tear apart a little boy."

payments lowered, a request that was denied. And now he stood there, a month later, asking for complete custody of the boy."

Lynn went on to refute Luft's claim that her son was happy with his new living arrangement. In this rebuttal, she quoted discussions she had had with Johnny. These talks had affirmed her assumption that the boy was actually seeing very little of his father.

Bari also questioned the stability of the Garland-Luft household, pointing out the couple had been on the verge of divorce twice within the past three years. She went on to mention that their well-publicized conflicts had purportedly been marked by violence.

Lynn's testimony was interrupted, at her attorney's request, one-hour-and-fifteen-minutes into the trial; Judy Garland had just arrived and would be called to the stand.

Continuing Bari's train of thought, her lawyer pressed Garland on the two divorce actions the singer had initiated against Luft; one having taken place in February 1956; the other, in March 1958. Judy acknowledged both. Her second complaint was then read aloud in the courtroom. It stated that Sid beat Garland and tried to strangle her, included a request that he be evicted from their home, and sought to prevent him from taking their two children (Lorna, five, and Joey, three) out of state.

> "Miss Garland, would you say your husband was a man of even and mild temper, or of violent and ungovernable temper?" Bari's attorney asked.
>
> "Pretty even-tempered," Judy responded.
>
> "Has Mr. Luft ever attempted to strangle you?"
>
> "No."
>
> "Did he ever beat you?"
>
> "No."

Garland was excused from the stand several minutes later. Lynn's side then rested their case. Over the next five hours, both parties' lawyers conferred with Superior Judge Philip H. Richards and talked among themselves.

Bari and Luft were finally called to the bench. Once again, Lynn was hopeful. Judge Richards issued a temporary decree:

> "It has been decided that John Luft is no longer in complete custody of his father. But, that from this day on, his mother shall have the opportunity of visiting the boy two days a week, and having him on alternate weekends and for half of his Christmas vacation."

Bari was stunned. She had worked so diligently with her legal team to bring about new evidence and testimony that would reverse the ruling of the previous trial — but all of their efforts had instead been met with a perfunctory judicial gesture. Lynn could no longer contain her emotions:

> "I'm not going to accept this. My son is my life. For ten years I've been his mother...*I* took care of him all the times he was sick. *I* was there when he began to walk, to talk, when he learned his prayers, when he got hurt and needed somebody to console him ...*I've* been everything to him and *he's* been everything to me... And I want him back, all the way...Do you hear?...*All the way!*"

Most fortunately for Bari, the near future held one more opportunity for the restoration of the original custody arrangement. Judge Richards ordered the entire case to be reviewed over a period of two weeks, during which time both sides could strengthen their pleas. A third court date was set for Friday, November 21.

In the days following her second court appearance, Lynn drove over to Johnny's school and had a talk with him.

> "I didn't tell him anything about the trial except to say that there had been one, and then when the trial seemed to be over, the judge had been good enough to continue it. ...I told him that the judge would give me another chance to get him back."

Johnny then presented his mother with a miniature glass bear, which he said would bring her good luck. Bari clenched the figurine and smiled, and the two said their goodbyes.

The charm had seemingly begun to work its magic by the morning of November 21. Additional hope had come to Lynn over the previous day, when her son had been invited into Judge Richards' chambers for a lengthy consultation.

Bari proudly displayed her glass bear to a swarm of waiting photographers as she once again entered Los Angeles Superior Court. Nathan Rickles and her legal team were at her side. The trial commenced, treading a familiar path.* Lynn's attorney, Bruce Sumner, depicted the atmosphere of the Garland-Luft home as being injurious to John Luft's well-being. He requested the court to remove the boy from this residence and reinstate him into the overall care of his responsible and loving mother.

Dr. Rickles was called to testify in his wife's defense. He termed Bari an "excellent mother," one who did her own housekeeping and cooking. With regard to her drinking, he stated she had in the past indulged in no more than an "occasional cocktail." Rickles went on to say that Lynn and Johnny had "an extremely warm and close relationship." He then noted the boy's demeanor and how it had changed since Sid Luft had been awarded his guardianship two months before. The psychiatrist claimed that a once "secure and happy child" was now beginning

---

* Testimony from this trial is derived from an article in the *Los Angeles Mirror-News*, November 21, 1958.

to evidence "increasing nervousness and restlessness." Rickles also perceived the health of the ten-year-old to be in a deteriorative state. This observation was later corroborated by the testimony of Mrs. Claire Little, mother of Johnny's roommate at Chadwick, who had witnessed "a normal, robust American boy" succumb to ill-health.

A motion to recall Judy Garland to the stand was met with an immediate objection by Luft's attorney, who stated that her appearance would subject the star "to further harassment by the press." After weighing the issue, Judge Richards found no practical reason for Garland to submit to further questioning.

Lynn's confidence was wavering as the trial neared a close; twice before her hopes had been dashed at the last moment, and the possibility of a third bombshell being thrown her way was cause for great unsettlement. Clasping her tiny bear, she approached the bench with Luft. The two stood before Richards as he began reading his final judgment on the custody of their son:

> "Whereas two months ago, young John Luft was a healthy, happy, well-adjusted boy at Chadwick School, the court cannot escape the conclusion from the evidence before it and from conversation with the boy, that he is now lonesome, confused and unhappy in a household where — to substantially all of its members — he is a stepchild." *
>
> "[John is a] fine, intelligent, warmhearted and well-mannered boy who harbors no ill feeling toward either parent and is trying his ten-year-old best to maintain his love and affection for each while caught in the maelstrom of their conflicting desires." **

Judge Richards returned Johnny to his mother and said the boy would finish out the term at his present day school, after which time he could reenroll in Chadwick. Luft was given the right to have his son on alternate weekends and for part of each summer.

Overcome with tearful emotion, Lynn glanced up at Richards and said, "Thank you," in almost inaudible tones. Her face started to assume a look of weary peacefulness as she left a cheering courtroom. Directly, she headed to a nearby area where Johnny was waiting.

A collective sigh of relief was sounded by Bari's many supporters, cherished family members and friends whose hearts had gone out to her throughout her period of anguish.

> JUNE GALE LEVANT: "Everybody had been shocked when they heard the news that Lynn's custody of her son was taken away from her — and happy when the case was settled in her favor."

* Quote compiled from a November 21, 1958 Associated Press release and the February 1959 *Modern Screen* article, "How to tear apart a little boy."
** Quote derived from a November 27, 1958, article in the *Los Angeles Times.*

On Thursday, November 27, the *Los Angeles Times* printed an article, "Lynn Bari's Happy Day: Son Johnny Back Home." The essay led off with the following:

> "Today will be the happiest of Thanksgiving Days for Actress Lynn Bari — her 10-year-old son Johnny will be home with her again.
>
> "As the result of a decision made last Friday by Superior Judge Philip H. Richards, Johnny was returned to Miss Bari yesterday after an absence of more than two months.
>
> "Waiting for Johnny in his home at 469 N. Palm Drive, Beverly Hills, was a huge sheet of paper bearing Thanksgiving Day greetings and messages of friendship from his fellow students in the fifth grade at Chadwick School, where he had been enrolled until two months ago.
>
> "The classmates indicated they'd be happy when Johnny comes back."

Lynn would be eternally grateful to Judge Richards for bringing to her a happy resolution to Sid Luft's custody action against her. On the other hand, she'd remain totally baffled by Judge Ware's earlier handling of the case. The way in which she had been treated by Ware, combined with the intent of her ex, had made for experiences in and out of court by which she'd long be unnerved. Thirty-plus years after the fact, there was a quiver in her voice as she remembered them:

One day I'd like to write a book about that custody case, which was *really unbelievable*. You can't imagine! It went on with private detectives and I had to get bodyguards. I was in court for three-and-one-half months, and I went from about one-hundred-and-twenty-five pounds down to one-hundred pounds. I looked like hell. I couldn't eat. I couldn't think. And I didn't drink a *drop* because they said I was this terrible lush and that I neglected the child and I stuck him in this school and that I only saw him every two weeks! It was ridiculous!

Revitalized by the outcome of the custody trial, Lynn regained her appetite and got herself back into shape. She contacted the Milt Rosner agency and told them she was ready to resume her career. Her plan now was to work on a steady basis. Nathan Rickles actually championed this, in part because he thought acting would be good therapy for Bari in the wake of her ordeal. It was also quite possible that the shrink was being somewhat self-serving here. The past several months had seen the press portray him as the devoted husband of a well-liked celebrity during her time of crisis. Having had a taste of favorable publicity, he perhaps thought he could remain in the public eye if Lynn made a wholehearted return to performing.

Bari's professional regeneration began on a rather sour note. While in the midst of her court battles, she had learned that Universal had been seriously considering her for *Pillow Talk* (1959). Doris Day and Rock Hudson were slated to star in the film, which would go on to become one of the studio's top moneymakers and a sex farce nonpareil. The script to the comedy featured two secondary female characters: Alma, Day's tipsy housekeeper, and Marie, who'd be introduced as Hudson's girlfriend. Thelma Ritter would eventually play the salty Alma. The far blander Marie had at one time looked to be in Lynn's pocket, but she quite likely lost the part (to Julia Meade) because of the negative fallout from her recent legal clashes. Although she had been dealt with sympathetically by the press, Bari had figured greatly into the nasty accusations of a much-publicized mess — making her something of a casting liability at the major studios.

Pillow Talk notwithstanding, thirty-nine-year-old Lynn had long since resigned herself to the fact that her days as a screen luminary were over. She had been witnessing actresses with far greater marquee value — some of them nearly a decade her junior — competing for the occasional substantial film role involving a woman over thirty. The odds were unfavorable, and they had convinced Bari to zero in on television and the stage. She would seldom have a problem obtaining work in these fields of entertainment, where her talent and professionalism would always stand her in good stead.

Lynn's first post-trial acting job was for Walt Disney, who had personally offered her a guest shot on *Disneyland*, the hour-long show he produced for ABC-TV. Disney also hosted the popular anthology, which was filmed in Technicolor. The format of *Disneyland* was varied, often embracing the miniseries genre. In October 1958 Disney had introduced the ten-part western, "The Nine Lives of Elfego Baca," about the real-life justice crusader of long ago. Bari was featured in the miniseries' fifth episode, "Elfego Baca, Attorney At Law," broadcast February 6, 1959.

Those shows were very interesting. Bob Loggia, a really good actor, played Elfego Baca. He was this enchanted man from below the border. Always escaping death, he settled scores for other people.

"Elfego Baca, Attorney At Law" also guest-starred Annette Funicello and James Dunn. The show would be edited together with another "Nine Lives" installment ("The Griswold Murder"), going on to be released in foreign markets as the theatrical feature, *Six Gun Law* (1962).

Lynn remained in the Old West for an episode of ABC's *Bronco* series, which would be televised in June 1959. Then, out of nowhere, Bari and Nathan Rickles decided to collaborate on a novel, *Try My Couch*. Their book idea would leave their minds almost as quickly as it had entered them.

Putting her pen aside, Lynn went into rehearsals for the Pasadena Playhouse production of *Plain and Fancy*. The show was a breezy musical, one that had had a respectable run on Broadway during 1955-56. A large portion of its action took place among the Amish in Southeast Pennsylvania. Traveling to Lancaster

County were Ruth Winters and Dan King, two urbane New Yorkers who had some property to sell a Mennonite local. Playing Ruth had led to a Theatre World Award for Shirl Conway — and it was Conway's role to which Bari had been assigned at the Playhouse.

Plain and Fancy posed a challenge to Lynn since it would require her participation in a half-dozen songs, one of which ("It's a Helluva Way to Run a Love Affair") was to be a solo. To this end, Bari worked tirelessly with a vocal coach while in rehearsals. Her efforts paid off; she went on to surprise theatergoers — and even herself — with a singing voice that was both powerful and affective.

> WILLIAM ROERICK: "I was astonished — I didn't know that she sang, and she sang very well. She had pizzazz!"

Critics who caught *Plain and Fancy's* May 29 opening were, without exception, enchanted by Bari. *The Los Angeles Examiner* wrote, "A sparkling performance by Lynn Bari … When she was on stage, the show took on a quality of delight. Her timing and sense of comedy approaches that of Kay Kendall." *The Hollywood Citizen-News* was equally captivated: "Miss Bari's reactions and remarks set the audience off into continuous laughter. A veteran of more than ninety films, she evidenced the ability to play the boards with the best of them and had a romp of it. Written with strong laughs, she made it even stronger. Several times the show was halted by the applause grabbed by Miss Bari's comedy moments." The *Valley Times* was all-encompassing in its praise for Lynn: "This remarkable actress and singer manages to sustain a comic pace that never falters — and manages to look completely lovely while doing it. Her songs in the show come through with the aplomb and charm that only a veteran of this type of thing could give them, and she sells her laugh lines and business with a silver tongued finesse that only a veteran of musical comedy could." The *Los Angeles Times* summed everything up by stating, "Miss Bari comes through with the same high class performance one would expect from an actress with her background."

Bari's sensational reviews would play a large part in the fortunes of *Plain and Fancy* — which would be held over at the Playhouse well into summer 1959. During its run, the show was promoted by Lynn's old friend, June Gale Levant, now a local talk-show hostess.

> JUNE GALE LEVANT: "In the late fifties I had a daily television show in LA and I contacted Lynn to be a guest. She came on the show and we had a nice reunion. Her voice had deepened over the years and when I mentioned it — on the air — she replied, 'Oh, it's just gotten tired!' — which made me laugh. It was fun to remember when we were once young and carefree."

Off camera, Lynn told her pal that she and Nathan Rickles had recently purchased a six-bedroom home from a member of Hollywood's Warner family. The two-story, Spanish-style mansion was located on North Alta Drive in Beverly

Lynn, during her run in Plain and Fancy *(1959).* COURTESY OF PHOTOGRAPHER ED COLBERT.

Hills. Bari had decided with Rickles to remodel the house. She would oversee its alterations during the latter part of the year, momentarily putting her career on hold.

One of Lynn's concerns became the design and operation of her husband's office, which would be moving from its Wilshire Drive quarters to the ground floor of their new abode. Although she followed through with her part in this relocation, Bari disliked the fact that the psychiatrist would be practicing under the family roof. The proximity of home and office perturbed her for several reasons, one of them being that Rickles had made known his desire to have her involved with his work on a continuing basis. Lynn was aghast at this, wanting nothing to do with her husband's professional affairs. The doctor, however, made it clear to her that she would be called upon to assist him whenever he deemed it necessary. Bari waved the white flag and she settled on North Alta Drive with Rickles and their children.

Lynn and her husband frequently attended auctions, and they'd decorate their home with antiques purchased at these sales. Many would be placed in their spacious living room, whose walls were a pale salmon-pink. The pastel coloring would draw attention to a portion of the couple's art collection; specifically, an assortment of Goya prints and framed miniature paintings, taken from Persian manuscripts. The centerpiece of the living room, however, was to be a magnificent Steinway grand piano. The Rickles' dear friend, composer André Previn, would often take to its keyboard at lively parties given on North Alta. Sometimes these get-togethers would feature repasts prepared by the hostess herself, an accomplished gourmet cook.

Despite her culinary inclinations, Bari would spend comparatively little time in her kitchen during the winter of 1959-60, for her career went back into high gear as soon as everything was properly furnished and pleasing to the eye. Around the time of her fortieth birthday, on December 18, she filmed two western shows at NBC: *The Overland Trail* and *The Law and the Plainsman*. Her guest stints on these series would air the following February. By then, Lynn had made a return to the stage in a Los Angeles production of *Simon and Laura*, a British romp centering on a squabbling show-business couple. Bari was prima donna Laura Foster, a role made famous by England's Kay Kendall.

The road then beckoned, with Lynn planning a summer tour of the 1954 Broadway hit, *Anniversary Waltz*. The play was not new to Bari, for she had had a limited run with it on the strawhat circuit a few years previously. Written by Jerome Chodorov, *Waltz* was a comedy involving Manhattan's smart set. Kitty Carlisle had been the show's original lead, cast as Alice Walters, the role Lynn was now set to enact for a second time.

As Bari happily rode a nonstop work wave, Nathan Rickles intervened and pulled the breaks on her career. The psychiatrist had not too long ago encouraged Bari's professional aspirations, but their actualization had caused him to change his tune. He felt once more that Lynn was consumed by acting and neglectful of what he perceived to be her wifely duties. In short, he wanted her at home. Bari sensed this had something to do with their present living situation, where she thought Rickles was affecting the air of a lord-and-master of a stately manor. It appeared to her that he wished her to be at his beck and call — and not only in a familial respect. The shrink was holding firmer to his resolve concerning his celebrated spouse and his own career. He had decided that Lynn should play an active role in his practice, managing his books and doing receptionist chores. Bari balked at this girl-Friday business, in addition to Rickles' other designs for her. The two seemed to be following a well-worn script involving similar matters, with battles ensuing and Lynn strategizing in secret. Bari finally succumbed to her husband, assuming she'd eventually find a way to extricate herself from what she considered to be a life of servitude.

By hook or by crook, Lynn was determined to follow through with the *Anniversary Waltz* tour. She would. But her umpteenth comeback was preceded by several housebound months where she enacted the role of Lynn Bari, Psychiatric Assistant. Bari performed admirably, charming her husband's expanding roster of patients in the process. The work at hand was not exactly to Lynn's liking, however, and she couldn't stand being within shouting distance of Rickles day after day. The couple's marriage became pervaded by tension, with Bari sitting tight until the shrink softened.

In April 1960, while Lynn was under Rickles' employ, her brother John came to her with distressing news: their sixty-six-year-old mother was seriously ill. Marge Fisher had just suffered a devastating stroke and was being treated at a county hospital in Manhattan Beach. The specifics surrounding what had befallen her were unclear because Marge was choosing not to be forthcoming about them. Once again, she was relying on certain tenets of Religious Science as a means of remaining silent about her medical problems.

Marge had given everyone the impression that her life had been marked by excellent physical health since her recovery from breast cancer in the early fifties. Those close to her, for the most part, believed this had been so — privately taking into account her unacknowledged dependency on alcohol. John and Eugenie Fisher, in fact, could only remember one other instance where she had appeared not at all well. This had occurred some time before her stroke. The couple had gone to her apartment for a casual visit and had been horrified to see her greet them with an angry bruise covering her face. Marge had reacted to their alarm nonchalantly, explaining she had taken a minor fall and was doing fine — and didn't want to discuss the matter any further. John and Eugenie would later surmise that she might have had a minor stroke which had caused her to fall face-forward onto her floor. Equally plausible to them, though, was the idea that she could have hurt herself while in a drunken stupor. In any event, her current disorder had come about suddenly, after a period of relative good health.

John told his sister the effects of Marge's stroke made highly doubtful her returning to a satisfactory physical state. He said her motor abilities had become severely impaired, adding that she was no longer mentally alert. Dispirited by what she was hearing, Lynn felt a strong need to be there for her mother — whom she had not seen in over six years.

Bari paid regular visits to Marge in the hospital. Her mother's debilitation was pronounced, but it didn't move Lynn to any outward displays of emotion. She instead dealt with her much as she would with one of her husband's patients, affecting a demeanor of cordiality and efficiency. Bari only seemed to relate to Marge with smiles and genteel good wishes, never extending to her anything truly heartfelt. To the hospital staff, she came across as an extremely well-organized woman, one who always stayed on top of her mother's care.

Marge had been languishing in the county hospital for several weeks when John Fisher concluded that it would be best for her to be transferred to a private health facility, where she'd hopefully receive more effective treatment. Lynn went along with the idea, but her husband refused to share in the expense that would be involved. As she and John were deciding on how to proceed, their mother's condition worsened dramatically. It was now apparent to both that the end was near. Marge Fisher died in Manhattan Beach on May 11, 1960.

Upon her mother's death, Bari conveyed to her family she was experiencing a sense of relief.

> EUGENIE FISHER: "There was no false grief or anything like that. Peggy was very bitter toward her mother, so she wasn't maudlin. It was sort of like, 'Well, that's over.' John had much more tender feelings for his mother, and I think he really loved her. But I think there was relief there, too. Marge had fouled herself up so many times that both he and Peggy were kind of beyond having *really* tender feelings toward her.
>
> "Just after she passed away, we were going through her things and I found something that she had written — she used to spend a lot of time at her old Underwood typewriter, writing stories and poetry which she would send off to the *Saturday Evening Post*; she was always getting pink-slipped. I was absolutely floored at what I read. It was the most saccharine, Victorian poem. It had something to do with sitting under a tree and gazing into this person's eyes and this upwelling of feelings. And it was written seriously: 'As I gazed at him and he looked at me…' It was so maudlin; I couldn't believe that it came from this woman.
>
> "There was a dichotomy to this person. She wanted to be liberated but she didn't have the tools, the education, maybe the economic means to do something for herself. There was some kind of awful frustration that *(laughing)* drove her crazy — and everyone else crazy!"

Marge was now gone, but Lynn's complex attachment to her would hold on. Her mother had shaped her life and she loved and hated her with equal intensity. Bari had kept a tight wrap on these emotions during Marge's hospital stay, not for a moment straying from a composed and self-assured bearing. In many ways, she had been behaving exactly as she had when she was young and in the face of stressful situations created by her mother. A self-possessed false front had remained Lynn's chief coping mechanism because she had failed to confront her maternal problems head-on; the thought of doing so had become increasingly more terrifying to her.

With a vitally important personal issue left unresolved, Bari hadn't been able to interact with her dying mother in a natural way. She had, in effect, negated the chance of bringing some sort of closure to their relationship. This would have a great impact on her — and Marge would forever loom large in her psyche.

Marge's death would resonate deep within Lynn, leading her down a path of self-destruction. The tumultuous times ahead would find Bari exhibiting a personality in startling likeness to that of her mother.

Lynn Bari finds herself enveloped in emotional turmoil, as Mrs. Donford, the high-strung wife and mother of The Young Runaways *(1968).*

CHAPTER SIXTEEN
THE GASLIGHT TREATMENT

Marge Fisher had left Lynn quite a legacy — most of it related to her drinking. Her alcoholism had formed the dynamics of the family in which her daughter had grown up. The problems engendered by her boozing had been countless, many of them affecting Bari directly. Lynn had also been negatively influenced by Marge's alcoholic sensibilities, which had gone on to become part of her own approach to life. This emulation had been furthered because Bari had not been able to properly detach herself from her mother. Having just lost her, Lynn was now on the verge of imitating her in a far more unsettling way — by becoming a full-blown alcoholic.

Bari had returned to what could be called "social drinking" shortly after her custody ordeal. In the wake of Marge's death, she'd begin to consume booze with increasing regularity and her world would grow a little bleaker with each passing day. Alcohol would frequently be shading her mind as it had with her mother; she'd be overcome by unrealistic fears, bitterness and hopelessness.

Nathan Rickles would play a large part in Lynn's distorted way of thinking. The unfavorable place her husband held in her life would burgeon in Marge's absence — and her alcohol abuse would make him a disproportionately monumental adversary. From there, her marriage would turn into a total shambles.

There was little hint about what was to come between Bari and Rickles in the months following Marge's death. Their marriage was maintaining relative calm, with the psychiatrist concerned about how his wife was coming to grips with her loss. Proving to be supportive of Lynn, he wished her well on her *Anniversary Waltz* tour. Bari began with the play, her run with it taking place in early summer 1960. While she was away, her husband planned for them an August vacation in Europe.

The couple traveled throughout the continent on this, Lynn's first trip overseas. Their itinerary was a source of immense enjoyment for Bari, who also seemed to derive some pleasure from her husband's company. The two shared a great enthusiasm for art and much of their time was spent in museums that Lynn had long wanted to visit. She and Rickles did many other touristy things along the way and their trip wound down with both in a state of happy exhaustion. Thousands of miles away from home, they had allowed their vacation to be a much-needed tonic for their relationship. Never again would they be so content together.

The couple's state of harmony, in fact, turned out to be extremely short-lived. Bari began pulling away from her husband as soon as they returned to the States. Her career once again became all-consuming and this time no admonishments

Summer 1960; Lynn, projecting good cheer, shortly before her European sojourn.
COURTESY OF PHOTOGRAPHER ED COLBERT.

from Rickles could slow her down. Lynn's vacation photos weren't yet developed when she started work on *The Aquanauts*, the CBS adventure series. Bari guest-starred with Paul Henreid on the show's fifth broadcast, "Deep Escape" (aired October 12, 1960). Her next television assignment found her making a splash as a murderess in "The Heiress," an episode of NBC's *Michael Shayne* detective series. Richard Denning was the video incarnation of the sleuth whom Lloyd Nolan had portrayed in seven Fox films — one of which, *Sleepers West*, had co-starred Lynn. Twenty years had passed since that picture had been made but Bari wouldn't look much worse for the wear, proving to be a most glamorous evildoer. Her performance as such would reach the home screen in February 1961.

"The Heiress" wrapped and Bari immediately went into rehearsals for *French Postcards*. The play was being mounted for the first time in the US, its premiere set for December 1960 at Los Angeles' Civic Playhouse. A comedy, it was based on *La Betise De Cambrai*, one of the last works of noted French playwright Jean De Letraz. Its original version had been successfully staged some years before at the Palais Royal Theater in Paris. Writers Mawby Green and Ed Feilbert later worked on its English translation, which came to be entitled *French Postcards*. As with its predecessor, Green and Feilbert's play took place at a seaside villa in Monte Carlo and was replete with breezy, sophisticated dialogue.

French Postcards was being produced by Rick Newberry and directed by Edward Ludlum. Both men had Broadway experience and they were approaching their current endeavor with great enthusiasm, hoping its Civic Playhouse production would lead to a New York run. Equally excited was Lynn who, as *Postcards'* Olivette Bouche, was headlining a cast that included Wanda Hendrix, Carleton Carpenter and Teddy Hart. Bari gave her all to the show, thinking it might very well return her to a position of prominence in the entertainment world.

The comedy opened to a star-studded audience in attendance. The first-nighters filled the Civic Playhouse with laughter and they applauded heartily at the end of each of the play's three acts. Lynn and her costars took their curtain calls amidst wild cheers, with Bari being brought back for a solo bow. Opening-night theatergoers, however, can be overly polite, often holding no barometer for a play's critical response. Such was the case with *French Postcards*, which went on to be lambasted in the Los Angeles papers. Bari was devastated by this, as were her friends and family.

> EUGENIE FISHER: "She was wonderful in [*French*] *Postcards*. I was impressed with her wit — she was really funny. But the show was panned terribly. Things like that hurt Peggy."

Advance sales helped to keep *French Postcards* from bombing totally but the play had a very short run, closing toward the end of January 1961. Lynn didn't deal at all well with her first theatrical failure — a bit of unpleasantness that had come too soon after her mother's death. The dreams that had died with the show left Bari feeling more imprisoned by her marriage. Her sense of self-worth took a swift plunge — with her drinking escalating just as quickly.

Lynn's publicity portrait for French Postcards *(1960-61).*

Lynn's boozing started to have its effect on her physical appearance. This became evident in her April guest turn on the popular CBS detective series, *Checkmate*. Bari was featured in an episode entitled "Good-Bye, Griff," playing the alcoholic wife of a wealthy publisher (Simon Oakland). Attired in glad rags, she slurred and stumbled about most convincingly. That was acting — for she didn't imbibe while on the job. However, it wasn't makeup that was contributing to the bloat in her face, causing her to appear washed-out and considerably older than her forty-one years. Lynn didn't look out of character, though, and she gave an appropriately melodramatic performance — one that was to attract much attention.

I had done that drunk over at Universal and *everybody* wrote in about how great it was. That gave me an awful big boost at the time.

"Good-Bye, Griff" would indeed lead to other work for Bari — but now she'd be typecast on television as a down-on-her-luck society wife. More unfortunately, Lynn's portrayals of these forlorn women would often be abetted by her own physical deterioration, brought on by her alcohol dependency. The home-screen camera lens would sometimes be anything but her friend, treating her rather mercilessly.

Faring better behind the footlights, Lynn joined a West Coast tour of *The Pleasure of His Company* in summer 1961. The frothy romantic comedy cast Bari as Kate Dougherty, the role that had been created on Broadway several years before by Cornelia Otis Skinner. Skinner had also authored *The Pleasure of His Company*, along with Samuel Taylor. Taylor had then gone on to pen the movie version of the show, which had just opened in wide release. The film starred Fred Astaire, Debbie Reynolds and Lilli Palmer (as Kate). Lynn's stage troupe did quite well in the face of their screen competition, playing to near-capacity crowds on the strawhat circuit. Bari would later thank Louella Parsons for having contributed to her show's success; the columnist had plugged her appearance in the comedy on more than one occasion.

Lynn was back in Hollywood in early September, filming an episode of *Everglades*, a syndicated police series that had yet to debut. By month's end, she had completed work on another upcoming cop show, ABC's *The New Breed*. Both of these guest stints aired in November. More noteworthy was Bari's next TV credit, "A Certain Time, a Certain Darkness," the December 11 broadcast of *Ben Casey*. The popular medical drama cast Lynn and Donald Woods as the self-absorbed parents of Joan Hackett, playing a young woman afflicted with epilepsy. The trio shared some very uncomfortable on-camera moments, among themselves and with series star Vince Edwards (as Dr. Ben Casey). All were served well by the direction of actor Abner Biberman (who had supported Bari and Woods in *The Bridge of San Luis Rey*). Hackett made the greatest impression, turning in a performance that would net her a 1962 Best Supporting Actress Emmy nomination.

Bari's *Ben Casey* appearance brought to her a number of offers from TV casting directors, all of whom wanted her for one-shot gigs on network shows. She turned every one of them down. Lynn, in fact, wouldn't be accepting — or pursuing — any acting jobs for six months. Her career had once again come to an abrupt halt because her marriage had reached yet another point of crisis. Same scenario, same outcome: Bari, having grudgingly given into her husband's demands, becomes a full-time housewife and office assistant. The only difference this time out was that she was relying more heavily on booze to take the edge off her discontentment. Not that that was working, though. Her drinking was sending her into frequent moods of self-pity, intensifying her anger towards Rickles

Lynn and Lorrie Richards in Trauma *(1963).*

and denying her a way to constructively approach their marriage.

Other "career breaks" would be ahead for Lynn — and, with each, she'd grow more dependent on booze and more despondent. There was no doubt that she functioned better as a working actress. The discipline she applied to her craft — and the self-esteem she derived from it — lifted her spirits and diminished her need for liquor. Acting would serve as a control for Bari's drinking for some time to come, slowing down her alcoholic progression — but not arresting it. Whether housebound or performing, Lynn would continue to relate to booze as a remedy for her various problems.

Bari's personal troubles were mounting when her husband relented and allowed her to act occasionally, more or less as occupational therapy. She resumed her career in summer 1962 by appearing in *Trauma* (1963), her first feature film in five years — and the most bare-bones affair with which she'd ever been connected. The picture was a dismal independent (produced by a company called Parade), a psychological thriller centered on the unresolved murder of a wealthy woman named Helen Garrison (Lynn). Its story was set almost entirely on the grounds of Helen's mansion, with most of the action taking place in the aftermath of her death by drowning. Young Lorrie Richards (in her only screen appearance) played Emmaline Garrison, the victim's niece and the sole witness to the crime that had been committed. John Conte costarred, as Emmaline's bridegroom — once the lover of the departed Helen. The plot to *Trauma* actually wasn't half-bad but it was executed in an incredibly slipshod manner, proving to be something of an embarrassment for its one celebrated participant.

You know, I was not supposed to get screen credit for *Trauma*. Two friends asked me if I would do a scene before the credits. I said, "Yes." Well, I get there and they've got this whole part written that's going to go before they put the title on this thing. So I said, "It's a little much; but okay, I'll do it." We did the opening scene. It went on and on. They added some pages. Pretty soon, I asked, "You're going to show *all* of this behind the title?" They said, "Oh yes, this is what 'they' do now."

Later, I was vacationing in Puerto Rico. One day, the man who ran the hotel where I was staying came up to me.

"You know, I've always been a fan, Miss Bari, but they ran the worst picture of yours the other day. What are you doing in a thing like that?" he said.

"What are you talking about?" I asked.

"*Trauma*."

"How did you know that I was in it?"

"It said: 'Lynn Bari and John Conte in *Trauma*.'"

I wound up with top billing and I don't know how. I expected just no credit, nothing. Well, I was in half of the picture! They kept cutting me into things and replaying a scene where my character asks for her pills. And I thought that I'd be drowned and out of the thing by the time the titles came on!

The whole thing was awful. They told me about this marvelous dramatic actress they'd discovered. She couldn't walk for two cents without falling on herself; this horrible girl. I guess somebody was getting lucky with her — *(laughing)* although I don't know who!

Trauma would have a very spotty release schedule, playing the lower half of double bills through 1964. Thankfully for Lynn, few people over twenty-one would see her in this potboiler. Those that remembered her from her heyday would have been shocked that she'd agreed to do something so subpar. Bari's contemporaries would no doubt have been equally disturbed by the way she'd photographed here. The eye of *Trauma's* camera had seemed to reflect all the turmoil in her personal life and she looked a very played-out forty-two-year-old. Apparently, the telltale effects of drinking and stress had mattered less to Lynn than her need to bolt from home and perform.

Bari's disinterest in her appearance was disconcerting to those close to her. Friends gasped when she informed them that she was about to tour the West Coast as the blowsy, emasculating mother, Mae Peterson, in *Bye Bye Birdie*. Lynn brushed off their concerns, reasoning that Kay Medford had brought the house down playing Mae on Broadway two years earlier. She felt she'd have a ball doing the musical comedy and looked forward to working with Sheree North, another erstwhile Fox star. Thirty-year-old North had been cast as her nemesis, Rose Grant (the girlfriend of Mae's son, Albert). The two actresses hit it off immediately, each enjoying the other's down-to-earth attitude and irreverent sense of humor. *Bye Bye Birdie* was a laugh-filled experience for Bari, both onstage and off. As had been expected, she had great fun schlepping about as the frowsy Mae — and she was very sorry to say goodbye to her character when her commitment to the show ended in September 1962.

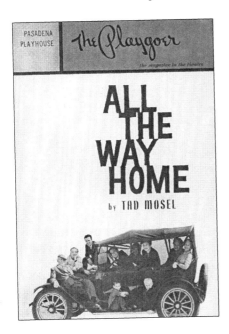

Bye, Bye Birdie had had a remarkably positive effect on Lynn, emboldening her in the aftermath of a period of great unsettlement. She felt better, looked better and was determined to forge ahead with her career. As luck would have it, a most satisfying project came her way right after the tour. The Pasadena Playhouse was again calling upon her, this time to star in its production of *All the Way Home*, set to open in November. The play was based on the late James Agee's autobiographical novel, the heart-stirring *A Death in the Family*. Set in 1915 Knoxville, TN, *A Death in the Family* had gone on to earn Agee a Pulitzer Prize, awarded to him posthumously in 1958. Three years later writer Tad Mosel had won a Pulitzer for his Broadway adaptation of Agee's book. *All the Way Home* had also garnered Mosel and four others Tony Awards. Included among this group had been actress Colleen Dewhurst, who'd portrayed Mary Follet — the role Lynn was now performing in Pasadena. Mary was the drama's emotional pillar, the mother who held her family together after her husband's death in an automobile accident.

All the Way Home **was a beautiful, beautiful play.**

The drama rekindled all of Bari's enthusiasm for acting. Mary Follet was a demanding part in which she completely — and soberly — immersed herself. Her efforts in this regard resulted in critical acclaim and the admiration of her confreres.

JUNE GALE LEVANT: "I recall reading about a play Lynn was appearing in at the Pasadena Playhouse, *All the Way Home*. I took the freeway to see her performance and was *thrilled* at how good a stage actress she'd become. I went backstage to congratulate her."

Revivified by *All the Way Home* and the curtailment of her drinking, Bari contacted her agents during the show's two-month run, telling them she was open to any and all reasonable offers. In February 1963 she filmed an episode of *Ripcord*, the syndicated TV series about skydivers. Other home-screen guest stints were pending, embracing a time frame that would allow for her to do summer stock.

Lynn's career was back in full swing — a situation that came to a screeching stop under the intense pressure of her irritated husband. The vicious circle had again come to the point where Nathan Rickles was fed up with Bari's inability to strike a balance between her professional and personal lives.

The joys of *All The Way Home* and *Bye Bye Birdie* now seemed buried deep in the past, as Lynn began what would be tantamount to a three-quarter-year ramble about her mansion. She'd be mildly productive in the months ahead, though; doing her psychiatric-assistant bit for her husband. However, this type of work would continue to be totally unrewarding, leaving Bari mad at herself, angrier at Rickles — and giving her license to hit the bottle with increasing regularity.

The marital treadmill moved Lynn into an advantageous place in October. Pulling herself together, she reached an agreeable understanding with the shrink about her desire to act. Late in the year she filmed "The Case of the Accosted Accountant," an episode of CBS's high-rated courtroom drama, *Perry Mason*. Bari's appearance as a social-climbing corporate wife would be singled out in the promotion of the show's January 9, 1964, broadcast, with several flattering captioned headshots of her being released to the press.

The holiday season on North Alta Drive was a relatively amicable one for Lynn and her family. John Luft was now living at home full-time, attending Beverly Hills High. Rena Rickles was currently on a winter break from the University of Washington, where she was majoring in drama. Both her father and stepmother, to their credit, had always tried their very best to make Christmas-time enjoyable for their children.

The New Year found the kids back in school and Bari enacting the central character in *The Late Liz* (1964), a syndicated television special sponsored by the Episcopal Church. The show was based on a 1950s bestseller of the same name, the autobiography of Gert Behanna. Behanna had been born into luxury, the daughter of a powerful New York business executive who'd given her everything but love. The first three decades of her adult life had been marked by promiscuity, alcoholism and a pill addiction. Then, at age fifty-three, she experienced a spiritual conversion and her dissolute behavior came to an end. *The Late Liz* embraced the most dramatic elements of Behanna's story, placing strong emphasis on her epiphany.* Bari had a field day etching a portrait of this decidedly colorful woman and she would remember her TV bio with great fondness.

> It was a damn good show. It was the story of a drunkard. She was an actual member of the church who was married to one of the big guys on the stock exchange. She became saved in the end through God. I know it sounds icky, but it was very well done. We had a good director, Tay Garnett. For me, it was a real tour de force. They had initially wanted to expand it into a series. But this one had cost so much money that they eventually called it quits.
>
> I was brought to Atlanta, where *The Late Liz* was screened for all the bigwigs in the church. I've never met so many people in my life. To be entertained as I was down there, all I can say is — boy, do those people know how to live!

The Late Liz aired in March 1964, shortly before Easter. Lynn had by then completed work on "Trial at Belle Springs," the April 21 episode of TV's syndicated *Death Valley Days.* The long-running western anthology cast her as Belle Wilgus, an outlaw who went head-to-head with Wyatt Earp's brother (Ken Scott).

Bari spent the summer touring the East Coast with Joseph Stein's *Enter Laughing*, a Broadway hit of the previous season. Set in 1930s New York, the show was an uproarious comedy based on the semi-autobiographical novel by Carl Reiner. Its protagonist was David Kolowitz, a young man who idolized Ronald Colman and pursued an acting career — despite the protestations of his parents, who had wanted for him a career as a pharmacist. David had been a star-making role for its original portrayer, Alan Arkin. The actor's performance had been ably abetted by Sylvia Sidney, playing David's overprotective mama, Emma Kolowitz. Sidney was admirably succeeded on the road by Lynn, who pulled out all the stops as Emma. Bari's most hilarious moments came with Billy Gray (late of TV's *Father Knows Best*), cast as her beleaguered son. Also featured in this edition of *Enter Laughing* was Lynn's frequent costar of films-gone-by, Alan Mowbray, in the part of the washed-up, alcoholic actor who gave David his start in show business.

Bari finished her run with *Enter Laughing* and whiled away the rest of her year at her husband's side, with an occasional family jaunt enlivening things. She broke away from Rickles briefly in January 1965, to shoot another *Perry Mason* episode, "The Case of the Fatal Fetish." The series again cast her as an executive's wife, a betrayed one this time. Assignment completed, it was back to the receptionist desk for a two-month stretch.

Lynn returned to the Pasadena Playhouse in the spring, going into rehearsals for *Ballad of the City*, an original work by Steve Allen. The play was comprised of a number of vignettes taking place in the Los Angeles area. The sketches were wide-ranging in nature, from broad comedy to poignant drama. Bari was featured in all. The most serious had her portraying a prostitute who became a murder victim. Completely different in tone was "The Interview," a playlet in which she was an aging, alcoholic movie star. The actress was visited at home by

* *The Late Liz* would be made into a theatrical feature in 1971, with Anne Baxter starring.

a frumpy female reporter. The writer and her subject broke into conversation —
and the contents of a martini shaker. Before long, the star's maid was trying in
vain to keep the booze away from her boss. The scene drew to a close with one
drink left in the shaker. The interviewer poured it for herself and raised her glass
to make a toast. The actress joined her in the salute, clutching her empty goblet.
The two women's hands then parted — with the host in possession of the last

Don't mess with Belle: Lynn, in "Trial at Belle Springs," a 1964 episode of Death
Valley Days.

This portrait of Lynn helped to promote her summer 1964 tour with Enter Laughing.

martini. This bit of comic dexterity would help to earn Bari hearty applause at curtain-call time. Her show would also click with audiences, being held over at the Playhouse for several months.

I got wonderful, wonderful notices on that one.

Ballad of the City brought Lynn together with Jerry Walston, a man with whom she'd maintain a close personal friendship over the course of the next fifteen years. Walston was in his late thirties at the time, a hairdresser who'd been residing in LA for more than a decade. The stylist had come to idolize Lynn Bari twenty-three years earlier, while attending a showing of *Orchestra Wives* in the northern Minnesota town where he had grown up. Quite by chance, Walston had been offered the job of Bari's hairdresser on *Ballad of the City*. He jumped at this opportunity, and a sometimes heartrending — but always loving — relationship began.

> JERRY WALSTON: "Lynn was a marvelous person. She had character, decency and honesty — all the beautiful things. I remember the first time I met her; she walked through the door of my shop and my heart came up in my throat. I was almost speechless. She looked at me and said, 'That bad, huh?' And we were friends from that moment on.
>
> "On my first big day as her hairdresser, she quit! She got into it with [*Ballad of the City* actress] Diane Ladd at the theater one night. I don't know exactly how Diane had put it, but her [Bari's] talent was questioned. I didn't hear it, but I think she also made a remark about a generation gap between herself and Lynn. Well, Lynn stood up and said, 'How *dare* you question me!' She then told Diane Ladd exactly who she [Ladd] was and what she was, and what she had to do in order to get the parts that she'd gotten — and who she did it with *(laughing)* — and, 'How dare you question me! You can take the part, the production and the theater and put it where the sun doesn't shine!' By the time she finished, Diane's mouth was hanging open and she didn't have anything left to say. Lynn said, 'I'm outta here. I don't need this.' She walked off and out the door she went. And I'm right behind her, thinking, 'What the hell is this?' Lynn turns around and says, 'What the hell are you doing here?' I said, 'Hell, I'm your hairdresser; if you leave, I'm with you.' She said, 'Let's get drunk.' And we did.
>
> "Lynn was back in *Ballad of the City* in a matter of days. The producers had called her back and Diane, who somehow or another was still in the production, had apologized to her. Lynn never would have walked out in the first place had not somebody *really* offended her. She was a very professional woman.
>
> "Lynn would study a script, get up and almost have it pat. I never saw her run lines — I never saw anything like it in my life!

On *Ballad of the City*, she did quick changes between each of the vignettes, going from a hooker to an elderly woman in just about five seconds. I would stand in the wings with my arm around her while the action would be going on onstage. She'd say to me, 'Hold me, hold me, hold me.' Then she'd say to herself, 'Control, control, control.' She'd hit her cue line and she'd hit my arms and she'd hit

Jerry Walston and Lynn, backstage at the Pasadena Playhouse, during the run of Ballad of the City *(1965).* COURTESY OF JERRY WALSTON.

those boards and there was *no one* who could hold a candle to her. She had such magnetism and presence. It was just *absolutely unbelievable* that this girl who had been trembling had transformed herself so. I'd never cease to be amazed.

"One of the things that made Lynn an outstanding actress was she *worked.* A lot of people who started in the business when she did did it because it was convenient at the time for them to do so. When they had to start *working* for a living, they just fell by the wayside. Lynn, however, studied — she worked. It was her *survival.* She knew she could not depend on her husbands. She knew she could not depend on her mother. She just had to depend on herself. She got where she got because of her *talent* and because she gave them a dollar's worth of work for every dollar she took home.

"I'm going to be perfectly blunt: *no one, no one* was ever allowed to use her body for a sewer. She just *never, never* would allow it. She was a *lady.* She had *dignity.* She stood up for her rights — God,

I admired her. She never played the sexpot; she was a dramatic actress. Even as 'Queen of the 'B's,' she was a dramatic actress. I put Lynn in the class with another great talent, Bette Davis. Davis once said, 'There's only one way to work — like hell!' And *that's* the way Lynn worked. She was intense. When she was on, she was intense. I don't care if she was sleeping, she did it intensely; every cell of her body was concentrated into doing just that one thing.

"Imagine what she could have been had she had more support, understanding and love; if she could have had someone in all of that insanity whom she could have trusted. She couldn't trust anybody — and if people got too close, she'd just go.

"Lynn had no idea how to look for a husband, number one. And if her mother told her that they were all bastards, what difference did it make? Maybe she thought that she had to have a husband because she wouldn't be whole without someone. But her marriages were a dollars-and-cents thing most of the time. There was no love, no respect, no consideration. I think that she was degraded so much by her husbands and her family that it never occurred to her that she was a talented actress; when you're in the middle of it, you don't see it. Lynn never got a chance to discover who she was. She always thought she was the person 'they' told her she was.

"Lynn had a way of having to be nice all the time. She wanted to be accepted. I think this had to do with where she came from and her childhood. She was always trying to please people. That got her into a lot of uncomfortable situations. She was always going the extra when nobody else would. Then people would treat her 'less than' because she would tolerate it.

"Lynn came to accept me as a person whom she could trust and depend on. The more she opened herself up to me, the more she allowed herself to become *vulnerable*. And then she would do the very thing that she would hate herself for — get drunk.

"I never saw Lynn drink socially. I always saw her drink *destructively*. She had a self-worth problem. She was *really* an incredible person; but as much as I wanted her to recognize that, she could never, never grasp that."

There was one other person to whom Lynn drew especially close in the mid-1960s. Her name was Gladys Issacson. A charming and sophisticated woman, Mrs. Issacson was then about sixty, the wife of a rabbi. She had known Bari twenty years, although it's not exactly clear how they had first met. Lynn had always thought Gladys to be an exceptionally warm and wise person, one who had the ability to set her mind at ease with a few well-chosen words. The two had kept in contact at irregular intervals during the time Marge Fisher had been alive. Their friendship had been set on a more intimate path after Marge's death, with a mother-daughter dynamic developing. Bari would, in fact, refer to Mrs. Issacson as her "spiritual mother." She looked to her for sound advice and a more positive outlook on life. Gladys happily offered her both, for she adored Lynn. By 1965, the women were engaging in conversation regularly, often in person. Their frequent communication with one another would be maintained

Jerry Walston is happily brought together with Eugenie and John Fisher in the mid-1960s. COURTESY OF JERRY WALSTON.

for years to come, with Bari placing phone calls to her friend when she'd be on tour with a play.

John Fisher encouraged Lynn's relationship with Mrs. Issacson. He was greatly impressed by her unselfish concern for his sister and the respectful manner in which she treated her. Accordingly, it was obvious to him that Gladys filled a longstanding void in Bari's life, being there for her in way that his mother never had been.

John was now fifty and the owner of a Volkswagen dealership in Lakewood, CA. Even-tempered, stalwart and practical, he continued to be something of a father figure for his sister. No one knew Lynn better than he did — and he was, to her, a source of unshakable dependability.

> JERRY WALSTON: "If Lynn needed anything, he'd be right there. He was very devoted to her, but he didn't try to run her life or get in her way. Lynn would say things and John would be so tickled inside; he'd just chuckle and laugh. He was big and warm — just like Lynn. I loved John because I could tell he loved her."

Bari and her brother were, in a certain sense, a family of two. Beyond Christmas cards and occasional phone calls, they hadn't really kept up with relatives who'd played a part in their childhoods. There was no enmity involved here. It was rather a case of time and distance loosening their familial ties; it had been well over thirty years since they'd moved to California and most of their kin were still based on the East Coast.

Living much closer by was their stepfather, Robert Bitzer. Dr. Bitzer was now sixty-nine and sixteen years the pastor of the Hollywood Church of Religious Science.* The Reverend had long been a highly-esteemed spiritual leader in the Los Angeles community. His inspirational books and teachings had proved influential worldwide — and he would come to be regarded as one of the 20th century's greatest metaphysicians.

Lynn and John had quietly kept track of Dr. Bitzer and were aware of his many accomplishments. Despite this, however, they'd never made a concerted effort to reunite with him. Marge's divorce from the Reverend had apparently helped to create a schism with a far-reaching effect.

It is almost certain that Bari and Robert Bitzer's paths crossed at least once in later years, but nothing truly substantive took place between them and they'd continue going their separate ways. Each, however, would always speak well of the other. With John, though, it was a different situation because his relationship with his stepfather had been far more strained than his sister's.

Eugenie Fisher remembers the day when the Reverend called her husband at their home in Newport Beach (to which they had moved in 1963):

> EUGENIE FISHER: "We had a neighbor here who went to Dr. Bitzer for counseling. Somehow, she mentioned to him that she lived next door to John Fisher. He phoned here. I got on the phone and he said, 'This is Robert Bitzer, John's stepfather — may I speak with him?' John got on the phone and he was rigid; there was a yes-no-and-oh kind of tenor to his conversation. He came back into the living room, and he was in tears and he was shaking. And I asked, 'What did he say?' And he said, 'Oh, nothing, nothing. He was very nice; he was just trying to be nice.' I said, 'I think that's wonderful; after all these years he had the courage to call you and try to initiate some sort of relationship. What are you supposed to do? Are you going to call him back?' He said, 'I don't ever expect to talk to him again.'
>
> "And that was the end of that. He simply wouldn't open the door there. Bitzer was trying to reestablish a relationship. On his part, the intentions and feelings were good. In John's case, I think there was a whole lot of shame mixed up with jealousy, unresolved feelings and memories."

---

* In 1949 Dr. Bitzer had founded the Hollywood Church of Religious Science, an offshoot of the Institute of Religious Sciences — the church to which he had previously been affiliated.

Both John and Lynn still carried the scars of their childhoods. These emotional injuries had worked to prevent them from reengaging with their stepfather — and an exceptional opportunity for coming to terms with their innermost conflicts never came to pass.

In October 1965 Bari embarked on what would be her most successful theatrical endeavor, the national tour of *Barefoot in the Park*. The Neil Simon comedy was still packing houses on Broadway, where it was about midway into its four-year run. Romantic, lighthearted and full of typically hilarious Simon one-liners, its story centered on Paul and Corie Bratter, newlyweds who settled into a Manhattan walk-up inhabited by eccentrics. Paul was a button-down young lawyer whose personality was completely unlike that of his ditsy bride. Corie's widowed mother, Ethel Banks, was also a dizzy one and her presence in the couple's life was looming. Eventually, Ethel's attentions were diverted to Victor Velasco, the oddball middle-aged Casanova who resided in the attic above the Bratter's tiny fifth-floor apartment. The roles of Victor, Paul and Corie had been originated by Kurt Kasznar, Robert Redford and Elizabeth Ashley, respectively. While Ashley had gone on to be nominated for a Tony Award for her performance, it had actually been Mildred Natwick who'd stolen the show as Mrs. Banks. Natwick's gift for comic timing had been perfectly suited for Ethel, *Barefoot in the Park's* funniest character. The play's producer, Saint Subber, had come to think that Lynn would be equally good in the part, having been impressed by her turn as the mother in *Enter Laughing*. He offered her Mrs. Banks and Lynn's 111-city adventure with *Barefoot in the Park* began.

Bari's contract with Subber had specified that she'd be top-billed in *Barefoot in the Park*, with her name being advertised in larger type than her costars. Joel Crothers and Joan McCall were Paul and Corie when the tour kicked off. Both performers were repeating roles they had played on Broadway, having been replacements for Redford and Ashley. Portraying Victor Velasco was Sándor Szabó, a Hungarian actor with an impressive list of New York stage credits. Szabó and Lynn had clicked instantly and each did Neil Simon proud with their altogether engaging interpretations of his characters.*

Bari, in fact, went on to be continually singled out as *Barefoot in the Park's* most winning attraction. *Variety* termed her performance a "standout," stating, "Her pleasant, husky voice and sure control of expression and movement sock over the mom role." *The Evansville Courier* wrote, "Svelte Lynn Bari need bow to none for bright, sassy, sharp timing and playing. Miss Bari's role [is] superbly done." The *Fort Worth Star-Telegram* described Lynn "a grand comedienne — and let us say that the view from the fifth row center reveals her as quite a dish."

---

* Sándor Szabó would eventually depart Lynn's *Barefoot in the Park* company and join up with one headlining Myrna Loy. Woody Romoff would take over as Victor Velasco in the Bari edition of the comedy.

After playing Dallas late in the year, *Barefoot in the Park* moved further westward. The tour had already wended its way through innumerable cities and many more engagements were to follow. Bari seemed to thrive on this frenzied booking schedule, her trait of working best when under pressure coming to the fore. She was, of course, also being fueled by her adoring audiences — and the first-rate theatrical vehicle in which she was starring.

Lynn gains the sympathies of Joan McCall and Joel Crothers in Barefoot in the Park. *Bari is seen here in October 1965, at the outset of her 111-city tour with the Neil Simon comedy.*

You couldn't miss with that one. You just had to walk out and move your foot and they laughed.

Lynn was about halfway into her *Barefoot in the Park* commitment when the tour's traveling pace slowed down for a two-week stay in San Francisco, which would be followed by a month at the Melodyland Theatre in Los Angeles. Tab Hunter had signed on to play Paul Bratter for these important engagements — Saint Subber having temporarily yanked Joel Crothers, an actor without Hunter's box-office appeal.

Hunter and *Barefoot in the Park* made for a smooth blend, and the comedy sold out in San Francisco. Local celebrity Gypsy Rose Lee had caught the show, especially wanting to see Bari. The two had palled around at Fox in the late thirties (when Lee had been billed onscreen as Louise Hovick), but had lost touch with one another since. A joyful backstage reunion took place, leading to appearances by both Lynn and Tab on *Gypsy*, Lee's nationally-syndicated TV talk show.

Bari and Hunter brought *Barefoot in the Park* to Melodyland in late January 1966. The *Los Angeles Times* sent two of their critics, Cecile Smith and Margaret Harford, to review the play. Both bestowed acting honors upon Lynn. Smith wrote that she was a "deft and skillful comedienne … much too handsome a female to be anyone's mother-in-law." Harford had this to say: "*Barefoot in the Park* draws chiefly on Lynn Bari's fine comedy talents. She is an artful comedienne, a real pro with a cool, ironic style and the wit to time a laugh just long enough without letting it get cold."

Other LA critics were similarly charmed by Bari's opening-night performance at Melodyland. Most spoke to the fact that she had carried herself off in an assured manner. If only they had seen her before the curtain had come up — for she had arrived to the theater in a mode of extreme agitation. According to Jerry Walston, Lynn's emotional stress had been due in large part to the actions of Nathan Rickles. Walston recalls what had happened that evening, as he gives forth with his observations about the psychiatrist and his marriage to Bari:

> JERRY WALSTON: "She opened at Melodyland in *Barefoot in the Park* and this jerk [Rickles] brings her in *half-an-hour* late — and he does it deliberately! So I said to Lynn, 'The next time you do anything here *I* will come and get you here early enough, so you're not in a state of insanity by the time you're ready to go on stage — you can't afford that.'
>
> "Rick wanted a movie star for a wife. In public, it was his chance to be 'on.' He always treated Lynn as though, 'Well, here she is — she's a star, but it's not that important.' — How could you bring a *star* in half-an-hour late? It's terrible; but that's why she was attracted to him. She could handle the rest of them, so she went out and got another one — just like the ones she'd had. Only this one had a couple of million dollars and a house in Beverly Hills. Lynn wanted security.

January 1966; Barefoot in the Park *reaches San Francisco and this portrait of Lynn graces the show's souvenir program.*

"She was married to 'one of the top ten psychiatrists in the country.' Although how the hell he ever got that title, I'll never know. He would tell you this, though. By trying to make himself look so good, he tried to make Lynn look less. I think that he didn't want to be 'Mr. Lynn Bari' — and that's how it ended up. All she had to do was walk in and he'd fade into nothingness. No matter where they went, people would come up to her and ask for autographs. [She'd sign them] and he'd just get rude. And yet, I don't think he realized what he was doing. I don't think he thought he was degrading her.

"Rick didn't want her to be independent. In the early times, he was always putting up 'the family thing.' It was just a farce. As far as I'm concerned, he was a manipulative, controlling, domineering person with less than social grace and very money-minded."

The control to which Jerry Walston refers might help to explain the course Lynn's career would take after her journey with *Barefoot in the Park* had come to an end. The tour had been an out-and-out triumph for Bari and she had left it in late April 1966 with her professional self-confidence fully restored. Looking forward to bigger and better things, she had for several months been in talks with her managers about staging a Lynn Bari publicity blitz that would emphasize her run in the Simon comedy. It was then decided full-page trade ads would be designed, each featuring becoming headshots of Bari alongside excerpts from her most glowing reviews. The campaign took off in May, in *Variety* and other widely-read industry publications. There was no doubt that Lynn was seizing the moment in a most constructive way. Once again, however, she'd succumb to an old behavioral pattern of success followed by self-sabotage. This would result in her being at home for the remainder of the year — under the domination of a person whose treatment of her reaffirmed her sense of low self-esteem.

It could be said that Nathan Rickles put the kibosh on his wife's career after *Barefoot in the Park*, but Bari had allowed this to happen. The neurotic needs of both were evidently being met, as their relationship deteriorated and entered into an unhealthy realm from which it would never emerge. Instead of making a big splash after the Simon play, Lynn became engulfed in a domestic psychodrama. Mind games were now carrying her marriage along, with Bari and her husband behaving in a hostilely interdependent manner. Lynn returned to working in Rickles' office, fired up about the ignominiousness of it all; here she had tossed away a brass ring to file psychological histories. Missed professional opportunities, anger and self-pity took their toll on Bari, leading her to the bottle with increasing regularity.

Making matters worse for Lynn and Rickles' relationship was the fact that their children were now much less involved in their day-to-day lives. Rena Rickles had recently married and John Luft had entered college, leaving Bari and the shrink more time to focus on doing battle with one another.

Lynn's career was, as always, at the center of the couple's most heated arguments. After having lost a few rounds on this topic, Bari determined she'd resume acting come hell or high water. It was now January 1967, over eight months since *Barefoot in the Park* — and the professional momentum it had engendered. To Lynn's great dismay, the only reasonable offer presented to her was a guest shot NBC-TV's campy secret-agent series, *The Girl from U.N.C.L.E.* She took on the assignment, playing a glamorous spy in "The Phi Beta Killer Affair" (aired March 14). Bari actually looked quite stunning on the show, far better than she had in her television gigs of the past half-dozen years. It was obvious that she had set her mind on taking greater care of herself, in the hopes that her *U.N.C.L.E.* appearance would help to reestablish her as a home-screen staple. It wouldn't. The sixties were then at their most swinging, TV had become more youth-oriented — and almost all forties film actresses had gotten lost in the shuffle.

Bari and her contemporaries were, indeed, finding the pickings slim on television. However, their situation there looked rosy in comparison to their prospects in motion pictures — which were next-to-nil. The theater was much more welcoming, particularly at summertime. In this regard, Lynn could certainly have made plans to hit the strawhat circuit. Nathan Rickles drew the line there, though, making it clear that out-of-town engagements were out of the question. Bari instead remained close by her husband, doing her bit in his office and socializing with the Beverly Hills crowd. As per usual, the two were constantly at loggerheads — a situation that had often given a perverse charge to their sex life. Make-up time found the couple charting out a second European vacation, which would be taken in the autumn.

Lynn's next acting job came about at the suggestion of her friend William Reynolds. Reynolds had met Bari on the set of *Has Anybody Seen My Gal*, where he'd been cast as her son. She had proved to be extremely encouraging to the young actor, then at the outset of his career. Never forgetting Lynn's kindnesses, Reynolds was now in a position of helping to secure her work on *The F.B.I.*, the hit ABC-TV series to which he had recently come aboard as costar. He broached Bari's name to the show's producer, Quinn Martin. Martin responded to him quite favorably, for he himself had happily landed Lynn for a guest turn on one of his earlier series, *The New Breed*. Reynolds' gesture resulted in a meeting between Bari and Martin, with the producer assigning her to "Line of Fire," the November 26, 1967, episode of *The F.B.I.*

Lynn filmed "Line of Fire" in the late summer, playing a bedraggled alcoholic named Ma. The widow of a Hispanic tavern owner, the character of Ma was older in years than Bari herself. The role was a seriocomic one, amounting to an arresting cameo opposite Reynolds and *F.B.I.* star Efrem Zimbalist, Jr. Quinn Martin took note of Bari's performance and promised to keep her in mind for other guest shots.

Lynn set off for Europe with her husband toward the end of October. The couple first spent a few days in New York, where Bari made the radio and television talk-show rounds, plugging her upcoming *F.B.I.* appearance. Once abroad, the Rickles spent the majority of their time in Italy, visiting Rome, Florence and Venice. The Venice floods had occurred just one year before, their devastation to the port city leaving Lynn rather unsettled. Nevertheless, she'd come to remember her Venetian sojourn most fondly. The last leg of her vacation was London. She and Rickles caught several shows on the West End, before flying into New York the third week of November.

Bari again went on the Gotham talk-show circuit. She dropped by the studios of WBAI, where author Richard Lamparski interviewed her for his popular syndicated radio show, *Whatever Became Of?* * Lynn reminisced with Lamparski about her career, mentioning it was still very much active. She told her host she was in New York to pursue the possibility of working on Broadway. Lamparski responded to this enthusiastically, commenting that she still exuded the glamour and verve of her heyday — something that would surely appeal to theatergoers. Whether Bari was actually entertaining any serious offers to appear on the New York stage remains unclear, but it is certain she headed back to Los Angeles without having committed herself to any type of theatrical endeavor.

Although no plays were pending, Lynn arrived home invigorated by her vacation. Thanksgiving was soon approaching and she was very much looking forward to spending time with her son. She felt happy — for a moment. Her upbeat frame of mind dissipated almost immediately and she became entrenched in moroseness. Genie Fisher gives credence to this fast downward spiral, recalling the communication she had had with her sister-in-law in the days following her return to Beverly Hills:

> EUGENIE FISHER: "She called me and mentioned this gallant, handsome Italian man she had met in Venice — he had made an indelible impression. My husband came home and I mentioned that we had talked, and mentioned this man from Venice. Well, John misunderstood and thought Venice, *California*. So when John and Peggy talked, there was a miscarriage of information.
>
> "Peggy called me and she was in her cups and she started in with this diatribe — it was just like I was listening to her mother — I was absolutely floored. The gist of it was that I had made fun of this man from Venice, Italy — which I *hadn't*; my husband had made a mistake and said something to her that was misconstrued. I remember I then very, very quietly hung up on her. That was that — there was a chill there for six months or so, and then it just went on to business as usual.
>
> "I think that when Peggy got drunk, she mouthed off with stories that weren't true — just like Marge. It was déjà vu. It was strange."

---

* Bari would twice be a subject of Richard Lamparksi's *Whatever Became Of?* book series, first appearing in its fourth entry, which would be published by Crown in 1973.

Lynn's dependency on alcohol intensified, the quality of her life deteriorating swiftly. She'd later come to consider 1968 as the beginning point of her darkest period — a hellish time involving the final years of her marriage to Nathan Rickles.

1968 would turn out to be Bari's last year as a motion-picture and television actress. In January she filmed what was to be her TV swan song, "The Mecha-

Lynn and James Edwards, in a scene from The Young Runaways *that wound up on the cutting-room floor.*

nized Accomplice," the March 31 episode of *The F.B.I.* The crime series once more featured her in a cameo, this one strictly of the comic-relief variety. She played Belinda, an aging hippie who ran a San Francisco bookstore into which ventured the characters portrayed by William Reynolds and Efrem Zimbalist, Jr. Interrogated by the pair, Belinda showed herself to be an out-and-out kook. Lynn had fun with the role, enacting it with zest — her face almost getting lost underneath a voluminous blonde wig. Tresses aside, she looked a fetching forty-eight.

Most unfortunately, Bari's physical appearance was soon to take a radical tumble, her mounting personal hardships dramatically manifesting themselves. She seemed downright haggard in May, when she reported for work on *The Young Runaways* (1968). The picture would be Lynn's final screen credit. It was produced by MGM — the studio where her movie career had begun thirty-five years before. *Runaways* was certainly not in the class of a *Dancing Lady*, being intended for the lower half of the double bills. Nonetheless, it was actually a fairly substantive and sensitive study of teenage unrest. *Variety* (9/11/68) would comment, "Excellent cast, direction, production for good script."

Patty McCormack, Brooke Bundy and Kevin Coughlin were the film's run-aways, equally-troubled youths whose stories were unrelated to one another. Bari and Norman Fell were cast as the Donfords, the parents of McCormack's character. Mrs. Donford was a shrill woman, very uptight about the sexual revolution and the influence it was having over her daughter. Lynn brought her to life forcefully, her worn visage working in her favor here. She went on to receive good billing for what was clearly a secondary role — one that had been whittled down in the cutting room. Taking the scissoring in stride, Bari was left satisfied by her performance and *The Young Runaways* itself.

We had a wonderful director on that picture, Arthur Dreifuss, and I had a good part. I knew Patty. I had performed with her before — on a live TV show ["An Episode of Sparrows"] which was taken from a beautiful book. We worked well together and I enjoyed seeing her again.

The Young Runaways wrapped in June and Lynn's career came to a standstill. For the next three years, she'd remain tied down to a home where both she and her marriage would degenerate in a disturbing manner.

I didn't go to work. I had to run the house. I was the maid, the nurse. I had to answer his phone — he practiced at home and I had to take care of the patients — they all called me when they had problems. It was just like everything closed in.

> JERRY WALSTON: "Lynn was living in a very, very sick environment. I was at her home quite a bit and Rick tolerated me. I remember I was once in the house when he was supposedly treating patients; and a very famous young actress was screaming throughout the house. I asked Lynn, 'How can you live here?' She said, 'I can't. Let's get the hell out of here!' So we left.
> "I was drinking quite heavily with Lynn at the time. Occasionally, we'd go out for a few in the afternoon and come back a few days later. Rick didn't mind at all. Once, I brought Lynn back after we'd been gone for some time. He said, 'I don't know where the hell you take my wife, but when she comes home she's all woman!'"

Absent from Bari's marital relationship was any sort of tender, loving attention. Jerry Walston provided her with this, in a platonic way. Lynn responded to him in kind, proving to be a source of great support to a friend who was hurting from the dissolution of a longtime romantic attachment. Both, however, could only be of so much help to the other since their perceptions were generally distorted by alcohol. Still, they were able to maintain a bond of trust which enabled them to enjoy many pleasant moments together. Bari certainly delighted in her overnight outings with her pal. The two would usually wind up sharing a room with twin beds in a hotel not too far from Beverly Hills. Sheltered there, Lynn would often feel a thrill — similar to that of a child who starts to run away from home, knowing full well she'd be back with her parents before dark.

Each time Bari returned from one of the excursions, she felt more imprisoned by her marriage. Her sense of conjugal victimization grew in intensity, exacerbated by her boozing. She began to perceive her husband as a most menacing antagonist. Accordingly, she caved into his demands, often without first putting up a good fight. Rickles may have been trying to strip Lynn of her identity, but in doing so he satisfied his wife's penchant for turmoil — a character trait that apparently knew no bounds once she had succumbed to alcohol.

> EUGENIE FISHER: "At that time, Peggy was going through menopause. I think that a lot of women have got to remove themselves from stress when they're going through that period — and she had a lot stress.
>
> "She was always disappointed in men — and there she was, disappointed at a very vulnerable time in her life. And then to have the alcohol and the cigarettes on top of that — I think it was very destructive to her, emotionally and physically. Given her nervous system, alcohol was devastating to her health — and, gradually, it played a part in her relationship with Rick. She just lost her equanimity."

It was now 1969 and Lynn was fast approaching fifty. She hadn't acted in over a year, her social life was dwindling, her drinking was on the upswing and she was carrying on a rather isolated existence at home. By virtue of this set of circumstances, her husband became a force that prevailed over her every waking moment. Almost all that she did, said and thought was in someway tied into him and their relationship, and each move the shrink made was met with suspicion. Bari's loved ones greeted her with great concern, recognizing the unhealthy nature of her preoccupation. However, Lynn did have just cause to mistrust Rickles — particularly after she discovered he was having an affair with one of his patients.

The woman with whom Rickles had become involved was six years Bari's junior. She was married to one of the most talented and respected names in the motion picture industry. This man had maintained an especially warm friendship with Lynn over the years — and both he and his wife had been frequent guests at the Rickles' home. The couple shared similar creative inclinations, although the husband — a multiple Academy Award-winner — was the infinitely more famous one in their common profession.

This man would leave his wife for a younger woman in 1970. His wife would later utilize her abandonment as the basis for an artistic work, one which would strike to the heart of women who'd been likewise thrown over. The younger woman was the patient of Rickles who'd been screaming throughout his house the day Jerry Walston had come to visit. She would eventually marry and divorce Lynn's award-winning friend and begin a long-term relationship with another celebrity of note. Ironically, this later union would be broken by her mate's involvement with a college-age girl — a headline-making story in the 1990s.

The beginnings of this chain of infidelity saw the Rickles' household plunge into frenzy. Bari, devastated by her husband's betrayal, lost all sense of self-control and went on the warpath. The shrink responded to her actions by behaving in an uncharacteristically desperate manner. Genie Fisher vividly recalls the unsettling situation that was then transpiring:

> EUGENIE FISHER: "When Peggy found out that this woman and Rick were having an affair, she snooped into his journals. They certainly were revealing; but, after all, he's a psychiatrist so whatever he was privy to was certainly none of her business — but she was looking for something. Anyway, she went into an absolute rage. She threw all of his journals out the window. She wrote four-letter words all over the inside of his study in lipstick and carried on like a crazy woman.
>
> "And he called here. I was at home — John was at work. Rick was beside himself about my 'sister-in-law' — not his wife. My 'sister-in-law' was just driving him crazy and she had done all these awful things and something had to be done, and he was on the verge of tears. I said, 'Let me get a hold of John, and John will get back with you.' John called him. Rick was in tears. 'What am I going to do with her? What am I going to do?' he said. He's a psychiatrist and this is his wife and he's wringing his hands on the phone, asking me and my husband what he's supposed to do with his wife. That was my last conversation with him."

Rickles was unable to placate Lynn. His marriage continued on a downward slide in 1970, despite the fact that his liaison had come to an end. Bari was now viewing the doctor as evil incarnate. She became convinced he was plotting to destroy her. Without hesitation, she made this belief known to close friends and family, usually while in an intoxicated state. Most would listen in helpless astonishment to her tales of persecution — melodramatic stories that could have been concocted during a script session at Fox's old Western Avenue studio.

> JERRY WALSTON: "There was a time through this when I took what she said with a grain of salt. Not that I didn't believe it; it could have very well happened, but I kind of took what she said with a grain of salt because she was *pretty* shook up."

> EUGENIE FISHER: "She got paranoid; I don't know if it was with good reason or not. She really thought Rick was out to get her. She said he was giving her the 'gaslight treatment.'* She would call me

* In 1939, and again in 1944, Patrick Hamilton's play *Angel Street* was filmed as *Gaslight*. The plot of *Gaslight* concerned a man who tried to drive his wife insane — hence Bari's expression, "the gaslight treatment."

and go out on the deep end with things that she would say. I felt like I was listening to Marge again. I hung up on her once because she was *unbelievable*. And we never talked about it again; I think because she was feeling self-conscious about it."

Lynn's disturbed relationship with Nathan Rickles reached a climax in early 1971. At this point, she truly believed the psychiatrist was attempting to do her in. Some of those dearest to her would hear her relate a nightmarish incident — one which would propel her to leave her husband for good.

Bari claimed the following sequence of events had occurred at her home: She and Rickles had gotten into a heated argument one evening. Her husband tried to calm things down by suggesting that they both take a sleeping pill and go to bed. Lynn agreed to the idea, swallowed a sleeping tablet and nodded off. Then, in the middle of the night, she awakened in stunned horror to find the psychiatrist poking barbiturates down her throat. She immediately wrested herself away from him, bolted from their bed, threw on some clothes and raced away,

John and Eugenie Fisher were the first to learn of this harrowing event, as Lynn sought refuge in their home on the night in question. Bari remained in Newport Beach briefly and then headed back to LA, where the hospitality of Jerry Walston would be awaiting her.

> JERRY WALSTON: "She needed to get away to a place where she could hide, so she came to live with me for a while. She was afraid. She told me that Rick was trying to drive her crazy.
>
> "Lynn didn't stay with me all that long. She said she wanted to go to Las Vegas to see some people. So we drove to Las Vegas and she called some people there to express her fear that he [Rickles] might be going to do something to her — and she didn't want him to get away with it, if he did.
>
> "I remember that we had gone to Las Vegas on Rick's credit cards. *(Laughing)* Lynn got the biggest kick out of charging all this stuff to his credit cards — she had a ball.
>
> "We spent a weekend there and came back. She was really worried that Rick was trying to kill her so that she wouldn't be able to get a settlement out of him. She said, 'What am I going to do? I've [only] got ten thousand dollars, a mink coat, and a car.' I told her, 'Don't worry about it; I'll sell the property I've got, my house if we have to, and I'll keep you going.' She said, 'Well, what am *I* going to do?' 'Well,' I said, 'you're going to have to do what I do — go to work.' She said, 'Well, all right.'"

Bari took Walston with her to her lawyers' offices; she discussed with her attorneys how she should proceed with the dissolution of her marriage. March 1971 found her living alone at the Malibu Outrigger, a condominium in which she was to reside for a few months. Nathan Rickles apparently made several attempts to contact her there, hoping to broach the subject of reconciliation. Lynn viewed these gestures as a threat to her well-being and her fear of her husband intensified. She then fled Malibu for the security of her brother and sister-in-law's.

> EUGENIE FISHER: "She spent about a week with us. She had lost a lot of weight. She was throwing up all the time; it was more nerves than drink. She was terrified that he [Rickles] was going to come in and *get* her. I couldn't understand why she was frightened of this older man — he was maybe fifteen years older than she. I couldn't imagine him having the strength or the will to haunt her that way. But she was very afraid of him."

The Fishers were able to provide Lynn with the type of support she needed to get a firmer grip on herself. John helped to find her a small apartment in Hollywood, north of Sunset Boulevard. For Bari, this area seemed better protected than Malibu, principally because it was more populated. She made the move there. Happily, her drinking started tapering off.

It was now summer. Friends and family were encouraging Lynn to resume her career. Uppermost in her mind was disentangling herself from Rickles, but she did reengage with her management and asked them to put out feelers on her behalf.

The first plausible offer presented to her was the role of the sultry and sardonic actress, Lorraine Sheldon, in a stage revival of Kaufman and Hart's *The Man Who Came to Dinner*. The comedy was going to be produced by the Mummers Theater in Oklahoma City, OK. Of local renown, the Mummers had been run as an amateur theatrical company for decades. It had become a professional venue in 1970, at which time it had begun operating out of a newly-built, five-million-dollar theater. The details of its present status were overly stressed to Bari by her agent, who was aware of her first-rate stage credentials. After considerable thought, Lynn signed on to *The Man Who Came to Dinner*, hopeful that Oklahoma City might be just the place for a low-key comeback.

The play was scheduled for a two-month run, opening in December 1971. Bari arrived in Oklahoma in November to begin rehearsals. Two days later she was back in Los Angeles. Shedding some light on her *Man Who Came to Dinner* experience is Tony Aylward, an actor in the show:

> TONY AYLWARD: "Lynn was there for the reading of the play and I thought she was just wonderful. She had that combination of affected star and real down-to-earth dame, which I thought the part really required. She was very funny and certainly had the voice and the presence. She looked good, her figure was good; I thought she'd look smashing in the show.
>
> "That night, she invited some of the actors to her apartment for drinks. She was very charming, very vivacious. The next day we

came to rehearsal and were told that she had fled! *(laughing)* The
story was given that someone had called and told her that her husband was having an affair with somebody."

One can only speculate the real reason behind Lynn's sudden exit. In all likelihood, any question she might have had about appearing in a Midwest-based
production — one being mounted by fledgling professionals — had been quickly
answered to her; she had most probably sized up the endeavor as something
beneath her theatrical standards. She had then thought fast, employing the two-
year-old secret of Rickles' infidelity to cast herself as a distraught woman scorned.
Consequently, she had been able to back out of a commitment by incurring sym-
pathy rather than ire, holding on to her stage reputation in the process.

Bari and Nathan Rickles were legally separated on December 23, 1971.
Shortly thereafter Lynn initiated a divorce action against her husband. *The Hollywood Reporter* ran the following on February 24, 1972:

> "Actress Lynn Bari has been through a tragic marital drama that
> could outscare a Hitchcock horror buff. After recently separating
> from her marriage of 17 years to psychiatrist Dr. Nathan Rick-
> els [sic], she told agent Bob Meiklejohn she wishes to resume her
> acting career. Spectators taking notes at her forthcoming divorce
> hearing will get a nightmarish script, and they can look for more
> than one top Hollywood name to be subpoenaed."

Bari's cloud of oppression began to evanesce as the termination of her marriage came into view. She was regaining control of her life, feeling optimistic
about her future for the first time in ages. Lynn's loved ones were, naturally,
cheered by this. Most sensed a diminishment in drinking had also been behind
her improvement. Healthier in body and spirit, Bari would steer herself on a
positive course for the better part of 1972. She decided to upgrade her living
situation early in the year, moving south of Sunset Boulevard to North Doheny
Drive, where she rented an attractive apartment (once the home of actor Zachary Scott). While settling in there, she set about finding herself work.

Her search had barely begun when she landed the lead in a touring company of Neil Simon's *The Gingerbread Lady*. The comedy-drama had premiered
on Broadway the previous theatrical season, with Maureen Stapleton starring.
Lynn's version of *Gingerbread* took to the road in the spring, concentrating mostly
on the Southwestern states. For six months, Bari would portray the alcoholic
Evy Meara, a has-been singer who returns to her Manhattan home after an
extended stay at a rehab.

Evy is in her mid-forties, a sharp and expansive person who's as self-destructive
as she is witty. *Gingerbread's* first act presents her as a "changed" woman, one who

is welcomed back from her convalescence by two close friends and seventeen-year-old Polly Meara, the daughter from whom she'd been somewhat estranged. Evy is buoyed by the support she's receiving, but things become unsettled when her abusive ex-boyfriend Lou drops in for a visit. All hopes for the singer fade as she drinks her way through the second act, alienating her pals and disrupting the relationship she has been trying to reestablish with Polly. The curtain falls with Evy making a phone call to Lou, telling him she is heading over to his place to spend the night. *Gingerbread's* third act unfolds the following morning in Evy's apartment. She is nowhere in sight, her friends and daughter anxiously awaiting her. Finally, she walks through the door hung over and beaten, attempting in vain to mask her condition with caustic one-liners. Her two buddies once again rally behind her — as does Polly, whom Evy acknowledges to be a far stronger person than she.

Lynn would later recall that *The Gingerbread Lady* had come along at just the right point in her life. After a three-year absence from performing, she had been given the chance to invest herself in a creative venture that would fulfill her on both a professional and personal level. The show enabled her to etch a character of great depth and complexity — a woman who was similar in temperament to herself. Across the board, she won high praise for playing Evy Meara. The *Dallas Times Herald* wrote:

> "She is a terrific actress. No one could question that after having seen Miss Bari so dominate the stage, giving so much power, poignancy and biting comic emphasis to the role."

Bari was in Dallas with *The Gingerbread Lady* on July 25, 1972 — the day she was granted a divorce. Her busyness with the tour had mercifully spared her a trial filled with tales of horror, "special guest stars," and other histrionics. However, in order to actually receive the divorce, she had to appear in Superior Court in Los Angeles. The timing of this hadn't been at all propitious. In 1973 Lynn would relate the following to *Modern Screen*:

> "I got the divorce while I was in the play. To get it, I had to fly back from Dallas to California. I left at 2:30 in the morning, got the divorce at 8:30 that same morning, then flew back and did the show that night."

The court proceedings had been brief and without fireworks. Bari, citing irreconcilable differences, had been handed her decree of divorce by Superior Judge Earl F. Riley. At her request, Riley had also reinstated her maiden name, Marjorie Fisher. The press reported that a property settlement agreement had been submitted, one which was to give Lynn $150,000 in cash and an automobile. News articles about this agreement also stated that no provision for alimony had been included.

Some of Bari's confidantes would later dispute the exact terms of the settlement but all would agree that it resulted in a raw deal for Lynn, in light of Rickles' wealth. Bari herself was well aware of this inequity at the time of her divorce decree. However, she was eager to put a quick finish to her marriage and get on with her life, having no reason to doubt that she could support herself handsomely as a working actress. The day would come, though, when she'd live to regret not having taken advantage of California's community property laws. In fact, she was soon to tell friends that Rickles had proved to be worth more than he had admitted, and this would add to her eventual disappointment over her hastiness.

Seventeen years after their divorce, and with sober hindsight, Lynn had offered this remembrance of the man who had become her third husband:

He was a *psychotic* psychiatrist. He gave *me* the gaslight treatment, *really* bad. You mustn't think that I just say this about all my ex-husbands *(laughing)* but it's true! What frightened me about the shrink was that *he* was so damned *unstable himself, how* the hell could he tell anybody what to do? I don't think he heard half of it [his patients]; he was deaf in one ear and he was too damned *vain* to wear an ear piece.

Bari's antipathy for Rickles would endure.

Lynn Bari, during her 1974 tour with The Gingerbread Lady. COURTESY OF PHOTOGRAPHER ED COLBERT.

CHAPTER SEVENTEEN
EARTHBOUND

Lynn felt she was once again on a purposeful path, her divorce action against Nathan Rickles having led her there. After seventeen years of marital discord, she thought herself more self-possessed and goal-oriented. Her creative spirit had returned in full force, due in no small part to her current success with *The Gingerbread Lady*. She continued reaping great satisfaction from the show until her tour completed its run in autumn 1972. At that point, though, she was glad her turn as Evy Meara had come to an end. The role had been quite a demanding one, ultimately leaving her emotionally and physically depleted. She still very much wanted to go forward with her career, but she knew a long period of rest would have to come first. Consequently, she declined an offer to take *The Gingerbread Lady* to Australia that winter.

Bari was certainly exhausted when she got back to LA, but her outlook was positive. She followed through with taking a break and would revel in her relaxation, a single woman at liberty. Quickly revived to a rather carefree state, she'd basically be in repose for six months. Her happy-go-lucky side came across to Dora Albert, when the writer interviewed her in April for a *Modern Screen* article. Albert's essay, "Catching up with Lynn Bari," would be published in the magazine's October 1973 issue. The piece would include many choice quotes from the subject herself. Among them:

> "My marriage to Dr. Rickles had disintegrated completely, and I didn't take it lightly. I was under great pressure and strain, and could hardly sleep at night."

> "I would never marry again. I think that after you've been married three times, you're out. Each time I felt I was marrying for a good reason, but I was wrong."

> "I don't want to have anything said that makes me sound like I was some little marshmallow who sat back and took anything and everything."

"Now is the first time in my life that I've ever been able to feel free to do what I want to do. I'm not lonely."

"I'll be doing another stage play soon and if anything interesting comes up in the way of a TV show or a movie, I'll take it."

"I've been to Vegas three times in the last month. I love to gamble — it's my biggest sin, I guess. Vegas is the most sordid place to live but I like to go there for short visits. I enjoy New Orleans; at Mardi Gras time I went there and stayed with friends. I have a brother who lives in Newport Beach; I could have that scene if I wanted it. But I'm having fun right here in Beverly Hills. Believe me, I ain't alone. Nobody has to feel sorry for me. I'm living life to the hilt. There will never again be one man in my life. I'm going to have a little fun for a change."

While Lynn's newfound emancipation was cause for good cheer, she was also very angry with those whom she felt had exploited her. This indignation would surface in Albert's article in a pronounced way. The essay wouldn't, however, make clear the fact that she was especially mad at Rickles — and the extent to which she had been shortchanged in their divorce settlement. Nonetheless, those close to Bari would read between the lines and see her taking direct aim at the shrink's double-dealing. This would evidence itself toward the beginning of the piece, after mention of Lynn's having earned a million dollars by the time she'd reached thirty. Albert would write:

"Today, she [Bari] still has that look of glamour — her merry face is framed by short reddish brown hair. Her long legs and slender shape show off the clothes she wears with great style. The day I caught up with her someone had called to ask her to pose for a commercial ad for jewelry — and she'd said yes. 'I can use the money,' she admitted. 'I threw away most of that million dollars on bad investments and jerks who ripped me off.'"

Lynn did not serve herself well by the above two-sentence statement. At that point her financial situation was anything but tight; Rickles may have hoodwinked her but he had left her quite comfortable. However, she had been given an opening for a potshot and she ran with it, albeit indirectly.

"Catching up with Lynn Bari," though essentially flattering, would bring to light an ever-troublesome fact about its subject: her achievements had always been shaded by disappointment, being largely in reaction to the negative forces in her life. For better or worse, however, Bari's antagonistic relationships had been what had kept her moving along.

As much as Lynn thought she'd enjoy being on her own, she would prove to have great difficulty adjusting to life without the stimulus of interpersonal conflict. The novelty of being single, footloose and fancy-free was soon to wear off and she'd become oppressed by feelings of inadequacy and victimization. Her self-esteem falling to new depths, she would find herself engulfed by bitterness. There'd be no one on whom she could vent her anger, so she'd turn her rage inward and give herself up to the bottle.

Lynn's publicity portrait for Follies *(1973).* COURTESY OF PHOTOFEST, INC.

Sometime in 1973 Bari entered into the terminal stage of alcoholism, which in her case would endure for a decade — and take her on a journey into hell. Over the course of the next ten years she'd destroy her career, discard many of her friendships, lose most of her savings and see her health permanently impaired.

Liquor would also adversely affect Lynn's appearance to an irreversible degree. This particular deterioration would evolve relatively slowly, though, not reaching noticeably unfavorable proportions until her sixtieth birthday. As Dora Albert had written, Bari was still a very attractive woman in 1973. Lines below her eyes and the trace of a jowl did evidence her passage into middle age, but those eyes were still a luminescent hazel and her smile was as cherubic as ever. Pretty and svelte, Lynn was certainly a youthful-looking fifty-three. It must be noted, however, that she had recently undergone a face lift. Her cosmetic surgery hadn't been at all radical, but she clearly hadn't looked so well in ages. Freedom from Dr. Rickles had also added a lift to her countenance, helping to make her an immediately-identifiable figure of days gone by.

Bari's film-star recognition factor no doubt figured into her securing the role of faded movie queen Carlotta Campion in the East Coast tour of *Follies*. The Stephen Sondheim musical had been the winner of seven Tony Awards in 1972. It was set in an about-to-be-demolished Broadway theater in which a revue, *Weismann's Follies*, had been staged many years before. The cast members of this production formed the nexus of *Follies*, coming together in present day for a nostalgic yet bittersweet reunion.

Follies had ended its Broadway run the previous July. Soon afterwards its first national company had taken to the road. It was followed in the US by Lynn's tour, which hit the boards in June 1973. The cast of this version included Vivian Blaine, Robert Alda, Jane Kean, Hildegarde and Selma Diamond. Bari played the part Yvonne De Carlo had created in New York. Carlotta was of secondary importance to the musical, but the role boasted the first-act showstopper, "I'm Still Here," a coruscating ode of showbiz fortitude.

Lynn was several weeks into *Follies* when the musical was lighting up the Tappan Zee Playhouse in Nyack, NY. In the midst of this engagement, on July 2, Betty Grable passed away. The next evening *Village Voice* critic Arthur Bell was on hand at the Tappan Zee. Nine days later Bell's review of *Follies* was published in the *Voice* — under the headline, "So *that's* what's become of Lynn Bari." He wrote:

> "Lynn Bari sings 'I'm Still Here,' and the effect was chilling. Bari was a Fox contract player in the '40s — one of her earliest movies was 'Pigskin Parade,' which featured Grable. In 'Follies,' with great vitality and aplomb, Lynn Bari sings about the vicissitudes of a Grable-like performer, medium on talent, high on personality, patting herself on the back for having survived it all. Under the circumstances, Bari's rendition sent shivers."

Lynn went on to garner additional praise for *Follies*, as the play traveled throughout the Northeast. Somewhere along the way, however, her personal problems would begin to hamper her ability to sustain a top level of performance — something that had never before occurred. She now felt lost without the presence of a significant other to whom she could relate, be it a husband or a mother. Her state of independence was fast crashing down on her and she started to break down emotionally. She became overwhelmed by a sense of isolation, a situation exacerbated by her being three-thousand miles away from home. Her free time on the road was being wasted away, as she drowned her sorrows in booze. By late summer, her spark and enthusiasm had totally fallen by the wayside. She was still acting with a modicum of dynamism, but she was putting forth great effort to affect this quality. Soon, though, it wouldn't be of any concern to her how she was coming across onstage. Her demons would go on to best her in a publicly embarrassing way — and she'd be out of *Follies* by October. In deference to Bari, the show's producers would explain to the press that she'd been in ill health and was being replaced by Julie Wilson.

Lynn returned to Los Angeles dazed, despondent and humiliated. Just one year ago she had felt her life was falling into place, and now she was experiencing something of a spiritual death. Hopelessness prevailed. Bari's friend Jerry Walston could identify with her despair because he himself had gone through a similar depression during the final stages of his own active alcoholism. Having put down his last drink two-and-one-half years earlier, he had come to rejoice in the many gifts of sobriety. It pained him greatly to see Lynn, a woman who had yet to deal with her addiction in a constructive manner. He knew full well she first had to surrender to the fact that she was an alcoholic — something she was presently unable to do.

> JERRY WALSTON: "After Lynn moved into the apartment on Doheny, I used to pick her up and we'd go out to lunch. I was sober. I remember we went to the Hamburger Hamlet one day. The girl came and asked if we wanted a drink. I said, 'No, I'll have some coffee.' Lynn said, 'I'll have a drink. He's the coffeeholic, I'm the...' And she never finished the sentence. She looked at me like: 'You bastard!' *(laughing)*
>
> "Lynn was the type who was *always* the lady. She was *charming* — you'd think sugar wouldn't melt in her mouth. As far as I was concerned, she was a sober saint; Lynn would do anything she could to do right. But the minute she'd have three or four drinks, this viciousness would come out and the language would change. And I remember, with myself, just *exactly* how it was.
>
> "She just could not handle alcohol — in just twenty minutes, she'd be drunk. She usually got very indignant — she was scared to death to let anyone find out about it. She'd say to me, 'I know and I know you know, but just give me some time.'
>
> "When I was seeing her constantly, I would go to her apartment and she'd be sitting there sewing. I mean, it wasn't her to sit and sew. I knew this was being staged for my benefit. One day I said, 'Come on, Lynn. Don't have any more to drink. Let's go out and get something to eat.' She said, 'What good does it do? You son of a bitch, I stayed sober for you three whole days and you didn't even notice!' And I thought, 'My God, that's what we all do to start — we stay sober for somebody else.' And it doesn't work until we start staying sober for ourselves."

Instead of confronting her alcoholism, Bari would go on to do herself and her career a grave disservice by returning to work at a time when she'd be in no condition to approach anything of consequence. She had made no attempt to seek employment in the months following her *Follies* debacle, her creative ambitions all but drowned out. Then, in spring 1974, she was presented with another offer to reprise the role of Evy Meara. This time she was being asked to commit to a summer's run of *The Gingerbread Lady* on the West Coast dinner-theater circuit. Lynn grasped at the opportunity. Her eagerness surprised her intimates, who'd seen her acting desire go on the wane. Perhaps Bari had thought the tour might stir her out of her malaise, being an answer to both her professional and personal problems. It would turn out to be neither, however. Under distressing circumstances, she'd drop out of the show midway through, having only played three two-week engagements.

It was a demanding role and it wiped me out. I was getting to be like the character *(laughing)* — getting *looped* every night.

Jerry Walston saw Lynn soon after her break with *The Gingerbread Lady*. It was heartbreakingly clear to him that his friend was in the midst of a major depression.

> JERRY WALSTON: "I remember when she came home from that. She was really feeling down and she was sitting in front of the mirror, trying to make herself look good to go out; and she threw all of her stuff down and started to cry. I think she felt that she couldn't look the way she used to look. She was also at a time in her life when acting was getting to be a real job, a real chore. There was a time when she loved it and looked forward to it, but she wasn't enjoying herself anymore."

Bari's apathetic attitude toward her work and her fragile state of mind had been made glaringly apparent to her brother and sister-in-law during her second go-around with *The Gingerbread Lady*.

> EUGENIE FISHER: "She came home one weekend. Her nerves were more on edge. There was a whole lot of emotional stuff going on, inwardly and outwardly. And she said in anger, not at me but just describing how she felt, 'You don't know what it's like to get up there in front of all those people and have to put yourself on the line.' And she went on about how *awful* it was and how difficult it was and how she didn't think she could go on with it.
> "And she blew that show. And I remember John saying, 'You know, you can't do this too many times in this business, because they'll blackball you.' And that was kind of the beginning of the end."

The 1974 *Gingerbread Lady* tour would, in fact, mark the demise of Lynn's career. Bari was taken aback by mention of this fifteen years later, before pausing and going on to describe her mind-set at the time:

> Oh, my God, there *is* nothing after that!…I didn't get any offers of work and I had enough money that I thought, "Well, I'm going to relax for a while and do what I damn well please." I was so sick of taking orders and cooking meals and entertaining that I just checked out for a while.

Lynn's final gesture at seeking work came in 1975. At some point that year she was reading through the trades and saw advertised an open audition for a national television commercial, one which would be spotlighting a woman of a certain age. She somewhat oddly chose not to pursue this job through an agent, whereby she could have secured a personal appointment with a casting director. Rather, she showed up for the audition anonymously, becoming lost in a large crowd of unknowns. An interminable wait followed. She was finally ushered into a room for an interview and cold reading. There, she was met by the astonished look of an old familiar face — the casting director. The man was full of apologies, so sorry Bari had been put through the paces of a cattle call. Quite naturally, he asked her why she hadn't gone through different channels to see him. Lynn said she hadn't wanted to trouble anyone. The two exchanged a few more pleasantries and Bari did a reading. Marjorie Reynolds would get the commercial.

Lynn would truly "check out" of showbiz soon after her halfhearted attempt to reenter it. By walling herself off from the entertainment industry, she'd deprive herself of the social aspect of a work environment, something that had for so very long been a mainstay to her. There would sadly be no compensation for this in her everyday life because she'd give in to her self-destructive impulses, becoming an increasingly more solitary individual.

Lynn's isolation took hold in a flat to which she had recently moved. Airy and modern, her home was a unit of a large apartment complex on La Cienega Boulevard, neighboring Beverly Hills. Bari would reside there until 1978, seldom venturing out at night. Evenings out-and-about with the Hollywood A-list crowd had been important to Nathan Rickles, but Lynn had come to be totally disinterested in this scene and was turning down any-and-all invitations to keep her a part of it. While eschewing the glitterati was one thing, Bari was also beginning to shy away from more personal contact, be it any time of day. She became disinclined to reach for an address book filled with names of good friends — and, in quick succession, she'd eliminate from her life the majority of her pals. Most of these people she had known for decades. All of them were to comprise what Eugenie Fisher would call Lynn's "graveyard of friendships."

Many of Bari's friendships reached back to her early days at Fox, having their roots in the happy camaraderie that had existed among her fellow stockgirls at the studio. These women had found themselves in the same boat, learning the rudiments of acting six long days a week in the rather closed society of a film company. By virtue of their work circumstances, most became close to one another — both on and off the set. Their friendships, by and large, had proved to be longstanding. Over the years they had had any number of large reunions, coming together at weddings and dinner parties. They had also met in smaller groups, for lunch and a movie or supper at one another's homes. These more intimate gatherings had seen them into middle age and were, in fact, still going strong in the mid-1970s.

The bonds of friendship Lynn had formed at the outset of her career had remained unbroken up until this point. There had never been a thought of leaving the other women behind, even though she became a movie star and they faded into obscurity; in this respect, Bari was quite unlike many who'd achieved fame. Unlike Lynn, a good number of her old comrades had gone on to marry top Fox personnel. Their lives had been spent away from the immediate glare of the spotlight, following a normal course in comparison to that of Bari's. Consequently, those who were now divorced or widowed were making far better adjustments to single life than their celebrated pal.

Lynn, awash in a state of alcoholic self-pity, had come to be upset by her friends' healthy adaptations. She became filled with resentment and started to have fallings-out with some of her chums. With others, she'd leave behind a trail of cancelled engagements and unanswered phone calls. The ones who'd manage to maintain contact with her would also be kept at distance, the effects of Bari's drinking making her insecure about setting up dates. The whole situation would grow worse and, within a few years, an entire social circle would be obliterated.

While there would be many moments when Lynn would want nothing better than to cut herself off from everyone, she'd continue to be responsive to some. Those with whom she'd remain in touch would include four from the show-business world: Dana Andrews, former Fox contract player Jean Rogers, and New York actors Tom Coley and William Roerick (her *Light Up the Sky* buddies). These particular friends would be less threatening to Bari because they hadn't been involved in the details of her decline; her relationships with them would afford her the room to affect a selective presentation of herself. All, however, knew Lynn ever-so well and would not be taken in by her posturing — something that would only serve to intensify their concern for her.

Dana Andrews had an acute understanding of Bari's problems because he himself had endured a long battle with alcoholism. He had now been sober fifteen years, having joined Alcoholics Anonymous in 1960. Andrews forever held a dear place in Lynn's heart and she'd always speak of him with admiration and affection:

Dana's remained a good friend. He's a wonderful actor, a nice guy. However, he just was so terribly mixed-up in the beginning — he went kind of wild. He got himself in Dutch when he was drinking so heavily. But he hasn't had a drink in something like twenty-five or thirty years now. He doesn't talk about it; he just doesn't do it.

Lynn had long since realized the extent to which Andrews' life had improved since he'd stopped drinking. Back in 1975, however, there was no comprehension of what sobriety could mean to her. She thought it terrific for people like Andrews and Jerry Walston, but her alcoholic self-denial made her case different; she felt she had no choice but to drink to survive. In their own ways, though, both Andrews and Walston served as powers-of-example for Bari, planting the idea of sobriety into her mind at a time when she had neither the strength nor the courage to put down the booze.

Jerry Walston remembers several instances when he suggested to Lynn that she attend AA meetings:

> JERRY WALSTON: "I'd say, 'You don't even know who you are. You're a marvelous person. Let's get sober and introduce you to yourself.' And she'd always say, 'Well, maybe, but not today.'"

Bari's loved ones were becoming alarmed by the progression of her alcoholism. Booze was now her sole point of focus and she was fast losing any motivation to carry on in a meaningful way. Her days came to be repetitiously barren; for the next three years, she wouldn't do much of anything — except to pour herself another drink. Sometimes, though, she'd manage to gather herself for a restaurant date. Her dinner partners would generally be sent into a state of worry by her deportment at these outings.

> JERRY WALSTON: "A lot times we'd be out some place and Lynn would stop before she'd go through the door and say, 'Wait a minute.' She'd take a deep breath and put her hand down in the pit of her stomach and say, 'All right — in we go.'
>
> "Once, we were finishing our lunch and she took out her purse to pay the check. I said, 'Put your purse away.' She said, 'Goddamn son of a bitch! Every asshole out there and his brother is trying to screw me out of every nickel they can get — and you won't even let me buy you lunch! What the hell's the matter with you?' And I said, 'If I did let you pay, I'd be just like all the rest of those assholes out there. And I'm not.'
>
> "There were times when she embarrassed herself so badly with me. And she'd call me the next day and say, 'Honey, I am so sorry for what I did.' And I'd say, 'Lynn, it never happened. I love you. Get yourself together and we'll go out to lunch.' And I said that *many* times."

More than once, Bari would respond affirmatively to Jerry Walston's suggestion that they rekindle the fun of the past by going on an overnight jaunt together. These latter-day excursions would be good for Lynn, taking her away from her seclusion with a sober person. Walston, for the most part, would enjoy traveling about with Bari. However, he'd also be brought to points of anguish, as his friend would unwittingly reveal to him her fundamental psychological torment.

JERRY WALSTON: "We'd go places and stay; and, naturally, we'd end up in twin beds in the same bedroom — never in the same bed, never. She'd go to sleep, and sometimes in her sleep she'd cry out for her mother. She'd say, 'Mama! Mama! Mama!' And, oh Jesus, I never felt so helpless in my life."

Sometime in 1978, Lynn was roused to effect a personal change. It wasn't, however, her drinking that she wished to modify. Bari's actions instead concerned her living circumstances. She was totally disenchanted with her apartment on La Cienega, primarily because she had grown to abhor the neighborhood in which it was situated. It's not entirely clear why she had come to feel so strongly about her environs. More than likely, though, her alcoholic way of thinking had made them a major thorn in her side, the source of her discontent. She in any event wanted out and — for the fifth time in seven years — she made a move, leasing a handsome apartment in Marina Del Rey, CA. Enhanced by a spectacular ocean view, this dwelling would be her home for five years.

Marina Del Rey was then an up-and-coming Los Angeles beach community, located between Venice and the LA International Airport. Its landscape was dotted with luxury condominiums and apartment buildings. A harbor for leisure craft outlined the area. The inhabitants of Marina Del Rey were mainly the upper-middle-class singles' set, professionals who liked to participate in outdoor sports and a swinging nightlife.

Being where the action was appealed to Lynn, now nearing fifty-nine. Perhaps she thought a hopping social scene would lift her out of her depressed state, as would the beauty of Marina Del Ray itself. She immediately developed an appreciation for what the town had to offer, but her sensitivities in this regard failed to alter her overall disposition and self-destructive behavior. Nothing, it seemed, could put the breaks on her alcoholic descent. Shunning the excitement of her new community, she became increasingly more housebound and sodden by liquor. Her addiction did away with her interest in practically everything, including food. Deprived of nourishment, she took on an emaciated appearance. It had become clear to all that Bari was on an agonizing journey with booze. Soon she'd be brought to a place where, as Eugenie Fisher would later observe, "She drank just to get drunk, toward oblivion."

Lynn was befallen with additional hardship shortly after the move to Marina Del Rey. She became ill with an undiagnosed arthritic condition. It struck her in the back, causing her periods of acute discomfort. Her pain progressively worsened throughout 1979. By year's end she'd been rendered virtually immobile on more than several occasions. A concerned John and Eugenie Fisher were now entertaining the thought of engaging for her a full-time nurse. Lynn had yet to agree to such an arrangement when her son weighed in, deciding that he would come and live with her.

Bari and John Luft had always been close, their relationship marked by a special devotion to one another. Lynn was not a clingy mother, though; she had pretty much let John do his own thing once he'd left for college. The custody case twenty years before had convinced her that she would try her best not to involve her son in her personal dramas, lest he become his mother's rescuer instead of

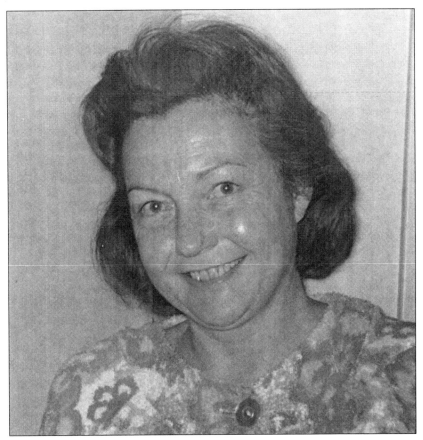

Lynn, in the late 1970s, at her Marina Del Rey home. COURTESY OF
PHOTOGRAPHER ED COLBERT.

his own man. John had gone on to pursue a career as an artist, proving to be a gifted sculptor. Now, at thirty-one, he was taking it upon himself to be there for Bari at a time when his caring presence could make a big difference in her life. And it would — his loving attention and support going on to be of immeasurable help in saving Lynn from a total self-annihilation.

John settled in Marina Del Rey and at once began accompanying his mother to various medical specialists. In 1980, Bari's malady was diagnosed as a certain chronic one. Nine years later Lynn would explain the affliction that had then been a part of her life for over a decade:

I've got ankylosing spondylitis. It's a rheumatoid arthritic condition of the spine. Did you read the Norman Cousins book, *The Art of Healing*? What happened to me is the same thing that happened to him [Cousins]. It *really* is a killer. I'm in constant pain and it affects my entire body. The back is the worst part because it supports everything that you do. I can move around all right, it's not hard — it just hurts when I do. If I've been out for a pleasant walk or something, the whole day has been killed for me.

Bari's arthritic disorder had deeply troubled her loved ones from the start. Quite compassionately, they'd all thought it grossly unfair that someone so decent and kind had been stricken by such a severe illness. Their hearts would soon be going out to Lynn in an even more pronounced way, for other ailments were about to descend upon her. In time, most would arrive at this unsettling conclusion: the unremitting stress of Bari's life had been the key factor in her physical decline.

> EUGENIE FISHER: "I think the reason things happened was because she'd always shouldered a lot of responsibility. I think that a lot of her physical problems, including the arthritis, were basically from an emotional source. There were just a whole lot of things that happened in the past. My husband also ended up with serious neurological problems."

> WILLIAM ROERICK: "Lynn tended to have things go wrong with her life. From the time that I knew her, *rarely* was she not involved in some traumatic situation. At the time, I just thought that she was courageous and made the best of a bad deal. However, if you're so upset and frustrated about something and can't do anything about it, you finally *do* make yourself ill."

Bari's state of health nose-dived in 1981. She developed respiratory problems that year and was told by her doctors that she was suffering from emphysema; her decades as a chain-smoker had taken their toll. Soon afterwards, she experienced a mild heart attack. A one-two punch had been delivered to Lynn, but her heavy cigarette habit would continue.

Bari spent much of 1982 in physicians' offices. Her doctors were many, each of them tending to a specific malady. Their method of treatment was almost exclusively drug-related. This approach was essentially life-imperiling to Lynn, in light of her alcoholism — which they had either failed to recognize or had not properly taken into consideration. The consequences of this mishandling would be distressing, the combination of booze and medication often sending Bari into a non-functioning state.

> JERRY WALSTON: "The doctors in Beverly Hills just had her on a round-robin; everyone was giving her something else. It was just terrible."

EUGENIE FISHER: "She had taken so many drugs that were devastating. Then she would need more because she was in so much
pain from the arthritis. Then they'd wean her off the drugs and
she'd have withdrawal symptoms — and the booze, of course, didn't
help at all."

Drugs of greater potency were prescribed to Lynn; she was now on many
heavy-duty pharmaceuticals. It quickly turned out that they didn't work well
together — to say the very least. Bari, in fact, experienced a near-fatal incident
because of their combined effect. This happened on a day in early 1983. Lynn
was at home with her son when she was overtaken by a fit of seizures. John Luft
immediately placed a call for emergency medical aid, as his mother laid in bed
gasping for air. Paramedics showed up on the scene at once. They managed to
arrest Bari's convulsions — with the cooperation of the patient herself. Lynn,
according to John, "fought like the Hulk" for her life.

At this point Bari was shocked into a realization: she had a strong desire to
live. She then decided it imperative that she really get her act together, vowing
to do whatever it would take to better herself.

———————————————

Lynn had become aware of the fact that her survival depended on a complete
turnaround in her lifestyle. Moving had long been an initial course of action in
her attempts to affect change, and so it would be again. This time, however, her
relocation would be relatively drastic in nature. She decided to say goodbye to
Los Angeles, her city of residence since age ten. LA had lost all of its appeal
for her; she had had her moments of glory there, but the town had come to
represent the stage on which she'd just completed a fifteen-year run in a most
self-destructive personal drama. Now acknowledging some responsibility for her
downfall, she thought it fruitful to jettison her victim mentality. Her efforts in
this regard would find her seeking a place to reestablish herself as an advocate
of a positive way of life.

Santa Barbara would become the setting of Bari's renaissance. Lynn had many
times visited friends there, being taken with the tranquility of the small city and
its idyllic landscape. A ninety-minute drive up the coast from LA, Santa Barbara
is encircled by the water and a postcardlike backdrop of hills. Lush California
vegetation abounds everywhere. Amidst a profusion of greenery and flowers
are early adobe homes, reminders of the Spanish town that once was. Taste-
fully-designed modern structures emphasize the city's metamorphosis into a
residential and resort area for California's genteel, old-money crowd.

An apartment complex on East Victoria Street was one of Santa Barbara's
newer dwellings in 1983. This is where Bari leased a flat in the summer of that
year. Her move there would be difficult, given her debilitation. She somehow
managed to summon up what little strength she had to make the relocation,
depending greatly on the enthusiastic support of her son and John and Eugenie

Fisher. John Luft, in particular, helped to ease what could have been an insurmountable transition. He had personally attended to all the logistics involved, during which time he'd determined it best to remain by his mother's side for an indefinite period. The two set up housekeeping on East Victoria, with Lynn filled with gratitude toward her son.

Bari arranged for a consultation with a local physician in the weeks following the move. The doctor had come recommended because he specialized in the treatment of arthritis. Lynn came to trust him almost immediately. She found him to be extremely knowledgeable, caring, and sincere. To her great relief, he was quite unlike her pill-dispensing LA physicians, being very conservative in his employment of medication. He instead placed emphasis on alternative techniques, including various physical therapies. His patient approach was basically humanistic; he treated the whole person, realizing one's ills were often manifestations of their psychological problems. Most fortunately for Bari, he was also well-versed in the field of alcoholism — and knew exactly with whom he was dealing in this regard.

The doctor had first off told Lynn the drugs she'd been prescribed had been intoxicating her system and that it was essential she be taken off of them. Once this was accomplished, she was assigned to less harmful medications. Bari was promised her reactions to them would be carefully monitored. She was then introduced to a regimen of physical therapy, which would encompass hydrotherapy, massage and exercises she could do on her own. A balanced diet would also play a major role in Lynn's treatment. Alcohol, however, would not be included on her menu. Her physician had laid down the law here, saying she would have to stop drinking if she wanted to see the quality of her life improve. Bari reached a turning point upon hearing this, finally having a willingness to become sober.

Lynn began to confront her alcoholism head-on, becoming acutely aware of booze's contribution to her physical, mental and spiritual declines. Staying sober would turn out to be far less difficult than she had ever imagined — having all to do with the fact that she had become sick and tired of abusing herself. She would never again pick up a drink.

Bari had understood from the outset that sobriety would not be a cure for her more serious physical problems; ankylosing spondylitis was a deteriorative condition and the damage done to her respiratory system was, for the most part, irreversible. Nevertheless, by remaining abstinent, she would have the ability to take care of herself in a sane, sensible and dedicated manner. Maintaining the best health possible became the order of the day, bringing to Lynn a sorely-needed positive focus and an upbeat way of thinking. It was her great hope that many years would be ahead for her. She was determined to make the most of all of them, accepting her medical situation with valor and seeing no good reason why her physical limitations should deny her a fulfilling life.

Bari's new outlook would change her for the better in almost every respect. She now derived pleasure from eating and became more robust of figure. Despite her ills, she found herself to be less complaining. A strong desire for contentment was present and she started to make peace with herself about the past. One by one, she began letting go of old resentments and disappointments. Her mind, in short, would no longer be plagued by undermining thoughts. The prospects were now greater for her to welcome what was enriching.

Emerging from her alcoholic isolation, Lynn found daily enjoyment in the scenic and cultural offerings of Santa Barbara. The city also brought to her a social life, one in which she'd engage whenever her health permitted. As for her old circle of friends, Bari would soon be getting back in touch with most all who'd been part of it. Her conciliatory gestures would be very much appreciated, leading to get-togethers in Los Angeles.

Lynn would make brief visits to LA several times a year. These sojourns would help to keep alive her enthusiasm for the entertainment industry. Now living ninety-five miles away from Hollywood, she was making a point of seeing the latest movies. Sometimes she'd pick up one of the trades, reading matter for an amused outsider. Bari herself would occasionally be the subject of an article in other types of publications, specifically those geared toward films of the golden age. To the authors of a few of these personal essays, she'd quite willingly make herself available for an interview. She found herself less inclined to accept invitations to industry functions, attending them only once in a great while. Lynn's level of energy was the main concern here, with vanity not a factor. Her illnesses and all those years of boozing had definitely played havoc with her physical appearance, but she had no qualms about presenting herself in public as a woman who hadn't aged gracefully.

Whether involving a Tinseltown shindig or a casual lunch near home, Bari's social agenda was something with which she proceeded very cautiously; all was determined under the wire by her state of health. The duration of those engagements she felt up to keeping would always be limited, for she was required to set aside ample rest time each day. Now in a generally serene frame of mind, she had no problem with remaining quiescent for hours on end. Reading was her main diversion while in repose.

> EUGENIE FISHER: "Peggy was the best-read woman I knew. She read *everything*. I think that she could have gotten a doctorate in literature."

Bari might have also aspired to a degree in political science. She had long been a keen observer of current events, especially those that pertained to US government policies. A great proponent of liberal causes, she detested everything that was being espoused by President Ronald Reagan. She made known her political leanings at the drop of a hat, and this would often lead to lively conversations among friends and family.

Lynn was at the center of many a kaffeeklatch in 1984 — the year in which she regained much of her old wit and spark. Next making a return would be her need for creative self-expression. A long-suppressed desire to write began to manifest and Bari would find herself positioned at her typewriter, pounding out short stories for her own amusement.

It had now become quite evident that Lynn was experiencing great success with her second shot at life, a happy situation directly related to her sobriety. She was becoming an integrated person, thinking with remarkable clarity and accepting herself as she was. Into her life came a new emotion — peace of mind.

Bari's attitudinal changes strengthened her sense of fortitude — something that was truly put to the test in 1985. That year, she was felled by another heart attack. The effects of this second coronary combined with her worsening arthritis to further restrict her movements. She was forced to give up driving and had to adhere to the guidelines of a safe-walking plan. Her doctor had told her she could only take short strolls, ones which were to include several rest stops. Lynn was committed to making these mini-excursions part of her daily routine. Sometimes, though, she was struck by agonizing pain and confined to her bed. Then there were those occasions when she was surprised to find herself capable of enjoying a few hours' pleasure away from home. There was never a way for Bari to predict how she'd be feeling on any given day; her health had now become characterized by a quality of instability. All the uncertainty involved became just one more thing that Lynn endured without protest.

Bari had no intention of letting her afflictions govern the manner in which she greeted life; that mode of thinking was for victims and she had had enough of that. She instead placed importance on being healthy in spirit — and her capacity for enjoyment increased as she degenerated physically. No one with whom she came in contact could deny that she was carrying on in a remarkable fashion.

Lynn's transformation was amazing — but not complete. While she had evolved to a place where she bore little ill will, she was not entirely resentment-free. This was made apparent in casual conversations, when the subject turned to Marge Fisher, Walter Kane, Sid Luft or Nathan Rickles.* Bari saw fit to disparage her ex-husbands and mother at the slightest provocation, much to the discomfort of her listening partners. Her anger toward this quartet was definitely a carryover from an earlier mind-set, for she was no longer anybody's fool. Lynn's friends had certainly recognized her progress, but they were also aware of her hypersensitivity and her difficulty with shaking old hurts — specifically, those that pertained to Marge and her marriages. Bari was, indeed, still wounded by four relationships from her past. She wouldn't admit this to anyone. She didn't have to — all of her hurled invectives did this for her.

Being human, Lynn was entitled to her share of unresolved feelings. Being sober, she had a better chance of working on them. Her desire to be in harmony with herself grew stronger and she became somewhat introspective about what was holding her back emotionally.

* Walter Kane and Nathan Rickles were now deceased; Kane had died in 1983 and Rickles, in 1982. Sid Luft would pass away in 2005.

Bari had for many years understood that her feelings of inadequacy had stemmed from the way in which her mother had related to her. Later on had come an awareness of how Marge had figured into her predisposition for personal conflict and inappropriate men. This realization was now being brought into sharper focus, as Lynn began to confront her ongoing contempt for her husbands and mother. She came to the determination that her rage had kept alive her involvement with these four old adversaries. It became important for her to diminish the space they occupied in her mind. Her efforts at detachment would be only halfway successful, reducing wrathful feelings to ones of mild anger. Part of the problem here had to do with her inability to recognize the degree to which she herself had fostered her negative relationships; coming to terms with this might very well have proved too painful for her to do. In any event, Lynn would never reach a point of resolution about those who had troubled her most.

There was, however, one delicate area which the more-contemplative Bari met with total openness. It had to do with the similarities between her mother and herself. With great candor, she was now acknowledging that she had inherited many of Marge's characteristics. She owned up to the fact that both were alcoholics and recognized each had serious problems with the opposite sex. Their journeys with booze, of course, had different outcomes — and for this Lynn would be eternally grateful. She had come to feel that her mother had helped her to become sober, her sorrowful ending serving as a frightening example of where drink could take one. With regard to men, Bari had always held them in higher regard — but she had to admit that neither she nor Marge had been cut out for marriage.

With some amusement, Lynn was coming to accept other ways in which she resembled her mother. She laughed when comparing her love for the Vegas gambling scene with Marge's penchant for playing the horses. It brought a smile to her face when she thought of her mother writing short stories in her later years — for she was now doing the same. A number of things about Marge were making Bari chuckle. One was her interest in numerology, the source of "Lynn Bari," Peggy Fisher's evenly divided, eight-letter stage name. Lynn used to think this occult study wacky — but she was soon to be consulting numerologists herself.

EUGENIE FISHER: "Peggy and her mother were so much alike, it's uncanny. She behaved like her mother, sounded like her mother, even their handwriting was similar. And, as she got older, she seemed to become more like her mother — *but* booze was the culprit there; because when she stopped drinking she really became so reflective and her values changed."

Bari's sober years would have their many rewards. Financial security, though, would not be one of them. Having not worked since 1974, Lynn's present income was based almost entirely on her Screen Actors Guild pension checks. She was also receiving payment for past television appearances, but these residuals were miniscule.

Although she had been frugal, Bari was left with a small cash reserve because of her enormous medical expenses. She accepted her status without self-pity or embarrassment. Nonetheless, it bothered her greatly that she could have been a woman of substantial means, had it not been for three exploitative marriages.

WILLIAM ROERICK: "When Lynn was in the money, she should have hired someone to pick her men for her — three *totally* disastrous marriages. The first one was her agent who stole her money; that was nice. Luft was really a horror. It was only when it came to Rick, however, that I thought she felt victimized. Because here he was: this millionaire psychiatrist having affairs with his patients. And when it came to the divorce, I think she may have gotten half of the house, but otherwise he managed to hide all of the money. So that quite properly pissed her off."

EUGENIE FISHER: "My husband used to worry about Peggy; he was concerned about her bad judgment in men. He used to beg her to sock some of her money away. Lots of times he'd say to me, 'God, I told Peggy to invest her money!' But she let people like Sid Luft get a hold of it and it was all just dissipated. Peggy was a woman who had lived in real style at one point in time, and she never put anything away. And her settlement from Rickles was just peanuts in today's world.

"Compared to the way she used to live, she was now living very, very simply. Yet I never heard her complain about her situation. She was such a great sport; so honest, really a very virtuous person. When you're a principled person and you find yourself involved very, very seriously with rather unscrupulous people, I think it must be so demoralizing. Can you imagine?"

In November 1985 Lynn journeyed to Los Angeles for the American Cinema Awards gala. She enjoyed the event, which gave her the chance to chat it up with many old Tinseltown friends. Silver-haired and attired in colorful dinner garb, she made herself available to press photographers. Their camerawork would reveal her to be rather ashen and dour-looking — in direct contrast to her lively demeanor that evening. Bari's facial appearance hadn't yet caught up with her state of health, which had actually begun to take a considerable turn for the better. Although still dealing with intense pain, she was becoming increasingly more energetic and ambulatory. Lynn was thrilled by this change, knowing it would enable her world to expand. She was also immensely thankful for her superior medical care and the doctor who had directed her toward a path of self-improvement.

Bari was finishing out an extremely difficult year on a high note, full of expectation for good times ahead. In December she made the trip to Newport Beach for Christmas at the Fishers'. The holiday turned out to be a thoroughly light-hearted one for Lynn and her family. New Year's came and Bari decided to devote greater attention to a recent interest. She enrolled in one of Santa Barbara's adult education programs, signing up for a course of study in creative writing. Lynn took to the classroom experience immediately.

Los Angeles, November 1985; Lynn attends the American Cinema Awards fete.
COURTESY OF PHOTOGRAPHER ED COLBERT.

> EUGENIE FISHER: "More than just the classes, the writing course opened her up to some social opportunities. It enabled her to meet people who were more or less her intellectual equals, who were creative and who believed in her."

Lynn approached her writing assignments with the same dedication she had applied to her acting. There was a difference now, however; she had developed a faith in herself that was allowing the creative process to be more soul-satisfying. Stimulated by this deeper appreciation, she became especially receptive to being enlightened — by a concept, a person, an activity, or any combination therein.

Bari's life was broadened in large part by books and journals, particularly those pertaining to world affairs. The type of reading matter she preferred gen-

December 1986; Lynn appears in sync with the spirit of Christmastime, as she stands at the entrance to her apartment on Santa Barbara's East Victoria Street.

erally reflected her liberal orientation. The majority of it fueled her antipathy for the Reagan administration. This distaste turned to outrage sometime in 1986, when she was made aware of the American government's intervention in Central America. She found untenable the human-rights abuses in El Salvador and the military aid given by the US to that country. Always pro-union, Lynn was now standing firm behind a dissident faction of the AFL-CIO, the NLC — the National Labor Committee in Support of Democracy and Human Rights in El Salvador. The NLC had fast been growing in strength. It was now receiving national press coverage, thanks to actor Ed Asner and other high-profile group activists. Bari was in contact with Asner and learned of plans for a well-organized demonstration by anti-interventionists; their protest would be taking the form of a march on Washington, DC, scheduled for April 25, 1987. Lynn very much wanted to be among those passing by the White House that day, but she knew a hectic cross-country trip would be imperiling to her health. Instead, she observed the demonstration on television, roused to excitement by the 100,000 who had assembled on the Capitol in opposition to the policies of a president she abhorred.

Bari didn't go to DC, but she was now entertaining the idea of taking an extended vacation. It didn't have to be far-flung one; she just wanted to visit a place where she could relax and enjoy a change of scenery. She felt such a trip possible, for she was moving about better and hadn't experienced any health setbacks in well over a year. Still, the thought of vacationing was a bit daunting to her because she'd come to live within carefully-set boundaries of activity. Her trepidations seemed to fall by the wayside when an invitation came from Beverly Petrachek, an old friend from the Fox make-up and hair department. Petrachek and her husband were living in Phoenix, Arizona. The couple was eager to have Lynn as their summer houseguest; they hoped she'd be able to stay with them for two weeks of leisure. Bari happily accepted their offer and started planning for a Phoenix getaway.

Lynn was in the midst of preparations for the trip when she began to feel uneasy. Doubts resurfaced, with Bari questioning the extent of her stamina. Not wanting to disappoint either her friends or herself, she went to her family for reassurance. They encouraged her to go through with the visit, feeling she was coping remarkably well with her physical problems — and knowing all the while how much she'd come to miss traveling. John Luft went on to deal with the details of his mother's itinerary. At Lynn's urging, he planned for himself a vacation, one which would be taken during her absence. Luft would depart from Santa Barbara before Bari, on his way to a fly-fishing excursion on the Yellowstone River. He left for Wyoming with his mother certain that she could easily make it to Arizona by herself.

The Petracheks showed up at the Phoenix airport to meet Lynn's flight at its appointed time of arrival — but the plane landed without their guest onboard. A frantic Beverly called the police. Ten hours later, Bari alighted from another Santa Barbara-to-Phoenix flight. She greeted her hosts in a state of exhaustion and total confusion, unable to explain what had happened to her. Her friends brought her to their home and put her to bed.

Lynn remained bedridden for the next ten days, suffering from pneumonia and respiratory congestion. Day eleven saw her in moderately decent shape. She called her brother in Newport Beach, apprising him of what had transpired. The two then discussed her return trip. It was decided that she'd fly into LAX airport, where Fisher would be waiting to pick her up. Bari left Phoenix full of apologies. The Petracheks said there was no cause for her be remorseful and bid her a warmhearted goodbye. The flight to LA went without incident. John Fisher drove his sister back to Santa Barbara. Once there, she met with her physician. He told her to curtail all of her activities for the present.

It took some time for Lynn to fully recover from her most recent ailments. Her journey to Phoenix had made glaringly apparent the fact that she was a frail woman. No one had to tell her that strict limitations would be placed on her life forever more. Bari accepted her situation as best one could; determined to carry on with a positive approach, she wasn't about to let anything diminish her appreciation of life's everyday joys.

Lynn turned sixty-eight in December 1987. She began her new year without a pack of cigarettes by her side; the Phoenix episode had convinced her to once and for all give up a habit that had done continual harm to her health.

The next nineteen months would find Bari experiencing intervals of renewed vitality, but her physical status would remain precarious.

> WILLIAM ROERICK: "Lynn was at this point in and out of illness all the time. She was slowed down, but never lost her brightness or good humor or wit — everybody loved her.
> "I remember I came to visit with her and we went to some pleasant fish place on the pier and sat upstairs. It was a very pretty day. On our way over there, Lynn was having a little trouble walking. I asked, 'Are you sure you want to climb up there?' She said, 'No, no, I'll do fine.' She did. And she did it without thinking about it. Afterwards, she said, 'You know, I felt so miserable the other day — I was wondering if I could even manage it. Now I feel great and it's done me a lot of good.'"

William Roerick was then a regular on *The Guiding Light*, the daytime serial on CBS-TV. Bari made it a point to catch him on the soap whenever she had the chance. She also kept up with the work of other old friends who were still active in show business. Their lasting success was something in which Lynn took great delight. In turn, they had expressed to her their hope that she'd one day be able to resume her acting career. Bari had been touched by this, but until now had neither the longing nor the physical strength to stage a comeback. However, in 1988, during a period of relative good health, she surprised herself by accepting a guest shot on Angela Lansbury's CBS series, *Murder, She Wrote*. She and Joan Leslie were set to play sisters, Helen and Lillian Appletree, in a *Murder* episode entitled "Mr. Penroy's Vacation."

A very nice fellow had called me about doing the show. I talked to my doctor about it. He said, "I think that you could do something that's not too strenuous, and you could do it painlessly." He said he would give me something that I could take so I'd be all right — and it would not be habit-forming. I told him,

"Fine; I'll see what I can do." But then there was a writer's strike and the whole thing fell through.

"Mr. Penroy's Vacation's" start date had been pushed back to a period when Bari hadn't been feeling at all well. Bowing out of the show, she had been replaced by Teresa Wright. This turn of events hadn't really perturbed Lynn. Despite her doctor's words, she had come to sense that things would have gone awry for her in a far more detrimental way had the shoot not been postponed. The television offer had, however, served to revive her interest in performing. She wanted to act again, but her medical situation would have to become less inconstant for her to do so.

Murder, She Wrote had also brought to light for Bari the prospect of earning a paycheck — compensation that would have come in very handy at this juncture. Lynn's finances had now reached an all-time low. Her savings had become virtually depleted and she was finding herself in the uncomfortable position of looking to her brother for support.

> EUGENIE FISHER: "John had been taking care of her the last few years. He supplemented her income and was happy to do that because she had been very generous with us. She was so deserving. He knew that she would have done it for him, anytime, if she could."

John, Genie and their son Jay drove to Santa Barbara to be with Bari and John Luft on December 18, 1988. The day was not only Lynn's sixty-ninth birthday, but also her nephew's thirty-sixth. The double-event was cause for a most festive celebration. The family reunited a week later for another Christmas at the Fisher home. Bari was then having a difficult time getting about, and she couldn't have made the trip to Newport Beach if it had not been for the able assistance of her loving son.

> EUGENIE FISHER: John [Luft] was simply wonderful to his mother. He knew every pill that was prescribed for her; when to take it and what it was made of. He also got her on good food. He was totally devoted to her."

John was soon to find his mother's health on the upswing. Lynn was physically stronger at the start of the New Year, walking with increasingly greater ease. She determined herself well enough to attend the 1989 American Cinema Awards function, to be held that January in Los Angeles. Her son escorted her there. The two sat at a table with Jane Withers, astronaut Buzz Aldrin and Aldrin's wife, Lois. Seated nearby were three longtime friends of Bari's: Cesar Romero, Francis Lederer and Roddy McDowall. Each in this trio embraced Lynn and extended to her their compliments about her appearance. She did, in fact, look infinitely better at this event than she had at the 1985 Cinema Awards ceremony. This time out she greeted press photographers with a broad smile and twinkling eyes. Her cheerful face was framed by a new hairstyle, a flattering grayish-blond bob. The colorfully-striped Armani blouse she was wearing seemed very much in keeping with the verve she was projecting throughout the evening. Bari's overall countenance would come through in portrait photos

John Luft (holding "Chester"), enjoying a warmhearted moment with John, Eugenie and Jay Fisher in 1990.

from the affair. She'd later admit to being very happy with the way these pictures had turned out, attributing any cosmetic improvement to three things: her physical therapy, the cessation of her smoking and, most importantly, her ongoing sobriety.

Lynn returned to Santa Barbara in buoyant mood. The Cinema Awards had done her a world of good, reminding her of her place in the Hollywood firmament in an altogether jolly social arena. Still savoring the fun and glamour of the evening, she looked forward to brightening her life with other types of companionable diversions. She wanted to continue learning from people, whether one-on-one or through literary and artistic forms of expression. There was present in Bari a strong desire to become a better-rounded individual. Motivated by this, she held an optimistic attitude about her future in the face of ongoing illness.

Lynn's disposition had changed so much over the past half-dozen years. Sometimes even she herself couldn't believe what a different person she'd become. Bari's transformation might have been a startling one, but it had evolved quite logically — through her willingness to turn her life around. The work she had done on herself had been considerable.

EUGENIE FISHER: "Peggy was trying very, very hard to make sense out of her life. In the last few years, she really became very spiritual and began to see things realistically. She understood her place and time as an actress and realized how lucky she was to have gotten the training that she did — and the success that went

Eugenie Fisher, 2008.

along with it. In many ways, she felt she had a good time, better than most people.

"I think that she was looking at it all very philosophically. Considering what she had undergone — the responsibilities and the kind of crap she had to put up with, with the mother and these husbands — it was amazing that she was as gracious and as vibrant and as wonderful as she was. She survived with a great deal of class and dignity. She was brave."

Los Angeles, January 1989; Lynn bubbles over with good humor at the American Cinema Awards gala. COURTESY OF PHOTOGRAPHER ED COLBERT.

Lynn Bari, 1941.

CHAPTER EIGHTEEN

AT LAST

I'm free to discuss anytime. You are the one who has to dissect all this garbage. Oh, listen; you'll have to get a truck. I can be a bloody bore. If you've got enough dribble for one day, and if I'm boring you, please tell me to "shut up" when I'm saying something that's just superfluous. And if you ever have a dull party and want to clear the room, just turn the tapes on. You write the thing. I have implicit faith in you.

Lynn made these remarks to me in July 1989, shortly after we began the conversations that would lead to this book. We held a series of lengthy interviews that summer, all conducted over the telephone and taped. Bari spoke to me from her home in Santa Barbara. I was in New York City, listening to the musings of a most expansive and forthcoming woman. Words flowed freely from Lynn, even when she became emotional. She was never for a moment the least bit boring; a talk with her was always a stimulating experience.

Bari's animated and provocative nature had been revealed to me some time before. We had, in fact, been in frequent phone contact over the several years preceding our formal discussions. Although Lynn's film work had brought us together in friendship, our chats up until May 1989 had generally revolved around everyday concerns and current-events topics. Bari's views on subjects making the news were as trenchant as they were definite. She was given to sounding off with her liberal take on most issues of the day, including a woman's right to an abortion, the flag-burning controversy and the situation in El Salvador. On Election Day 1988, she had left a message on my answering machine. I laughed out loud when I heard its concluding words:

Whatever you do, for God's sake, don't vote Republican!

Six months later we were both bemoaning the outcome of the last presidential race when somehow the conversation drifted from politics to the movies. In fascinating detail, Lynn recounted the circumstances surrounding Warner Oland's disappearance from the set of *Charlie Chan at Ringside*. This led to, of all things, her heartfelt remembrances of Peggy Ann Garner — and, once again, I was impressed by Bari's sharp memory and storytelling abilities. Shortly after our dialogue came to an end, I was struck by several thoughts. It occurred to me I'd have difficulty finding other stars from Hollywood's golden age that possessed Lynn's vivid sense of recall. Perhaps there were a few still around who had amazing memories, but surely next-to-none were as engaging and intelligent as Bari. My conjecturing immediately brought to mind the idea of recording Lynn's reflections on her career in a formal-interview setting. I let the notion sit for two weeks and then called Bari, asking her if she would be willing to share her reminiscences with me for the purpose of an article in a film journal. My request delighted her; I could even hear eagerness in her voice. We both got out our appointment books and scheduled interview number one for an afternoon in June.

And, unbeknownst to us both, we were soon to embark on a project of vast dimension — and profound meaningfulness.

The film career of Lynn Bari had long since held great interest for me. When I was a teenager, my passion for vintage movies became focused on the Twentieth Century-Fox Film Corporation; I was tremendously attracted to the studio because of the crisp air and contrasty photography of their pictures. Seldom did I miss the chance to catch an old Fox flick on television or at a revival house. I came to be intrigued by Lynn, having seen her face pop up practically everywhere. Her seemingly ubiquitous presence would later lead me to the conclusion that her fourteen-year association with Fox had resulted in one of the most comprehensive acting careers in film history.

I had come to view Bari in an impressive light, as the definitive contract player of Hollywood's golden age. Her credits for Fox were untold and, to me, she represented the best of what her studio had offered on the acting end; she was a skilled and versatile performer, to be sure. Beautiful, she was also attractive in that intangible way that spells screen charisma. Lynn's assets were many, indeed, and she had what it took to become a major star. But she didn't — and I couldn't fathom why.

In 1973, I purchased Richard Lamparski's then-latest volume of his *Whatever Became Of...?* series. Included in this book of personal interviews was a section on Lynn. Two photos of Bari bracketed its text. One was a publicity portrait from the late forties. The other had been taken on *The Gingerbread Lady* tour, featuring a warm opening-night embrace with devoted friends Dana and Mary Andrews. Lamparski's words were peppered with revelations and bon mots from his subject. Lynn came across in a captivating manner, as a woman of tremendous wit, candor and individuality. Her comments on her frenetic Fox shooting schedules: "I made as many as three [pictures] at a time. I'd go from one set to another shooting people and stealing husbands. [The pace was] so fast I never knew what the hell the plots were." Lamparski followed this quote with an assessment of Bari's career and personal life. His essay ended, "The staunch liberal voted for Dr. Spock in the 1972 Presidential election." Never let it be said that Lynn didn't stand out among Tinseltown's old guard.

My admiration for Bari increased over the course of the next dozen years. Occasionally, I'd meet showbiz folk who had worked with her in the past. All would characterize her as a very bright, funny and honest person.

During this period, I was in the midst of gathering movie posters and other memorabilia pertaining to Twentieth Century-Fox. My collection grew to extensive proportions, with Bari being a significant part of this assemblage. Video recorders then came into our homes and tapes of Fox films began to complement my studio archive. Many of these videos would be hard-to-find titles, acquired through private channels. Among the rarities would be a good number of Lynn's Western Avenue movies.

One of these films, *Sleepers West*, made it back to the big screen in the fall of 1986. The Mike Shayne mystery was revived in New York, at Broadway's Regency Theatre. The print unreeled was a sparkling one. Incandescent, too, was the performance of the picture's leading lady. Having left the showing thoroughly gladdened, I was prompted to write my one and only fan letter. It was to Bari. The note was several times rewritten and then sent (its destination address having been secured from a friend of Richard Lamparski's).

Lynn responded to my missive swiftly — much to my delight. Her letter to me was gracious in tone, marked by a sincere form of humility. She veered away from the gooey, punctuating many of her thoughts with gentle witticisms. Clearly, she also expressed an interest in me — in a way that invited further correspondence. And correspond we did. Pen pals turned into telephone chums — and a friendship cemented itself.

The cello voice that had helped to define Bari's screen persona remained unmistakable over the phone, but her years of smoking had deepened its pitch and roughened her enunciations. Still, her speech resounded with vitality. Her peppy intonations weren't forced; however, they did belie her state of health.

Lynn would never expose to me the full extent of her physical disabilities; she gave me the impression that she suffered from a painful and debilitating arthritic condition — and nothing else. Perhaps the fact that we had yet to meet face-to-face had made it easier for her to conceal her other maladies and past medical history. Bari would discuss her ankylosing spondylitis straightforwardly, but in a measured way. When she'd see fit to wind down about it, she'd apologize for boring me and immediately turn to a completely different topic.

Lynn's subterfuge about her health was harmless and in keeping with her character. In every other respect, though, she was totally forthright with me. She

Posing for this Walking Down Broadway *pictorial promo are the six lovelies of the 1938 film: (left to right) Dixie Dunbar, Jayne Regan, Claire Trevor, Phyllis Brooks, Lynn and Leah Ray.*

also communicated a genuine concern for all those with whom she was presently in contact. An extremely empathetic person, Bari worried about the underprivileged, the politically oppressed and others less fortunate than she.

Lynn preferred talking about matters of today in our pre-interview days; the past didn't seem to hold too much fascination for her. However, when prompted, she did acknowledge her stardom and she spoke of it with a sense of pride. It was also apparent to me that Bari occasionally enjoyed taking a look back at her career through the wonders of video tape. She very much appreciated the fact that I was able to augment her film library with cassettes of pictures she hadn't seen in decades.

Hotel for Women was the first video I had sent Lynn. Two weeks after its posting, I received this letter:

Dear Jeff: Tried to call you this AM and got your answering machine. I don't know why anything mechanical gives me the hives, but I get all giggly and girlish when I talk into one. Hence this note. If you think that a bit weird, you should see me with my VCR (which has always sounded like something vaguely catching to me). I braved it the minute your tape arrived and got a big kick out of seeing "Hotel" again — after so long. — I called Jean Rogers. She is a lovely person and has been very ill but seems to be in good spirits, so I'm sure the film would cheer her.*

A year later *Meet the Girls* was on its way to Santa Barbara. Lynn lit up:

I'm dying to see that. Every day we've been watching for it. Every time I hear the mailman, I run out to see if it's arrived.

The film soon turned up on Bari's doorstep and she took great pleasure in viewing it. Shortly afterwards, I mailed her *Walking Down Broadway*. Lynn was amused to see herself in one of her first credited assignments.

Our chat about the fifty-year-old drama included Bari's fond reminiscences of costars Claire Trevor, Phyllis Brooks, Leah Ray, Dixie Dunbar and Jayne Regan. I remarked to Lynn that all five were still very much alive. She exclaimed:

I know! Isn't that great!

The thought then occurred to me that a reunion of some sort could be staged — and Bari responded mischievously.

Oh, please; something horrible would happen!

Lynn was to receive a total of two dozen films from me. She'd express her thanks for each and every one of them, via a phone call or handwritten note. Of course, some of the movies would appeal to her more than others. Then there were those she had no interest in revisiting. She declined *Secret Agent of Japan* in a teasing manner:

I don't know if I'm old enough to see it.

Equally humorous, but more to the point, was her refusal of *The Women of Pitcairn Island:*

Do you want to keep our friendship?

---

* Jean Rogers had costarred with Bari in *Hotel for Women*. Retired since 1951, Rogers would pass away in 1991.

Bari was in better health at the time she agreed to be interviewed by me. She had recently guested on a local TV talk show and had made it through the experience just fine. More active than usual, she had an upcoming theater date and several other social engagements to which she was looking forward. Lynn continued to plan ahead carefully, though, spacing out her appointments so she wouldn't exhaust herself. Quiet time often found her reading or composing short stories. She also made it a point to keep up with her correspondence.

January 1989; Lynn, enjoying being part of the American Cinema Awards event in Los Angeles. COURTESY OF PHOTOGRAPHER ED COLBERT.

Bari received a parcel from me in early June 1989. Included in this mailing were portraits of her from January's American Cinema Awards gala. Also tucked into the package were a few photos of myself. Up until this point Lynn had no idea what I looked like, something that hadn't been of concern to me. My feelings about this had now changed because I had come to think it important to the interview process that she associate a face with the voice of her long-distance friend.

Neither Bari nor I had given much thought to how many discussions we'd be holding. At the outset, though, both of us were of the opinion that their number would probably be two.

The initial interview would last ninety minutes — and we'd barely touch upon Lynn's earliest days as a Fox stockgirl. Midway through, it was obvious to me that Bari had a limitless amount of information to share about her career. She was also evidencing a remarkable willingness to discuss her personal history, her words etching a disturbing childhood. The subject of her father's suicide was brought up immediately, with Bari confiding she'd never spoken of this to anyone outside her family. The topic then turned to her mother. I mentioned that I'd seen photos of her. Her patrician appearance had given me the impression of her having been a very refined woman. Well, Lynn greeted my notion with a torrent of highly-charged comments about Marge — one person to whom she'd return again and again during our talks. Bari's introduction of her mother was ever-so emotional, yet at the same time it served a constructive purpose. By presenting Marge as she did, Lynn was right off conveying a reason why she had failed to become a top-ranking star; this message was delivered to me in a totally unambiguous way.

There were also, as mentioned, those aspects to her mother which she now found amusing. Bari could, in fact, put a humorous spin on most everything. She was downright funny in the final minutes of this first discussion, letting loose with some outrageous Hollywood anecdotes. The phone call ended in laughter, with the two of us having scheduled a second interview for the following week.

Several hours later I reviewed our dialogue on my tape recorder. This listening convinced me that Bari's story should be told in book form, rather than as a magazine article. I broached my sentiments to Lynn shortly thereafter. She was very receptive to the book idea, understanding the expansion would entail many more interviews than had originally been envisioned.

Our conversations took place once or twice a week, covering the period from mid-June through the end of July. These talks were free-floating, but basically chronologically-directed. They each lasted about one-and-one-half hours. All were conducted in the afternoon — Bari's time. Lynn felt she was more alert before nightfall. She explained:

As the day wears on, "Mama's" brain starts going — because I'm not on the pills.

Bari's state of health that summer was up and down. There was nothing seriously imperiling her, but she was periodically rendered incapacitated by the painful effects of her ankylosing spondylitis. Matter-of-factly, she related:

Some days I just can't move.

Several interviews had to be rescheduled because acute pain had befallen her. Lynn had begged off of these appointments full of needless apologies. As it would turn out, no discussion had to be rebooked twice, for Bari had always managed to rebound in the days after a cancellation.

Lynn made for a perfect interview subject. On her own accord, she did her "homework" between talks, our chronological progression having helped to guide her. She came to each conversation prepared. Often, she'd open with a previously-discussed topic that she felt needed further clarification. The cadence of her voice was generally animated, reflecting her enthusiasm for the project at hand. There was a genuine sparkle to Bari's intonations — something by which I was amazed, given what I knew of her physical situation. Also wondrous to me was the fact that she almost never mentioned the discomfort she was enduring. I brought this to her attention once, while making a comment about her sounding so well over the phone. Her response:

I'm glad I sound that way, because I don't want to bore people with it [her ankylosing spondylitis]. And I'm going to get back into a pain management program so I can sit down at the typewriter without going berserk. I've been living with this for ten years. So, by now, you have to learn to live with it — or you might as well drop dead. But I'm too mean to die! *(laughing)*

Lynn loved to laugh, often at her own expense. Her cracks were priceless and her imitations, hilarious. Possessed with the gift of mimicry, she frequently spiced up her remembrances with uncanny vocal impersonations of the celebrated. I could barely contain myself as I listened to her dead-on characterizations of Sonja Henie, Peter Lorre, Harry Cohn, Ronald Colman, Joan Rivers and Jay Leno. There was a bit of the clown in Bari, a quality that made more endearing her cheerful and chatty countenance.

Lynn had much to say, but she wasn't at all garrulous. Her responses to my queries were immediate and without an ounce of fat. Her digressions were also interesting and to the point. She approached everything with directness, spontaneity and thoughtfulness. Because of this, we were able to cover a great amount of territory in each of our talks.

Although Bari was given to good humor, her mood would either flare up or become somber when a troubling aspect of her life was being addressed. She once brought up a series of upsetting events, spilling a part of her soul as she did. Then she took a deep breath, composed herself and said softly:

I don't know why I'm laying all these stories on you. But I think you'd know a little bit more about me by my telling you.

A moment of quiet followed, with Lynn taking a sip from her ever-present glass of Coca-Cola. The soda was the only thing for which she reached when things got serious. Bari proudly told me:

I'm a Coke-a-holic now — I don't drink *anything* booze-wise.

Clear of mind, Lynn placed significance on viewing things in their broadest perspective. She tried very hard to be objective about herself. This intent had come to play a key role in her journey of self-actualization. Nothing could deter her from pursuing fulfillment. In the face of adversity, she found much pleasure by zeroing in on life's positive elements. "Everything is copasetic" had come to be one of her pet phrases. I will always identify this catchword with Bari, for it says volumes about her extraordinary spirit.

Maintaining a positive outlook was one of Lynn's greatest strengths in her later years. Holding firmly to her beliefs was another. Many ideological matters were of consequence to Bari, and she'd speak to them all in resolute and impassioned tones. A portion of our June 29, 1989, conversation illustrates this. The subject had turned to politics — and Lynn was off and running:

I was called a "Commie" for a long time. God knows why. Oh, but don't worry, they said I was once. And you know what I said to them — "I can't even *spell* Communist! I've never written the word and I don't have anything to do with it."

I've been a Democrat since Roosevelt. I didn't get to vote for him until the last time he ran, but I went out and campaigned for him. My mother was a *big* Republican. My brother still is, but he's nice (laugh*ing*) — I think he's coming over.

I'm a liberal, a progressive Democrat. We're not a dying breed; we're a sleeping breed. Wait until we have another few years of this crap and *believe* me... Up here [in Santa Barbara], you can't say those things. Except they all hate Reagan now, especially the blue-haired set; he's done them dirt with their pensions and such.

People just don't understand that, if you keep going on and tightening and tightening on certain situations, you're going to go back to the witch-hunting; that's what we'll get into again. Maybe I'm a jerk as far as that's concerned, maybe I'm not thinking rationally — but I don't intend to change my politics.

You know, Kennebunkport, Maine [where then-President George H.W. Bush had a summer home], was one of my favorite places to play — and now I wouldn't go near it. I could never stand the townspeople there anyway; they're all so goddamned rich and *so* Republican. But *(laughing)*, it is the loveliest place in the world if you want to take a nice vacation and eat fresh fish!

———————————————————————

During the course of our discussions, Bari was in the midst of an active real-estate search. She was looking for another place to live in Santa Barbara because she had grown dissatisfied with her dwelling on East Victoria Street. There were several reasons for her discontent. One had to do with topography. Her apartment was situated at ground level, but the building in which it was housed stood on a hill — with many daunting steps leading to its main-floor entrance. Lynn said:

Stairs are the worst — I mean, they kill me.

Bari explained she might have been able to come to peace with this obstacle had it been the only problem with her living circumstances. Also troubling her was the fact that her neighborhood had become very noisy at night. Then there was her landlady, whom she described as uncooperative and unpleasant. The whole situation on East Victoria had for some time been bringing to Lynn a discomfort she could ill afford. Several months before, she'd voiced her concerns to her beloved brother. John Fisher had urged her to move to a more agreeable environment, going on to say her choice of relocation should not be based on the cost of rent; he himself would see to it that her monthly payments would be met.

Bari had set about with her apartment hunt in late spring. John Luft had been doing most of the leg work entailed — and, once again, Lynn was greatly indebted to him for his efforts on her behalf. Bari always spoke of her son with tremendous pride; she marveled at his artistic abilities and thought the world of him as a human being. She expressed the following to me on more than one occasion:

Johnny's saved my life. My God, he's been wonderful. We have a fine relationship.

Bolstered by her two Johns, Bari became increasingly more eager to relocate. The prospect of finding a new home had reinvigorated her sense of enthusiasm and, by July, there was a certain joie de vivre about her. The zeal and vitality she was displaying were giving everyone the impression that her physical situation had stabilized, if not improved.

As an interview subject, Lynn was growing more animated with each conversation. She appeared to be exuberant on July 13, opening our discussion with these words:

I have exciting news. John [Luft] found us an apartment yesterday. We're moving in on the fifth of August — and I'm so excited. It's on the Mesa, way up in the sky, with all the beautiful oak trees and flowers. You look down on the whole town of Santa Barbara and all around the ocean; the view is quite something. The apartment is really lovely — although I don't intend to be in it too much, as I'm going to go roaming outside.

On July 26, Bari had this to relate:

Saturday, I would like to get up to the new place and take measurements and stuff. And I have a new address [on Las Manos Lane] I'm going to give you. *(Laughing)* I don't want you sending me long-stemmed roses to the wrong address, letting them get wilted.

Lynn was especially high-spirited when I called her on July 30, talking a mile a minute. Our greetings to one another had included this update on her move:

I'm sitting here in my room with nothing but boxes all around, most of them full. I haven't done a one. My son has done the whole thing; Johnny's been marvelous taking care of "Mom." We're going off to the place tomorrow. I don't want to waste your money, so I'll send you a picture! *(laughing)*

Lynn never lost her knack for timing; our last formal interview was the one of Sunday, July 30 — held just six days before her much-anticipated move. It had been decided that the content of this final discussion would involve the following from Bari: a career overview, insights about herself she had yet to share, and thoughts on her present-day life. Ever prepared, Lynn had much to impart. She began:

I've got a lot of friends up here. Last Sunday I went to a house-opening. Yesterday the local radio guy, Tom Carroll, came over and took me to lunch on the wharf. He showed me lots of places in Santa Barbara that I'd never been to before. It's a real laid-back town and I'm finding something new here every day.

I also imagine doing a lot of other things, but they don't happen. I never had the time to go anywhere or do anything when I was a kid. I never got out of town. Now they take you to Bulgaria to shoot the entrance to the movie!

If I were well, I would like to return to acting. In fact, I'd love it. I'd also like to make some money. I think that work would give me some of the self-esteem that you need. I know that I could put some pressure on friends if I wanted to work. I haven't had an agent for years, and one won't look at you unless you're sellable. *(Laughing)* Look, at my age, what am I going to do? I know that I'd love to do a play called *Night Must Fall.* That's all done in a wheelchair, you know; she only gets up once — to walk around the room. However, it's all to be seen if I do return. What will be, will be.

Most of the time now, I'm pretty much confined close to home. You see, I can only sit a certain length of time — it's too painful, and it's a bore to have someone leave in the middle of something, which has never happened with me. I did go to see a show last weekend, *42nd Street,* and I really had a ball; I met some nice people and all. But I gave up going to the movies and I don't care because of the VCR. I stayed up till three o'clock the other morning watching *Turtle Diary* (1985), with Glenda Jackson. I'd seen it before, but I'd never seen a performance like that.

These days I'm trying to get back into writing. About two or three years ago, I took a course in creative writing. I've written about twenty short stories. My teacher was amazed at my stuff and said, "With your wild imagination, any one of these will work. Start a novel on this one." I have started to write two or three books, and then I've been discouraged. I've got to decide what the hell I'm going to do and just sit down and do it.

An autobiography would be too painful — I really couldn't do it. I've thought about it, but I just couldn't go back into that — the thing with my mother and the thing with Sid, and this last husband — he was the worst and that's too near. You know, the only good autobiography I read was Doris Day's. She had a helluva writer [A.E. Hotchner] do it with her. Doris is a smart woman and a very nice lady. We both belonged to the Beverly Hills Tennis Club and used to sit and talk. I'd meet her at parties, too. She was always gracious, unassuming and unpretentious. I liked her very much.

I told Lynn she possessed the very same qualities she'd ascribed to Day, remarking that she herself was a wonderful person. Bari responded:

Oh, come on. Well, thank you very much. I'm really not. I've done some rotten things in my life, I suppose. My husbands were always telling me I was nothing. *Nothing! (laughing)*

I gently suggested to Lynn she get a better perspective on herself and mentioned to her that many held her in most fond regard. Her reply:

Well, that's nice. Well, I guess you've also got to listen to the right people. So the next time I feel down in the dumps, I'll call you and say, "Okay kid, tell me how great I am."

I assured her that I would. We then turned to her career — a topic with which Bari had no problem giving forth.

I think I had a wonderful career! What in the world would I have done otherwise? I'd have finished high school, maybe gone to college if the Depression had been over. Then I'd probably have married a shoe salesman and had twenty kids and died at the age of fifty-two. *(laughing)* I mean, that was the life that you had, especially during hard times. And we certainly lived through the hardest period, cash-wise.

Radio was the easiest medium and it was very lucrative, as well. Stage pays very small money, but I loved it. I worked for practically nothing at places like the Pasadena Playhouse.

But I learned the fundamentals of acting in pictures. I know how to get around in front of a camera. The director of the play *Who's Afraid of Virginia Woolf?* [Alan Schneider] was just starting in films when he came onto the set of my last picture, *The Young Runaways*. My director told him that if he wanted to learn how a movie actress works in front of a camera, he should come right over and see me. And I'd never been so thrilled. Wasn't that nice? Well, I can brag about myself!

With some of my pictures, I'm astounded that they've held up so well. Others are just camp stuff and funny. I'm completely detached from it now. It's like watching yourself in another world, in another space and time — and you are you now. I feel the same as I did then, only I hurt a lot more.

I did a radio show last week. It was just the usual pap. The audience called in and asked a question or two, which was nice. But then this particular chap asked me to pick the three pictures I disliked the most. Right away, it's like a cold fish in your face. Why not talk about the positive things in your life, about the fun that you had on different pictures, something of that sort?

And I certainly had a lot of fun working at Fox, where it was kind of like "Old Lynn," "Get Lynn." Everybody there called me by my first name, which was lovely — in fact, it was great.

Fox did feel like a home to me. The studio even let me take my little camera onto the sets. The cameramen would give me film and I would have fun making pictures just for my own amazement. Nobody else was allowed to do this, but I was a nice kid and everyone knew that I'd never sell the photos.

There were lots of wonderful people at Fox, and so many of the actors were marvelous to know. I mean, everybody was happy and gay, but you *worked!* Forty weeks a year. Because of the tight schedules, my 'B' pictures were a lot more demanding than the 'A's I made — and most of them were just as good. When I worked, I didn't kid around as far as my job was concerned; I took it very seriously no matter what it was. I was even on the test stage every other day, working with new people that the studio wanted to sign up. There, I met directors like [Jean] Renoir who did some of the screen tests. I guess, as far as pictures are concerned, I did do practically everything.

This 1941 memory from Fox's publicity department had heralded the three young stars of The Perfect Snob: *Cornel Wilde (top), Lynn and Anthony Quinn.*

I remarked to Lynn that she'd appeared in an astonishing number of films, well over one-hundred-and-twenty-five. Had she at any point been overwhelmed by the volume of her work?

No. I think of poor old John Wayne; he made a million, too. Listen, I'm a ham. I loved doing them. *All* of them!

Given her staggering list of credits, I assumed Bari's library to be bulging with scrapbooks and other career memorabilia. Lynn said she only wished this was the case, offering to me this explanation:

Some time ago Walter Kane had sent me a scrapbook, one he had finally let go of. Johnny asked, "Well, where are the rest of them?" I said, "Listen, it's lucky he sent me this. When we separated, he even kept my ice skates!" Unfortunately, I had a lot of other stuff that I wish I'd kept, but my last husband told me that I was living in the past, that it wasn't good for anybody. So, I threw it all out. But I've collected a lot since then.

Moving from the ephemeral to the symbolic, I brought up the subject of Bari's screen image. To me, she had more often than not projected an air of sophistication. Lynn quipped:

Yeah, but taxi drivers think that they're sophisticated; they'll tell you *all about* how sophisticated they are.

Bari roared with laughter when I then recounted the recent experience of a mutual friend. He had stepped into a Manhattan taxicab, only to find pictures of herself and Hedy Lamarr pasted all over the back of the driver's seat.

Oh, my God — the two brains of the industry! Two airheads! But I *am* the taxi driver's dream, and I know it for certain now that I've heard this story. Whenever I'm in New York, every time it's, "Hey, Lynn, baby! Seen ya picture on television!"
I think that my audiences *were* the taxi drivers. I'm not kidding. Middle-class people liked me. They felt that they *could* say, "Hey, Lynn baby." I don't think that I represented anything that was threatening to them.

A writer had once tagged Bari as "a woman of Dresden and steel." The description caught on, repeatedly finding its way into print. Its popularity seemed understandable to Lynn.

I think it's pretty hokey, but maybe it's right. I used to be very shy. When I was a kid, I used to bluff it out by acting tough — but I quickly stopped that. I don't let people take advantage of me anymore, which I used to do. I learned that when I want something, I go out and get it. I might be tough now, but that's just from a lot of wear. *(laughing)* The "Dresden" thing, I guess that's true; I'm hurt very easily. People don't think that I'm sensitive. That was especially so at the studio. Once, they were bringing up names for a part in a new picture. Someone suggested me and this writer said, "Lynn Bari! My God, Lynn looks as if she were lost in a forest, she'd eat a tree!" That *really* hurt me terribly.

But you've got to have a sense of humor if you're going to be in pictures. *(Laughing)* I always did the wrong thing, but I usually rectified it. And, as I said, I used to let people take terrible advantage of me. There are so many phonies in the world. I just think that some people are born amoral; they do not know what it means to have morals. They're just slobs with warped brains, and they don't care. They only think about what you can do for them or what they can take from you. I defy anyone to say, "I've never been taken in by anyone," because if this was so, they would have to have been a hermit.

Bari had collided with some major users in her time, enduring the type of Sturm und Drang one would find in a Eugene O'Neill play. The melodrama she experienced was decidedly unique, but she was certainly not the only female star to have suffered greatly at the hands of exploiters. However, unlike most others so abused, she survived the pitfalls of Hollywood and became emotionally sound. I wondered to Lynn if her intelligent and perceptive nature had played a part in this personal victory. She answered:

No, because every once in a while I question whether I have all my marbles. *(laughing)* Common sense, I think I never had. I guess I'm just lucky. I really do mean that.

I thank God every night that I'm still here. My brother is older than I and he's still going strong. We both have a lot of things wrong with us physically, but I'm not giving into them and he isn't either.* I fully expect to see the year 2000 — in a wheelchair, if necessary.

There was great assuredness in Bari's voice when she expressed these last comments, her conviction making me feel optimistic about her future. Her words also made apparent her desire to end our interviews on a high note. The conversation drew to a gradual close, with my wishing her well with her imminent move. I also conveyed to her my deepest appreciation for all the time she'd devoted to my book project. She responded to me most cordially:

I was delighted to do it.

I gave Lynn a brief rundown on how I'd be proceeding with her biography. Once transcribed, the content of our interviews would be reordered to a point of precise chronological progression. My next step would entail necessary thematic rearrangements. I'd then embark on the manuscript's first draft. This draft, when completed, would be sent to Bari for corrections and additional comments. Lynn

---

* John Fisher would pass away in October 1992.

said she'd be happy to help out in any way she could. Thanking her, I felt she should have an idea of when the manuscript would be ready for submission. I couldn't give her anything approaching an exact finish date, but I knew I'd be working away for many months. Bari greeted this with understanding, having assumed the writing process wouldn't be brief in duration. She then let out a giggle and said:

Oh well, take your time — just so you don't publish it posthumously.

I called Lynn the second week in August, soon after she'd relocated. She sounded well and was quite pleased with her new apartment. However, she confessed to being very "uptight" during the move — so much so that she'd picked up cigarettes for the first time in ages. Her smoking had lasted all of two days, but it had left her very annoyed with herself. Determined to pay greater attention to her health, she told me she was enrolling in a pain management program. She was also looking forward to participating in more convivial activities and had set up a few dates with friends. After making mention of this, Bari asked how I was doing. I updated her on myself and we went on to cover the news of the day. Our chat ended with cheerful goodbyes.

Sometime that month, Lynn posed for two snapshots. The photos turned out to be to her liking and she had them copied in an 8"x10" format. Her brother John was among those to whom she sent these portraits. Both he and his wife were a bit taken aback by one of them.

> EUGENIE FISHER: "It certainly portrays her honestly because it's not a flattering picture. She's sitting in a polyester jogging suit, wearing a straw hat. The hat's kind of cocked slightly to the side and she seems to be tipping it at you, as if she were saying, 'Adios.' There's nothing glamorous about it, and yet she had it enlarged and sent to her brother. Considering that she was once a great beauty, you'd never think that she'd be honest enough to see herself — and want other people to see her — the way she really was."

Lynn didn't seem to be her usual self when I spoke with her in early September. Working on the manuscript, I had called her with the intent of asking some additional questions. None of them would be posed, though. From the moment we said our hellos, I could tell Bari was in an extremely weakened state. She said her ankylosing was acting up. She also felt tired, admitting she'd overdone it with the combination of the move and her exercise therapy. Taking a deep sigh, Lynn apologized for not being in a more conversational mood. She then asked me to phone her back in another week or two, after some scheduled doctors' appointments.

We next talked the third week of September. The call began with a few pleasantries, after which I gathered from Bari that she was in a great deal of pain. To

Santa Barbara, August 1989; Lynn tips her hat — in what would be her final turn before a camera.

some extent, we discussed what was ailing her. This was definitely not an opportune moment to delve into the biographical — or much else, for that matter.

Hours later I contacted my brother, Jimmy, a DC-based physician who specialized in holistic medicine. I told him I was concerned about my friend and asked if he knew of anyone in the Santa Barbara area who could help her. He said that he did, coming up with the name of a doctor who was a renowned pain therapist. It was clear to me that Jimmy wanted to discuss this man with Lynn, feeling she should know why he believed him appropriate for her. I relayed my brother's thoughts to Bari in the days that followed. Genuinely appreciative, she said she'd be phoning Jimmy right away. Our call didn't last long but Lynn was lively throughout, appearing to be on the rebound.

Bari's improvement was fleeting, however. I spoke with her on October 3, disheartened to learn that her health had plummeted.

I've been so sick since I've talked to you last. Well…it's a long one, but that's okay. I haven't gotten in touch with that doctor, and your brother was so nice to me. I'm so apologetic about not calling that man. I feel so down. I've got something wrong with my eyes now; it's giving me migraine headaches. And I started a new program over at the Hospital of Physical Therapy — and I guess I overdid that. And this move was a traumatic thing, too. It was a jolt to my system, particularly when I haven't been doing a damn thing. But we're in it fine.

Lynn wanted to know what was new with me and I told her how the manuscript was progressing. In spite of her physical situation, she had lost none of her interest in my book project. We briefly discussed its form and content, with Bari coming up with a few insightful suggestions. Although I had no intention of burdening her with specific questions, Lynn had a need to explain why she wasn't in a position to contribute more.

I have to see my doctors, so they can figure out what to do with me. I've been taking *very* large doses of Percocet now because these headaches have just about pushed me over the rim. And I'll have to get off of that. I just don't think properly when I'm like this. So, I think we'd better make it [a mini-interview date] in at least ten days, or two weeks even — if you don't mind; then, it won't be a waste of time.

I assured Bari that that would be fine. We had now been speaking for about ten minutes and I thought it best to let her go. Saying goodbye, I asked Lynn in passing if she'd received *City of Chance*, a video I'd recently mailed her. She said she had. Then, all of a sudden, her voice perked up and she started tearing into the 1940 movie.

Oh, that was terrible. *(Laughing)* It was! Well, that director, Ricardo Cortez, had me doing things in that I should have been *arrested* for. Saying like, "Oh, gee, aren't I cute?" I'm too big to be cute! That's for Shirley Temple. Awful, awful! Oh, *(laughing)* what the hell. It was an eighteen-day picture, you know.

I interjected the film had been well-received in a trade review I'd come across.

Oh, really? *(Laughing)* **It must have been a drunken reporter!**

I said the critic had been crazy about her, thinking delightful her portrayal of a young Southern reporter.

Lynn and C. Aubrey Smith in City of Chance.

Oh, yeah — but that Southern accent came and went; I sounded Southern one moment, and the next…oh, it was so cornball! And the terrible thing is that I was born in the South! It was so hokey what I was doing.

And poor C. Aubrey Smith [her *City of Chance* costar] would clear his throat before every take — and he had the *loudest* noise that came out of his mouth! And I would jump right up to the sky before every scene! *(laughing)* Oh, and he was as deaf as a post, poor man. But he was a lovely man, a fine man. They knighted him later on.

Listening to Lynn's bubbly *City of Chance* recollections, I felt I was talking to someone other than the person with whom I had entered into a conversation. Listless no longer, she then gave forth with some kind words and bade me a hearty farewell.

Bari's phone-call revival had no correlation to any type of physical resiliency; she was now past the point of bouncing back from severe illness. Her health was, in fact, deep in the midst of a progressive downslide. I wasn't aware of this at the time, for she had chosen to be selective in disclosing to me the details of her medical condition.

I next dialed Lynn's home on October 19. John Luft answered the phone. Friendly and well-spoken, he gently shared some unsettling news about his mother: she was presently convalescing at a local hospital. It was explained to me that she had been admitted there because she had weakened considerably over the past month, and this had created a problem with her metabolism that had to be carefully addressed. In reassuring tones, John told me Bari was responding nicely to her doctors' care; it would only be a matter of days before she'd back in her apartment. She would probably enjoy hearing from me upon her return, Luft said.

I would later discover that Lynn had been dealing with more than a metabolism issue. She had also been stricken with a heart attack. The coronary had, in turn, engendered other medical problems. Saddled with misfortune, Bari remained in the hospital two weeks.

I reached Lynn on October 25 — and was devastated by her utterly frail hello. She then whispered:

Oh, Jeff, I've been so sick.

Gathering a bit more strength, Bari wanted to know if John had spelled out to me the reasons behind her hospitalization. I said he had mentioned a metabolism problem. Lynn chuckled in muffled tones:

***That* is only the beginning.**

With that, Bari immediately changed the subject.

How are you, honey?

I said I was doing fine, but was very concerned about her. I expressed to her my hope that a goodly number of people were tending to her — and Lynn responded affirmatively.

Oh, everybody; my God, I can't believe it. I spent this *awful* time in the hospital and I couldn't *wait* to get out of there. And now I'm home. And, God, I'm sweeping my friends away. I've know I've got some lovely friends, you included. Well, honey, you be of good cheer. I love you, honey, and you're very sweet to call.

I phoned Lynn again six days later, hoping she had improved. Her opening remarks made apparent she was more robust of voice, yet she sounded different; her words were now shaded with tones of anguish and frustration. It was wrenching listening to her. I told her I wasn't going to keep her on the line more than a moment, but I did want to know how she was feeling.

Not too good. I'm awful sick; I just ache all over. It's the damned ankylosing spondylitis. This happens every few years. It lasts forever — it seems like forever. Johnny went out and got me a new bed today; I wasn't able to sleep in the old one. I don't know ... I'm going nuts. I sound like Marilyn Monroe: "Tear down the mountain!" In the hospital, they had all these broads poking me. Oh, they're all full of baloney. They really are terrible, honey. Well, thank you for calling, honey. And I do love you.

Sensing (but still not knowing) the severity of Bari's situation, I felt for the first time she was failing.

We next spoke on Monday, November 6. This would turn out to be our last conversation. At its outset, Lynn in some ways gave the impression of being stronger. Her intonations were more resonant, free of grievousness. I could tell she was moving about as we chatted, something she had not done since August. It also appeared she wanted to remain on the phone. For some time, she'd actually be quite engaged with me. This level of involvement wouldn't endure to the end of our dialogue, however, for there'd come a point when Bari would begin to wither. She began:

Oh Jeff, I'm in terrible shape. I don't seem to be getting any better; if it's not one thing, it's another. Things keep popping up and I'm just about to lose what's left of my so-called, alleged brain. So, tell me, what's going on in your young life?

I told her she would soon be receiving the first draft of her biography, rough as it was. This seemed to please her. With regard to her reviewing it, she said softly:

You're not in any particular hurry — because what I've got to go through here, it's pretty hard.

I replied she could take as much time as she needed; there was absolutely no rush. I then asked her if it would be okay for me to write about her ankylosing.

I don't give a damn. I don't want to look like a big jerk, but I do think that if you have something wrong, it's all right to say something. You might help someone else.

We went on to talk of things less consequential, with Lynn in a relatively agreeable mood. Then, out of nowhere, her voice became filled with frustration. She let out with her disappointment — although I wasn't sure if it was to me whom she was airing it.

Oh boy, am I ever feeling sorry for myself! I'm terrible. I'm screaming and carrying on, and I know what I'm doing but it's unfortunate.

My heart ached for Bari, but I just didn't know how to respond to her. A feeling of helplessness had taken over and I was rendered silent for a moment that seemed an eternity. Desperately searching my mind for a proper thing to say, I could only come up with a platitude.

I said to her gently, "I hope it will pass soon," and she sobbed:

I will — it will. Honey, I gotta go now. Bye-bye.

Lynn had literally faded away from me there and then, as I would later come to realize.

Terribly shaken by this call, I had the urge to phone Bari back with truly consoling words. Good judgment thankfully prevailed; I sat on my impulses, quickly realizing the intrusiveness of such an act.

The next two weeks would find me over and over trying to reason out Lynn's deportment during the final minutes of our last conversation. She had obviously been depressed of late, and justifiably so. Had intense pain suddenly descended, causing her to crumble? Perhaps, but I came to sense there had been far more to Bari's breakdown. This had left me with an extremely uneasy feeling about her prospects. Nevertheless, I tried to bring her into positive focus by carrying on with her biography.

Lynn had given so much of herself to me, enthusiastically and openly. Her generosity had spurred me on with my manuscript in an unexpectedly rapid fashion. I had taken great delight in immersing myself in the book's first draft, particularly in August and September. There were still joys to the writing process, but since October my work approach had become increasingly more frenetic. I felt like a stressed-out reporter, racing to meet a deadline.

Thoughts of Lynn filled my mind on Monday, November 20. The first draft of her biography was now finished, ready to be photocopied and sent to Santa Barbara. After bolting down my breakfast, I dropped off my manuscript at a copy shop. I returned there two hours later to pick up my order. My next stop was the post office, where I grabbed an Express Mail label. Arriving home, I promptly addressed the label to Bari.

I had decided I would phone Lynn later in the afternoon, to tell her of what would be coming her way. The call, of course, would also provide me with the opportunity to find out how she was feeling. The silence that had existed between us over the past two weeks had done nothing but exacerbate my anxiety about her condition.

At about 2:00 PM, my two dogs and I went for our daily walk in Central Park. A certain grayish sky cast a pronounced quiet over the area that Monday; perhaps the first hint of winter had subdued the two- and four-legged ones roaming the park. My little troop was treading a well-worn path when we came upon two young women involved in a wondrous activity — the gathering of a magnificent

The warmth and incandescence of Lynn Bari, shining through in a 1944 portrait.

autumn's multi-hued leaves. With clumps of amber, green and yellow bursting from their hands, the pair told me the leaves were going to be mailed to relatives in Texas and Oklahoma. People in their part of the Southwest, they explained, seldom experienced a real change of seasons. The three of us then exchanged a few pleasant words about New York and went our separate ways. Leaving the park, I looked skyward and felt a lovely sense of serenity.

I returned home and wrote a tender note of thanks to Lynn. The missive and a copy of the manuscript were placed into a manila envelope, which was then sealed. For some reason, it was important to me that Bari be sent this parcel that very day. It wouldn't, however, be mailed until I had spoken with her. The post office would close in about an hour, at 6 PM.

I dialed Santa Barbara at 5:00 PM. The line was busy; a good sign, I thought. It was clear at five-thirty. John Luft answered with a tentative hello. I asked him how his mother was doing and found myself waiting on his response. Choosing his words thoughtfully, he told me she had passed away several hours earlier, of congestive heart failure. I became somewhat disoriented, sad, pained.

John and I somehow managed a fifteen-minute conversation. He said Lynn had entered a rehabilitation institute (at the Goleta Valley Community Hospital) on November 16. Over the course of the following three days she had received physical therapy, hydrotherapy and sedation. By November 19, she had taken a "180-degree" turn for the better. The next day she was gone.

"It totally blew my mind," John said of his mother's death. "She was responding so well to the treatment. I guess it wasn't in the cards. The last two months she was a different person entirely. It was her time because her heart was very weak — and her lungs, too. And she'd been in such agony. So it was a blessing in disguise. It really is for the better because we did all that medical science could do for the last eight-to-ten years. Now she's at peace; she's happy, I would assume.

"She was an interesting person, full of compassion, sensitivity and [she] had a lack of selfishness concerning her illness. She was a powerful woman; she made the most of her life, saw friends, wrote and took walks on the beach. There were certainly times of fun and laughs those last few years; she had plenty of pleasure in there. Her spirit was phenomenal. You'd be lucky to meet another person who's as nice and special as she was. The book will be a nice memento. She was such a great actress and a fine person and she left a great legacy."

I asked John if there were people nearby with whom he could share his grief. He assured me there were, adding that the Fishers were coming up from Newport Beach on Wednesday. Sometime that day, Lynn's family would be scattering her ashes off the coast of Santa Barbara. Thursday afternoon everyone would be sharing in a Thanksgiving dinner. Gladdened by this, I knew the time was right to say my goodbyes to John. I extended to him and his family my deepest sympathies and he responded appreciatively. In closing, I asked if I might be able to call him again. He said that that would be fine and we arranged to speak the following evening.

John and I talked for two hours that next night, mostly about his mother. Now and again, though, we drifted off into trivial matters. The proverbial topic of the weather came up, causing me to mention the two women I had the day before encountered in the park. John paused for a few seconds and went on to tell me about one of the very last letters his mother had received. It had been sent by William Roerick, her dear friend from New York. Roerick had written her a chatty note — and, below its pages, he had placed a cluster of dried leaves. John explained that Lynn had once expressed to her pal how much she missed the varying foliage of her Eastern childhood — and, every year since then, Roerick had gifted her with a medley of autumn leaves.

My feelings of despondency over Bari's death became somewhat assuaged by thoughts of this letter, because the fallen leaves included brought to mind the natural completion of life's cycle. During her final months, Lynn had afforded herself the chance to look back on her own life — and she had done so from the perspective of one who had achieved an inner peace. Like the harvesting of those leaves, she had gathered together the many colorful threads of her existence, weaving them into a beautiful fabric for the first and last time.

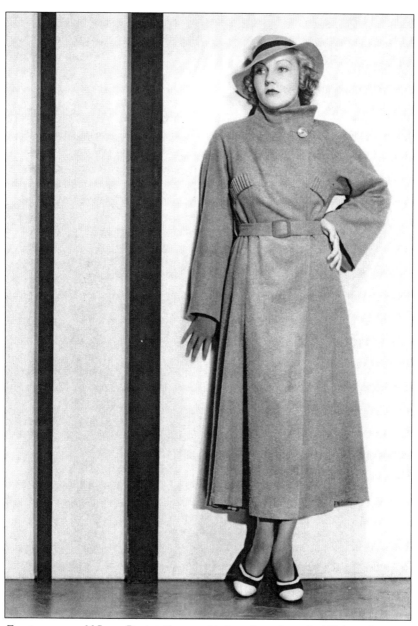

Fourteen-year-old Lynn Bari strikes a sophisticated pose in early 1934, at the outset of her tenure with the Fox Film Corporation.

FILMOGRAPHY

The following are listed by release date. This chronology does not always correspond to the order of production. For instance, while *Dancing Lady* marked Lynn Bari's film debut, *Meet the Baron* was her first motion-picture release.

UNCREDITED APPEARANCES

(Between 1934 and 1937, Lynn Bari was featured as an extra, showgirl and/or bit player in approximately twenty Fox films per year. The entries in this section represent a partial listing — those movies where her appearances have been verified.)

1933. *Meet the Baron*. DIRECTOR: Walter Lang. CAST: Jimmy Durante, Jack Pearl, Ted Healy and his Stooges, ZaSu Pitts, Edna May Oliver. (MGM)

1933. *Dancing Lady*. DIRECTOR: Robert Z. Leonard. CAST: Joan Crawford, Clark Gable, Franchot Tone, Fred Astaire, Nelson Eddy, Ted Healy and his Stooges, Eve Arden. (MGM)

1934. *I Am Suzanne*. DIRECTOR: Rowland V. Lee. CAST: Lillian Harvey, Gene Raymond, Leslie Banks, Georgia Caine. (Fox)

1934. *Search for Beauty*. DIRECTOR: Erle Kenton. CAST: Buster Crabbe, Ida Lupino, Robert Armstrong, Gertrude Michael, James Gleason, Clara Lou (Ann) Sheridan. (Paramount)

1934. *David Harum*. DIRECTOR: James Cruze. CAST: Will Rogers, Kent Taylor, Evelyn Venable, Louise Dresser, Stepin Fetchit. (Fox)

1934. *Coming Out Party*. DIRECTOR: John Blystone. CAST: Frances Dee, Gene Raymond, Alison Skipworth, Nigel Bruce, Edward Norris. (Fox)

1934. *Bottoms Up*. DIRECTOR: David Butler. CAST: Spencer Tracy, John Boles, Pat Paterson, Harry Green, Thelma Todd, Lucille Ball. (Fox)

1934. *Stand Up and Cheer*. DIRECTOR: Hamilton MacFadden. CAST: Warner Baxter, Shirley Temple, Madge Evans, James Dunn, John Boles, Stepin Fetchit. (Fox)

1934. *The World Moves On*. DIRECTOR: John Ford. CAST: Madeleine Carroll, Franchot Tone, Reginald Denny, Louise Dresser, Sig Rumann. (Fox)

1934. *Handy Andy*. DIRECTOR: David Butler. CAST: Will Rogers, Peggy Wood, Mary Carlisle, Robert Taylor, Conchita Montenegro. (Fox)

1934. *Caravan*. DIRECTOR: Erik Charell. CAST: Charles Boyer, Loretta Young, Jean Parker, Phillips Holmes, Louise Fazenda, C. Aubrey Smith. (Fox)

1934. *Caravane* (French language). DIRECTOR: Erik Charell. CAST: Charles Boyer, Annabella, Conchita Montenegro, Pierre Brasseur, Andre Berley. (Fox)

1934. *365 Nights in Hollywood*. DIRECTOR: George Marshall. CAST: James Dunn, Alice Faye, Frank Mitchell, Jack Durant, John Bradford, Grant Mitchell, John Qualen. (Fox)

1934. *Music in the Air*. DIRECTOR: Joe May. CAST: Gloria Swanson, John Boles, June Lang, Douglass Montgomery, Reginald Owen. (Fox)

1934. *Bachelor of Arts*. DIRECTOR: Louis King. CAST: Anita Louise, Tom Brown, Arline Judge, Henry B. Walthall, Mae Marsh, Frank Albertson, Berton Churchill. (Fox)

1935. *Charlie Chan in Paris*. DIRECTOR: Lewis Seiler. CAST: Warner Oland, Mary Brian, Thomas Beck, Keye Luke, Erik Rhodes. (Fox)

1935. *Lottery Lover*. DIRECTOR: William Thiele. CAST: Lew Ayres, Pat Paterson, Peggy Fears, Sterling Holloway, Walter Woolf King, Alan Dinehart, Reginald Denny. (Fox)

1935. *Under Pressure*. DIRECTOR: Raoul Walsh. CAST: Edmund Lowe, Victor McLaglen, Florence Rice, Marjorie Rambeau, Charles Bickford. (Fox)

1935. *The Great Hotel Murder*. DIRECTOR: Eugene Forde. CAST: Edmund Lowe, Victor McLaglen, Rosemary Ames, Mary Carlisle. (Fox)

1935. *George White's 1935 Scandals*. DIRECTOR: George White. CAST: Alice Faye, James Dunn, Lyda Roberti, Ned Sparks, Arline Judge, Eleanor Powell. (Fox)

1935. *Ten Dollar Raise*. DIRECTOR: George Marshall. CAST: Edward Everett Horton, Karen Morley, Alan Dinehart, Jed Prouty, Berton Churchill, Rosina Lawrence, Ray Walker. (Fox)

1935. *Spring Tonic*. DIRECTOR: Clyde Bruckman. CAST: Lew Ayres, Claire Trevor, Jack Haley, ZaSu Pitts, Tara Birell. (Fox)

1935. *Ladies Love Danger*. DIRECTOR: H. Bruce Humberstone. CAST: Gilbert Roland, Mona Barrie, Adrienne Ames, Donald Cook. (Fox)

1935. *Doubting Thomas*. DIRECTOR: David Butler. CAST: Will Rogers, Billie Burke, Gail Patrick, Alison Skipworth, Frank Albertson, Sterling Holloway. (Fox)

1935. *The Daring Young Man*. DIRECTOR: William A. Seiter. CAST: James Dunn, Mae Clarke, Neil Hamilton, Sidney Toler, Warren Hymer, Stanley Fields, Madge Bellamy. (Fox)

1935. *Dante's Inferno*. DIRECTOR: Harry Lachman. CAST: Spencer Tracy, Claire Trevor, Henry B. Walthall, Alan Dinehart, Rita Cansino (Hayworth), Scotty Beckett, Andrea Leeds. (Fox)

1935. *Orchids to You*. DIRECTOR: William A. Seiter. CAST: John Boles, Jean Muir, Charles Butterworth, Arthur Lake. (Fox)

1935. *Curly Top*. DIRECTOR: Irving Cummings. CAST: Shirley Temple, John Boles, Rochelle Hudson, Jane Darwell, Arthur Treacher. (Fox)

1935. *Welcome Home*. DIRECTOR: James Tinling. CAST: James Dunn, Arline Judge, Raymond Walburn, Rosina Lawrence, William Frawley. (Fox)

1935. *Redheads on Parade*. DIRECTOR: Norman Z. McLeod. CAST: John Boles, Dixie Lee, Jack Haley, Raymond Walburn. (Fox)

1935. *Music Is Magic*. DIRECTOR: George Marshall. CAST: Alice Faye, Bebe Daniels, Ray Walker, Hattie McDaniel, Thomas Beck. (Fox)

1935. *The Gay Deception*. DIRECTOR: William Wyler. CAST: Francis Lederer, Frances Dee, Benita Hume, Alan Mowbray, Akim Tamiroff, Lionel Stander, Luis Alberni. (Fox)

1935. *Charlie Chan in Shanghai*. DIRECTOR: James Tinling. CAST: Warner Oland, Irene Hervey, Charles Locher (Jon Hall), Keye Luke, Russell Hicks. (20th Century-Fox)

1935. *Metropolitan*. DIRECTOR: Richard Bolesawski. CAST: Lawrence Tibbett, Virginia Bruce, Alice Brady, Cesar Romero, Thurston Hall. (20th Fox – a Darryl F. Zanuck (DFZ) production)

1935. *Way Down East*. DIRECTOR: Henry King. CAST: Rochelle Hudson, Henry Fonda, Andy Devine, Margaret Hamilton, Russell Simpson, Spring Byington, Slim Summerville. (Fox)

1935. *Thanks a Million*. DIRECTOR: Roy Del Ruth. CAST: Dick Powell, Ann Dvorak, Fred Allen, Patsy Kelly, Paul Whiteman, Raymond Walburn. (Twentieth Century; released by 20th Fox – a DFZ production)

1935. *The Man Who Broke the Bank at Monte Carlo*. DIRECTOR: Stephen Roberts. CAST: Ronald Colman, Joan Bennett, Colin Clive, Nigel Bruce. (20th Fox – a DFZ production)

1935. *Show Them No Mercy!*. DIRECTOR: George Marshall. CAST: Rochelle Hudson, Cesar Romero, Bruce Cabot, Edward Norris, Ed Brophy. (20th Fox – a DFZ production)

1935. *Professional Soldier*. DIRECTOR: Tay Garnett. CAST: Victor McLaglen, Freddie Bartholomew, Gloria Stuart, Constance Collier, Michael Whalen, C. Henry Gordon, Pedro de Cordoba, Dixie Dunbar. (20th Fox – a DFZ production)

1936. *King of Burlesque*. DIRECTOR: Sidney Lanfield. CAST: Warner Baxter, Alice Faye, Jack Oakie, Mona Barrie, Arline Judge, Gregory Ratoff, Fats Waller, Dixie Dunbar, Jane Wyman. (20th Fox – a DFZ production)

1936. *It Had to Happen*. DIRECTOR: Roy Del Ruth. CAST: George Raft, Rosalind Russell, Leo Carrillo, Arline Judge, Alan Dinehart. (20th Fox – a DFZ production)

1936. *My Marriage*. DIRECTOR: George Archainbaud. CAST: Claire Trevor, Kent Taylor, Pauline Frederick, Paul Kelly, Thomas Beck, Helen Wood. (20th Fox)

1936. *Song and Dance Man*. DIRECTOR: Allan Dwan. CAST: Claire Trevor, Paul Kelly, Michael Whalen, Ruth Donnelly. (20th Fox)

1936. *Everybody's Old Man*. DIRECTOR: James Food. CAST: Irvin S. Cobb, Rochelle Hudson, Johnny Downs, Norman Foster, Alan Dinehart. (20th Fox)

1936. *The Great Ziegfeld*. DIRECTOR: Robert Z. Leonard. CAST: William Powell, Myrna Loy, Luise Rainer, Frank Morgan, Fannie Brice, Virginia Bruce, Ray Bolger, Stanley Morner (Dennis Morgan), Virginia Grey. (MGM)

1936. *Gentle Julia*. DIRECTOR: John Blystone. CAST: Jane Withers, Tom Brown, Marsha Hunt, Jackie Searl, Francis Ford, George Meeker. (20th Fox)

1936. *Private Number*. DIRECTOR: Roy Del Ruth. CAST: Robert Taylor, Loretta Young, Patsy Kelly, Basil Rathbone, Jane Darwell, Kane Richmond. (20th Fox – a DFZ production)

1936. *Poor Little Rich Girl*. DIRECTOR: Irving Cummings. CAST: Shirley Temple, Alice Faye, Gloria Stuart, Michael Whalen, Jack Haley, Tony Martin, Jane Darwell, Sara Haden, Henry Armetta, Claude Gillingwater. (20th Fox – a DFZ production)

1936. *36 Hours to Kill*. DIRECTOR: Eugene Forde. CAST: Brian Donlevy, Gloria Stuart, Douglas Fowley, Isabel Jewell, Stepin Fetchit. (20th Fox)

1936. *Girls' Dormitory*. DIRECTOR: Irving Cummings. CAST: Herbert Marshall, Ruth Chatterton, Simone Simon, Constance Collier, J. Edward Bromberg, Dixie Dunbar, Tyrone Power. (20th Fox – a DFZ production)

1936. *Star for a Night*. DIRECTOR: Lewis Seiler. CAST: Claire Trevor, Jane Darwell, Evelyn Venable, Arline Judge, J. Edward Bromberg, Joyce Compton, Chick Chandler, Dean Jagger, Hattie McDaniel. (20th Fox)

1936. *Sing, Baby, Sing*. DIRECTOR: Sidney Lanfield. CAST: Alice Faye, Adolphe Menjou, Gregory Ratoff, Michael Whalen, Ted Healy, Patsy Kelly, The Ritz Brothers, Dixie Dunbar, Douglas Fowley, Tony Martin. (20th Fox – a DFZ production)

1936. *15 Maiden Lane*. DIRECTOR: Allan Dwan. CAST: Claire Trevor, Cesar Romero, Douglas Fowley, Lloyd Nolan. (20th Fox)

1936. *Ladies in Love*. DIRECTOR: Edward H. Griffith. CAST: Janet Gaynor, Loretta Young, Constance Bennett, Simone Simon, Don Ameche, Paul Lukas, Tyrone Power, J. Edward Bromberg. (20th Fox – a DFZ production)

1936. *Under Your Spell*. DIRECTOR: Otto Preminger. CAST: Lawrence Tibbett, Wendy Barrie, Gregory Ratoff, Arthur Treacher, Gregory Gaye, Berton Churchill, Jed Prouty. (20th Fox)

1936. *Pigskin Parade*. DIRECTOR: David Butler. CAST: Stuart Erwin, Patsy Kelly, Jack Haley, Johnny Downs, Betty Grable, Arline Judge, Dixie Dunbar, Judy Garland, Tony Martin, Elisha Cook, Jr., Alan Ladd. (20th Fox – a DFZ production)

1936. *Crack-Up*. DIRECTOR: Malcolm St. Clair. CAST: Peter Lorre, Brian Donlevy, Ralph Morgan, Thomas Beck, Helen Wood, Kay Linaker. (20th Fox)

1937. *Woman-Wise*. DIRECTOR: Allan Dwan. CAST: Rochelle Hudson, Michael Whalen, Thomas Beck, Alan Dinehart, Douglas Fowley, Chick Chandler, Astrid Allwyn. (20th Fox)

1937. *On the Avenue*. DIRECTOR: Roy Del Ruth. CAST: Dick Powell, Madeleine Carroll, Alice Faye, The Ritz Brothers, George Barbier, Alan Mowbray, Joan Davis, Douglas Fowley, Stepin Fetchit, Cora Witherspoon, Sig Rumann. (20th Fox – a DFZ production)

1937. *Love Is News*. DIRECTOR: Tay Garnett. CAST: Tyrone Power, Loretta Young, Don Ameche, Slim Summerville, Pauline Moore, George Sanders, Jane Darwell, Stepin Fetchit, Dudley Digges. (20th Fox – a DFZ production)

1937. *Time Out for Romance*. DIRECTOR: Malcolm St. Clair. CAST: Claire Trevor, Michael Whalen, Joan Davis, Chick Chandler, Douglas Fowley. (20th Fox)

1937. *Fair Warning*. DIRECTOR: Norman Foster. CAST: J. Edward Bromberg, Betty Furness, John Payne, Victor Kilian, Billy (Bill) Burrud, Gavin Muir, Gloria Roy, Andrew Tombes. (20th Fox)

1937. *Wake Up and Live*. DIRECTOR: Sidney Lanfield. CAST: Alice Faye, Walter Winchell, Ben Bernie, Patsy Kelly, Ned Sparks, Jack Haley, Joan Davis, Leah Ray, Douglas Fowley, Walter Catlett, Grace Bradley, Robert Lowery. (20th Fox – a DFZ production)

1937. *Café Metropole*. DIRECTOR: Edward H. Griffith. CAST: Loretta Young, Tyrone, Power, Adolphe Menjou, Gregory Ratoff, Helen Westley, Charles Winninger. (20th Fox – a DFZ production)

1937. *This Is My Affair*. DIRECTOR: William A. Seiter. CAST: Barbara Stanwyck, Robert Taylor, Victor McLaglen, Brian Donlevy, John Carradine, Douglas Fowley, Sidney Blackmer, Marjorie Weaver, Alan Dinehart. (20th Fox – a DFZ production)

1937. *Sing and Be Happy*. DIRECTOR: James Tinling. CAST: Tony Martin, Leah Ray, Helen Westley, Joan Davis, Allan Lane, Dixie Dunbar, Chick Chandler. (20th Fox)

1937. *Wee Willie Winkie*. DIRECTOR: John Ford. CAST: Shirley Temple, Victor McLaglen, June Lang, Michael Whalen, C. Aubrey Smith, Cesar Romero, Constance Collier. (20th Fox – a DFZ production)

1937. *She Had to Eat*. DIRECTOR: Malcolm St. Clair. CAST: Rochelle Hudson, Jack Haley, Arthur Treacher, Eugene Palette, Douglas Fowley. (20th Fox)

1937. *The Lady Escapes*. DIRECTOR: Eugene Forde. CAST: Gloria Stuart, Michael Whalen, George Sanders, Cora Witherspoon, Regis Toomey, Franklin Pangborn. (20th Fox)

1937. *You Can't Have Everything*. DIRECTOR: Norman Taurog. CAST: Alice Faye, The Ritz Brothers, Don Ameche, Tony Martin, Phyllis Brooks, Arthur Treacher, Louse Hovick (aka Gypsy Rose Lee), Charles Winninger, Wally Vernon, Louis Prima. (20th Fox – a DFZ production)

1937. *Life Begins in College*. DIRECTOR: William A. Seiter. CAST: The Ritz Brothers, Gloria Stuart, Dick Baldwin, Joan Davis, Tony Martin, Marjorie Weaver, Nat Pendleton, Jed Prouty. (20th Fox – a DFZ production)

1937. *Wife, Doctor and Nurse*. DIRECTOR: Walter Lang. CAST: Loretta Young, Warner Baxter, Virginia Bruce, Jane Darwell, Sidney Blackmer, Maurice Cass, Minna Gombell. (20th Fox – a DFZ production)

1937. *Ali Baba Goes to Town*. DIRECTOR: David Butler. CAST: Eddie Cantor, June Lang, Tony Martin, Roland Young, Louise Hovick (aka Gypsy Rose Lee), John Carradine, Alan Dinehart, Virginia Field. (20th Fox – a DFZ production)

1937. *45 Fathers*. DIRECTOR: James Tinling. CAST: Jane Withers, Thomas Beck, Louise Henry, Hattie McDaniel, Leon Ames, Sammy Cohen. (20th Fox)

1937. *Love and Hisses*. DIRECTOR: Sidney Lanfield. CAST: Walter Winchell, Ben Bernie, Simone Simon, Dick Baldwin, Bert Lahr, Joan Davis, Ruth Terry, Douglas Fowley, Chick Chandler. (20th Fox – a DFZ production)

1938. *City Girl*. DIRECTOR: Alfred Werker. CAST: Phyllis Brooks, Ricardo Cortez, Robert Wilcox, Douglas Fowley, Marjorie Main, Chick Chandler, Esther Muir, Adrienne Ames, Robert Lowery. (20th Fox)

1938. *Rebecca of Sunnybrook Farm*. DIRECTOR: Allan Dwan. CAST: Shirley Temple, Randolph Scott, Gloria Stuart, Phyllis Brooks, Jack Haley, Helen Westley, Bill Robinson, Slim Summerville, J. Edward Bromberg, Dixie Dunbar, William Demarest, Alan Dinehart, Ruth Gillette, Franklin Pangborn, Paul Harvey. (20th Fox — a DFZ production)

A publicity portrait of Lynn, promoting her appearance in Lancer Spy *(1937) — the film in which Bari received her first on-screen credit.*

FILMS AS A FEATURED PLAYER

(Unless indicated otherwise, all are Twentieth Century-Fox releases.)

1937. *Lancer Spy*. DIRECTOR: Gregory Ratoff. ASSOCIATE PRODUCER: Samuel G. Engel. SCREENPLAY: Philip Dunne, from a story by Marthe McKenna. CAST: Dolores Del Rio, George Sanders, Peter Lorre, Joseph Schildkraut, Virginia Field, Sig Rumann, Maurice Moscovich, Lionel Atwill, Luther Adler, Fritz Feld, Lynn Bari. A Darryl F. Zanuck (DFZ) production

1938. *The Baroness and the Butler*. DIRECTOR: Walter Lang. ASSOCIATE PRODUCER: Raymond Griffith. SCREENPLAY: Sam Hellman, Lamar Trotti and Kathryn Scola, from a story by Ladislaus Bus-Fekete. CAST: William Powell, Annabella, Helen Westley, Henry Stephenson, Joseph Schildkraut, J. Edward Bromberg, Nigel Bruce, Lynn Bari, Maurice Cass. A DFZ production

1938. *Walking Down Broadway*. DIRECTOR: Norman Foster. EXECUTIVE PRODUCER: Sol M. Wurtzel. SCREENPLAY: Robert Chapin and Karen DeWolf. CAST: Claire Trevor, Phyllis Brooks, Leah Ray, Dixie Dunbar, Lynn Bari, Jayne Regan, Michael Whalen, Thomas Beck, Douglas Fowley, Walter Woolf King, Jed Prouty, Leon Ames, Robert Kellard, Maurice Cass.

1938. *Mr. Moto's Gamble*. DIRECTOR: James Tinling. EXECUTIVE PRODUCER: Sol M. Wurtzel. ASSOCIATE PRODUCER: John Stone. SCREENPLAY: Charles Belden and Jerry Cady; partially based on the character, "Mr. Moto," created by John P. Marquand. CAST: Peter Lorre, Lynn Bari, Keye Luke, Dick Baldwin, Douglas Fowley, Jayne Regan, Harold Huber, Maxie Rosenboom, Ward Bond, Lon Chaney, Jr.

1938. *Battle of Broadway*. DIRECTOR: George Marshall. EXECUTIVE PRODUCER: Sol M. Wurtzel. SCREENPLAY: Lou Breslow and John Patrick, from a story by Norman Houston. CAST: Victor McLaglen, Brian Donlevy, Louise Hovick (*aka* Gypsy Rose Lee), Raymond Walburn, Lynn Bari, Jane Darwell, Robert Kellard, Sammy Cohen, Esther Muir, Hattie McDaniel.

1938. *Josette*. DIRECTOR: Allan Dwan. ASSOCIATE PRODUCER: Gene Markey. SCREENPLAY: James Edward Grant, from a play by Paul Frank and George

Fraser; based on a story by Ladislaus Vadnai. CAST: Don Ameche, Simone Simon, Robert Young, Bert Lahr, Joan Davis, Lynn Bari, Paul Hurst, William Collier, Sr., Tala Birell, William Demarest, Ruth Gillette. A DFZ production

1938. *Always Goodbye.* DIRECTOR: Sidney Lanfield. ASSOCIATE PRODUCER: Raymond Griffith. SCREENPLAY: Kathryn Scola and Edith Skouras, from a story by Gilbert Emery and Douglas Doty. CAST: Barbara Stanwyck, Herbert Marshall, Ian Hunter, Cesar Romero, Lynn Bari, Binnie Barnes, Johnny Russell, Mary Forbes, Mary Treen, Franklin Pangborn, Robert Lowery. A DFZ production

1938. *I'll Give a Million.* DIRECTOR: Walter Lang. ASSOCIATE PRODUCER: Kenneth Macgowan. SCREENPLAY: Boris Ingster and Milton Sperling, from a story by Cesare Zavattini and Giaci Mondaini. CAST: Warner Baxter, Marjorie Weaver, Peter Lorre, Jean Hersholt, John Carradine, J. Edward Bromberg, Lynn Bari, Fritz Feld, Sig Rumann. A DFZ production

1938. *Meet the Girls.* DIRECTOR: Eugene Forde. EXECUTIVE PRODUCER: Sol M. Wurtzel. ASSOCIATE PRODUCER: Howard J. Green. SCREENPLAY: Marguerite Roberts. CAST: June Lang, Lynn Bari, Robert Allen, Ruth Donnelly, Gene Lockhart, Wally Vernon, Erik Rhodes, Jack Norton.

1938. *Speed to Burn.* DIRECTOR: Otto Brower. EXECUTIVE PRODUCER: Sol M. Wurtzel. ASSOCIATE PRODUCER: Jerry Hoffman. SCREENPLAY: Robert Ellis and Helen Logan, from a story by Edwin Dial Torgenson. CAST: Michael Whalen, Lynn Bari, Marvin Stephens, Henry Armetta, Chick Chandler, Sidney Blackmer, Lon Chaney, Jr.

1938. *Sharpshooters.* DIRECTOR: James Tinling. EXECUTIVE PRODUCER: Sol M. Wurtzel. SCREENPLAY: Robert Ellis and Helen Logan, from a story by Maurice Raph and Lester Ziffren. CAST: Brian Donlevy, Lynn Bari, Wally Vernon, John King, Douglas Dumbrille, C. Henry Gordon, Sidney Blackmer.

1939. *Pardon Our Nerve.* DIRECTOR: H. Bruce Humberstone. EXECUTIVE PRODUCER: Sol M. Wurtzel. SCREENPLAY: Robert Ellis and Helen Logan, from a story by Hilda Stone and Betty Reinhardt. CAST: Lynn Bari, June Gale, Guinn Williams, Michael Whalen, Edward Brophy, John Miljan, Ward Bond, Theodore Von Eltz, Chester Clute, Helen Ericson.

1939. *The Return of the Cisco Kid.* DIRECTOR: Herbert I. Leeds. ASSOCIATE PRODUCER: Kenneth Macgowan. SCREENPLAY: Milton Sperling, from a story by O. Henry. CAST: Warner Baxter, Lynn Bari, Cesar Romero, Henry Hull, Kane Richmond, C. Henry Gordon, Robert Barrat, Chris-Pin Martin, Victor Kilian, Ruth Gillette, Ward Bond. A DFZ production

1939. *Chasing Danger.* DIRECTOR: Ricardo Cortez. EXECUTIVE PRODUCER: Sol M. Wurtzel. SCREENPLAY: Robert Ellis and Helen Logan, from a story by Leonardo Bercovici. CAST: Preston Foster, Lynn Bari, Wally Vernon, Henry Wilcoxon, Joan Woodbury, Harold Huber, Pedro de Cordoba.

1939. *News Is Made at Night.* DIRECTOR: Alfred Werker. EXECUTIVE PRODUCER: Sol M. Wurtzel. ASSOCIATE PRODUCER: Edward Kaufman. SCREENPLAY: John Larkin. CAST: Preston Foster, Lynn Bari, Russell Gleason, George Barbier, Eddie Collins, Minor Watson, Betty Compson, Charles Halton, Paul Harvey, Richard Lane, Charles Lane.

1939. *Hotel for Women* (aka *Elsa Maxwell's Hotel for Women*). DIRECTOR: Gregory Ratoff. ASSOCIATE PRODUCER: Raymond Griffith. SCREENPLAY: Kathryn Scola and Darrell Ware, from a story by Scola and Elsa Maxwell. CAST: Linda Darnell, Ann Sothern, Lynn Bari, Jean Rogers, James Ellison, June Gale, Joyce Compton, John Halliday, Katharine Aldridge, Alan Dinehart, Sidney Blackmer, Ruth Terry, Amanda Duff, Chick Chandler and Elsa Maxwell. A DFZ production

1939. *Hollywood Cavalcade.* DIRECTOR: Irving Cummings. ASSOCIATE PRODUCER: Harry Joe Brown. SCREENPLAY: Ernest Pascal, from a story by Hilary Lynn and Brown Holmes. CAST: Alice Faye, Don Ameche, J. Edward Bromberg, Alan Curtis, Lynn Bari, Stuart Erwin, Jed Prouty, Donald Meek, George Givot, Eddie Collins, Chick Chandler, Robert Lowery.* GUEST STARS: Buster Keaton, Ben Turpin, Chester Conklin, Al Jolson, Mack Sennett, the Keystone Kops. (Technicolor) A DFZ production

1939. *Pack Up Your Troubles.* DIRECTOR: H. Bruce Humberstone. EXECUTIVE PRODUCER: Sol M. Wurtzel. SCREENPLAY: Lou Breslow and Owen Francis. CAST: The Ritz Brothers, Jane Withers, Lynn Bari, Joseph Schildkraut, Stanley Fields, Fritz Leiber, Leon Ames.

1939. *Charlie Chan in City in Darkness.* DIRECTOR: Herbert I. Leeds. EXECUTIVE PRODUCER: Sol M. Wurtzel. ASSOCIATE PRODUCER: John Stone. SCREENPLAY: Robert Ellis and Helen Logan, from a play by Gina Kaus and Ladislaus Fodor — and also based on the character, "Charlie Chan," created by Earl Derr Biggers. CAST: Sidney Toler, Lynn Bari, Richard Clarke, Harold Huber, Pedro de Cordoba, Dorothy Tree, C. Henry Gordon, Douglas Dumbrille, Noel Madison, Leo G. Carroll, Lon, Chaney, Jr.

---

* Advance publicity had Lynn Bari receiving fifth billing as silent screen vamp Trixie Farrell. By the time of *Hollywood Cavalcade*'s release, however, all but one of Lynn's scenes had been deleted and she went uncredited.

1940. *City of Chance.* DIRECTOR: Ricardo Cortez. EXECUTIVE PRODUCER: Sol
M. Wurtzel. SCREENPLAY: John Larkin and Barry Trivers. CAST: Lynn Bari,
C. Aubrey Smith, Donald Woods, June Gale, Amanda Duff, Richard Lane,
Robert Lowery, Alex D'Arcy, Robert Allen, Robert Emmett Keane, Harry
Shannon. Prologue narration: Jack Carson.

1940. *Free, Blonde and 21.* DIRECTOR: Ricardo Cortez. EXECUTIVE PRODUCER:
Sol M. Wurtzel. SCREENPLAY: Frances Hyland. CAST: Lynn Bari, Mary
Beth Hughes, Joan Davis, Henry Wilcoxon, Robert Lowery, Alan Baxter,
Katharine Aldridge, Helen Ericson, Chick Chandler, Joan Valerie, Elyse
Knox, Kay Linaker, Richard Lane.

1940. *Lillian Russell.* DIRECTOR: Irving Cummings. ASSOCIATE PRODUCER:
Gene Markey. SCREENPLAY: William Anthony McGuire. CAST: Alice
Faye, Don Ameche, Henry Fonda, Edward Arnold, Warren William, Leo
Carrillo, Helen Westley, Dorothy Peterson, Ernest Truex, Lynn Bari, Nigel
Bruce, Claude Allister, Joe Weber, Lew Fields, Una O'Connor, Eddie Foy,
Jr., Joan Valerie, Elyse Knox. A DFZ production

1940. *Earthbound.* DIRECTOR: Irving Pichel. EXECUTIVE PRODUCER: Sol M.
Wurtzel. SCREENPLAY: John Howard Lawson and Samuel G. Engel, from
a story by Basil King. CAST: Warner Baxter, Andrea Leeds, Lynn Bari,
Charley Grapewin, Henry Wilcoxon, Elizabeth Patterson, Russell Hicks.

1940. *Pier 13.* DIRECTOR: Eugene Forde. EXECUTIVE PRODUCER: Sol M.
Wurtzel. SCREENPLAY: Stanley Rush and Clark Andrews, from a story
by Harry Connors and Philip Klein. CAST: Lynn Bari, Lloyd Nolan, Joan
Valerie, Douglas Fowley, Chick Chandler, Louis Jean Heydt, Frank Orth,
Oscar O'Shea, Mantan Moreland, Maurice Cass.

1940. *Kit Carson.* DIRECTOR: George B. Seitz. PRODUCER: Edward Small.
SCREENPLAY: George Bruce, from a story by Evelyn Wells. CAST: Jon Hall,
Lynn Bari, Dana Andrews, Ward Bond, Harold Huber, Raymond Hatton,
C. Henry Gordon, Clayton Moore, Renie Riano. (United Artists)

1940. *Charter Pilot.* DIRECTOR: Eugene Forde. EXECUTIVE PRODUCER: Sol M.
Wurtzel. SCREENPLAY: Stanley Rauh and Lester Ziffren, from a story by J.
Robert Bren and Norman Houston. CAST: Lynn Bari, Lloyd Nolan, Arleen
Whelan, George Montgomery, Hobart Cavanaugh, Henry Victor, Etta
McDaniel, Andrew Tombes, Charles Wilson, Chick Chandler.

1941. *Sleepers West.* DIRECTOR: Eugene Forde. EXECUTIVE PRODUCER: Sol M.
Wurtzel. SCREENPLAY: Lou Breslow and Stanley Rauh, based on the novel,
Sleepers East, by Frederick Nebel — and the character, "Michael Shayne,"
created by Brett Halliday. CAST: Lloyd Nolan, Lynn Bari, Mary Beth

Hughes, Louis Jean Heydt, Ed Brophy, Ben Carter, Don Costello, Oscar O'Shea, Don Douglas, Mantan Moreland.

1941. *Blood and Sand*. DIRECTOR: Rouben Mamoulian. ASSOCIATE PRODUCER: Robert T. Kane. SCREENPLAY: Jo Swerling, from the novel by Vincente Blasco Ibanez. CAST: Tyrone Power, Linda Darnell, Rita Hayworth, Anthony Quinn, Nazimova, Lynn Bari, J. Carrol Naish, John Carradine, Laird Cregar, Vincente Gomez, William Montague (aka Monty Banks), George Reeves, Pedro de Cordoba, Ann E. Todd, Kay Linaker. (Technicolor) A DFZ production

1941. *Sun Valley Serenade*. DIRECTOR: H. Bruce Humberstone. PRODUCER: Milton Sperling. SCREENPLAY: Robert Ellis and Helen Logan, from a story by Art Arthur and Robert Harari. CAST: Sonja Henie, John Payne, Lynn Bari, Milton Berle, Joan Davis, the Nicholas Brothers, Dorothy Dandridge, Sheila Ryan, Lynne Roberts, Ann Doran, Gary Gray, Chester Clute, and Glenn Miller and his Orchestra.

1941. *We Go Fast*. DIRECTOR: William McGann. EXECUTIVE PRODUCER: Sol M. Wurtzel. ASSOCIATE PRODUCER: Lou Ostrow. SCREENPLAY: Thomas Lennon and Adrian Scott, from a story by Doug Welch. CAST: Lynn Bari, Alan Curtis, Sheila Ryan, Don DeForest (DeFore), Ernest Truex, Gerald Mohr.

1941. *Moon Over Her Shoulder*. DIRECTOR: Alfred Werker. PRODUCER: Walter Morosco. SCREENPLAY: Walter Bullock, from a story by Helen Vreeland Smith and Eve Golden. CAST: Lynn Bari, John Sutton, Dan Dailey, Alan Mowbray, Joyce Compton, Kay Linaker, Irving Bacon, Leonard Carey, Lillian Yarbo.

1941. *The Perfect Snob*. DIRECTOR: Ray McCarey. PRODUCER: Walter Morosco. SCREENPLAY: Lee Loeb and Harold Buchman. CAST: Lynn Bari, Cornel Wilde, Charlie Ruggles, Charlotte Greenwood, Anthony Quinn, Alan Mowbray, Chester Clute.

1942. *Secret Agent of Japan*. DIRECTOR: Irving Pichel. EXECUTIVE PRODUCER: Sol M. Wurtzel. SCREENPLAY: John Larkin. CAST: Preston Foster, Lynn Bari, Noel Madison, Sen Yung, Janis Carter, Steven Geray, Kurt Katch, Addison Richards.

1942. *The Night Before the Divorce*. DIRECTOR: Robert Siodmak. PRODUCER: Ralph Dietrich. SCREENPLAY: Jerry Sackheim, from a play by Gina Kaus and Ladislas Fodor. CAST: Lynn Bari, Mary Beth Hughes, Joseph Allen, Jr., Nils Asther, Truman Bradley, Kay Linaker, Mary Treen, Thurston Hall, Spencer Charters, Leon Belasco, Dorothy Dandridge, Robert Emmett Keane.

1942. *The Falcon Takes Over.* DIRECTOR: Irving Reis. PRODUCER: Howard Benedict. SCREENPLAY: Lynn Root and Frank Fenton, from the novel, *Farewell, My Lovely,* by Raymond Chandler. CAST: George Sanders, Lynn Bari, James Gleason, Allen Jenkins, Anne Revere, Helen Gilbert, Ward Bond, Edward Gargan, George Cleveland, Turhan Bey. (RKO)

1942. *The Magnificent Dope.* DIRECTOR: Walter Lang. PRODUCER: William Perlberg. SCREENPLAY: George Seaton, from a story by Joseph Schrank. CAST: Henry Fonda, Lynn Bari, Don Ameche, Edward Everett Horton, George Barbier, Frank Orth, Marietta Canty, Hobart Cavanaugh, Chick Chandler.

1942. *Orchestra Wives.* DIRECTOR: Archie Mayo. PRODUCER: William Le Baron. SCREENPLAY: Karl Tunberg and Darrell Ware, from a story by James Prindle. CAST: George Montgomery, Ann Rutherford, Lynn Bari, Carole Landis, Cesar Romero, Virginia Gilmore, Mary Beth Hughes, the Nicholas Brothers, Jackie Gleason, Tamara Geva, Frank Orth, Marion Hutton, Grant Mitchell, Harry Morgan, Dale Evans, Kay Linaker, Trudy Marshall, Robert Emmett Keane, Iris Adrian, and Glenn Miller and his Orchestra.

1942. *That Other Woman.* DIRECTOR: Ray McCarey. PRODUCER: Walter Morosco. SCREENPLAY: Jack Jungmeyer, Jr. CAST: Lynn Bari, James Ellison, Dan Duryea, Janis Carter, Alma Kruger, Lon McCallister. NOTE: Lynn Bari's involvement with this film came to an end in June 1942, when the project went on hiatus during the second week of production. Cameras started rolling again in July, with Virginia Gilmore replacing Bari in the role of Emily Borden.

1943. *China Girl.* DIRECTOR: Henry Hathaway. PRODUCER: Ben Hecht. SCREENPLAY: Hecht, from a story by Melville Crossman (Darryl F. Zanuck). CAST: Gene Tierney, George Montgomery, Lynn Bari, Victor McLaglen, Alan Baxter, Sig Rumann, Myron McCormick, Bobby Blake, Ann Pennington, Philip Ahn, Tom Neal. A DFZ production

1943. *Hello, Frisco, Hello.* DIRECTOR: H. Bruce Humberstone. PRODUCER: Milton Sperling. SCREENPLAY: Robert Ellis, Helen Logan and Richard Macauley, from a story by Gene Markey and Harry Tugend. CAST: Alice Faye, John Payne, Lynn Bari, Jack Oakie, June Havoc, Laird Cregar, Ward Bond, George Barbier, Michael "Ted" North, Aubrey Mather, John Archer, Frank Orth, Kirby Grant, Esther Dale, Fortunio Bonanova. (Technicolor)

1944. *The Bridge of San Luis Rey.* DIRECTOR: Rowland V. Lee. PRODUCER: Benedict Bogeaus. SCREENPLAY: Howard Estabrook, from the novel by Thornton Wilder. CAST: Lynn Bari, Francis Lederer, Akim Tamiroff, Nazimova, Louis Calhern, Blanche Yurka, Donald Woods, Emma Dunn, Barton Hepburn, Joan Lorring, Abner Biberman, Minerva Urecal. (United Artists)

1944. *Tampico*. DIRECTOR: Lothar Mendes. PRODUCER: Robert Bassler. SCREENPLAY: Kenneth Gamet, Fred Niblo, Jr. and Richard Macauley, from a story by Ladislas Fodor. CAST: Edward G. Robinson, Lynn Bari, Victor McLaglen, Robert Bailey, Marc Lawrence, E.J. Ballantine, Mona Maris, Tonio Selwart, Carl Ekberg, Ralph Byrd.

1944. *Sweet and Low-Down*. DIRECTOR: Archie Mayo. PRODUCER: William Le Baron. SCREENPLAY: Richard English. CAST: Linda Darnell, Lynn Bari, Jack Oakie, James Cardwell, Allyn Joslyn, John Campbell, Dickie Moore, Helen Koford (Terry Moore), Roy Benson, and Benny Goodman and his Band.

1944. *Bon Voyage*. DIRECTOR: Lee Strasberg. CAST: Jeanne Crain, Lynn Bari, Joan Blondell, C. Aubrey Smith, Glenn Langan, Edward Ryan, Jane Nigh, Trudy Marshall. A DFZ production. NOTE: This film was shelved on October 9, 1944, after one week before the cameras. Production was never resumed.

1945. *Captain Eddie*. DIRECTOR: Lloyd Bacon. PRODUCER: Winfield Sheehan. SCREENPLAY: John Tucker Battle. CAST: Fred MacMurray, Lynn Bari, Charles Bickford, Thomas Mitchell, Lloyd Nolan, James Gleason, Mary Philips, Darryl Hickman, Spring Byington, Richard Conte, Charles Russell, Richard Crane, Stanley Ridges, Clem Bevans, Grady Sutton, Chick Chandler.

1946. *Shock*. DIRECTOR: Alfred Werker. PRODUCER: Aubrey Schenck. SCREENPLAY: Eugene Ling and Martin Berkeley, from a story by Albert deMond. CAST: Vincent Price, Lynn Bari, Frank Latimore, Anabel Shaw, Michael Dunne, Reed Hadley, Renee Carson, Charles Trowbridge.

1946. *Home Sweet Homicide*. DIRECTOR: Lloyd Bacon. PRODUCER: Louis D. Lighton. SCREENPLAY: F. Hugh Herbert, from the novel by Craig Rice. CAST: Randolph Scott, Lynn Bari, Peggy Ann Garner, Dean Stockwell, Barbara Whiting, Connie Marshall, James Gleason, Anabel Shaw, John Shepperd (Shepperd Strudwick), Marietta Canty.

1946. *Margie*. DIRECTOR: Henry King. PRODUCER: Walter Morosco. SCREENPLAY: F. Hugh Herbert, from the stories of Ruth McKenney and Richard Bransten. CAST: Jeanne Crain, Glenn Langan, Lynn Bari, Alan Young, Conrad Janis, Barbara Lawrence, Esther Dale, Hobart Cavanaugh, Hattie McDaniel, Ann E. Todd, Vanessa Brown. (Technicolor) A DFZ production

1947. *Nocturne*. DIRECTOR: Edwin L. Marin. PRODUCER: Joan Harrison. SCREENPLAY: Jonathan Latimer, from a story by Frank Fenton and Rowland Brown. CAST: George Raft, Lynn Bari, Virginia Huston, Joseph Pevney, Myrna Dell, Edward Ashley, Walter Sande, Mabel Paige, Bernard Hoffman, Queenie Smith. (RKO)

1948. *The Man from Texas.* DIRECTOR: Leigh Jason. PRODUCER: Joseph Fields. SCREENPLAY: Fields and Jerome Chodorov, from the play, *The Missouri Legend,* by E.B. Ginty. CAST: James Craig, Lynn Bari, Johnnie Johnston, Una Merkel, Wallace Ford, Harry Davenport, Sara Allgood, Reed Hadley. (Eagle-Lion)

1948. *The Spiritualist.* DIRECTOR: Bernard Vorhaus. PRODUCER: Ben Stoloff. SCREENPLAY: Muriel Roy Bolton and Ian Hunter. CAST: Lynn Bari, Turhan Bey, Cathy O'Donnell, Richard Carlson, Donald Curtis, Virginia Gregg. (Eagle-Lion) NOTE: After its first wave of release, this film saw its title changed to *The Amazing Mr. X* in the US.

1949. *The Kid from Cleveland.* DIRECTOR: Herbert Kline. PRODUCER: Walter Colmes. SCREENPLAY: John Bright, from a story by Kline and Bright. CAST: George Brent, Lynn Bari, Rusty (Russ) Tamblyn, Tommy Cook, Ann Doran, Louis Jean Heydt, K. Elmo Loew, Johnny Berardino, Maeve McGuire, and the Cleveland Indians. (Republic)

1951. *I'd Climb the Highest Mountain.* DIRECTOR: Henry King. PRODUCER: Lamar Trotti. SCREENPLAY: Trotti, from the novel, *The Circuit Rider's Wife,* by Corra Harris. CAST: Susan Hayward, William Lundigan, Rory Calhoun, Lynn Bari, Alexander Knox, Barbara Bates, Gene Lockhart, Ruth Donnelly, Kathleen Lockhart, Jean Inness, Frank Tweddell. (Technicolor)

1951. *Sunny Side of the Street.* DIRECTOR: Richard Quine. PRODUCER: Jonie Taps. SCREENPLAY: Lee Loeb. CAST: Frank Laine, Terry Moore, Lynn Bari, Billy Daniels, Jerome Courtland, Toni Arden, Audrey Long, Dick Wesson. (Columbia; in Super CineColor)

1951. *On the Loose.* DIRECTOR: Charles Lederer. PRODUCER: Collier Young. SCREENPLAY: Dale Eunson and Katherine Albert, from a story by Young and Malvin Wald. CAST: Melvyn Douglas, Lynn Bari, Joan Evans, Robert Arthur, Hugh O'Brian, Susan Morrow, Constance Hilton, Michael Kuhn. Prologue narration: Ida Lupino. (RKO)

1952. *I Dream of Jeanie.* DIRECTOR: Allan Dwan. PRODUCER: Herbert J. Yates. SCREENPLAY: Alan Le May. CAST: Ray Middleton, Bill Shirley, Eileen Christy, Lynn Bari, Muriel Lawrence, Louise Beavers, James Kirkwood. (Republic; in Trucolor)

1952. *Has Anybody Seen My Gal.* DIRECTOR: Douglas Sirk. PRODUCER: Ted Richmond. SCREENPLAY: Joseph Hoffman. CAST: Piper Laurie, Rock Hudson, Charles Coburn, Lynn Bari, Gigi Perreau, William Reynolds, Larry Gates, Skip Homeier, Frank Ferguson, Fritz Feld, James Dean, Gloria Holden, Paul Harvey. (Universal-International; in Technicolor)

1954. Documentary on Israel. DIRECTOR/PRODUCER: Frederick de Cordova. Narrators: Lynn Bari and Lloyd Nolan. (An independently-produced short subject, released by Universal-International)

1954. *Francis Joins The WACS*. DIRECTOR: Arthur Lubin. PRODUCER: Ted Richmond. SCREENPLAY: Devery Freeman and James B. Allardice, from a story by Herbert Baker; based on characters created by David Stern. CAST: Donald O'Connor, Julia (Julie) Adams, Lynn Bari, Chill Wills, Mamie Van Doren, ZaSu Pitts, Allison Hayes, Mara Corday, Joan Shawlee. (Universal-International)

1955. *Abbott and Costello Meet the Keystone Kops*. DIRECTOR: Charles Lamont. PRODUCER: Howard Christie. SCREENPLAY: John Grant, from a story by Lee Loeb. CAST: Bud Abbott, Lou Costello, Lynn Bari, Fred Clark, Frank Wilcox, Maxie Rosenbloom, Roscoe Ates, Joe Besser. Guest Stars: Mack Sennett, Heinie Conklin, Hank Mann. (Universal-International)

1957. *The Women of Pitcairn Island*. DIRECTOR: Jean Yarbrough. PRODUCER: Yarbrough and Aubrey Wisberg. SCREENPLAY: Wisberg. CAST: Lynn Bari, James Craig, John Smith, Arleen Whelan, Sue England, Carol Thurston, Harry Lauter.

1958. *Damn Citizen!* DIRECTOR: Robert Gordon. PRODUCER: Herman Webber. SCREENPLAY: Stirling Silliphant. CAST: Keith Andes, Lynn Bari, Maggie Hayes, Gene Evans, Jeffrey Stone, Ann Robinson, Edward C. Platt. (Universal-International)

1962. *Elfego Baca: Six-Gun Law*. DIRECTOR: Christian Nyby. PRODUCER: James Pratt. SCREENPLAY: Maurice Tombragel. CAST: Robert Loggia, Lynn Bari, James Dunn, Annette Funicello, Patric Knowles, Audrey Dalton, James Drury, Kenneth Tobey, Jay C. Flippen, Grant Withers, R.G. Armstrong, Phillip Terry, Edward Colmans. (Walt Disney/Buena Vista; in Technicolor)

1963. *Trauma*. DIRECTOR: Robert Malcolm Young. PRODUCER: Joseph Cranston. SCREENPLAY: Young. CAST: Lynn Bari, John Conte, David Garner, Lorrie Richards, Warren Kemmerling, William Bissell, Robert Totten. (Parade)

1968. *The Young Runaways*. DIRECTOR: Arthur Dreifuss. PRODUCER: Sam Katzman. SCREENPLAY: Orville H. Hampton. CAST: Patty McCormack, Brooke Bundy, Kevin Coughlin, Lynn Bari, Lloyd Bochner, Norman Fell, Richard Dreyfuss, Dick Sargent, James Edwards, Quentin Dean, Isabel Sanford. (MGM; in Metrocolor)

Lynn Bari, as she appeared in Pulitzer Prize Playhouse's *"The Big Break,"* *broadcast by ABC-TV in June 1951.*

TELEVISION APPEARANCES

The following are listed by air date. This chronology does not always correspond to the order of production. In some instances, broadcast dates and episode titles are not known. The entries in this section represent the majority of Lynn Bari's television credits — but not all.

1950. *The Ken Murray Show* (CBS, April 29). SERIES HOST: Ken Murray. GUEST STARS (as themselves): Lynn Bari, Henry Wilcoxon, David Street, Charles Chaplin, Jr., Eileen Barton.

1950. *The Toast of the Town/The Ed Sullivan Show* (CBS, date unknown). SERIES HOST: Ed Sullivan. GUEST STAR (as herself): Lynn Bari.

1950. *The Detective's Wife* (CBS, July 7-September 29). SERIES STARS: Lynn Bari (as Connie Conway), Donald Curtis.

1951. *Lux Video Theatre* (CBS. June 11). EPISODE: "The Weather for Today." GUEST STARS: Lynn Bari (as Kay Plumber), Lee Bowman, Butterfly McQueen.

1951. *Pulitzer Prize Playhouse* (ABC, June 29). EPISODE: "The Big Break." GUEST STARS: Lynn Bari, James Dunn.

1951. *Bigelow Theatre* (Dumont, November 22). EPISODE: "Agent from Scotland Yard." GUEST STARS: Lynn Bari, Patric Knowles, Alan Mowbray.

1952. *Boss Lady* (NBC, July 1-September 23). SERIES STAR: Lynn Bari (as Gwendolyn F. Allen). SERIES REGULARS: Glenn Langan, Lee Patrick, Richard Gaines, Charles Smith, Nicholas Joy.

1952. *The Schaefer Century Theatre* (NBC, September 9). EPISODE: "The Other Woman." GUEST STARS: Lynn Bari, Douglas Kennedy.

1953. *Ford Theatre* (NBC, February 26). EPISODE: "All's Fair in Love." GUEST STARS: Lynn Bari (as Myra Pelham), Cesar Romero, June Vincent, Sherry Jackson.

1954. *City Detective* (syndicated, date unknown). EPISODE: "Case of the Long Lost Wife." SERIES STAR: Rod Cameron. GUEST STAR: Lynn Bari (as Anita).

1954. *Pantomime Quiz* (CBS, July-August). SERIES HOST: Mike Stokey. GUEST STARS (as themselves): Lynn Bari, James Lydon, Jeff Donnell, Richard Erdman.

1954. *Viceroy Star Theatre* (CBS, July 30). EPISODE: "I'll Never Know When." GUEST STARS: Lynn Bari (as Millie Karns), Virginia Christine, Louis Jean Heydt, Joseph Crehan.

1954. *Lux Video Theatre* (NBC, October 14). EPISODE: "A Visit from Evelyn." SERIES HOST: James Mason. GUEST STARS: Lynn Bari (as Evelyn), Ann Harding.

1955. *Pepsi-Cola Playhouse* (ABC, May 8). EPISODE: "Stake My Life." GUEST STARS: Lynn Bari (as Linda Rainey), Hugh Beaumont, Steven Geray, Claude Akins, Nana Bryant.

1955. *City Detective* (syndicated, May 10). EPISODE: "The Beautiful Miss X." SERIES STAR: Rod Cameron. GUEST STARS: Lynn Bari (as Cynthia), Marguerite Chapman, Paul Langton, Walter Reed.

1955. *Lux Video Theatre* (NBC, May 19). EPISODE: "Make Way for Tomorrow." SERIES HOST: James Mason. GUEST STARS: Lynn Bari (as Anita), Michael Whalen, Ernest Truex, Sylvia Field, William Bakewell.

1955. *Science Fiction Theatre* (syndicated, July 1). EPISODE: "Hour of Nightmare." SERIES HOST: Truman Bradley. GUEST STARS: Lynn Bari (as Verda Wingate), William Bishop.

1955. *Screen Directors Playhouse* (NBC, October 26). EPISODE: "Arroyo." GUEST STARS: Jack Carson, Lynn Bari (as Hattie Mae Warren), Neville Brand, Lola Albright, Lloyd Corrigan, John Baer, Bob Steele, William Schallert.

1955. *Studio 57* (syndicated, November 22). EPISODE: "Forest Magic." GUEST STARS: Lynn Bari (as Diane Breen), Hugh Corcoran, Stephen [Michael] Dunne, Beverly Washburn.

1956. *Climax!* (CBS, March 29). EPISODE: "An Episode of Sparrows." SERIES HOST: William Lundigan. GUEST STARS: Lynn Bari (as Mrs. Combie), Patty McCormack, J. Carrol Naish, Brandon de Wilde, Jessie Royce Landis.

1956. *Studio 57* (syndicated, April 3). EPISODE: "A Tombstone for Taro." GUEST STARS: Lynn Bari (as Karen), Rod Cameron, Claude Akins, Lawrence Dobkin.

1956. *Lux Video Theatre* (NBC, November 29). EPISODE: "Old Acquaintance." SERIES HOST: Otto Kruger. GUEST STARS: Lynn Bari (as Millie Drake), Ruth Hussey, Joan Evans.

1958. *The Red Skelton Show* (CBS, April 8). SERIES STAR: Red Skelton. GUEST STARS: Lynn Bari (as herself/Clara Appleby), Barbara Nichols.

1958. *Matinee Theatre* (NBC, date unknown). EPISODE: "Washington Whispers Murder" (working title). SERIES HOST: John Conte. GUEST STAR: Lynn Bari.

1959. *Disneyland* (ABC, February 6). EPISODE: "El Fago Baca: Attorney At Law." SERIES HOST: Walt Disney. RECURRING STARS: Robert Loggia, Annette Funicello. GUEST STARS: Lynn Bari (as Liz Simmons), James Dunn, James Drury, Grant Withers, Kenneth Tobey.

1959. *Bronco* (ABC, June 2). EPISODE: "Hero of the Town." SERIES STAR: Ty Hardin. GUEST STARS: Lynn Bari (as Amy Biggs), Harry Lauter.

1960. *The Overland Trail* (NBC, February 7). EPISODE: "Perilous Passage." SERIES STARS: William Bendix, Doug McClure. GUEST STARS: Lynn Bari (as Myra Belle Shirley/Belle Starr), Harry Guardino.

1960. *Law of the Plainsman* (NBC, February 18). EPISODE: "The Matriarch." SERIES STAR: Michael Ansara. GUEST STARS: Lynn Bari (as Constance Valeri), Denver Pyle.

1960. *The Aquanauts* (CBS, October 12). EPISODE: "Deep Escape." SERIES STARS: Keith Larsen, Jeremy Slate, Ron Ely. GUEST STARS: Lynn Bari (as Ann Nincel), Paul Henreid, Joyce Meadows.

1961. *Michael Shayne* (NBC, February 3). EPISODE: "The Heiress." SERIES STARS: Richard Denning, Jerry Paris, Herbert Rudley. GUEST STARS: Lynn Bari (as Dolores Dane), Susan Oliver, Richard Crane, Frank Albertson, Celia Lovsky.

1961. *Checkmate* (CBS, April 15). EPISODE: "Good-Bye, Griff." SERIES STARS: Anthony George, Doug McClure, Sebastian Cabot. GUEST STARS: Julie London, Lynn Bari (as Marjorie Bates), Harry Guardino, Simon Oakland.

1961. *The New Breed* (ABC, November 14). EPISODE: "The Butcher." SERIES STARS: Leslie Nielsen, John Beradino. GUEST STARS: Lynn Bari (as Mrs. Grace), Jeanne Cooper, Peter Whitney.

1961. *Everglades* (syndicated, November 20). EPISODE: "Clay Island Murder." SERIES STARS: Ron Hayes, Steve Brodie. GUEST STARS: Lynn Bari (as Sarah Clay), Hardie Albright.

1961. *Ben Casey* (ABC, December 11). EPISODE: "A Certain Time, a Certain Darkness." SERIES STARS: Vince Edwards, Sam Jaffe, Jeanne Bates. GUEST STARS: Joan Hackett, Lynn Bari (as Ethel Dixon), Donald Woods, Dyan Cannon.

1963. *Ripcord* (syndicated, date unknown). EPISODE: "The Trouble with Denny Collins." SERIES STARS: Ken Curtis, Larry Pennell. GUEST STAR: Lynn Bari (as Meg Collins).

1964. *Perry Mason* (CBS, January 9). EPISODE: "The Case of the Accosted Accountant." SERIES STARS: Raymond Burr, Barbara Hale, William Hopper, William Talman, Wesley Lau. GUEST STARS: Richard Anderson, Lynn Bari (as Sylvia Cord), Robert Armstrong, Murray Matheson.

1964. *The Late Liz* (syndicated religious special, March). STARRING: Lynn Bari (as Liz), Dick Foran, Lyle Bettger.

1964. *Death Valley Days* (syndicated, April 21). EPISODE: "Trial at Belle Springs." SERIES HOST: Stanley Andrews. GUEST STARS: Lynn Bari (as Belle Wilgus), Ken Scott.

1965. *Perry Mason* (CBS, March 4). EPISODE: "The Case of the Fatal Fetish." SERIES STARS: Raymond Burr, Barbara Hale, William Hopper, William Talman, Wesley Lau. GUEST STARS: Fay Wray, Lynn Bari (as Ruth Duncan), Gary Collins, Karen Steele, Douglas Kennedy.

1966. *Gypsy* (syndicated, January). SERIES HOST: Gypsy Rose Lee. GUEST STARS (as themselves): Lynn Bari, Tab Hunter.

1967. *The Girl from U.N.C.L.E.* (NBC, March 14). EPISODE: "The Phi Beta Killer Affair." SERIES STARS: Stefanie Powers, Noel Harrison, Leo G. Carroll. GUEST STARS: Lynn Bari (as Miss Twickum), Victor Buono, Barbara Nichols, Jack La Rue, Donald Curtis.

1967. *The Joe Franklin Show* (syndicated, October 27). SERIES HOST: Joe Franklin. GUEST STARS (as themselves): Lynn Bari, Jessica Walter.

1967. *The F.B.I.* (ABC, November 26). EPISODE: "Line of Fire." SERIES STARS: Efrem Zimbalist, Jr., Philip Abbott, William Reynolds. GUEST STARS: Lynn Bari (as Chino's widow), Henry Silva, Dean Harens, Lynda Day (George).

1968. *The F.B.I.* (ABC, March 31). EPISODE: "The Mechanized Accomplice." SERIES STARS: Efrem Zimbalist, Jr., Philip Abbott, William Reynolds. GUEST STARS: Andrew Prine, Lynn Bari (as Belinda), Bobby Sherman, Connie Gilchrist.

1989. *The Tom Carroll Show* (syndicated talk-show pilot). SERIES HOST: Tom Carroll. GUEST STAR (as herself): Lynn Bari.

INDEX

Abbott and Costello Meet the Keystone Kops 335,
335-337, *336*

Abbott, Bud 335, *335,* 337

Adams, Julie 333

Agee, James 382

Alda, Robert 412

Aldrin, Buzz 431

Ali Baba Goes to Town 73

All the Way Home 382, 382-383

Allen, Steve 384

Alton, John 292-293

Always Goodbye 86-90, *88, 89,* 135, 163, 206

Amazing Mr. X, The (see: *Spiritualist, The*)

Ameche, Don 13, 86, 97, 129, 131-132, 179-
180, *181,* 183, 209, 247

Anders, Glenn *301*

Anderson, Mary 237

Andes, Keith 349

Andrews, Dana 144, *146,* 237, 416-417, 438

Andriot, Lucien 135, 163

Ankers, Evelyn 175

Anna and the King of Siam 270

Anna Christie 65

Annabella *52,* 78-79

Anniversary Waltz 370-371, 375

Aquanauts, The 377

Armetta, Henry *87*

Arnold, Edward 132, *132*

Art of Healing, The 420

Arthur, Jean 37, 183-184, 205, 246

Arthur, Robert 247-248

Asner, Ed 429

Astaire, Fred 44, 46

"At Last" 13, 154, 158, 187-188

Atwill, Lionel 77

Aubert, Lenore 275

Aylward, Tony 404-405

"Baby, Take a Bow" 58

Bacall, Lauren 205

Bacon, Lloyd 244, 270, 275

Bad Seed, The 343-345

Baldwin, Dick *85,* 99-100

Ball, Lucille 175, 260, 320

Ballad of the City 384-385, 387-388, *388*

Ballard, Lucien 184, 187

Bankhead, Tallulah 238

Banton, Travis 154

Bara, Theda 131

Barbier, George *105*

Barefoot in the Park 392-397, *393, 395*

Barkley, Lillian 62, 65

Barnett, Sanford 210

Baroness and the Butler, The 77-79, *78,* 183

Barrie, James 29, 44

Bat, The 37

Battle of Broadway 85-86, *86*

Baxter, Anne 145, 189, 196, 251, 268, 278, 332,
384

Baxter, Warner 58-59, 66, 86, 103-104, *104,*
134-135, *135*

Behanna, Gert 383-384

Ben Casey 379

Bendix, William 216

Beneke, Tex *185*

Bennett, Constance *68*

Bennett, Joan 296, 307

Berle, Milton 152, *152*

Bey, Turhan 291-292, *292*

Biberman, Abner 226, 379

Bigelow Theatre, The 321

Billy Rose's Diamond Horseshoe 247

Bishop, William *340*

Bitzer, Robert 35, 37-42, *40,* 51,114, 198, 250,
253, 391

Blaine, Vivian 412

Blondell, Joan 237-238, 240

Blood and Sand 125, 132-134, *133*, 167, 267

Boardman, Eleanor 29

Bogeaus, Benedict 223-227

Boles, John 58

Bon Voyage 237-240, *239*, 243, 251

Boomerang! 275

Boss Lady 326-327, *327*

Bowery After Dark 216

Bowman, Lee 320

Boyer, Charles *52*

Boyle, John W. 225

Brahm, John 184, 187-188

Brand, Harry 100, 200, 219-220

Brasher Doubloon, The 277

Brent, George 298-299

Bridge of San Luis Rey, The 216-217, 223-229, *224*, *226*, 231, 379

"Broadway's Gone Hillbilly" 58

Bronco 367

Bronson, Betty 29

Brooks, Phyllis 80, *81*, *440*, 441

Bryan, Jane 288

Bullock, Walter 161

Bundy, Brooke 400

Bye Bye Birdie 382-383

Cabanne, Julie 62

Café Metropole 70

Calhern, Louis 226-227

Cantor, Eddie *73*

Canyon Passage 251

Captain Eddie 242, 243-246, *244*, *245*, 248, 250-251, 253-254, 258, 263, 275

Caravane 52

Cardwell, James 233

Carlisle, Kitty 370

Carpenter, Carleton 377

Carroll, Madeleine 183

Carroll, Tom 447

Carter, Janis 173

Chandler, Chick *87*

Charlie Chan at Ringside 84, 437

Charlie Chan in City in Darkness 108-110, *109*

Charlie Chan in Paris 55

Charter Pilot 137, 139-140, *142*, *143*, 147, *147*, 281

Chasing Danger 91, 91-92

Checkmate 379

China Girl 13, 147, 192-196, *193*, *195*, 232, 282

Chodorov, Jerome 370

Christy, Eileen 321

City of Chance 136-137, *137*, 454-455, *455*

Clark, Fred 335, *335*

Clarke, Charles G. *95*

Clearing in the Woods, A 349

Cleveland Indians, The 298-299

Climax! *338*, 343, 400

Clive, E.E. 37

Cobb, Irvin S. 68-69

Coburn, Charles 324, *325*, 326, *326*

Cohn, Harry 215-216, 444

Colbert, Claudette 100, 246

Coley, Tom 300, 302, 416

Colman, Ronald 13-17, *15*, 29, *63*, 196, 198, 307, 444

Como, Perry 216

Conreid, Hans 288

Conte, John 381

Conte, Richard 244, 247

Conway, Shirl 368

Conway, Tim 92

Coogan, Jackie 285, 293

Cook, Fielder 320

Cooper, Jackie 285, 293

Cooper, Sandra "Rocky" 310

Corday, Mara 333

Cortez, Ricardo 137, 454

Costello, Lou 335, *335*, 337

Coughlin, Kevin 400

Cousins, Norman 420

Crack-Up 66, 67

Craig, James *287*, 288, 345, 347

Crain, Jeanne 237-238, 240, 246-247, 264, *265*, 266-267, 279, 281-282

Crawford, Joan 43-44, 46

Cregar, Laird 145

Cronjager, Edward 153-154

Crosby, Bing 153

Crothers, Joel 392, *393*, 394

Cukor, George 237, 329

Curtis, Alan 129, 158

Curtis, Donald 291, 311-312

Dailey, Dan 160, *161*, 163

Damn Citizen! *348*, 348-349, *354*

Dancing Lady 43-49, *45*, 51, 100, 399

Dark Corner, The 258, 260, 263

Darnell, Linda *125*, 125-127, *127*, 132, 145, 189, 196, 205, *206*, 233-234, 248, 279, 281

Dart, Justin 288

David Harum 54

Davis, Bette 196, 299, 389

Day, Doris 367, 447

De Carlo, Yvonne 412

de Cordova, Frederick 334

DeFore, Don 158

De Letraz, Jean 377

DeMille, Cecil B. 209-210

deMond, Albert 255

DeSylva, Buddy 65

Dead End 83

Dean, James 326

Dearing, Dorothy *53*

Death Valley Days 384, *385*

Del Rio, Dolores 77-78

Del Ruth, Roy 69

Denning, Richard 377

Detective's Wife, The 311-313, *312*

Dewhurst, Colleen 382

Dietrich, Ralph 164

Disney, Walt 367

Disneyland 367

Do You Love Me 263, 279

Documentary on Israel 334

Dolly Sisters, The 247

Donlevy, Brian 84, 91-92

Donnell, Jeff *334*

Douglas, Melvyn 272, 317, 319, *319*

Dreifuss, Arthur 400, 448

Drew, Ellen 175

Dunbar, Dixie 80, *81*, 99, *440*, 441

Dunn, James *57*, 58, 320, 367

Dunne, Irene 13, *15*

Durante, Jimmy 46

Dwan, Allan 56, 70, 86, 247, 321

Earthbound 134-136, *135*, *136*, 143

Eberle, Ray 154, 187-188

Eddis, Theodore 296, 307

Eddy, Nelson 44, 46

Edwards, James *399*

Edwards, Vince 379

Elliot, Lorraine 233

Ellison, James 125, 192

Enter Laughing 384, *386*, 392

Erdman, Richard *334*

Ericson, Helen *73*

Escape Me Never 260

Estabrook, Howard 225-226

Evans, Gene 349

Evans, Joan 272, 317, *319*, 347

Everglades 379

Everybody's Old Man 68-69

Eythe, William 247

Falcon Takes Over, The 169, *169*

Fallen Angel 248

Farewell, My Lovely 169

Faye, Alice 57, 59, 66, 69-70, 128-129, 131-132, 145, 203, *204*, 205, 247-248, 282

F.B.I., The 397, 399

Feilbert, Ed 377

Fell, Norman 400

Fetherston, Eddie *67*

Field, Betty 307

Field, Sylvia 341

Field, Virginia 300

Fields, Gracie 237

Finklehoff, Freddie 300

Fisher, Eugenie 296-297, 305-307, 313, 331-332, 337, 339-340, 351-352, 361-362, 371-372, 377, *390*, 391, 398, 401-404, 414-415, 418, 420-423, 425-427, 431, *432*, 433, *433*, 452, 460

Fisher, Jay 331, 351, 431, *432*

Fisher, John Maynard (Lynn Bari's father) 19-21, 23-25, 27-32, 38, 253, 442

Fisher, John Owen (Lynn Bari's brother) 19-20, 24-34, *25*, *26*, 27, *28*, *30*, *33*, 38-41, *40*, 114, 198-200, *199*, 250, *253*, 253-254, 293, 295-297, 305-307, 313, 331-332, 337, 351, 361, 371-372, *390*, 390-392, 398, 402-404, 414, 418, 420-422, 426-427, 429-431, *432*, 445-446, 451-452, 460

Fisher, Marge 14-17, *18*, 19-35, *36*, 37-44, *40*, 51, 113-115, 117, 119-120, 183, 198-201, 248, 250, 253, 293, *295*, 295-297, 299-300, 302, 305-307, 313, 315, 320, 322, 330-332, 337, 350-351, 361-362, 371-373, 375, 390-391, 398, 418, 424-425, 442-443, 445, 447

Fitzgerald, Ella 234

Fitzgerald, Geraldine 216

Follies 411, 412-414

Follow Thru 37

Fonda, Henry 13, *56*, 80, *131*, 132, 180, *180*, 183, 209, 277

Fontanne, Lynn 44

Ford Theatre 327-328, *328*

Ford, John 60, 79-80, 247

Forde, Eugene 95-96, 137, 139
42nd Street 447
Foster, Norman 80
Foster, Preston 91-92, *105*, 105-106, *107*, 160, 172, 174, 263
Four Men and a Prayer 79
Fox, William 59
Foy, Bryan 164, 285-286
Francis Joins the WACS 333, 333-334
Free, Blonde and 21 80, 137, *138*, *139*
French Leave 293
French Postcards 377, *378*
Friday, Pat 153-154, 156, 184, 188
Funicello, Annette 367
Gable, Clark 43-44, 46, 324
Gale, June (see: Levant, June Gale)
Garbo, Greta 37, 48, 78, 205
Garfield, John 233, 275
Garland, Judy 268, 314-315, 322-324, 329, 341, 356-357, 359-360, 362-365
Garner, Peggy Ann 268, *270*, 270-272, 437
Garnett, Tay 384
Garson, Greer 13, *15*, 122, *197*
Gaslight 402, 407
Gates, Larry *325, 326*
Gaynor, Janet 59
Getty, J. Paul 292
Geva, Tamara 189
Gilmore, Virginia 145, *185*, 189, 192, *197*
Gingerbread Lady, The 405-406, *408*, 409, 414-415, 438
Girl from U.N.C.L.E., The 397
"Girl with the Sugar Brown Hair, The" 161
Girls' Dormitory 134
Gleason, Jackie, *185, 186*
Gleason, James 269
Gleason, Russell 105, *105*
Goetz, William 185, 193, 215, 324
Golden Boy 275
Golden, Eve 160
Goodbye, My Fancy 329
Goodman, Benny 154-156, 233-235
Goodwin, Bill 220
Gordon, Elizabeth "Cookie" *119*, 219
Gordon, Mack 153-154, 156, 187, 219, 233, 254
Grable, Betty 144, 216, 247, 268, 278-279, 281, 412
Granville, Bonita 268, 327

Grapes of Wrath, The 80
Gray, Billy 384
Great Ziegfeld, The 65
Green Grass of Wyoming 247
Green, Mawby 377
Greenwood, Charlotte 164-165
Guiding Light, The 430
Gypsy 394
Hackett, Joan 379
Hahn, S.S. *330*
Hall, Charlie 117, 192
Hall, Jon 144, *146*
Halliday, John 125
Hamilton, Alexander 22
Harding, Ann 337
Harris, Jed 44
Harrison, Joan 272, 274
Hart, Margie *301*
Hart, Moss 237, 300
Hart, Teddy 377
Has Anybody Seen My Gal 323-326, *325, 326*, 332, 392
Hassell, George *70*
Hasso, Signe 205, 263
Hathaway, Henry 13, 192-196, 256, 258, 260
Haver, June 247, 250, 275, 282
Havoc, June 203
Hayes, Allison 333
Hayes, Maggie 349
Haymes, Dick 247, 263
Hayward, Susan 251, 268, *309*, 309-310
Hayworth, Rita 132-133
Hecht, Ben 193-194
Hello, Frisco, Hello 96, *202*, 203-205, *204, 206*, 281
Hendrix, Wanda 377
Henie, Sonja 145, 152, 156-158, *157*, 233, 444
Herbert, F. Hugh 264, 268
Herschel 163, 204
Hilber, Phillippa 220
Hitchcock, Alfred 272, 274
Hollywood Cavalcade 125, 128-131, *130*
Hollywood Players, The 275
Hollywood Startime 210, 257
Holmes, Ernest 37
Home in Indiana 237
Home Sweet Homicide 218, 268-272, *269, 270*, 275-276
Hopper, Hedda 362

Horton, Edward Everett 183

Hotchner, A.E. 447

Hotel for Women 125, 125-128, *127*, *129*, 135, 137, 440-441

Hough, Stanley, 266

Hudson, Rochelle *56*

Hudson, Rock 324, 326, *326, 367*

Hughes, Howard 113, 117, 120-122, 320, 351, 361

Hughes, Mary Beth *139*, 140, *144*, 145, 171, *171*, *185*, 189, *190*

Humberstone, Bruce *95*, 96-97, 108, 157

Hunt, Marsha *214*

Hunter, Ian 87

Hunter, Tab 394

Hussey, Ruth 307-308, 347

Hutton, Marion *185*

I Am Suzanne 49

I Dream of Jeanie 304, 321

"I Know Why (And So Do You)" 153

I Love Lucy 320

I Wonder Who's Kissing Her Now 274-275

I'd Climb the Highest Mountain 308-311, *309*

I'll Give a Million 86

"I'm Making Believe" 233-234

Iceland 158

Ink Spots, The 234

Irving, Charles 311

Issacson, Gladys 389-390

It Had to Happen 66

Jackson, Glenda 206, 447

James, Harry 263

Janis, Conrad 265-267, 282-283

Jergens' Hollywood Playhouse 207

Jessel, George 237, 247

Josette 86

Joslyn, Allyn 233

Joyce, Brenda 145, 189

Junior Miss 270-271

Kane, Walter 14, 94, 96, 113-114, 117-123, *118, 119*, 183, 192, 201, 216, 218, 220, 320, 351, 361, 424-426, 450

Kazan, Elia 240, 247, 275

Keighley, William 209

Kelly, Grace 126

Kelly, Nancy 343

Kendall, Kay 368, 370

Kennedy, Douglas 326

Kent, Sidney R. 59, 215

Kid from Cleveland, The 298-299, *299*

Kilroy Was Here 285, 289, 293

King of Burlesque 66, *66*, 203

King of Hearts 341

King, Henry 56, 60, 235, 264, *264*, 266-267, 308-310

Kit Carson 143-144, *145*, *146*, 225

Knox, Alexander 235

Koch, Howard W. 266

Kornman, Gene 101

Ladd, Diane 387

Ladies in Love 68

Lamarr, Hedy 13, *15*, 147, 450

Lamont, Charles 337

Lamparski, Richard 398, 438-439

Lancer Spy 77, 132, *470*

Landis, Carole 184, *185*, 189-191, *190*, 277, 288

Lanfield, Sidney 88-89, 163

Lang, Fritz 225, 247

Lang, Jennings 320

Lang, June *93*, 93-94, *94*, 96

Lang, Walter 47, 60, 78, 86, 179, 183, 278

Langan, Glenn 264, *265,* 266, 282, 326-327

Lansbury, Angela 430

Larkin, John 172

Late Liz, The 383-384

Laura 216

Laurie, Piper 324, *325*, 326, *326*

Law and the Plainsman, The 320

Lawrence, Barbara 266-267

Lazar, Swifty 300

LeBaron, William 184

Le Maire, Charles 308

Leachman, Cloris 341

Lederer, Charles 317, 319, 339, 341

Lederer, Francis 226, *226*, 431

Lee, Gypsy Rose 394

Lee, Roland V. 225, 227

Lee, Sammy 42-44, 49, 51

Leeds, Andrea 134

Leeds, Herbert I. 104, 110

Leno, Jay 444

Leonard, Robert Z. 44

Leslie, Joan *197*, 430

Letter to Three Wives, A 127

Levant, June Gale 93, *95,* 96-97, *97*, 126, 136, *137*, 365, 368, 383

Levant, Oscar 96, 126

Levene, Sam 300, *301,* 302

Levy, Jules 254

Lewis, Milton 312

Life Begins in College 73, 99

Lifeboat 238

Light Up the Sky 300-302, *301*, 307-308, 344

Lighton, Louis D. 270

Lillian Russell 125, *131*, 131-132, *132*

Livingston, Philip 22

Loggia, Robert 367

Lorre, Peter 77, 84-85, *85*, 163, 444

Lorring, Joan 226

Lottery Lover 53

Louisa 308

Love and Hisses 54

Loy, Myrna 158, 246, 312, 392

Ludlum, Edward 377

Luft, Joey 356

Luft, John *295*, 296, 300, 302, 306, 311, 313-
315, 319-320, 322-324, *323*, 329, 331, 337,
339, 341, 343, 346, 349-351, 355-360, 362-
366, 383, 396, 398, 418-419, 421-422, 429,
431, *432*, 445-446, 450, 456-457, 460-461

Luft, Lorna 356

Luft, Sid *217*, 217-221, 235, *236*, 248-250,
249, 253-255, 258, 263, 267, 276, 285, 287,
289-291, *290*, 293, *295*, 298, 308, 313-316,
319, 321-324, 329, 337, 341, 355-366, 424-
426, 447

Luke, Keye 84-85

Lundigan, William 309-310

Lupino, Ida 196, 260

Lux Radio Theatre 208, 209-210, 275-276, 278

Lux Video Theatre 320, 337, 341, 347

Lydon, James *334*

Lyon, Ben 278-279, 308

McCall, Joan 392, *393*

McCallister, Lon 237, 247, 272

McCarey, Ray 192

McCormack, Patty 343, 400

MacDonald, Grace *214*

MacDonald, Joe 244

McDowall, Roddy *168*, 168-169, 214, 236-237,
240, 247, 281, 431

McGann, William C. 159

McKaye, Fred 210

McLaglen, Victor *193*, 193-194, 230-232

McLean, Barbara 62

MacMurray, Fred 243-244, *244*, *245*, 246, 249-
251, 253-254

McQueen, Butterfly 320

MacWilliams, Glen 237-238

Magnificent Dope, The 13, 174-175, 179-184,
180, *181*, *182*, 191, 196, 247, 250, 279

Mamoulian, Rouben 133, 225, 247

Man from Texas, The 286, *287*, 287-288, 291,
293

Man O' War 298

Man Who Broke the Bank at Monte Carlo, The
63

Man Who Came to Dinner, The 404-405

Mankiewicz, Joseph L. 247

Margie 262, 264-268, *265*, 275, 282, 326

Margo 226

Marin, Edwin L. 272

Marley, Peverell 171, 183

Marquand, J.P. 85

Marshall, Connie 268, *270*, 270-271

Marshall, George 85

Marshall, Herbert 87

Martin, Quinn 397

Martin, Tony *72*

Marx, Zeppo 249

Mason, James 329

Massen, Osa 189, 192

Mature, Victor 277

Maxwell, Elsa 126

Maxwell, Marilyn *214*

Mayer, Louis B. 203

Mayer, Ray 214

Mayo, Archie 188, 190, *235*, 247

Meade, Julia 367

Medford, Kay 382

Meet the Baron 46-49

Meet the Girls 92, 92-95, *93*, *94*, 139, 441

Mendes, Lothar 231

Mercer, Johnny 214

Mescall, John 225

Metropolitan 62, 123

Michael Shayne 377

Miller, Alan 320

Miller, Glenn 13, 151-158, *152*, *154*, 184-188,
185, *186*, 191-192, 233

Minnelli, Liza 357

Minnelli, Vincente 322

Miranda, Carmen 144, 237, 277

Monaco, James V. 233

Monroe, Marilyn 457

Montague, William (Monty Banks) *133*

Montgomery, George 140, 145-148, *147*, 184, *185*, 186, *186*, 193-195, *195*, 221, 277-278, 281-282

Moon Over Her Shoulder 44, 151, 159-164, *160*, *161*, *162*, 272, 281

Moon Over Miami 151

Moore, Dickie 233

Moore, Terry 233, *314*, 316, *317*

Morosco, Walter 164

Mosel, Tad 382

Mother Wore Tights 278

Mowbray, Alan *161*, 166, 384

Mr. Moto's Gamble 84-85, *85*, 163

Murder, My Sweet 169

Murder, She Wrote 430-431

Music Is Magic 57

Mutiny on the Bounty 345

My Darling Clementine 247

My Little Margie 327

NBC University Theater of the Air 298

Natwick, Mildred 392

Nazimova, Alla 132, 226-227

New Breed, The 379, 397

Newberry, Rick 377

Newman, Alfred 62, 134, 161

Newman, Emil 153

News Is Made at Night 105, 105-107, *106*, *107*

Night Before the Divorce, The 170, 171, *171*, 174

Night Must Fall 447

Nocturne 272-274, *273*

Nolan, Lloyd 128, 137, 139-140, 143, *143*, *144*, *147*, 244, 254, 334, 377

North, Sheree 382

O'Brien, Pat 209, 276, 288

O'Connor, Donald 333

O'Donnell, Cathy 291-292

O'Hara, Maureen 179, 233, 263, 281

O'Keefe, Dennis 209-209

O'Neill, Eugene 65, 451

Oakie, Jack 203, 233-235

Oakland, Simon 379

Oland, Warner 84-85, 437

Olivier, Laurence 48

On the Avenue 69, *71*

On the Loose 248, 272, 317-319, *318*, *319*

On the Sunny Side 168

Orchestra Wives 13, 147, 153-156, 184-192, *185*, *186*, *189*, *190*, 196, 201, 203, 387

Orson Welles' Almanac 209

Overland Trail, The 370

Pack Up Your Troubles 108, *108*

Paige, Mabel 274

Painting with Light 292-293

Pantomime Quiz 334, *334*

Pardon Our Nerve 92-97, *95*, *98*

Parsons, Louella 115, 151, 249, 315, 341, 379

Patrick, Lee 326

Payne, John 25, 145, 151, 154, *154*, 156, *157*, 203, *204*, 209, 237, 277

Peck, Gregory 247

Pepsi-Cola Playhouse 341

Perfect Snob, The 164-168, *165*, *166*, *167*, *449*

Perlberg, William 179, 184, 219, 250

Perreau, Gigi 324, *326*

Perry Mason 383-384

Peter Pan 29

Peters, Jean 266

Petrachek, Beverly 429-430

Phantom Lady 272

Pichel, Irving 134

Pied Piper, The 168

Pier 13 137, 139-140, *140*, *141*

Pigskin Parade 69, 412

Pillow Talk 367

Pin-Up Girl 216

Pitts, ZaSu 333

Plain and Fancy 367-368, *369*

Platt, Ed 349

Pleasure of His Company, The 379

Powell, Dick 169

Powell, Eleanor 221

Powell, William *78*, 78-79, 183, 312

Power, Tyrone 97, 132, *133*, 134, 207

Powolny, Frank 101

"Pretty Girl Is Like a Melody, A" 65

Previn, André 316, 370

Price, Vincent 210, 255-258, *256*

Pulitzer Prize Playhouse 320-321, *480*

Purtill, Moe *185*

Queen Christina 48

Quine, Richard 316

Quinn, Anthony 132, 166-168 *167*, 175, *449*

Raft, George 209, 272, *273*, 274

Ratoff, Gregory 70, 77, *127*

Ray, Leah 80, *81*, 99, *440,* 441

Razor's Edge, The 267-268

Reagan, Ronald 308, 423, 426, 429, 445

Rebecca of Sunnybrook Farm 70

"Red Red Robin, The" 325
Red Skelton Show, The 355
Redgrave, Michael 216
Reed, Florence 131
Regan, Jayne 80, *81, 85,* 86, 99, *440,* 441
Renoir, Jean 165, 449
Return of the Cisco Kid, The 103-104, *104,* 120
Rexall Summer Theatre, The 288-289, 291
Reynolds, Marjorie 415
Reynolds, William 324, *326,* 397, 399
Rhodes, Erik *93*
Rice, Craig 268, 271
Richards, Lorrie *380,* 381
Richardson, Ralph 207
Rickenbacker, Eddie 243-244, *244,* 246
Rickles, Nathan 339-352, *342,* 355, 357-362,
    361, 364-371, 375-377, 380, 383-384, 394,
    396-407, 409-410, 412, 415, 424-426, 447
Ripcord 383
Risdon, Elisabeth 209
Ritz Brothers, The 108, *108*
Rivers, Joan 444
Robbins, Gale *206*
Robinson, Edward G. 216, 229-233, *232,* 274,
    296
Roerick, William 300-302, 344, 368, 416, 420,
    426, 430, 461
Rogers, Ginger 147
Rogers, Jean *125,* 126, 416, 441
Rogers, Will 54, 58-59, 69
Romero, Cesar 104, 151, 184, *185, 186,* 328,
    328, 431
Romoff, Woody 392
Roomful of Roses, A 345
Rooney, Mickey 131
Roosevelt, Franklin D. 214, 445
Rose, Helen 203-204
Ruggles, Charlie 164-166, *165*
Russell, Johnny 87, *88*
Russell, Rosalind 196
Rusty 216
Rutherford, Ann 184, *185,* 186, 189, *197*
Sanders, George 77, 169, *169*
Schaefer Century Theatre, The 326
Schenck, Aubrey 205, 255
Schenck, Joseph M. 59, 215
Schildkraut, Joseph 108
Schneider, Alan 448
Schreiber, Lew 89-90, 122, 128, 278

Science Fiction Theatre 340
Scott, Ken 384
Scott, Randolph 216, *269,* 269-271
Scott, Zachary 405
Screen Guild Players 207-209, 275
Search for Beauty 49
Sears, Fred *314*
Seaton, George 179, 247
Seaton, Phyllis 194
Secret Agent of Japan 171-174, *172, 174,* 441
Seitz, George B. 144, *145*
Selznick, David O. 44, 46, 243
"Serenade in Blue" 13, 187-188, *189,* 191
Sersen, Fred 244
Shanghai Gesture, The 131
Shannon, Harry *137*
Sharpshooters 84, *90,* 91-92
Shawlee, Joan 333
Sheehan, Winfield 51, 59, 243-244, 246, 251
Shepperd, John (Shepperd Strudwick) 269
Shirley, Anne 339, 341
Shirley, Bill 321
Shock 210, 238, 255-258, *256, 257, 259*
Shunn, Iris *53*
Sidney, Sylvia 384
Simon and Laura 370
Simon, Neil 392, 405
Simon, Simone 78, 86
Sinbad the Sailor 274
Siodmak, Robert 171
Sirk, Douglas 324-325
Six Gun Law 367
Skinner, Cornelia Otis 379
Skouras, Spyros P. 215
Sleepers West 137, 139-140, 143, *144,* 229, 377,
    439, 439
Small, Edward 143
Smith, C. Aubrey 136, 238, 455, *455*
Smith, Helen 160
Smith, John 345, *346,* 347
Smoky 251, 263
Sondheim, Stephen 412
Sothern, Ann *125,* 126, 175
Speed to Burn 86-88, *87,* 97
Sperling, Milton 152
Spier, William 288
Spiritualist, The (The Amazing Mr. X) 291-293,
    292, 311
Spock, Benjamin 438

Spring Tonic 82
Stage Door 80
Stand Up and Cheer 58, *58*
Stanley, Kim 349
Stanwyck, Barbara 86-88, *89*, 100, 151, 206
Stapleton, Maureen 405
Star Is Born, A 329, 356
Stars Over Hollywood 329
Steele, Joe 15-16
Stein, Joseph 384
Stevens, Mark 275
Stewart, Martha 275
Stockwell, Dean 268, *270*, 270-271
Stokey, Mike *334*
Strange Triangle 205, 263
Strasberg, Lee 238, 240
Subber, Saint 392, 394
Sullivan, Ed 123
Sun Valley Serenade 96, *150*, 151-159, *152*, *154*, *155*, *157*, 164, 184, 191
Sunny Side of the Street 314, *314*, 316, *317*
Suspense 288
Susskind, David 313
Sutton, John 145, 160, 163, 281
Swamp Water 165
Sweet and Low-Down 154, 188, 214, 233-235, *234*, *235*
Szabó, Sándor 392
Tamblyn, Russ 298, *299*
Tamiroff, Akim 226-227
Tampico 216-217, 229-233, *230*, *232*, 274
Temple, Shirley 58-59, 70, 454
Ten Gentlemen from West Point 281
That Other Woman 192
13th Chair, The 37
Three Little Girls in Blue 277
Three Stooges, The 44, 128
Tibbett, Lawrence 62
Tierney, Gene 13, 145, 189, 193-196, *195*, 216, 229, 279, 281-282
Tiomkin, Dimitri 225, 227
Toler, Sidney 109, *109*
Tone, Franchot 43, 46, 209
Tracy, Spencer 59
Trauma 380, 380-381
Tree Grows in Brooklyn, A 240, 270
Trevor, Claire 80-85, *81*, 93, *440*
Trotti, Lamar 308
Truex, Ernest 341

Try My Couch 367
Tunberg, Karl 185
Turner, Lana 117, 183, 332
Turtle Diary 447
Van Doren, Mamie 333
Velez, Lupe 227
Vernon, Wally 91, *94*
Viceroy Star Theatre 334
Vincent, June *328*
Walker, Nancy 317, 320
Walking Down Broadway 76, 77, 79-80, *81*, 97, 99, *440*, 441
Walsh, Christy 243-244
Walston, Jerry 387-390, *388*, *390*, 394, 396, 400-403, 413-414, 417-418, 420
Wanger, Walter 251
Ware, Darrell 185
Warren, Earl *206*
Warren, Harry 153-154, 156, 187
Wasserman, Lew 332
Way Down East 56
Wayne, John 84, 450
We Go Fast 158-159, *159*
Weaver, Marjorie 86
Webb, Clifton 247
Welcome Home 57
Weld, Tuesday 281
Welles, Orson 209
Werker, Alfred 105-106, 163, 256
Westmore, Bud 233, 325, *348*
Westmore, Frank *286*
Westmore, Wally 233
Whalen, Michael *70*, 97, 341
Whatever Became Of? 398, 438
Whelan, Arleen *147*, 345
Where Do We Go from Here? 250-251, 263
Whiting, Barbara 218-219, 268, *270*, 270-272, 282, 344-345
Whiting, Eleanor 218-219
Whiting, Margaret 218-219
Who's Afraid of Virginia Woolf? 448
Wilcoxon, Henry 134, *136*, 137
Wild, Harry J. 274
Wilde, Cornel 164, *166*, 166-167, 247, *449*
Wilder, Thornton 216, 224-225
Wilkerson, Billy 94-95, 117, 221
William, Warren 132, *132*
Wills, Chill 333
Wilson 216, 235-237

Wilson, Julie 413
Winchell, Walter 207
Winged Victory 237
Wintertime 158
Withers, Jane 108, 168, 271, 431
Woman-Wise 70
Women, The 185
Women of Pitcairn Island, The 345, 345-347,
    346, 441
Wood, Helen *67*
Wood, Yvonne 120-121, 203-204, 233
Woods, Donald 136, 226, 379
World of Robert Burns, The 355
Wrather, Jack 326-327
Wright, Jr., Cobina 151
Wright, Teresa 307, 431
Wurtzel, Sol M. 79-80, 83, 90, 110, 134, 136,
    156, 164

Wyatt, Jane 275
Wyman, Jane 175
Yates, Hal *167*
You Can't Have Everything 72
Young Runaways, The 374, 399, 399-400, 448
Young, Alan 266-267
Young, Collier 317
Young, Loretta 69, 79, 127, 281
Young, Robert 86
Yurka, Blanche 226
Zanuck, Darryl F. 54, 59-62, *60*, 79, 83, 86, 103,
    115, 117, 123, 125-134, 152, 156-158, 164,
    172, 184-185, 193, 205, 215-216, 228, 231,
    235-238, 243, 247-248, 260, 263-268, 271,
    276, 279, 281-283, 285
Zimbalist, Jr., Efrem 397, 399

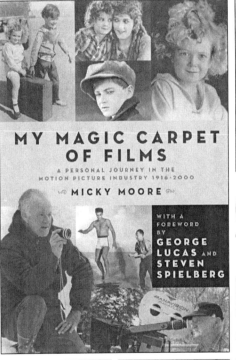

Breinigsville, PA USA
12 April 2010
235980BV00003B/9/P